Global Media Ethics

Global Media Ethics

Problems and Perspectives

Edited by

Stephen J. A. Ward

**WILEY-BLACKWELL**

A John Wiley & Sons, Ltd., Publication

Library of Congress Cataloging-in-Publication Data
Global media ethics : problems and perspectives / edited by Stephen J.A. Ward.
       pages cm
   Includes bibliographical references and index.
   ISBN 978-1-4051-8392-5 (hardback) – ISBN 978-1-4051-8391-8 (paperback)
1. Journalistic ethics. 2. Mass media – Moral and ethical aspects. I. Ward,
Stephen J. A. (Stephen John Anthony), 1951– editor of compilation.
   PN4756.G56 2013
   174′.907–dc23
                                                                2012037007

A catalog record for this book is available from the British Library.

To Glenda Louise Thomson: steadfast companion, love of my life, global advocate for justice; a kind and beautiful soul.

Contents

Notes on Contributors

Katherine M. Bell is an assistant professor in the Communication Department at California State University, East Bay. She is a career journalist who worked with the Canadian Press news agency as a reporter, editor, and news manager. She holds a PhD in Communication from the University of Washington in Seattle, where she specialized in celebrity and media studies.

Ralph D. Berenger is an associate professor of mass communication at the American University of Sharjah, United Arab Emirates, where he teaches journalism writing and editing, international mass communication, and theory courses. He has previously taught at universities in Cairo, and has lived and worked in the Middle East for 13 years. In addition to a score of book chapters, he has also published four books on mass media and is finishing his fifth on social media during the Arab Spring, to be published in 2012. He holds a doctorate from Idaho State University in political science. Prior to joining academia he spent nearly four decades as a newspaper reporter, editor, and publisher in the United States and elsewhere.

Clifford G. Christians is a Research Professor of Communications, Professor of Journalism, and Professor of Media Studies Emeritus, University of Illinois at Urbana-Champaign. His most recent coauthored book is *Ethics for Public Communication: Defining Moments in Media History* (with John Ferre and Mark Fackler, 2012). His coauthored *Media Ethics: Cases and Moral Reasoning* (2011) is in its ninth edition. He edited *Key Concepts in Critical Cultural Communication* (with Linda Steiner, 2010).

Nick Couldry is Professor of Media and Communications at Goldsmiths, University of London and Director of its Centre for the study of Global Media and Democracy. He is the author or editor of 10 books, including most recently *Media, Society, World: Social Theory and Digital Media Practice* (2012) and *Why Voice Matters: Culture and Politics After Neoliberalism* (2010).

Sharon Dunwoody is Evjue-Bascom Professor of Journalism and Mass Communication at the University of Wisconsin-Madison. Her research explores news making about science from the perspectives of both scientists and journalists, as well as the ways in which individuals use media messages to make sense of risky things. She earned her BA from Indiana University, her MA from Temple University, and her PhD from Indiana University.

Charles M. Ess is Associate Professor in Media Studies, Department of Media and Communication, University of Oslo. He has also served as a guest professor at Aarhus University and IT-University (Denmark), Trier University (Germany), the Norwegian University of Science and Technology at Trondheim, and Nîmes (France). He has received awards for excellence in both teaching and scholarship, and has published extensively in both philosophy and media studies.

Jo Ellen Fair is a professor in the School of Journalism and Mass Communication at the University of Wisconsin-Madison. She has served as a trainer in several journalism workshops across Africa. The Vilas Associates program of the Graduate School at University of Wisconsin-Madison supported this research.

Thomas Hanitzsch is Professor of Communication at the University of Munich, Germany. He founded and chaired the Journalism Studies Division of the International Communication Association. His teaching and research focuses on global journalism cultures, war coverage, celebrity news, and comparative communication research. He is the editor-in-chief of Communication Theory (2012–14), and has coedited *The Handbook of Journalism Studies* (2009) and *The Handbook of Comparative Communication Research* (2012). He also has published more than 70 journal articles and book chapters. He is a former newspaper and radio journalist and received his PhD from Ilmenau University of Technology, Germany in 2004.

Brant Houston is the Knight Chair in Investigative Reporting at the University of Illinois where he teaches and oversees regional newsroom projects. He is cofounder of the Investigative News Network and the Global Investigative Journalism Network. He coauthored *The Investigative Reporter's Handbook* (2009) and is author of *Computer-Assisted Reporting* (2003). He served as executive director of Investigative Reporters and Editors for a decade and was an investigative reporter at Metropolitan Newspapers for 17 years.

Magda Konieczna is a PhD student in the School of Journalism and Mass Communication at the University of Wisconsin-Madison. Her research focuses on media economics and political economy, specifically examining how changing funding structures of journalism are affecting communities. She has a Masters of Journalism from the University of British Columbia and has worked as a journalist for Canadian magazines and newspapers.

Tim Macafee is a doctoral student in the School of Journalism and Mass Communication at the University of Wisconsin-Madison. His research interests involve the implications of political social network site use, motivations for using social network sites in political ways, and the role of information exchange in emergent forms of online political participation.

Mervi Pantti is Associate Professor in the Department of Social Sciences, Media and Communication Studies at the University of Helsinki, and director of the International Master's Program Media and Global Communication. She is the author of *Disaster and the Media* (with Karin Wahl-Jorgensen and Simon Cottle, 2012) and has published widely in international journals on mediated emotions and disaster reporting. She is the editor of *Amateur Images and Global News* (with Kari Andén-Papadopoulos, 2011).

Patrick Lee Plaisance is associate professor at Colorado State University. His research focuses on media ethics theory, moral psychology, journalism values, and media sociology. He is author of *Media Ethics: Key Principles for Responsible Practice* (2009). He also has published several book chapters and more than a dozen articles in journals including *Communication Theory, Journalism & Mass Communication Quarterly, Journal of Mass Media Ethics*, and *Journalism Studies*. His book project, *Virtue in Media: The Moral Psychology of Excellence in News and PR*, is forthcoming. He worked as a journalist at numerous American newspapers for nearly 15 years and received his PhD from Syracuse University in 2002.

Shakuntala Rao is Professor of Communication Studies at State University of New York, Plattsburgh. Her research areas are global media, ethics, and popular culture. She has published extensively and influentially in many communication, journalism, and interdisciplinary journals. Her most recent book is an edited anthology titled *Explorations in Global Media Ethics* (with Muhammad Ayish, 2012).

Hernando Rojas is an associate professor in the School of Journalism and Mass Communication at the University of Wisconsin–Madison. His research interests include the deployment of new communication technologies for social mobilization in a variety of contexts, the influence of audience perceptions of media (and audience perceptions of media effects) on both public opinion and the structure of the public sphere, and the conditions under which media support democratic governance.

Elizabeth A. Skewes is an associate professor of Journalism and Mass Communication at the University of Colorado–Boulder. Her research focuses on media sociology and news practices, the media's role in electoral politics, factors that influence media content about political campaigns, and politics in popular culture. She is the author of *Message Control: How News is Made on the Presidential Campaign Trail* (2007) and the author or coauthor of several book chapters and journal articles. She is a former newspaper reporter and magazine editor, and she received her PhD in mass communications from Syracuse University in 2001.

Mustafa Taha is an assistant professor of mass communication at the American University of Sharjah, United Arab Emirates. He holds a doctorate from Ohio University and has taught public relations and mass communication for more than 11 years at universities in the UAE. His areas of research and teaching include public relations, media representation, new media and society, media and conflict, image management, and public diplomacy. Prior to his academic career, he worked as a diplomat at the Sudan mission to the United Nations, New York, UN peacekeeping missions in Somalia and Liberia, and as Sudan's consul general in Ethiopia. In 2012, he published a book on media behavior in the 2000 US General Election.

Howard Tumber is Professor of Journalism and Communication, and Director of the Centre for Law, Justice and Journalism at City University London. He has published widely in the field of the sociology of news and journalism and is the author, coauthor/editor of eight books including *Critical Concepts in Journalism* (four vols., 2008), *Journalists under Fire* (2006), *Media at War: The Iraq Crisis* (2004), *Media Power, Policies and Professionals* (2000), *News: A Reader* (1999), *Reporting Crime* (1994), *Journalists at War* (1988), and *Television and Riots* (1982). He is a founder and coeditor of the journal, *Journalism: Theory, Practice and Criticism*.

Karin Wahl-Jorgensen is Reader in the Cardiff School of Journalism, Media and Cultural Studies at Cardiff University. She is the author of *Citizens or Consumers* (with Justin Lewis and Sanna Inthorn, 2005), *Journalists and the Public* (2007) and the recently completed *Disaster and the Media* (with Mervi Pantti and Simon Cottle, in press). She is the editor of several volumes, including *The Handbook of Journalism Studies* (2009) and is currently at work on a book about media, political participation, and emotion.

Stephen J. A. Ward is Director of the George S. Turnbull Center in Portland, Oregon. The center is the Portland base of the University of Oregon's School of Journalism and Communication. Previously, he was the Burgess Chair of Journalism Ethics and Director of the Center for Journalism Ethics at the University of Wisconsin-Madison. He is the author of the award-winning *The Invention of Journalism Ethics: The Path to Objectivity and Beyond* (2005). In addition, he wrote *Ethics and the Media: An Introduction* (2011), and *Global Journalism Ethics* (2010). He is coeditor of *Media Ethics Beyond Borders: A Global Perspective* (2010). Professor Ward is associate editor of the *Journal of Mass Media Ethics*. His articles and reviews have appeared in such journals as *Journalism Studies, Ecquid Novi: African Journalism Studies, Harvard International*

Journal of Press/Politics and the *Journal of Mass Media Ethics*. He was a reporter, war correspondent, and newsroom manager for 14 years.

Herman Wasserman worked as a print journalist in South Africa before earning his doctorate from Stellenbosch University in 2000 and embarking on an academic career. He has published widely on media in postapartheid South Africa, including the monograph *Tabloid Journalism in South Africa* (2010). Edited collections include *Popular Media Democracy and Development in Africa* (2011) and *Media Ethics Beyond Borders* (with Stephen Ward, 2010). He is currently Professor and Deputy Head of the School of Journalism and Media Studies at Rhodes University in Grahamstown, South Africa. He edits the journal *Ecquid Novi: African Journalism Studies*.

Introduction

Media Ethics as Global

Stephen J. A. Ward

Global media ethics seeks to articulate and critique the responsibilities of a news media that is now global in content, reach, and impact. It is the project of developing aims, principles, and norms of practice specifically formulated for a global, media-linked world.

The context for global media ethics is the current, often disorientating, revolution in media (Ward 2011a). Two major trends of this revolution are worth noting. First, the emergence of a "mixed news media" that is interactive and online. News media is "mixed" for two reasons. First, it is mixed because practitioners use many types of technology to create media content, for example, printed newspapers, blogs, websites, and social media such as Facebook and Twitter. Second, it is mixed because of the democratization of media – the fact that citizens have access to publishing technology. As a result, the number of media practitioners has increased dramatically in recent years, going far beyond the ranks of professional journalists to include web writers for NGOs, scientists with blogs, and citizen journalists.

A second and related trend is the globalization of news media, and media in general. We live in a world where "reality" is defined and mediated by a ubiquitous and powerful global media. News media are global in content because they report on global issues or events, whether the issue is immigration, climate change, world trade policies, or international security. News media are global in reach because they have the technology to gather information from around the world with incredible speed, and to use this information to create stories for a global public. News media are global in impact because the production of stories has impact across borders, sparking riots in distant lands or prompting global responses to natural disasters.

These two trends, mixed media and globalization, define the subject matter for global media ethics. The two trends create the problems and

Global Media Ethics: Problems and Perspectives, First Edition. Edited by Stephen J. A. Ward.
© 2013 Blackwell Publishing Ltd. Published 2013 by Blackwell Publishing Ltd.

opportunities that motivate scholars and others to study global media ethics. However, to be clear, global media ethics is *not* the empirical study of globalization as a complex phenomenon affecting culture, economics, and communication. It is the analysis of the normative implications of globalization on a news media whose practices and norms were created for a nonglobal, nonmixed media.

The argument for global media ethics can be summarized in one short sentence: Global power entails global responsibilities. It is therefore appropriate – some would say urgent – to ask about the ethics of global media, and to what extent it differs from the previous ethics of a nonglobal media rooted in individual nations and regions of the world. The need for a global ethics is due not only to technological innovation and new ownership patterns; it is due to changes in the world that journalism inhabits. Of primary importance is the fact that our media-connected world brings together a plurality of different religions, traditions, ethnic groups, values, and organizations with varying political agendas, social ideals, and conceptions of the good. Media content deemed offensive by certain groups can spark not just domestic unrest but global tension. As happened with the publication of the cartoons of Mohammed by a Danish newspaper, news media (and other media) can spark cultural tensions and violence that ripples across borders. In such a climate, the role of media, and its ethics, must be re-examined.

A globally minded media is of great value because a biased and parochial media can wreak havoc in a tightly linked global world. North American readers may fail to understand the causes of violence in the Middle East or of a drought in Africa if they are not reported properly. Jingoistic reports can portray the inhabitants of other regions of the world as a threat. Reports may incite ethnic groups to attack each other. In times of insecurity, a narrow-minded, patriotic news media can amplify the views of leaders who stampede populations into war or the removal of civil rights for minorities. We need a cosmopolitan media that reports issues in a way that reflects this global plurality of views and helps groups understand each other better. We need globally responsible media to help citizens understand the daunting global problems of poverty, environmental degradation, and political instability.

However, one may ask: Why not apply existing principles of media ethics to the problems raised by a globalization of media? The answer is: Traditional media ethics is insufficient because traditional media ethics was, and is, parochial, not global. For traditional media ethics, the media owed responsibilities to a public within the borders of a nation. For traditional media ethics, journalists were first and foremost citizens of specific countries who should be patriotic in serving their country's national interest, not global citizens seeking to create global understandings or global justice. Therefore, we must reconceive media ethics as dealing with issues surrounding transnational publics and global problems.

For some or all of these reasons, global media ethicists believe that the rise of global media calls for a simultaneous development of a global media ethics. In my concluding Chapter 15, I discuss to what extent this project of global media ethics might be realized. Yet, whatever the answer is to the question of realization, the fact remains that the world needs a global ethics for its media.

Plurality of Approaches

Even if we understand the need for global media ethics, this does not mean that "global media ethics" refers to something clear and singular. As a field of study, "global media ethics" does not refer to a well-defined science with a consensus on methods and aims. It is not a mature academic discipline which builds, rigorously and systematically, upon previous established knowledge. "Global media ethics" does not refer to one *thing*, such as one, internationally accepted, code of media ethics. Instead, global media ethics refers to an evolving field. It is a "felt need" that motivates a loosely connected set of activities and studies united by the belief that ethics must go global, for the reasons cited above.

Another commonality among advocates of global media ethics is the view that journalists and other media practitioners need to undergo a global revolution in their self-consciousness and in the way they practice their craft. For example, some global ethicists argue (Ward 2010) that journalists and news outlets need to regard themselves as global citizens. They need to see their responsibilities from a cosmopolitan view that challenges the often negative influence of various forms of parochialism, such as narrow patriotism or extreme nationalism. If journalists become globally minded, they will change how they cover global issues and events.

These common beliefs leave plenty of room for different answers to questions about the most effective methods of inquiry, the most important problems, and the most important principles of a global media ethics. Today, global media ethics is characterized by a plurality of approaches, a plurality of types of theorizing, and a plurality of contending views concerning what global media ethics is or should be.

As the chapters in this book indicate, there are numerous types of inquiry in the field of global media ethics. Types of inquiry can be divided roughly into four kinds, depending on the degree of normative and philosophical emphasis in the studies: empirical, empirical-normative, applied, and philosophical.

The empirical category includes comparative studies of media cultures and surveys (Weaver 1998) of the attitudes, working conditions, and practices of journalists and other media practitioners in different countries. Empirical-normative studies include surveys and cross-culture comparisons, but these studies are more focused on the implications of such studies on our conception of global media ethics. Empirical-normative studies also examine the normative similarities and differences among media practitioners. For example, Chapter 2 of this book, by Hanitzsch, Plaisance, and Skewes, draws conclusions about universals and differences in journalism based on a multinational survey of journalists.

The third form of inquiry works in the area traditionally known as applied ethics – the study and critique of the principles of media professions. Applied ethics, in global media ethics, means a creative and bold extension of existing ideas to media as global. Global applied ethics means the construction of new principles, the critique of existing principles, and the reinterpretation of norms for the guidance of global media. For example, in this book several chapters question the relevance of traditional notions of journalistic objectivity and neutrality for certain types of media coverage and for different media cultures.

The fourth type of inquiry works at the meta-ethical (or philosophical) level. Inquirers examine the theoretical foundation of global media ethics. Foundational topics include the goals and basic principles of global media ethics, the existence of media universals, and the challenge of ethical relativism. For instance, in Chapter 14 of this book, Clifford G. Christians argues against relativism as a major obstacle to the construction of global ethics.[1]

Given these lines of research, global media ethics is best described as a project. A project is a practical affair. It brings together people of varied skills and interests in an attempt to realize valued objectives. To be a project is to be an ideal not yet realized. Global media ethics is a project in this sense, in that it is an ideal not yet realized. Global media ethics – as a widely accepted explicit set of principles – does not exist. What is more, the project of global media ethics is controversial. Advocates see the construction of global ethics as a worthy project, required by today's media. Yet plenty of ethicists and media practitioners are not engaged in the project. As I discuss in Chapter 15, some people regard the project as utopian or undesirable.

The project, then, must establish a beachhead for global media ethics in the face of parochial (nonglobal) ethics and skeptics of the very idea of global ethics, especially in media. To establish a beachhead, the project sometimes takes the form of an ethical movement, usually described as the "search" for a global media ethics (Ward and Wasserman 2010). At the center of the movement are scholars and media practitioners deeply interested in exploring the fundamental ideas of global media ethics. For example, one group have, since 2007, held international round-tables to stimulate discussion on what global ethics means for different media cultures. The roundtables have resulted in seminal publications.[2] In addition, an increasing number of books and journal articles appear with global media ethics as their topic. The movement is supported by global media institutes and globally minded websites with an interest in global journalism and its ethics (Ward 2011b). These centers hold global media conferences and publish articles and newsletters which add to the conversation about global media ethics.

Skepticism of global media ethics because of its varied and contending perspectives is misplaced. It betrays a simplistic view of applied ethics and how it evolves. Global media ethics is a valid form of "emergent" applied ethics. A practice is emergent if its key normative elements are less developed than a more mature practice.[3] A mature practice enjoys substantive agreement on the goals, methods, and norms of the practice. The normative concepts of emergent ethics may be less developed for two reasons: either because the practice is new, or because the practice is not new but agreement on key concepts has broken down and in a state of flux or reformulation. Reformulation is prompted by engagement with new problems of practice. The need for changes in the applied ethics of technology, the sciences, or professions is based on ever-evolving new conditions in these areas of society. For example, the development of bioethics and the ethics of technology with worrisome military applications are examples of emergent ethics. Some areas of ethics are not emergent and are relatively stable for long periods of time. The ethics of a religion may remain unchanged in essentials over many decades, or centuries. However, among such practices as journalism, emergent ethics is a familiar phenomenon because of regular and rapid changes in the conditions of practice. In the media professions, the need to address new normative problems is so practically urgent that they force practitioners to reformulate ethical guidelines and to gradually codify (and philosophically ground) these responses to problems. Emergent ethics, in media and elsewhere, evolve through a gradual resolution of key issues forged in the crucible of daily practice and public debate. For global media ethics, the new problems created by mixed media and globalization of media force journalists and media scholars to engage in an emergent process that redefines basic concepts.

Structure of the Book

This book takes seriously the idea of global media ethics as a project with many types of contributors and many types of contributions. The four parts of the book were selected to reflect the book's subtitle – the many *problems* and *perspectives* in this new field of global media ethics.

Part I introduces the reader to media ethics worldwide. Couldry and Tumber argue for the continuing relevance of ethics for global media in general and for reporting international conflicts. Tumber says the best description of the ethical role of war reporters today is that of "responsible engagement" with events and issues, rather than the view that the role of such reporters is that of the neutral or objective observer. Hanitzsch, Plaisance, and Skewes examine the idea of universals and differences across media cultures; Houston indicates how an emergent ethics is developing among global networks of nonprofit journalists.

Part II analyzes media ethics in different regions of the world. Berenger and Taha examine Arab mass media, while Rojas and Macafee study the impact of new media on the Colombian public sphere. Wasserman explains the ethical tensions among South African media, and Fair questions the approach of international media development agencies in Liberia.

Part III considers how a global media ethics might change practice, especially the coverage of global issues. Dunwoody and Konieczna recommend a number of approaches that would improve media coverage of climate change. Wahl-Jorgensen and Pantti argue for a more cosmopolitan approach to covering natural disasters. Bell questions the use of celebrities as sources on global issues, and Rao shows how Amartya Sen's theory of comparative justice could be used to guide how Indian journalists (and journalists elsewhere) cover stories that involve issues of justice, wrongdoing by officials, and social class.

The book's concluding Part IV addresses philosophical questions raised by the preceding parts. Ess argues for a widening of media ethics to include consideration of how communication technology is altering how citizens interact with others, and how this "new media" is affecting conceptions of self. Christians examines the problem of relativism for global media ethics. Ward defends the project of global media ethics against a range of objections, including claims that the project is utopian and will never be realized.

Themes

We obtain a better appreciation of the concerns and the varied lines of inquiry in global media ethics by noting some common themes among the 15 chapters. The chapters show that the controversies in global media ethics are instantiations of much broader controversies in ethics, cultural studies, and philosophy. One of the main controversies is the debate between universalists, who focus on common values among media cultures, and antiuniversalists (or global skeptics), who focus on normative differences among media cultures. Moreover, we see that global media ethics cannot avoid engagement with the difficult philosophical issues around the idea of universalism in ethics. Through this engagement, theory building in global media ethics becomes embroiled in complex discussions and intense debates surrounding the relationship of the local and the global with respect to culture and ethics.

Here are five themes found in the book's chapters that define the current state of inquiry and debate in global media ethics:

Universalism or contextualism?

In this book, the debate between the local and global arises from the assumption that a global media ethics must be a form of universalism.

That is, it must assert that there are at least some universal principles that apply to media around the world. But this assertion runs up against at least two forms of skepticism. First, the existence and prevalence of universals: Are the principles of media ethics relative to particular societies? Are there any universal principles in media ethics (or in ethics)? Does the variety of types of media practice and media standards cast doubt on the possibility of universal media ethics? Second, universals and cultural difference: Is ethical universalism a form of cultural imperialism or cultural insensitivity? When we try to apply universal principles across borders do we show disrespect to local and regional variations among media cultures?

In this book, Hanitzsch, Plaisance, and Skewes argue that empirical research shows that there are *both* universals and differences across media cultures. Berenger and Taha contend that an abstract universalism of principles fails to capture significant ethical differences in the practice of Arab mass media. They prefer an approach called "contextualism" which studies how media norms operate in specific media cultures.

What type of ethical approach?

A second theme is best posed as a question: What approach to global media ethics will be most conducive to finding common values? Ess, Couldry, and Rojas and Macafee agree that media ethics remains important but the scope of media ethics should widen beyond professional journalists to citizens. Couldry argues that the plurality and complexity of media practice today makes a "top-down" approach unattractive in ethics. A top-down approach seeks common values by imposing principles on diverse media practices. Couldry promotes a flexible, "bottom-up" approach based in virtue ethics as the best way to begin a cross-cultural conversation on media ethics.

Interpreting global principles

A third theme is that global media ethics should provide nuanced and culturally sensitive interpretations of whatever concepts are put forward for inclusion in global media ethics. Among the candidates for inclusion are (1) ethical principles such as truth telling and objectivity, (2) forms of journalism such as watchdog investigative journalism, and (3) ideals such as "serving the public" or democracy. Wasserman examines the ways that journalists (and others) in transitional democracies like South Africa interpret the idea of media serving democracy. Should "serving democracy" in South Africa mean adopting a Western-style watchdog journalism focused on official wrongdoing or should it a mean a journalism focused on human dignity and social inequalities? Wasserman shows there is no simple, clear application of the abstract ideal of "media serving democracy."

Fair draws the same type of moral from her study of how international media development agencies have attempted to create a Western-style free media in Liberia. The notion of a free democratic press, imported from the West, cannot (and should not) be imposed on the complex history, ethnic composition, and political terrain of an African country such as Liberia.

Global approaches to global issues

Another theme is how media, steeped in traditional forms of practice, result in suboptimal coverage of global issues. Dunwoody and Konieczna argue that coverage of climate change is episodic and influenced by a narrow definition of news. Reporters tend to apply a traditional notion of "balance" to climate change stories, which results in reports that give too much credibility to questionable views and experts. They recommend a "weight of evidence" approach to reporting differing viewpoints, and endorse a form of coverage that brings the local and global together.

Wahl-Jorgensen and Pantti contend that coverage of natural disasters is restricted by an attempt to report in an unemotional "objective" manner. In addition, news media cover disasters in a parochial manner. Which disasters they cover and how they cover them is overdetermined by the impact of the disaster on their own country. They recommend that journalists adopt a more cosmopolitan approach toward coverage of disasters, an approach that brings together the emotions and the rationality of journalists.

Parochialism partially transcended

These themes lead back to one fundamental point upon which most of the authors agree: Even if we cannot say with precision what a global media ethics should be, media practitioners should become more globally minded and seek to transcend, at least partially, their parochial attachments. These attachments can distort coverage of events and inhibit the global public's understanding of trends. Even if the project of global media ethics is only beginning, a media that is global in content, reach, and impact cannot escape the responsibility – today – to improve their coverage of global issues.

Notes

1. See Ward (2010) for the foundations of global journalism ethics.
2. Among the roundtable leaders are Profs. Clifford G. Christians of the University of Illinois, Shakuntala Rao of the State University of New York-Plattsburgh, Herman Wasserman of Rhodes University, South Africa, Lee Wilkins of Wayne State University-Detroit, and myself. Roundtables have been held in Stellenbosch, South Africa, in 2007, Dubai in 2010, and Delhi, India, in 2011. Presentations at the South African roundtable became the content for *Media Ethics Beyond Borders* (Ward and Wasserman 2010). Papers from the Dubai meeting formed the content of a special issue on

global media ethics in *Journalism Studies* in December 2011, Vol. 12(6). Papers from the Indian roundtable will be published by Oxford University Press.
3. Beitz (2009: 43), for example, describes human rights practice as an emergent practice.

References

Beitz, C. R. 2009. *The Idea of Human Rights*. Oxford: Oxford University Press.

Ward, S. J. A. 2010. *Global Journalism Ethics*. Montreal: McGill-Queen's University Press.

Ward, S. J. A. 2011a. *Ethics and the Media: An Introduction*. Cambridge: Cambridge University Press.

Ward, S. J. A. 2011b. "Center for Journalism Ethics, School of Journalism and Mass Communication, University of Wisconsin-Madison." *Journalism Studies* 12(3): 392–8.

Ward, S. J. A. and Wasserman, H. Eds. 2010. *Media Ethics Beyond Borders: A Global Perspective*. New York: Routledge.

Weaver, D. Ed. 1998. *The Global Journalist*. New York: Hampton Press.

Part I

Media Ethics Worldwide

1

Why Media Ethics Still Matters

Nick Couldry

Journalists who work for British tabloid or midmarket newspapers, which have nearly four-fifths of circulation in Britain,[1] are trusted to tell the truth by less than a quarter of its population (10% for tabloid journalists, 22% for journalists on the midmarket press). It is small comfort that less than a third of people in Britain trust leading politicians, trade union leaders, or senior civil servants. Only BBC news journalists are trusted to tell the truth by a majority of Britain's population, although trust in them also fell drastically between 2003 and 2010 (Kellner 2010). And yet it is taken for granted that free media are essential to a working democracy.

There is more than a hint of paradox here. Media's freedom to publish does not automatically aid democracy: What if media regularly publish lies or untruths, as so many of the British population believe or suspect? As philosopher Onora O'Neill puts it, "the press has no licence to deceive; and we have no reasons to think that a free press needs such a licence" (O'Neill 2002: 100). The paradox goes further, since an untrustworthy media cannot provide a secure basis for trusting other public figures or processes. As O'Neill notes, "if we can't trust what the press report, how can we tell whether to trust those on whom they report?" (O'Neill 2002: 90). There is easily enough provocation here toward the development of a rigorous framework of media ethics, and indeed codes of journalistic ethics have existed for more than a century in many countries (Bertrand 2000).

I want, however, to argue in this chapter that the status of media ethics in media research is, in many respects, problematic and in need of robust defense. This is for at least two reasons. First, there is the increasingly ambiguous status of institutional media themselves within the proliferating complexity of the digital media age; second, and connectedly, there is the rising demand for a broader ethics of communication that would give no special prominence to the ethical problems raised by institutional media. The best response, I suggest, is to develop a media ethics that is flexible enough to provide starting points for new debate, and not

Global Media Ethics: Problems and Perspectives, First Edition. Edited by Stephen J. A. Ward.
© 2013 Blackwell Publishing Ltd. Published 2013 by Blackwell Publishing Ltd.

merely the reaffirmation of old rules and norms. Making this argument will bring out the special contribution of the philosophical tradition of *ethics*, by contrast with other approaches to the normative sphere, such as deontology. The distinction is important, although sometimes blurred in debate about media norms: By "ethics" I mean normative discourse focused on issues of the good and dispositions aimed at the good (virtue), while by "deontology" I mean normative discourse focused on duties (for a sharp treatment of the contrast, see Ricoeur 2007). Getting this distinction clear and so getting clear about the distinctive contribution that an ethics approach can bring to the normative dilemmas posed by media practice may, in turn, lay the foundations for a more robust communication ethics over the longer term.

Some Background

It might seem strange to anyone who followed, whether in Britain or internationally, the phone-hacking scandal that engulfed News Corporation in 2011, to say that media ethics needs justifying or defending as a topic. What could be more obvious than that practices at the media corporation in question needed to be more ethical? Indeed it is striking when no less a figure than Rupert Murdoch is forced to acknowledge in public the paradox mentioned earlier of democracy relying on an unreliable press. But that is exactly what he did when in a full-page advertisement printed in Britain's newspapers on 16 July 2011 he wrote that "The *News of the World* was in the business of holding others to account. It failed when it came to itself." And yet what has followed the phone-hacking revelations is not clear action to clean up the media and root out unethical practice: Practical proposals are still awaited and an inquiry led by Lord Leveson will sit for many months in an attempt to find a way forward. Existing journalistic codes and the weak "self-regulation" that is supposed to enforce them (overseen by the toothless Press Complaints Commission) have done little or nothing to prevent unethical practices from occurring. One key reason, as Angela Phillips already noted before the scandal broke, is that the *practical* conditions of working journalists are increasingly inimical to ethical practice (Phillips 2011). As yet, there are no clear starting points of media ethics for putting this right. There is no public consensus around the specific ethical expectations we can legitimately have of journalists in a democracy. This suggests that the problems raised by the contemporary practice of journalism are deep, and not susceptible to simple fixing by codification.

An abyss threatens to open up in Britain where people have minimal reasons to trust media, and so have minimal reasons to trust anyone else in the public world. Public life in general becomes irreversibly corroded. Fatalism about the limits and weaknesses of the media ("that's the media for you!") is a standard response, but offers no solution; indeed by normalizing mistrust in media it intensifies the problem, so blocking any ways forward.

An alternative approach, following Paul Ricoeur, is to note that it is precisely when the complexities of human and social life throw up outcomes that are problematic and unsustainable that new forms of ethics have to be built. Ricoeur calls such turning-points "limit situations": As one example, he gives the danger to human life from medical care that is not careful about its own norms, so generating the need for medical ethics (Ricoeur 2007: 34–5). We have entered, I suggest, a limit situation today with respect to the practice of journalism, at least in a country such as Britain where the institutional conditions for producing what counts as journalistic output directly undermine the purposes for which we need journalists in the first place: to circulate information that is necessary for the good conduct of our common life together. As a result, a need – not just institutional or bureaucratic, but a deep social and human need – emerges for a media ethics that is focused in particular on the practices of institutionalized media production, and also is applicable to *anyone* who contributes as a producer or commentator to our public world. As the late Susan Sontag pointed out, in an age of smart phones and endless digital platforms for contributing to public culture, that really could be any of us (Sontag 2004).

On the face of it, the prospects for such a media ethics are good. Academic publications on media ethics have in the past decade broadened out from the field's pioneers (Christians, Ferré, and Fackler 1993, Christians, Rotzoll, and Fackler 1991) who emerged in the context of the long-standing tradition of ethical debate in US journalism schools (Zelizer 2011) to a broader range of authors in a number of countries: Pinchevski (2005), Couldry (2006: chapter 8), Silverstone (2007), Ward and Wasserman (2008), Phillips (2011). This current book is itself evidence of a growing international debate about the frameworks for media ethics.

In addition, as digital media's role in the texture of our lives has become increasingly apparent with the installing, for example, of social media platform "apps" on our smartphones, concerns have started to be raised by prominent analysts or pioneers of the digital revolution about its ethical consequences. Sherry Turkle's 2011 book *Alone Together* is a prolonged meditation on whether our relations with digital technology are "offering us the lives we want to lead," a profoundly ethical question (Turkle 2011: 17); while virtual reality pioneer Jaron Lanier's book *You Are Not a Gadget* (Lanier 2011) asks searching questions about whether the growing drive to put more and more of our lives online and to rely increasingly on digital systems for conducting and managing our lives is a positive trend.

The underlying point can be put quite simply. We no longer have a way of living together – of conducting any domain of life – *without* media but we don't yet know how to live *well* with media. Using Habermas's in some ways outdated dichotomy between "lifeworld" and "system," there is no lifeworld any more that is not saturated at every level by system, including the systems that are "media." However, systems are not places within which we can live. The intense functional determination of systems means that, of themselves, system spaces are incompatible with any tolerable life. The point is not that system has *no* role in a life lived well, but rather that a life *saturated* with system injunctions quickly becomes intolerable.

It is tempting at this point to conclude that the increasing recruitment of all of us as information producers and circulators in a vast hypertextual universe requires us to bypass media ethics and concentrate on building a broader *communication* ethics in which the issues of institutional media play a smaller role. Certainly there are many ethical issues raised by everyday use of digital platforms which do not derive from the constraints of journalistic practice. For example, mutual coveillance penetrates ever deeper into everyday practices of work, identity, and sociality, and we leave archive trails of our lives (with uncertain ethical consequences) on social networking sites and wherever we buy or observe anything (Andrejevic 2008, Zittrain 2008: 219–20, Turkle 2011). Meanwhile there are sweeping arguments that, in the digital age, the old separation of producer and audience disappears, so that all of us become "produsers" of one sort or another (Rosen 2006, Bruns 2008). If so, do we require a common ethical framework whose starting points cannot be the particular conditions of those still *paid* to be journalists or image producers? The uncertainties affecting the digital media are multiple, including the economic viability of large-scale media operations and their continued social status and legitimacy versus the growing status and legitimacy of decentered social networks online (Couldry, 2012: chapter 1).

At the most basic level, we might conclude that, since we no longer straightforwardly know what "media" are, the whole project of *media* ethics should be dropped in favor of a broader communication ethics that has little contact any more with journalism ethics. That at least is the implication of some recent invocations of communication ethics which make no reference to issues of journalism (Hayles 2009, Stiegler 2009). But that, I believe, would be a profound mistake. In the rest of this chapter I want to defend both the necessity of media ethics and its generative importance for the emergent field of communication ethics. I will do so by putting emphasis on both words in the term "media ethics," arguing first for the distinctive contribution of *media* ethics and second for the usefulness of media *ethics* (as opposed to other philosophical approaches to media-related norms), for grasping the practical dilemmas with which the media and communication platforms (Gillespie 2010) of the early twenty-first century confront humankind.

The Need for *Media* Ethics

Truth seeking is a value for *all* effective forms of human organization, whether or not organized along democratic lines: Without practices aimed at truth (of which media are among the most important), co-operative human activity and the fulfillment of individual capabilities are impossible.

My argument's implications are, however, particularly sharp for those societies that claim to be democracies, such as the United States and Britain, since, as Sheldon Wolin (2008: 263) notes, "it seems paradoxical to say that democracy should deliberately deceive itself."

Notwithstanding the expanding role of commentary and "user-generated content" in digital cultures (Couldry 2012: chapter 2), most information we receive about the events and processes – governmental, economic, environmental, social – affecting our lives are institutionally produced. The emergence of media institutions (or "the media") is virtually universal in human societies during modernity, but with varying relations to government, markets, and civil society (Starr 2004, Hallin and Mancini 2004). It follows that the overall consequences of such institutions for truth seeking and truth finding are an issue of potential ethical significance for any such society.

The irreducible importance of ethical norms for media institutions has recently emerged particularly sharply at the global level. A global scale implies a space of irreducible moral disagreement and diversity. Media do not reduce or resolve such disagreement: On the contrary, they bring it into view. So an initial question is: How can we live *sustainably* with each other through media, even though media unavoidably expose us to our moral differences? Bruno Latour (2004: 40) expresses the challenge with great clarity:

> An entirely new set of questions has now emerged [on the political stage]: "Can we cohabitate with you?" "Is there a way for all of us to survive together while none of our contradictory claims, interests and passions can be eliminated?" ... "What should now be simultaneously present?"

We do not need a set of explicit rules about media practice, but a framework of thinking that can build, at a global level, shared norms and values in relation to media practice in spite of our differences.

We need not, however, only look at the global scale. *Any* large-scale form of human organization raises ethical complexities. Media are one of the ethically significant "practices" in which humans are involved, at least when they organize on a large scale. Our formulations of a specific ethics of media must be shaped by the distinctive human needs that media can fulfill and the distinctive harms that media can cause: respectively, the need for information and the harm of misrecognition, or lack of recognition.

There are at least three reasons why we need a distinctive *media* ethics. First, there is no ethics distinctive to a single medium, because media narratives – always to some degree, and emphatically now, in the digital age – involve references to other media content, often in different media formats (Hepp 2010). Second, media ethics is broader than journalism ethics, by which I mean the already partly codified rules for institution-ally empowered storytellers (journalists). Such codes are important and they have ethical content, but they emerge from particular institutional circumstances; instead I want to explore how far a *general* ethics of media can be built that is, in part at least, independent of the particular institutional contexts in which journalism now finds itself. That broader media ethics would consider the general issues that media as a human practice raises for *anyone* involved in it, whether working in an institution or not. Such an ethics would be derived from considerations of media's potential contribution to human life.

Third, there is still a need for a *media* ethics, as distinct from a general ethics of communication, that is, the distinctive ethical issues raised by the institutional concentration of communicative resources that we call "media" (even still "the media"), and the deeply embedded expectations we have of such institutions and our interactions with them. Those issues do not disappear just because we now receive and make media across some of the same platforms on which we present our personal lives to our family and friends.

It can be argued, for some countries such as the USA, that an ethics of journalism was already embedded within that practice from the start, as journalism's role in sustaining a large-scale society was increasingly interrogated from the late nineteenth century onwards (Zelizer 2011). But it can equally be argued, by reference for example to the contemporary conditions of journalism in Britain, that the *absence* of effective ethical norms is more usual because of the growing difficulties of funding and organizing intensive news gathering and news production.

Two simultaneous trends increase those difficulties. First, there are the proliferating possibilities for producing and circulating (even recirculating) information or opinion about public events and matters of public interest, which in turn makes *economically* viable operations particularly difficult to achieve. As Terhi Rantanen asks, does the constant availability of news-like "information" make it "more and more difficult to make a profit from general news services"? Does this presage perhaps a return to the mass of undifferentiated "new stories" that characterized the world before "news" was invented (Rantanen 2009: 129–32)? Second, there are the growing complexities of the social process itself, the processes on which media must report. Social life itself is increasingly saturated by new forms of information production and information storage at all levels, whether official or unofficial (Bimber 2003). Organizational and governmental work is characterized by increasingly complex interrelations and systemic interdependencies at and between all scales (Elias 1994, Sassen 2006). As a result, it becomes increasingly difficult, without the backing of major economic investment, for *anyone* to know continuously what are the appropriate sources for understanding or reporting any process, or indeed on what scale, or from where, one should operate to get the least misleading view of what is going on. How, for example, can the truth about the arms industries or pharmaceutical industries be discovered without institutions that sustain investment in news gathering?

This is not to deny the increasing role of noninstitutional researchers in specialist understandings of what is going on in the world: the rise of what John Keane (2009) calls "monitory democracy." But that does not outweigh the pressure to maintain *some* effective institutional forms of information production – for governments, corporations, social groups – and the ethical issues that such forms of production raise. We need as citizens to know that someone somewhere is committing what Bernard Williams calls the "investigative investment" (Williams 2002) necessary for effective truth seeking. Otherwise the opacity of the social world is guaranteed and the mechanisms of democracy are at best illusory, as the tradition of elite democratic theory has complained for nearly a century (Lippman 1925, Schattschneider 1960). The seriousness of such problems for ethics should not be underestimated.

The 2011 phone-hacking scandal in News Corporation is only an entry point to a much broader and more ethically complex world of compromise, underresourcing, system reliance, impossible deadlines, and business as usual. Recent studies of journalism practice reveal an alarming gap between the conditions under which journalists work in various countries and the conditions under which ethical action is possible. Let's leave aside more obvious cases where good journalistic ethics is in direct conflict with the demands of authoritarian power, and concentrate on democracies where it is generally supposed that government–press relations work well.

Drawing on extensive interviews with UK broadsheet journalists, press agency employees, and freelancers, Nick Davies argues that journalists in the UK "work in structures which positively prevent them discovering the truth" (Davies 2008: 28). This result is at odds with more optimistic views of where digital journalism is heading: toward more democratization and mutualism and towards less elitism, gate-watching rather than gate-keeping, a world of empowered producers. The problem is not that journalists have changed their values, since "for journalists the defining value [remains] honesty – the attempt to tell the truth" (Davies 2008: 12). The problem is that the conditions under which journalists work are not ones where that value can be consistently or reliably *acted upon*.

Davies links his diagnosis to wider global trends in an age of web-based journalism where stories from elsewhere get recycled in an unseemly form of "churnalism," resulting in "a global collapse of information-gathering and truth-telling" (Davies 2008: 154). Production imperatives – the need to get the story "up" in the quickest possible time, and maximize "hits" in an accelerated multiplatform news environment – lead to ever greater reliance on stories sourced from other journalists (Phillips 2011). Similar concerns about the US press have been voiced in recent years, for example in relation to the commercial pressures interfering with journalist practice at the *Los Angeles Times* (Carroll 2007). These pessimistic views are not by any means the *only* perspective on today's changing conditions of journalism in the United States and Britain. There is some plausibility in the argument that more niches now exist for journalistic voices (individual or collective) to emerge *outside* the major institutions of journalism, for example citizen-reporters or bloggers (Benkler 2006, Bruns 2008): The pharmaceutical industry for example, mentioned earlier, has generated critical voices in the blogosphere (discussed in Couldry 2009). But given the sheer size of contemporary journalism's task in tracking a complex world and the investment required for managing that task, these more optimistic views seem to deal with marginal features, not the central dynamics, of journalism today.

The bigger story is about a seismic shift in the conditions of news production itself in *many* countries. Pablo Boczkowski, discussing the online Argentinean press, puts the paradox starkly: We face, he says, a "remarkable increase in the amount of news available and a perplexing decrease in the diversity of its content" (Boczkowski 2010: 6). A recent ethnography of German newsrooms (Boyer 2010: 6) is even more vivid, quoting one journalist who felt his engagement with the news was being "hollowed out" when his time was "occupied [in] filtering, sorting and selectively elaborating on an increasing mountain of incoming information" that leaves "little time to think."

All this cuts journalists off from the practice they want to conduct: It is too simple to blame reduced investment in news-making resources by distant and uncomprehending owners. *All* social actors are competing to attract journalists' attention and so influence the news cycle: The result is a virtually unmanageable flow. Content management systems (Quandt 2008) that stem the resulting flow only increase journalists' distance from the human sources that might provoke ethical reflection. These systemic pressures derive from multiple aspects of digitalization: increased economic competition between media outlets as they seek audience attention, the possibilities of symbolic production far beyond the newsrooms' walls, and reduced budgets for news-gathering. The newsroom has become in the digital age congested to a degree that undermines more than ever before the conditions of ethical reflection. And yet it was the possibility of a journalism oriented toward truth that was the original purpose of a free press.

Where the information circulating in a society that passes for its truth – about the economy and financial operations, about civic and social life, about the workings of government – is not trustworthy, there is a systemic problem far broader than the ethical lapses of a single individual. When no obvious solutions appear to that systemic problem, there is a limit situation, in Ricoeur's term, that requires new ethical insight. Not everyone would see the problem with contemporary journalistic practice the same way of course: The opacity of social life *benefits* those interests that prefer to work under cover of darkness. Quite apart, however, from the harm that is usually done to less powerful people when powerful forces work without public scrutiny, there is the danger to *any of us* from not having key information about our common conditions of life – the state of the global environment as the planet heats up is the most obvious example – and so not knowing what we should do about it.

We can restate, more generally, Sheldon Wolin's principle quoted above that it surely is paradoxical to say that *any society* "should deliberately deceive itself." The problem of media ethics is therefore inescapable in all large societies with large-scale media. This is not to say that we have yet an ethical framework to address this problem or, even if we did, that we have any institutional means for enforcing that ethical framework. It is to the last two points that I now turn in considering the productiveness of a media *ethics*.

The Need for Media *Ethics*

The ethical deficit of contemporary journalism grows regardless of the existence of formal journalistic codes or general moral norms. The reason must be either that existing codes (and their enforcement mechanisms) fail to address this particular ethical deficit on the ground or that the basic conditions of contemporary journalistic practice – its financial, spatial, and temporal resources, the working rules and norms by which it "goes on" – are at odds with the very *possibility* of individual journalists exercising ethical reflection, so that the unethical nature of much media practice is buried under cover of "business as usual." It is the latter, more disturbing, possibility that has emerged from the brief discussion of recent literature on journalistic practice, and, quite separately, from the phone-hacking scandal. Perhaps there are *as yet* no relevant *working* norms adequate to the contradictory conditions in which journalists now operate in large corporations, often with minimal job security and horrendous time deadlines, and across multiple platforms. If so, it is clear that a way forward cannot lie *only* in the formulation of new ethical norms for journalism: Something needs changing in the material conditions of journalism themselves. But how can we provoke change in those conditions without the external shock that ethical challenge has the potential to provide? This normative deficit in the local or national newsroom parallels the normative deficit apparent when we consider media ethics on a global scale. The problem Roger Silverstone (2007) raised is how media can responsibly sustain and manage a global media interface between diverse peoples that overall secures peaceful interaction and mutual recognition rather than hostility and incomprehension. Silverstone's term for this multidimensional space is "mediapolis," but it is clear that there are no common moral frameworks or rules from which we can build the norms of the mediapolis. By definition, being global brings together all peoples, and there is no consensus in the world about morality or even about the rational framework within which moral questions can be posed.

A project of constructing norms for global media must therefore be indirect, building, if it can, from basic understandings of the power, purpose, and potentialities (for good or ill) of global media on which consensus might be reached (compare Couldry 2006: chapter 8). There are no ready-made answers to what journalists should do when a story they believe is true and plausible will, if circulated more widely, be likely to offend other communities, perhaps not the first but subsequent audiences of that story. The Danish cartoon controversy (on which see Eide, Kunelius, and Phillips 2008) was an ethical quandary of this sort, disguised by its origins in the use of humor to make a political point, rather than factual statement. But such conflictual dilemmas can occur at any scale since so many places host multiple ethnic and other communities. Indeed this lack of normative consensus is, in John Rawls's review, inherent to the liberal nation-state (Rawls 1996).

What I am suggesting is that the partial indeterminacy (for now) of ethics for the case of globally circulated media may, instead of being exceptional, characterize normative debate about media practice *on all scales*, given the new complexities of circulation in the digital age. Media ethics is always therefore – whether we are talking about media that circulates globally like the Danish cartoon, or remains at a local scale – something we must evolve through collective dialogue and questioning, starting out from agreed facts, and only gradually expecting to build norms that might over time become the subject of consensus. All this suggests that the appropriate way of framing the normative issues and dilemmas posed by contemporary media is via the tradition of ethics, and not deontology. Let me explain.

There is a broad, if crude, choice to be made between the deontological approach to morality (from the Greek word-root for "ought": *deont-*) and the approach known as "ethics" (from the Greek word-root for "way of life": *ethik-*) (Ricoeur 2007). A deontological approach asks: How *ought* I to behave in this *specific* situation? Or, perhaps, how am I rationally required to behave in this specific situation? But an ethical approach asks more broadly: What kind of life would it be *best* to lead? And (given that): What kind of person would it be *best* to be? The difference between the deontological and ethics traditions has been exaggerated (O'Neill 1996), and their focus certainly at times overlaps. Reaching a considered view on the type of life it is best to lead generates principles about the types of behavior that should be pursued and avoided (often expressed simply in terms of dos and don'ts); equally, as Paul Ricoeur (2007, 1992: 197, 238–9) notes, questions of "ought" (moral rules) depend on a prior specification of what is "good" (the sorts of things that humans aim for). In writing about media ethics, I place less emphasis therefore on the Kantian tradition of moral philosophy which is primarily concerned with what in any situation I am rationally *required* to do, and more on the broadly Aristotelian tradition of ethics, as developed recently by philosophers such as Bernard Williams, John McDowell, and Sabina Lovibond. This tradition asks, more broadly and simply, what a good human life is.

The reasons for this choice derive from the specific aims and reference points of these two traditions. Kant, writing at the height of the European Enlightenment, was concerned to discover the moral principles to which a "good will" – *any* good will, however rationally embodied – would assent, on pain of not contradicting itself. Kant therefore puts great emphasis on the principle of "universalizability," which he expresses as follows: "I ought never to act except in such a way that I could also will that my maxim should become a universal law" (Kant 1997: 15). *Some* idea of universalizability is important in any normative framework (norms, after all, are attempts to identify rules for all of us, not guidelines we can apply to others but evade ourselves). But Kant's aim was very specific: to find laws of absolute generality that would be compelling for any "good will" under any circumstances.

Kant too was looking to build a normative framework from minimal principles, but his choice of what to exclude from view was drastic: First, as the opening sentence of the *Groundwork of the Metaphysic of Morals* states, he leaves out of consideration a variety of possible goods, insisting that "it is impossible to think of anything at all in the world . . . that could be considered good without limitation *except* a good will" (Kant 1997: 7, emphasis added). Second, Kant excludes from the considerations relevant to specifying rules for conduct all the factual conditions of everyday life which might, we would have thought, shape norms that make sense to us: "*inexperienced* in the course of the world, *incapable* of being prepared for whatever might come to pass in it, I ask myself only: can you also will that your maxim become a universal law?" (Kant 1997: 16, emphasis added). Work that draws from the thought of Emanuel Levinas, in a version of Kant's argument that bypasses the "good will," insists that all of us, regardless of our empirical circumstances, are subject to a prior and absolute injunction toward "the other" that is the only starting point for morality (Levinas 1989, Bauman 1992, Pinchevski 2005).

By contrast, the tradition of ethics starts out by reflecting on the kind of life it is *possible and good* for human beings to lead. Injunctions to do what is possible for human beings fall away automatically; so too do absolute obligations that do not, as practiced, fit into some wider notion of what type of life is good for human beings or, as it is often expressed in neo-Aristotelian writing, for "human flourishing." Neo-Aristotelian ethics takes as its reference-point not universal law, or a "good will" abstracted from the flow of human practice, but the types of lives – actual lives, fully embedded in the circumstances of the world – that overall it is good for human beings to lead.

The Aristotelian approach has a number of advantages for us in formulating a normative framework for media in a global age. First, it does not even attempt to specify what absolutely we *ought* to do, and so brackets out areas of disagreement (for example, about obligations to God or to humanity) where we *know* there is no agreement. Second, the Aristotelian approach avoids the claim that it is ever possible to specify *in advance* what one ought to do in a specific situation, and seeks instead to specify the dispositions (or "virtues") that we expect of the person who is likely, on balance, to live a good life and contribute to a shared good life. What actually should be done in any particular circumstance is delegated, in the Aristotelian approach, to the discretion of the person who exhibits the particular virtues and, where conflicts arise between the requirements of different virtues, who exhibits the master virtue of "practical wisdom" (*phronesis*). Practical wisdom means being able to weigh up the often competing requirements and impetuses of different virtues in a complex factual situation. As a starting point for considering the vast and *contradictory* complexity of contemporary media practice, this is useful.

We get a clear sense of how neo-Aristotelian ethics might in general terms proceed from Warren Quinn:

> One tries to determine what, given the circumstances, it would be good or bad in itself to do or to aim at. These questions are referred to larger ones: what kind of life it would be best to lead and what kind of person it would be best to be. The sense of "good" and "best" presupposed in this noncalculative form of practical thought is very general. (Quinn 1995: 186)

Ethics is based on the idea that we can come to agree on certain general things about what a good life would be like without needing to pass through the seemingly more immediate question of how should I behave in this or that particular situation. That indeed is how the ethical tradition gets conversation going even when no consensus about moral rules seems possible or even imaginable.

This neo-Aristotelian starting point for any normative discussion asks: How should any of us live? It therefore looks for consensus around the shared conditions of human life, and certain qualities of a good life that flow from those conditions. Indeed, if one basic condition of human life is that it is lived not in isolation but with others, then any practical good life must involve elements that converge (things that are good *both* for you and me). The question "how should any of us live?" is given its point by the assumption that there are conditions which frame *all* human life, regardless of people's moral and religious beliefs, and that we can identify those conditions (including those we call "human nature"). Those conditions have consequences for our shared circumstances of life and the best general response to those circumstances that we *can* agree upon, *without* relying on a formal moral principle. The generality to which the neo-Aristotelian approach appeals has some similarity in its *outcomes* to Kant's categorical imperative, but it is reached by a different route.

In the neo-Aristotelian approach, definitive answers to the question "how should I behave in a situation of this exact type?" are delegated to the judgments made in practice by those with the right dispositions or "virtues." This ethics is guided by the eminently practical insight that right behavior cannot be identified in advance, abstracted from the often competing requirements of specific contexts. This is what McDowell calls the principle of "noncodifiability": The range of answers that ethics in practice generates cannot be codified in advance (MacDowell 1998: 50–73, especially 65, 73). The only answers that ethics can provide in advance are to questions posed at a different level: What is a good life for human beings in the conditions under which human life is, as a matter of practical necessity, lived? And what are the types of stable disposition required of someone who will prove in the long run to have lived a good life, that is, a life that we would agree *contributes to* a good life for us all, lived together? Note also that we are not concerned here with identifying all the features of a good life, only some minimal features. The basic question for media ethics flows quite readily: How should we act in relation to media, so that we contribute to lives that, both individually and together, we would value on all scales, up to and including the global?

From here virtue ethics routes all normative questions through an investigation of what stable dispositions ("virtues") do each of us *need* to have in order for us to live well together in relation to media.

There is one further point to be made about how a neo-Aristotelian approach would think about the norms appropriate to media as a practice. While neo-Aristotelian references to "human flourishing" might seem very general, much of human activity is not general, but organized into specific types of practice. A "practice" as defined by Alasdair MacIntyre, a Catholic philosopher who drew heavily on aspects of the neo-Aristotelian tradition, is a coherent and complex form of co-operative human activity whose internal goods involve distinctive standards of excellence, which, if achieved, extend our possibilities of human flourishing or excellence (MacIntyre 1981: 175). Media, I would argue, are a practice in this specific philosophical sense. What we do with media *matters* for how humans flourish overall in an era where we are dependent on the exchange of vast amounts of information through media. Media ethics in the digital age involves *all of us*, not just media professionals.

We can now formulate the starting question for media ethics more precisely as follows: *What are the virtues or stable dispositions likely to contribute to us conducting the practice of media well?* – "well," that is, by reference both to the specific aims of media as a human practice and to the wider aim of contributing to a flourishing human life together.

Conclusion

It is only now, as I start my conclusion, that I am in a position to state what I see as the three virtues for media-related practice in a digital era. They are accuracy, sincerity, and care. My argument for accuracy and care, set up in much more detail elsewhere (Couldry 2012: chapter 8), draws on the work of Bernard Williams (2002). By accuracy I mean the disposition to aim at truth and to make the necessary investigative investment to achieve truth. By sincerity, I mean the disposition to only make statements which match with whatever else I believe. By care – and here I go beyond Williams and draw on Ricoeur's (2007) work on "solicitude" and also, more distantly, on that of Roger Silverstone (2007) on "hospitality" – I mean the disposition to show care for the common fabric and spaces of interaction that media make possible.

I have left the specification of these virtues until last because the point of my argument has been not to defend any particular answer to the question of what dispositions we expect of journalists or anyone else who contributes to the practice of media people but to insist, at a preliminary level, that this is the right *type* of question to pose in relation to the normative dilemmas raised by media. My argument is that virtues (or stable dispositions), however we might specify them in detail, are the types of things we should be trying to formulate when developing a normative perspective on the conditions of journalism today.

It is here that the cutting edge of the media ethics tradition becomes clear. Far from claiming to start out from some accepted and already authoritative norm by which contemporary journalists can be judged, media ethics in the neo-Aristotelian tradition asks what, in today's factual conditions, can we expect that media as a practice *might* contribute to our possibilities of living well together and, from that starting point, how we would want those who conduct that practice – which could include all of us at various moments even if we are not journalists – to be disposed to act. I have argued that the very features of the neo-Aristotelian tradition that suit it well to provide starting points for media ethics on a global scale, where consensus over more specific moral norms *clearly* does not exist, suits it equally well to provide starting points for media ethics on a national or local scale where the time and resources for applying pre-existing journalistic norms clearly have been undermined, even perhaps eradicated. In both cases, we need a way of restarting the ethical conversation: Simply pointing to the rulebook (actual or imagined) in the corner is not enough. My wager is that the neo-Aristotelian tradition provides it.

This approach might to some seem rather tame: It will not deliver answers in advance as to what a journalist should do in a specific situation. But it will enable us to see that the conditions of contemporary journalism are in many cases *at odds* with living an ethical life, a life that can be valued. What greater provocation could there be to a more serious collective debate on whether the media institutions we have are the media institutions we need and, if not, what we might, in the interest of living better together, start doing about it? For that debate to begin, we must remain committed to the project of media ethics.

Note

1. Newspaper circulation figures in the introduction are from October 14, 2011: http://www.pressgazette.co.uk/story.asp?sectioncode=1&storycode=48050 &c=1.

Further Reading

An excellent starting point on the paradoxes of contemporary public journalism is chapter 5 of leading moral philosopher Onora O'Neill's book *A Question of Trust* (2002), based on her BBC Reith Lectures broadcast in 2002. On the paradoxes of journalism's role in global politics and a global public world, a pioneering contribution is the late Roger Silverstone's last book, *Media and Morality* (2007). Important discussions of the growing practical difficulties of being ethical as a journalist are *Guardian* journalist Nick Davies's book *Flat Earth News* (2008) and my Goldsmiths colleague Angela Phillips's "Transparency and the New Ethics of Journalism" (Phillips 2011). An eloquent example of the growing concerns about the ethical implications of our dependence on and involvement with digital communications is Sherry Turkle's *Alone Together* (2011).

References

Andrejevic, M. 2008. *I-Spy*. Lawrence: Kansas University Press.

Bauman, Z. 1992. *Postmodern Ethics*. Oxford: Blackwell.

Benkler, Y. 2006. *The Wealth of Networks*. New Haven, CT: Yale University Press.

Bertrand, C.-J. 2000. *Media Ethics and Accountability Systems*. New York: Transaction.

Bimber, B. 2003. *Information and American Democracy*. Cambridge: Cambridge University Press.

Boczkowski, P. 2010. *News at Work: Imitation in an Age of Information Abundance*. Chicago: Chicago University Press.

Boyer, D. 2010. "Making (Sense of) News in the Era of Digital Information." In S. E. Bird, ed., *The Anthropology of News and Journalism: Global Perspectives*. Bloomington, IN: Indiana University Press, 241–56.

Bruns, A. 2008. *Blogs, Wikipedia, Second Life and Beyond: From Production to Produsage*. New York: Peter Lang.

Carroll, J. 2007. "John S. Carroll on Why Newspapers Matter," http://www.niemanwatchdog.org/index.cfm?fuseaction=ask_this.view&askthisid=203, accessed August 24, 2012.

Christians, C., Ferré, J., and Fackler, M. 1993. *Good News: Social Ethics and the Press*. New York: Longman.

Christians, C., Rotzoll, K., and Fackler, M. 1991. *Media Ethics: Cases and Moral Reasoning*, 3rd edn. New York: Longman.

Couldry, N. 2006. *Listening Beyond the Echoes*. Austin, TX: Paradigm Books.

Couldry, N. 2009. "New Online Sources and Writer-Gatherers." In N. Fenton, ed., *New Media: Old News*. Thousand Oaks, CA: Sage, 138–52.

Couldry, N. 2012. *Media, Society, World: Social Theory and Digital Media Practice*. Cambridge: Polity.

Davies, N. 2008. *Flat Earth News*. London: Chatto and Windus.

Eide, E., Kunelius, R., and Phillips, A. Eds. 2008. *Transnational Media Events: The Mohammed Cartoons and the Imagined Clash of Civilizations*. Nordicom: Göteborg.

Elias, N. [1939] 1994. *The Civilizing Process*. Oxford: Blackwell.

Gillespie, T. 2010. "The Politics of 'Platforms'." *New Media & Society* 12(3): 347–64.

Hallin, D. and Mancini, P. 2004. *Comparing Media Systems*. Cambridge: Cambridge University Press.

Hayles, N. K. 2009. "RFID: Human Agency and Meaning in Information-Intensive Environments." *Theory, Culture & Society* 26(2–3): 47–72.

Hepp, A. 2010. "Researching 'Mediatized Worlds': Non-mediacentric Media and Communication Research as a Challenge." In N. Carpentier et al., eds., *Media and Communication Studies: Interventions and Intersections*. Tartu, Estonia: Tartu University Press, 37–48.

Kant, I. [1785] 1997. *Groundwork of the Metaphysic of Morals*, trans. M. Gregor. Cambridge: Cambridge University Press.

Keane, J. 2009. *The Life and Death of Democracy*. New York: Simon and Schuster.

Kellner, P. 2010. "Number Cruncher: A Matter of Trust," Prospect, September 22, http://www.prospectmagazine.co.uk/magazine/peter-kellner-yougov-trust-journalists/, accessed August 24, 2012.

Lanier, J. 2011. *You Are Not a Gadget*. New York: Penguin.

Latour, B. 2004. "From Realpolitik to Dingpolitik, or How to Make Things Public." In B. Latour and P. Weibul, eds., *Making Things Public: Atmospheres of Democracy*. Cambridge, MA: MIT Press, 14–43.

Levinas, E. 1989. The Levinas Reader, *ed.* S. Hand. Oxford: Blackwell.

Lippman, W. 1925. *The Phantom Public*. Orlando, FL: Harcourt Brace.

MacIntyre, A. 1981. *After Virtue*. London: Duckworth.

McDowell, J. 1998. *Mind, Value and Reality*. Cambridge, MA: Harvard University Press.

O'Neill, O. 1996. *Towards Justice and Virtue*. Cambridge: Cambridge University Press.

O'Neill, O. 2002. *A Question of Trust*. Cambridge: Cambridge University Press.

Phillips, A. 2011. "Transparency and the New Ethics of Journalism." In P. Lee-Wright, A. Phillips, and T. Witschge, *Changing Journalism*. New York: Routledge, 135–48.

Pinchevski, A. 2005. *By Way of Interruption: Levinas and the Ethics of Communication*. Pittsburgh, PA: Duquesne University Press.

Quandt, T. 2008. "News Tuning and Content Management: An Observation Study of Old and New Routines in German Online Newsrooms." In C. Paterson and D. Domingo, eds., *Making Online News*. New York: Peter Lang, 77–98.

Quinn, W. 1995. "Putting Rationality in its Place." In R. Hursthouse, G. Lawrence, and W. Quinn, eds., *Virtues and Reasons*. Oxford: Oxford University Press, 181–208.

Rantanen, T. 2009. *When News Was New*. Malden, MA: Wiley-Blackwell.

Rawls, J. 1996. *Political Liberalism*. Cambridge: Cambridge University Press.

Ricoeur, P. 1992. *Oneself as Another*. Chicago: Chicago University Press.

Ricoeur, P. 2007. *Reflections on the Just*. Chicago: Chicago University Press.

Rosen, J. 2006. "The People Formerly Known as the Audience." http://archive .pressthink.org/2006/06/27/ppl_frmr.html, accessed August 24, 2012.

Sassen, S. 2006. *Territory Authority Rights*. Princeton, NJ: Princeton University Press.

Schattschneider, E. 1960. *The Semi-Sovereign People*. Chicago: Holt, Rinehart and Winston.

Silverstone, R. 2007. *Media and Morality*. Cambridge: Polity.

Sontag, S. 2004. *Regarding the Pain of Others*. New York: Picador.

Starr, P. 2004. *The Creation of the Media*. New York: Basic Books.

Stiegler, B. 2009. "Teleologies of the Snail: The Errant Self Wired to a Wimax Network." *Theory, Culture & Society* 26(2–3): 33–45.

Turkle, S. 2011. *Alone Together*. New York: Basic Books.

Ward, S. and Wasserman, H. Eds. 2008. *Media Ethics Beyond Borders: A Global Perspective*. Cape Town: Heinemann.

Williams, B. 2002. *Truth and Truthfulness: An Essay in Genealogy*. Princeton, NJ: Princeton University Press.

Wolin, S. 2008. *Democracy Inc*. Princeton, NJ: Princeton University Press.

Zelizer, B. 2011. "Journalism in the Service of Communication." *Journal of Communication* 61(1): 1–21.

Zittrain, J. 2008. *The Future of the Internet and How to Stop It*. New Haven, CT: Yale University Press.

2

Universals and Differences in Global Journalism Ethics

Thomas Hanitzsch, Patrick Lee Plaisance, and Elizabeth A. Skewes

Some of the most prevalent and recurrent issues in journalism ethics include questions of whether reporting strategies pose invasions of privacy, whether news organizations are sufficiently transparent in their news-gathering efforts and presentation of content, and when graphic images or other sensitive content might be considered harmful or disrespectful. All are important and urgent issues. Since many researchers in media ethics focus their efforts on studying the deliberative process among journalists within news organizations, the field of study necessarily straddles applied philosophy and media sociology. What we are seeing in media ethics research is a slow but burgeoning and increasingly systematic movement toward the use of empirical, social psychological, and moral psychological approaches using long-established measurements to help in theory building.

While the maturation of media ethics theory in Europe, the United States, and Canada has produced an extensive literature that systematically seeks to apply a philosophy of ethics principles and normative frameworks to news production, much that falls under the umbrella of the field remains relatively straightforward articulations of professional norms, values, and conduct policies. Across the globe, it follows that the sophistication and ambition of professional journalism ethics might reflect the relative state of development of countries' journalism cultures. This wide diversity of professional cultures has resulted in a wide range of research approaches – content analyses of ethics codes (Himelboim and Limor 2011), ethnographic studies (e.g., Ryfe 2009), survey treatments (Weaver and Wilhoit 1996, Weaver et al. 2007). It also has come to preoccupy the work of normative theorists seeking to explicate a normative theory of universal values for media practice. An ethic of universal being, which Christians has argued is the central goal of media theorists, is "held together by a pretheoretical commitment to the purposiveness of life in nature, defined in human terms as the sacredness of life" (Christians 2008a: 7).

Christians (2008a) has identified what he calls proto-norms that provide the underpinnings for a media ethics theory that should strive to transcend political and cultural borders. And Christians is not alone in this endeavor: Efforts to articulate universal philosophical principles, thereby refining communication ethics theory and ensuring its relevance in an increasingly globalized media system, is the subject of a burgeoning amount of research (Christians 2008a, 2008b, 2010, Christians and Cooper 2008, Ward 2010, Ward and Wasserman 2008).

This chapter presents a discussion of journalists' professional values that underpin their ethical deliberations and decisions as seen from a global and comparative perspective. Two important aspects of comparative media ethics will be put in focus by this chapter: We will first engage with the quest for universal standards that may mark a globally shared understanding of the fundamental values that underlie journalists' ethical decisions. We will then move our focus to cross-national differences in journalists' ethical values. Our analysis primarily relies on data that was collected as part of the cross-national *Worlds of Journalism Study*. In this collaborative project, a total of 2,000 journalists were interviewed between 2007 and 2009 by a multinational consortium of researchers in 20 countries. The countries included in the study were: Australia, Austria, Brazil, Bulgaria, Chile, China, Egypt, Germany, Greece, Indonesia, Israel, Mexico, Pakistan, Romania, Russia, Spain, Switzerland, Turkey, Uganda, and the United States.

The Quest for Ethical Universals

A wide range of factors serve as influences on one's notion of professionalism and on one's behavior. The socialization of journalists often begins in academic or vocational programs and continues through immersion in newsroom culture. That culture remains the subject of research and inquiry, which methodologically often transverses the individual, organizational, and societal levels of analysis: Individuals' actions, values, and interpersonal interactions can be considered, and yet those same individuals typically are behaving within and are constrained by a web of social and professional norms and expectations. The focus of media ethics research too often shifts among these levels. Concerned as it is with normative practices and behaviors of individual players and specific dilemmas, normative research simultaneously draws from theories in the philosophy of ethics that rely on social and cultural claims of justice, of harm, of human dignity and of duties. Developments in media ethics research have increasingly highlighted this dichotomous focus and the tension it produces.

Recent journalism studies initiatives around the globe appear to suggest a growing consensus around claims that theories of cognitive processing, professional socialization, and cultural ideology point toward elements of universalism in journalistic behavior. In their study of US and Chinese journalists, Zhong and Newhagen used a cognition-based model of news production to suggest a trend toward "ever-increasing globalization of journalistic standards" (2009: 603). Deuze (2005: 278) has argued that we can identify a professional ideology among journalists that "presumes the corresponding ideas and values are carried" across cultural boundaries, and "thus suggests a certain kind of similarity or even universality in the characteristics of media practitioners" (278).

A similar evolution is taking place in the explication of media ethics principles. Elliott (1988, 2009) argued for the existence of normative journalistic values that are sustained across cultures. Hamelink (2000) calls for media systems to rely on a framework of international human rights to support normative professional standards. Ward (2005, 2010) also builds a global journalism ethics, relying on a modified contractualism. Christians (2008a, 2008b) argues that veneration of human life is the touchstone of a universal ethic for media practice. Rao and Wasserman (2007), cautioning against the cross-cultural imposition of Enlightenment media ethics norms, urge "a more pluralistic search for global ethics" in which "truth-telling, no harm to the innocent, empowerment and human dignity, among others, need to be examined and, if necessary, re-interpreted depending on the context and culture to which they are being applied" (2007: 46–7). All of these and others strive to ensure that cultural diversity is not subsumed by a metaphysics, yet it remains uncertain how in practice that threat is to be nullified. Journalism ethicist Stephen Ward (2005) neatly outlines this tension:

> Global journalism ethics will have to amount to more than a dreamy spiritualism about the brotherhood of man and universal benevolence. Conceptually, there is work to be done. Global journalism ethics must show, in detail, how its ideas imply changes to norms and practices. What exactly do journalists "owe" citizens in a distant land? How can global journalists integrate their partial and impartial perspectives? How can journalists support global values while remaining impartial communicators? (Ward 2005: 17)

Hence, while there is little question over whether ethical frameworks are used in journalistic decision making, the universal nature of ethical values is still subject to debate. Most of the proposals for prototype values of a universal code of ethics in journalism have evolved in a Western cultural context and are often, perhaps inadequately so, applied to non-Western cultures. In many of these cultures, people give priority to the concepts of social harmony and unity, which may render ineffective at least some of the "universal" ethical values in certain cultural contexts (Perkins 2002). Overall, comparative evidence suggests some considerable variation in ethical values systems of journalists between countries (Berkowitz, Limor and Singer 2004, Plaisance, Skewes and Hanitzsch 2012, Weaver 1998).

Such cultural diversity notwithstanding, a review of the literature suggests a number of major areas of worldwide concern within the field of ethical reasoning in journalism. These areas include truth, accuracy, factualness, objectivity, credibility, balance, completeness, verification, independence, impartiality, fairness, integrity, responsibility, accountability, honesty, and respect. The obvious problem of this list is that many of these values overlap conceptually, and they operate at different levels: at the level of journalism as an institution, as well as on the level of the individual journalist. Let us briefly summarize the literature.

The first of the above listed ethical values is concerned with the journalists' quest for *truth*. "Journalism's first obligation is to the truth," write Kovach and Rosenstiel (2001: 12) in their influential book *The Elements of Journalism*. There is a wide consensus in global media ethics research that truth, truthfulness, truth seeking, and truth telling are of central importance to the profession (Cooper 1990, Herrscher 2002, Perkins 2002, Randall 2000). Sanders (2003) argues that journalists' commitment to truth is one of the very few normative values that all good journalism should share. Based on a comparative assessment of ethics codes in Europe, North Africa, the Middle East, and Muslim Asia, Hafez (2002) found a broad intercultural consensus regarding the importance of truth and objectivity.

Accuracy is another value fairly often mentioned in the literature. Most of the time, however, accuracy is not listed separately but largely connected to discussions of *objectivity* (Cooper 1990) and *factualness* (Perkins 2002). Ward (2005) adds *credibility* to this list, but he places under this norm the subprinciples of truth seeking and independence. Truth seeking, in this view, includes standards such as accuracy, *balance, verification*, and *completeness* of facts. Verification and completeness are also mentioned quite frequently in media ethics research (Herrscher 2002, Kovach and Rosenstiel 2001).

The above discussed values broadly fall within the area of journalistic epistemology and generally refer to the pursuit of truth (Hanitzsch 2007). *Independence*, by way of contrast, is concerned with the conditions and constraints of editorial practice. It is for this reason that independence is not necessarily an ethical value, though it is frequently evoked in discussions of professional ethics (Cooper 1990, Herrscher 2002, Kovach and Rosenstiel 2001). Most of the time, the notion of independence in the context of journalistic ethics refers to freedom from government interference, censorship, and advertiser influence, and avoidance of conflicts of interest, but it is also used in connection with personal integrity, *impartiality*, and *fairness* (Perkins 2002, Randall 2000, Ward 2005).

The understanding of *integrity* does vary considerably in media ethics theory. On the one hand it stipulates that journalists should not have a personal interest in the causes, businesses, or parties of their sources (Herrscher 2002). In other words, ethical standards of professional conduct often explicitly prohibit conflicts of interest (Ward 2005). Another perception of integrity is related to practices by which journalists personally benefit from the publication of a story (Randall 2000). Practices in which journalists accept money or other material privileges for positive coverage are in particular commonly considered unethical, yet they are widespread in a number of countries (Hanitzsch 2006, Kruckeberg and Tsetsura 2003, Ristow 2010).

Closely related to integrity is *responsibility*, or at least a "desire for responsibility" (Cooper 1990: 3). The norm of responsibility is often evoked in the context of discussions about media freedom, in which journalists are commonly urged to use their freedom in a responsible manner (Perkins 2002). The influential report of the Commission on Freedom of the Press from 1947 carries in its title the notion of a "free and responsible press," arguing that "Freedom of the press means freedom from and freedom for" (1947: 18). Directed at journalism as a social institution, responsibility – or its related term *accountability* – essentially implies that the press is expected to meet the public's need and serve the greater good (Commission on Freedom of the Press 1947). At the level of the individual journalist, it means that journalists ought to bear responsibility for the consequences of their actions (Strentz 2002). In other words, journalists need to be able to justify the consequences of their actions, in accordance with their social contract (Ward 2005).

Still at the individual level, the media ethics literature sometimes refers to a number of traits that are seen as essential attributes of good journalists. *Honesty* certainly belongs to the most popular traits of this kind, often tied to transparency as to how information was obtained and why it was considered important and relevant (Herrscher 2002). In addition to honesty, Herrscher also lists *respect*. In this context, respect can refer to the recognition of people's privacy and sense of honor, as well as to the respectful treatment of diverse ethnic, gender, minority, and religious groups.

As the above reviewed sources indicate, most if not all of these ethical values originated from Western scholarship in the field of media ethics. To what extent these values also apply to journalists from non-Western contexts is an empirical question, one that calls for comparative assessment. In Chapter 5 of this volume, Berenger and Taha argue that a careful review of the values of media in the Arab world shows that we need to take a "contextual" approach to media ethics. A contextual approach is contrasted with a universalism that tries to impose one universal set of principles on different media cultures. The questionnaire of the *Worlds of Journalism* study therefore contained two parts that were specifically tailored to journalists' reflections on professional ethics. The first part was placed at a very early stage in the interview and framed as an open-ended question: "Could you please tell me the journalistic standards and values that are most fundamental to your own work?" We omitted an explicit reference to ethics in the question's wording in order to avoid any potential additional bias that might be introduced by such a normatively loaded concept. The journalists were not given specific hints or further instructions. We simply wanted to know the standards and values that spontaneously came to mind when journalists were confronted with the question.

The results do speak to some of the concepts and values reviewed above. Of the 2,000 journalists interviewed in the 20 countries, 415 made an explicit reference to *truth*. Many journalists in our sample expressed their "respect for the truth," a "drive to tell the truth," and one reporter explicitly mentioned that "the first loyalty of journalism is the truth." Furthermore, it was said that journalists should "cling to the truth," "stick to the truth at all costs," even though it can be a "walk on a tightrope" at times.

Accuracy, or one of its components, was explicitly mentioned by 506 journalists, and it seems to be of particular importance to news people in Australia (53%) and the United States (49%). In the journalists' responses, accuracy was connected to the "correctness" or "rightness" of facts, and faultless news reports. Another major aspect of accuracy was precision and exactness; several journalists mentioned that timeliness should not come at the expense of precision. Furthermore, accuracy could also mean to report the facts or things "as they are" or, in other words, to establish a "congruence" or "correspondence" between the "reality" and the way it is reported in the news.

Partially overlapping with accuracy is *objectivity*. Across all journalists interviewed, a total of 594 respondents referred or alluded to the notion of objectivity, either explicitly or implicitly. The words "objective" or "objectivity" were explicitly mentioned by 396 journalists, which shows that the norm of objectivity seems to have fairly global appeal – even beyond the Western world. Considering the fact that objectivity first evolved in American journalism during the nineteenth century (Donsbach and Klett 1993), one would expect objectivity to be mentioned more often by Western or – more specifically – Anglo-Saxon journalists than by those in other regions in the world. The empirical pattern, however, is quite uneven and does not follow the usual political and cultural divides. Objectivity was in fact most often mentioned by journalists in Romania (42%), Egypt (38%), Austria, Greece, and Pakistan (32%). As an implicit reference to objectivity we classified references to impartiality (149 listings), neutrality (or "no bias," 70) and "distance" (or "equidistance," 22).

As expected, *independence* was also mentioned by the journalists interviewed, but not nearly as frequent as the above values: 153 times. Many respondents framed it in terms of independence from economic interests, media owners, advertisers, politics and – interestingly – the audience.

Credibility was listed 142 times, and was partly connected to reliability and trustworthiness. *Balance* – broadly framed as "give equal say to all parties" – was mentioned 149 times, and *fairness* was cited 112 times.

The journalists also mentioned quite a number of individual traits that are commonly referred to as essential attributes of good journalists. Of these traits, *honesty* was most frequently cited (by 249 journalists), followed by *integrity* (108). Honesty – and in a few cases sincerity – was connected to several levels: It could mean being honest toward the audience, but also toward colleagues and sources. Integrity was mostly mentioned explicitly as such, though in some contexts it was more specifically framed in terms of "incorruptibility," "avoidance of bribes" or "bribe-taking," as well as "zero tolerance of corruption."

Among the other values that were mentioned at least 40 times were *rigor* (e.g., "sound research," "research and scrutiny," "verification," and "double-check," 103); *pluralism* ("diversity of viewpoints," "present all positions," and "all sides of the story," 61); *respect* (for privacy, others, "the rights of the afflicted," 54); *responsibility* (also "accountability," "social responsibility," and "care about consequences of news stories," 43); and *transparency* (42). Several other values were cited less often, some of which refer to desirable attributes of news coverage, including authenticity, contextualization, originality, thoroughness, and completeness. Other values refer to attributes of good journalists: courage, tolerance, open-mindedness, creativity, seriousness, conscience, dedication, passion, wisdom, and justice. Finally, a limited set of ethical values seems to refer to specific national conditions of journalists' work, such as "not harming state security" (in Israel), "social commitment" (in Mexico), and "respecting Islamic values" (in Pakistan).

From the qualitative responses of the 2,000 journalists interviewed we can conclude that it is especially the notions of objectivity, accuracy, and truth that are perceived to be the core elements of a very practical understanding of professional ethics around the world. These values seem to belong to the cornerstones of a commonly shared normative ethics of journalists, one that refers to an idealized understanding of good journalism that in many cases may be difficult to achieve in practice. Journalists have been socialized into these norms through formal journalism education or by way of interacting with other journalists.

It is interesting to note that the stress on objectivity comes at a time when objective reporting as an ideology and a practice has become increasingly subject to heavy criticism among many practitioners and scholars across the Western world. It has been said that objective journalism is impossible to achieve and that it fails to meet journalism's emancipatory goals (Durham 1998, Fuller 1996). Glasser (1992: 176) most forcefully argues that objective reporting is biased in favor of the status quo, so that it "effectively erodes the very foundation on which rests a responsible press." Considering such strong criticism voiced against objectivity in journalism, the journalists' emphasis on the importance of objectivity is surely a notable outcome of this study.

Mapping Differences in Professional Ethics

The emphasis on articulating universal ethics values for media theory has largely been a deductive, philosophical, and sociocultural level endeavor, with broad calls for behavior to be guided by the proper application of normative frameworks. It is largely theory imposed from above, as opposed to systematic, observational, and inductive work intended to build or revise existing theory. This work of philosophical explication has helped mature this area of communication research, bringing to bear in sophisticated ways the philosophy of ethics on professional practice. And yet the essence of ethical theory remains largely relational: that is, concerned with how we account for our decisions and their effects on others in a given situation or dilemma. In this sense, ethics is focused intensely on the individual level. Empirical investigations of individual-level behavior, contextualized within cultural, social, and institutional influences, can further complement, and in some cases offer opportunities to refine, the deductive normative explicative work that now dominates media ethics theory.

For more than a decade, theorists have urged a pluralistic approach to understand the nature of our moral cognition in specific settings (Blasi 1994, Doris and Stich 2005, Flanagan, Sarkissian, and Wong 2008). Too often, they charge, ethicists have made normative claims without an adequate grounding in, and in some cases explicitly shunning, relevant social science research:

> The thought that moral philosophy can proceed unencumbered by facts seems to us an unlikely one: there are just too many places where answers to important ethical questions require – and very often presuppose – answers to empirical questions. (Doris and Stich 2005: 115–16)

Others are even more forceful in questioning broad deductive endeavors to establish universal values:

> Thinking of normative ethical knowledge as something to be gleaned from thinking about human good relative to particular ecological niches will make it easier for us to see that there are forces of many kinds, operating at many levels, as humans seek their good; that individual human good can compete with the good of human groups and nonhuman systems; and finally, that only some ethical knowledge is global – most is local, and appropriately so. (Flanagan, Sarkissian, and Wong 2008: 19)

The comparative research with journalists around the world conducted through the *Worlds of Journalism Study*, discussed below, underscores the truth of this claim. True, a connective tissue of normative standards is found among most all journalistic cultures around the globe, but more prominent seem to be a web of national-level and sociocultural-level factors that shape distinguishing features of media systems, and the relationships among these factors are just now beginning to be fully understood.

Systematic efforts to bring long-established moral psychology instruments to bear on media sociology are emerging. The valuable body of work by Renita Coleman (2003, 2011), as well as her collaborations with Lee Wilkins (Coleman and Wilkins 2009, Wilkins and Coleman 2005), constitutes peerless research that reveals the theoretical links between the moral reasoning skills of media professionals and their approaches to various ethical dilemmas – all based on applying a long-established moral development instrument to media research. Plaisance (2011) has mapped the theoretical basis for an empirical model being used to examine the perspectives and behaviors of media "exemplars," or professionals judged by their peers not only to be successful but whose work and behavior embody key principles such as pursuit of quality and public service. The model comprises life-story data, personality traits, moral reasoning skills, ethical ideologies, and other factors. The *Worlds of Journalism Study* drew upon one of these, an ideological outlook measure of idealistic and relativistic tendencies known as the Forsyth Ethical Position Questionnaire or EPQ (Forsyth 1980), to examine the differential influence of country-level and individual-level variables across a wide array of countries (Plaisance, Hanitzsch, and Skewes 2012).

Developed by Donelson Forsyth in the 1970s, the 20-item EPQ has been used with a variety of populations and has been shown to be highly indicative of how individuals are likely to approach and resolve ethical dilemmas without depending on assumptions that any single pattern of responses is more "ethical" than any others. The EPQ is theoretically robust because the two dimensions it measures – relativism and idealism – reflect the deontology–teleology dichotomy found in the moral philosophy literature. One approach rests on claims that external moral laws or principles exist and are the basis for our moral duties; the other suggests that the "good," in contrast, must be defined along largely utilitarian notions based primarily on the consequences of a given act.

The EPQ measures both "the degree of idealism to which the individual subscribes" and "the extent to which the individual rejects universal moral rules in favor of relativism" (Forsyth 1980: 176). Forsyth developed a widely used taxonomy that identifies four types of ethical ideologies based on "high" and "low" degrees of expressed idealism and relativism (see Figure 2.1). The "situationist" exhibits a high degree of both relativism and idealism, and thus rejects claims that we can identify universal moral principles to help us determine the "rightness" of an act, and yet also embraces the idea that all actions should be based on a concern or love for

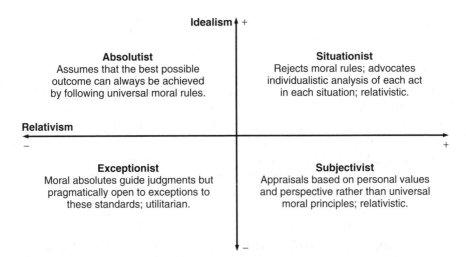

Figure 2.1   Classification of Ethical Ideologies according to Forsyth (1980: 176)

others. The "subjectivist," too, exhibits a high degree of relativism, yet as he or she also scores low on the idealism items, the absence of external moral standards means that what is "right" can only be determined by one's own personal perspective. The "absolutist" exhibits a high degree of idealism and a low score on the relativism measures, rejecting the notion that the "rightness" of an act depends on its consequences and instead advocating that to behave morally means to live by principles regardless of the possible harmful consequences. Finally, the "exceptionist," scoring low on both measures, mirrors a pragmatic approach, believing universal moral rules are important, yet applying such rules by taking into account mitigating contexts and circumstances.

Based on responses to 20 items on a nine-point Likert scale (10 items related to relativistic claims, 10 items related to idealistic claims), the EPQ has been tested widely and shown to be reliable, valid, and not correlated with social desirability. It has been used to explain a range of behaviors and beliefs among a wide variety of populations. For example, Forsyth (1980) found significant differences across the four ideologies with respect to attitudes toward abortion, euthanasia, homosexuality, and human in vitro fertilization. EPQ responses also suggest that people who demonstrate high idealism scores are more likely to judge perceived unethical behavior more harshly and have a greater ethic of caring (Forsyth, Nye, and Kelley 1988). People with high relativism scores tend to show more Machiavellian tendencies, that is, they tend to consider moral and ethical concerns irrelevant in social life (Leary, Knight, and Barnes 1986). Applied extensively in research on business and marketing sectors, the EPQ also has led researchers to claim that potential corporate whistle-blowers described as nonrelativistic were more likely to report peer wrongdoing (Barnett, Bass, and Brown 1996), and that ethical ideology responses reflect employees' abilities to identify verbally sexually harassing behaviors (Keyton and Rhodes 1997). Researchers also have used the EPQ to establish relationships between ethical orientations and right-wing authoritarianism (McHoskey 1996), nihilistic tendencies (McHoskey et al. 2000), support for animal experimentation (Wuensch and Poteat 1998), and discriminatory attitudes (Wilson 2003). Most recently, a meta-analysis of research examining variables influencing ethically questionable business decisions concluded that measures based on Forsyth's idealistic–relativistic typology served as reliable predictors of perceived ethical and unethical conduct. Individuals with strong internal beliefs that call for avoiding harm to others were found less likely to make unethical choices. Furthermore, a relativistic moral philosophy was also positively related to unethical choice (Kish-Gephart, Harrison and Klebe Treviño 2010).

Until its application in the *Worlds of Journalism Study*, the EPQ had not been widely used in journalism ethics research. Plaisance (2007) applied the EPQ to media ethics students to explore the effect of course content on their degrees of reported idealism and relativism, and has incorporated the instrument into a model to study professional "exemplars" in journalism and public relations (2011). While we were unable to use all 20 Forsyth idealism and relativism measurement items in our survey of 2,000 journalists around the globe, and while we also were required to modify some items due to translational and cultural imperatives, we found interesting cross-national differences in journalists' reported levels of idealism and relativism, as well as important relationships among journalists' reported levels of idealism and relativism and national-level factors.

The measures we used in order to map differences in journalists' ethical reasoning were adapted to the comparative purposes of the study in order to work more effectively across the countries included in the project. The six measures of ethical ideologies used Likert scales that ranged from strongly agree to strongly disagree, to ask respondents to assess three statements related to relativism and three related to idealism, where strongly agree indicates high relativism or high idealism. The three statements assessing relativism were:

- "What is ethical in journalism varies from one situation to another."
- "Ethical dilemmas in news coverage are often so complex that journalists should be allowed to formulate their own individual codes of conduct."
- "There are ethical principles which are so important that they should be followed by all journalists, regardless of situation and context." (signifies low relativism)

And the three statements assessing idealism were:

- "Journalists should avoid questionable methods of reporting in any case, even if this means not getting the story."

- "Reporting and publishing a story that can potentially harm others is always wrong, irrespective of the benefits to be gained."
- "There are situations in which harm is justifiable if it results in a story that produces a greater good." (indicates low idealism)

The results indicate that most journalists in the surveyed countries tend to obey universal principles that should be followed regardless of situation and context. They also agreed on the importance of avoiding questionable methods of reporting, even if this means not getting the story. Much less approval – although the extent of it varied between countries – could be found with respect to the view that due to the inherent complexity of ethical dilemmas, journalists should have more personal latitude in solving these problems. This desire for flexibility also relates to the relative importance of means versus ends. Many journalists think that in certain situations, some harm to others could be justified if the result supports a greater public good.

A comparative assessment therefore shows a relatively broad consensus among journalists from the various countries with respect to the general adherence to ethical principles. News workers in Western contexts exhibit a stronger tendency to disapprove of a contextual and situational ethics. This attitude, however, also exists in non-Western contexts, though less strongly. Chinese, Pakistani, and Russian journalists, on the other hand, tend to be most open to situational ethical practices. Consistent with this result, interviewees in Western contexts showed little support for the idea that journalists should be allowed to set their own individual ethical standards.

Similarities between journalists from Western countries also exist with regard to idealism. Although journalists in all countries agreed on the view that questionable methods of reporting should be avoided, those working in Western contexts appreciate this idea more than their colleagues in a developmental and transitional environment. Regarding the acceptance of harmful consequences of reporting for the sake of a greater public good, journalists in most Western countries – but also their colleagues in Brazil, Indonesia, Mexico, Pakistan, Turkey, and Uganda – tend to keep all options on the table. Journalists in Bulgaria, Chile, China, Egypt, Romania, and Russia, on the other hand, exhibit a relatively strong normative orientation with regard to the acceptance of harmful consequences.

Figure 2.2 not only visualizes similarities between countries but also points to an abstract structure that underpins the configuration. The plot was generated through the CoPlot technique, which is essentially an extension of multidimensional scaling.[1] In Figure 2.2, the relative (dis)similarities between countries are plotted against the six indicators relating to ethical ideologies. The indicators appear as vectors on the plot. These vectors emanate from a shared origin, and the angle between two vectors represents the correlation between the two variables in the overall solution (Bravata et al. 2008).

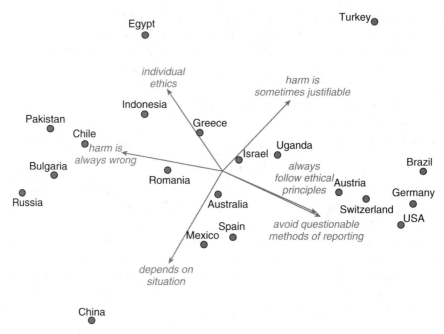

Figure 2.2   Cross-national Differences in Ethical Ideologies

The solution very much corresponds to the theoretical expectations of Forsyth's four types of ethical ideologies. On the left side of the map, a situational approach to ethical decisions is clearly distinguished from a subjectivist perspective. However, most countries are actually located in between the two poles. On the right side of Figure 2.2, there are journalistic cultures (Austria, Brazil, Germany, Switzerland, and the United States) that fall within what Forsyth calls the "absolutist" paradigm, while Turkey shows a strong tendency to the "exceptionist" approach. Generally, we can say that journalists in countries on the right side of the map tend to follow universal rules of ethical-professional conduct, but in some countries they are more open to exceptions from these rules than in others. Journalists in countries on the right side of the map are more considerate of the potential consequences of their reporting, and their differences are related to the extent to which they opt for either a situational or a subjective approach to ethical dilemmas.

Relating journalists' ethical ideologies to larger contextual forces we found that country-level, ideologically based factors such as degree of press freedom, democratic institutionalization, and private ownership appeared to have significant influences on journalists' degrees of relativistic and idealistic thinking (Plaisance, Skewes and Hanitzsch 2012). The high international polity and freedom measures of countries appeared to explain a significant amount of journalists' embracing of idealistic thinking. Those two factors, as well as private media ownership, also appear to be positive determining factors in the adherence of relativistic thinking of journalists. This, in large part, simply reflects the fact that the assumptions informing individuals' perceptions of reality, combined with hegemonic and value judgments about collective responsibility and individualism that are unquestioned, are rooted in deeply ingrained ideological framing of culture. Where people come from, in other words, depends upon the cultural – and moral – assumptions of their milieu. Overall, the results from our attempt to explain general ethical orientations of journalists thinking appear to reaffirm hierarchical theories of influences on news making as articulated by Shoemaker and Reese (1996), McQuail (2000), Voakes (1997), and others.

Conclusions

This chapter set out to comparatively assess journalists' professional values that underpin their ethical deliberations and decisions as seen from a global perspective. In this context we paid specific attention to increasingly used empirical methodologies drawn from social and moral psychology by media ethics theorists to systematically examine relationships among factors in decision making. We argue that this development is critical to the continued maturation of the field in that it promises to provide more solid foundation for normative theorizing. Our claims about how journalists *should* think about key ethical principles and dilemmas will simply carry more credibility when they are grounded in a more inductive understanding of the range of factors that influence why journalists do the things they do now. There is an important distinction to be made here, however, regarding the role and value of such empirical approaches. The peril of committing the naturalistic fallacy is a real one. One cannot derive a normative "ought" statement from mere description of practice on the ground. We are not implying that the constellation of principles and ethical ideologies revealed by such research is in any way "proof" that these journalists have got it right and that our ethical norms for media should be amended to reflect their wisdom. Rather, our normative and empirical work in media ethics should be discursive in nature – our spadework of systematic, inductive observation continually testing and refining the normative and predictive qualities of our broad theories. What we are suggesting is the need for more of a balance in media ethics research: The maturation of the field arguably depends on our ability to harness the methodologies of moral psychology to better inform the normative claims that we are often so quick to make. We suggest that striving for this discursive balance in media ethics research will ultimately result in better theory building, and in moving us toward what Doris and Stich call "a generally applicable, empirically adequate account of moral functioning" (2006: 16).

From the qualitative responses of the 2,000 journalists who were interviewed as part of the cross-national *Worlds of Journalism Study*, we found the notions of objectivity, accuracy, and truth to be at the core of a shared normative understanding of professional ethics among journalists from around the world. Even though these norms may often be difficult to achieve in practice, they are important elements of a global imaginary of good journalism. These norms are thriving in journalism textbooks, they are taught at journalism schools, and constitute key elements in professional codes of conduct. They belong to the "occupational ideology" (Golding and Elliott 1979: 115) and "instrumental myth" (Sigelman 1973: 133) of journalism, and as professional narratives about the past they populate the collectively shared memory of journalists.

These striking normative similarities notwithstanding, our analysis also points to substantial cross-national differences in the ethical frameworks of journalists. We tried to map these differences by drawing on Forsyth's (1980) well-received distinction between four general types of ethical ideologies: absolutist, situationist, subjectivist, and exceptionist. The results of our analysis attests to the usefulness of this typology. Most of the 20 investigated national journalism cultures can indeed be grouped into four broad paradigms: A cluster of countries that follows the absolutist paradigm includes Austria, Germany, Switzerland, the United States, and Brazil. Turkey, on the other hand, is very different from the other investigated societies in that journalists exhibit a strong tendency to follow the exceptionist approach. A fairly heterogeneous group of countries, which includes Bulgaria, China, Mexico, Russia, and Spain, represents the situationist type, while Egyptian and Indonesian journalists follow the subjectivist paradigm.

Furthermore, the clustering of countries also reveals a more general pattern that can be tied to an explanatory framework emphasizing journalism's legal and political context. Journalists in most Western countries operate in politically and legally relatively stable contexts, which makes it much easier for them to routinely rely on universal standards of professional conduct and effectively pursue their journalistic mission. In other countries, most notably in developing and transitional contexts, the legal and political context of journalism tend to be weak. Journalists are forced to invest more deliberation when facing the concrete of ethical dilemmas, and their differences are related to the extent to which they opt for either a situational or a subjective approach. This explanation is further supported by our analysis of the principal determinants of journalists' degrees of relativistic and idealistic thinking. It appeared that degrees of media freedom, democratic performance, as well as media ownership, bear a significant influence on journalists' ethical ideologies.

Overall, the implications for claims asserting global journalism ethical norms are clear, and significant: While "ethical knowledge" might not necessarily be local, significant national and cultural factors enforce important distinctions that in turn govern how journalists respond to ethical issues. This is not to say that resulting values and moral judgment cannot shift or evolve, and perhaps even gravitate toward "universal" normative standards. But it is critical that theorists have a firm understanding of what those cultural and moral frameworks are, and how a relevant shift toward such universal standards might be articulated, before any such norms are "imposed." Our results, consequently, should be read as affirmation for the ethical model of "pluralistic universalism" espoused by Christians, Ward, and others – a model that provides an avenue to build a public service ethos around core notions of dignity, integrity, and responsibility, even while the manifestations of such key values vary culturally. Theorists advocating universal standards must acknowledge that journalistic norms are rooted in deeply invested social value systems that serve a variety of needs. "It is important to interrogate the logic of universality and explore alternatives to it," Alleyne suggests (2009: 386). As with any effective argument, the empirical must inform the normative. The maturation of media ethics theory, and of journalism ethics in particular, requires more of this inductive research.

Note

1. We used the specialized software tool Visual CoPlot developed by Adi Raveh and David Talby. The program is freely available from http://www.davidtalby .com/vcoplot/.

Further Reading

Readers looking for an introduction to journalism and media ethics may start with Lee Wilkins and Clifford Christians's edited *Handbook of Mass Media Ethics* (New York: Routledge, 2009), Karen Sanders's *Ethics and Journalism* (2003), or *Journalism Ethics: A Philosophical Approach*, edited by Christopher Meyers (New York: Oxford University Press, 2010). Those specifically interested in recurrent discourses in the area of journalism ethics might find it interesting to use the book *Philosophical Issues in Journalism*, edited by Elliot Cohen (New York: Oxford University Press, 1992) as an insightful starting point.

An excellent reference for transnational media ethics is Stephen Ward's recent book *Global Journalism Ethics* (2010). A concise discussion and evaluation of the problems posed by universal standards of journalism ethics can be found in an article by Roberto Herrscher in the *Journal of Mass Media Ethics* (Herrscher 2002). Readers looking for comparative evidence on selected aspects of questionable reporting practices may look at David Weaver's multinational survey of journalists in *The Global Journalist: News People Around the World* (Cresskill, NJ: Hampton Press, 1998).

The discussion of global differences in journalism ethics in this chapter is heavily based on Donelson Forsyth's taxonomy of "ethical ideologies." A concise introduction to his theory can be found in his *Journal of Personality and Social Psychology* article (Forsyth 1980). The application of Forsyth's work to the field of journalism ethics was pioneered by Patrick Lee Plaisance in an article in

Journalism & Mass Communication Educator (Plaisance 2007). Those interested in getting more detailed information about the conceptual and methodological framework of the *Worlds of Journalism Study* may start their reading with an article by Hanitzsch et al. that appeared in 2011 in *Journalism Studies* 12(3): 273–93 and the study's website at www.worldsofjournalism.org.

References

Alleyne, M. D. 2009. "Global Media Ecology: Why There is No Global Ethics Standard." In L. Wilkins and C. G. Christians, eds., *Handbook of Mass Media Ethics*. New York: Routledge, 382–93.

Barnett, T., Bass, K., and Brown, G. 1996. "Religiosity, Ethical Ideology and Intentions to Report a Peer's Wrongdoing." *Journal of Business Ethics* 15: 1164–74.

Berkowitz, D., Limor, Y., and Singer, J. 2004. "A Cross-Cultural Look at Serving the Public Interest: American and Israeli Journalists Consider Ethical Scenarios." *Journalism* 5(2): 159–81.

Blasi, A. 1994. "Moral Identity: Its Role in Moral Functioning." In B. Puka, ed., *Fundamental Research in Moral Development*, vol. 2. New York: Garland, 168–79.

Bravata, D. M., Shojania, K. G., Olkin, I., and Adi, R. 2008. "CoPlot: A Tool for Visualizing Multivariate Data in Medicine." *Statistics in Medicine* 27: 2234–47.

Christians, C. G. 2008a. "The Ethics of Universal Being." In S. J. A. Ward and H. Wasserman, eds., *Media Ethics Beyond Borders: A Global Perspective*. Johannesburg: Heinemann, 6–23.

Christians, C. G. 2008b. "Universals and the Human." In K. Glenister Roberts and R. C Arnett, eds., *Communication Ethics: Between Cosmopolitanism and Provinciality*. New York: Peter Lang, 5–21.

Christians, C. G. 2010. "On Living in Nirvana." *Journal of Mass Media Ethics* 25(2): 139–59.

Christians, C. G. and Cooper, T. 2008. "On the Need and Requirements for a Global Ethic of Communication." In J. V. Ciprut, ed., *Ethics, Politics and Democracy: From Primordial Principles to Prospective Practices*. Cambridge, MA: MIT Press, 293–318.

Coleman, R. 2003. "Race and Ethical Reasoning: The Importance of Race to Journalistic Decision Making." *Journalism & Mass Communication Quarterly* 80(2): 295–310.

Coleman, R. 2011. "Color Blind: Race and the Ethical Reasoning of Blacks on Journalism Dilemmas." *Journalism & Mass Communication Quarterly* 88(2): 337–51.

Coleman, R. and Wilkins, L. 2009. "The Moral Development of Public Relations Practitioners: A Comparison with Other Professions and Influences on Higher Quality Ethical Reasoning." *Journal of Public Relations Research* 21(3): 318–40.

Commission on Freedom of the Press. 1947. *A Free and Responsible Press. A General Report on Mass Communication: Newspapers, Radio, Motion Pictures, Magazines, and Books*. Chicago: University of Chicago Press.

Cooper, T. 1990. "Comparative International Media Ethics." *Journal of Mass Media Ethics* 5(1): 3–14.

Deuze, M. 2005 "What is Journalism? Professional Identity and Ideology of Journalists Reconsidered." *Journalism: Theory, Practice & Criticism*, 6(4): 442–64.

Donsbach, W. and Klett, B. 1993. "Subjective Objectivity: How Journalists in Four Countries Define a Key Term of Their Profession." *Gazette* 51(1): 53–83.

Doris, J. M. and Stich, S. P. 2005. "As a Matter of Fact: Empirical Perspectives on Ethics." In F. Jackson and M. Smith, eds., *The Oxford Handbook of Contemporary Philosophy*. Oxford: Oxford University Press, 114–52.

Doris, J. M. and Stich, S. 2006. "Moral Psychology: Empirical Approaches," *Stanford Encyclopedia of Philosophy*, http://plato.stanford.edu/entries/moral-psych-emp/, accessed 3 February, 2012.

Durham, M. G. 1998. "On the Relevance of Standpoint Epistemology to the Practice of Journalism: The Case for 'Strong Objectivity'." *Communication Theory* 8(2): 117–40.

Elliott, D. 1988. "All is Not Relative: Essential Shared Values and the Press." *Journal of Mass Media Ethics* 3(1): 28–32.

Elliott, D. 2009. "Essential Shared Values and 21st Century Journalism." In L. Wilkins and C. G. Christians, eds., *Handbook of Mass Media Ethics*. New York: Routledge, 28–39.

Flanagan, O., Sarkissian, H., and Wong, D. 2008. "Naturalizing Ethics." In W. Sinnott-Armstrong, ed., *Moral Psychology. Vol.1: The Evolution of Morality: Adaptations and Innateness*. Cambridge, MA: MIT Press, 1–25.

Forsyth, D. R. 1980. "A Taxonomy of Ethical Ideologies." *Journal of Personality and Social Psychology* 39(1): 175–84.

Forsyth, D. R., Nye, J. L., and Kelley, K. 1988. "Idealism, Relativism and the Ethic of Caring." *Journal of Psychology* 122: 243–8.

Fuller, J. 1996. *News Values: Ideas for an Information Age*. Chicago: University of Chicago Press.

Glasser, T. L. 1992. "Objectivity and News Bias." In E. Cohen, ed., *Philosophical Issues in Journalism*. New York: Oxford University Press, 176–83.

Golding, P. and Elliott, P. 1979. *Making the News*. London: Longman.

Hafez, K. 2002. "Journalism Ethics Revisited: A Comparison of Ethics Codes in Europe, North Africa, the Middle East, and Muslim Asia." *Political Communication* 19(2): 225–50.

Hamelink, C. 2000. *The Ethics of Cyberspace*. Thousand Oaks, CA: Sage.

Hanitzsch, T. 2006. "Selling the Autonomy of Journalism: The Malpractice of Corruption Among Indonesian Journalists." In H. Xiaoming and S. K. Datta-Ray, eds., *Issues and Challenges in Asian Journalism*. Singapore: Marshall Cavendish Academic, 169–88.

Hanitzsch, T. 2007. "Deconstructing Journalism Culture: Towards a Universal Theory." *Communication Theory* 17(4): 367–85.

Herrscher, R. 2002. "A Universal Code of Journalism Ethics: Problems, Limitations, and Proposals." *Journal of Mass Media Ethics* 17(4): 277–89.

Himelboim, I. and Limor, Y. 2011. "Media Institutions, News Organizations, and the Journalistic Social Role Worldwide: A Cross-National and Cross-Organizational Study of Codes of Ethics." *Mass Communication and Society* 14: 71–2.

Keyton, J. and Rhodes, S. C. 1997. "Sexual Harassment: A Matter of Individual Rights, Legal Definitions or Organizational Policy?" *Journal of Business Ethics* 16: 129–46.

Kish-Gephart, J. J., Harrison, D. A., and Klebe Treviño, L. 2010. "Bad Apples, Bad Cases and Bad Barrels: Meta-Analytic Evidence about Sources of Unethical Decisions at Work." *Journal of Applied Psychology* 95(1): 1–31.

Kovach, B. and Rosenstiel, T. 2001. *The Elements of Journalism*. New York: Three Rivers Press.

Kruckeberg, D. and Tsetsura, K. 2003. "International Index of Bribery for News Coverage: A Composite Index by Country of Variables Related to the Likelihood of the Existence of "Cash for News Coverage," Institute for Public Relations, http://www.instituteforpr.org/topics/bribery-news-coverage-2003/, accessed August 27, 2012.

Leary, M. R., Knight, P. D., and Barnes, B. J. 1986. "Ethical Ideologies of the Machiavellian." *Personality and Social Psychology Bulletin* 12: 75–80.

McHoskey, J. W. 1996. "Authoritarianism and Ethical Ideology." *Journal of Social Psychology* 136(6): 709–17.

McHoskey, J. W., Betris, T., Worzel, W., Szyarto, C., Kelly, K., Eggert, T., Miley, J., Suggs, T., Tesler, A., Gainey, N., and Anderson, H. 2000. "Relativism, Nihilism and Quest." *Journal of Social Behavior and Personality* 14(3): 445–62.

McQuail, D. 2000. *McQuail's Mass Communication Theory*. London: Sage.

Perkins, M. 2002. "International Law and the Search for Universal Principles in Journalism Ethics." *Journal of Mass Media Ethics* 17(3): 193–208.

Plaisance, P. L. 2007. "An Assessment of Media Ethics Education: Course Content and the Values and Ethical Ideologies of Media Ethics Students." *Journalism & Mass Communication Educator* 61(4): 378–96.

Plaisance, P. L. 2011. "Moral Agency in Media: Toward a Model to Explore Key Components of Ethical Practice." *Journal of Mass Media Ethics* 26(2): 96–113.

Plaisance, P. L., Skewes, E. A., and Hanitzsch, T. 2012. "Ethical Orientations of Journalists Around the Globe: Implications from a Cross-National Survey." *Communication Research*, 39: 641–61.

Randall, D. 2000. *The Universal Journalist*, 2nd edn. London: Pluto.

Rao, S. and Wasserman, E. 2007. "Global Media Ethics Revisited: A Postcolonial Critique." *Global Media and Communication* 3(1): 29–50.

Ristow, B. 2010. "Cash for Coverage: Bribery of Journalists Around the World," Center for International Media Assistance, http://cima.ned.org/sites/default/files/CIMA-Bribery_of_Journalists-Report.pdf.

Ryfe, D. M. 2009. "Broader and Deeper: A Study of Newsroom Culture in a Time of Change." *Journalism* 10(2): 197–216.

Sanders, K. 2003. *Ethics and Journalism*. London: Sage.

Shoemaker, P. J. and Reese, S. D. 1996. *Mediating the Message: Theories of Influence on Mass Media Content*, 2nd edn. White Plains, NY: Longman.

Sigelman, L. 1973. "Reporting the News: An Organizational Analysis." *American Journal of Sociology* 79(1): 132–51.

Strentz, H. 2002. "Universal Ethical Standards?" *Journal of Mass Media Ethics* 14(4): 263–76.

Voakes, P. S. 1997. "Social Influences on Journalists' Decision Making in Ethical Situations." *Journal of Mass Media Ethics* 12(1): 18–35.

Ward, S. J. A. 2005. "Philosophical Foundations for Global Journalism Ethics." *Journal of Mass Media Ethics* 20(1): 3–21.

Ward, S. J. A. 2010. *Global Journalism Ethics*. Montreal: McGill-Queen's University Press.

Ward, S. J. A and Wasserman, H. Eds. 2008. *Media Ethics Beyond Borders: A Global Perspective*. Johannesburg: Heinemann.

Weaver, D. 1998. "Journalist Around the World: Commonalities and Differences." In D. H. Weaver, ed., *The Global Journalist: News People Around the World*. Cresskill, NJ: Hampton Press, 455–80.

Weaver, D. H., Beam, R. A., Brownlee, B. J., Voakes, P. S., and Wilhoit, C. G. 2007. *The American Journalist in the 21st Century*. Mahwah, NJ: Erlbaum.

Weaver, D. H. and Wilhoit, C. G. 1996. *The American Journalist in the 1990s*. Mahwah, NJ: Erlbaum.

Wilkins, L. and Coleman, R. 2005. *The Moral Media: How Journalists Reason about Ethics*. Mahwah, NJ: Erlbaum.

Wilson, M. S. 2003. "Social Dominance and Ethical Ideology: The End Justifies the Means?" *Journal of Social Psychology* 143(5): 549–58.

Wuensch, K. L. and Poteat, M. G. 1998. "Evaluating the Morality of Animal Research: Effects of Ethical Ideology, Gender and Purpose." *Journal of Social Behavior and Personality* 1(1): 139–50.

Zhong, B. and Newhagen, J. E. 2009. "How Journalists Think While They Write: A Transcultural Model of News Decision Making." *Journal of Communication* 59: 587–608.

3

The Role of the Journalist in Reporting International Conflicts

Howard Tumber

Poet and journalist Kwame Dawes working in Jamaica and Haiti said:

> I am taking a chance to even suggest that therefore these poems are about a subject, about something that we understand in a journalistic way. Yet they are exactly that because they are about my witnessing not intellectually but mostly emotionally what is happening before me. I stand as a witness to the silences – to what goes unspoken and ignored – to the things that float away as if insubstantial but that are filled with the simple breaths of people trying to make sense of their existence. This act of witnessing allows us to reach to other levels of meaning that can only be reached through the poem. (Dawes 2010: 22–3)

How should we define the role of the journalist in reporting conflict? Definition is always difficult to assess. Definitions of the war correspondent run the gamut from dictionary definitions which describe their association with news organizations: "a correspondent employed to report news concerning the conduct of a war and especially of events at the scene of battle" (Merriam Webster); or the rather stark: "a journalist who reports from a scene of war" (Oxford Dictionaries), or the one that touches on control and embedding (Dictionnaire de droit international public):

> a specialized journalist who is present, with the authorization and under the protection of the armed forces of a belligerent, on the theatre of operations and whose mission is to provide information on events relating to ongoing hostilities.

Military dictionaries and companions use similar terminology: "a newspaper or periodical writer or radio or television journalist assigned to report on a war or combat situation from direct observation" (The Oxford Essential Dictionary of the US Military).

Away from these somewhat technical definitions of the role, when we move to self-definition emanating from the myriad of autobiographies and

Global Media Ethics: Problems and Perspectives, First Edition. Edited by Stephen J. A. Ward.

reminiscences produced by journalists, a more colorful description and essence of the role emerges, in some instances portraying war reporting as an art. "The miserable parent of a luckless tribe" is how William Howard Russell, the first war correspondent who was reporting on the Crimean War for *The Times* between 1854 and 1856, described himself (Bellamy and Holmes 2001: 971).

Pease (1942) described the role of the ancient war correspondent in Greece as not only confined to reporting but playing an important role in the unfolding of the events being covered. Fame was driving the risky task of reporting war events, which consisted of detailed descriptions accompanied with fictitious and exaggerated elements which were not exempt from forms of censorship. Objectivity was not an issue in the literary pieces of ancient Greek generals: "the truly marvellous work of the war correspondent in the present war, with its world-wide scope, its imminent risk of death, wounding, disease, capture, starvation" (Pease 1942: 63).

The ambiguous status of the war correspondent has been defined by Mowrer (1943: 119) who, writing during World War II, believed this was a well-defined role both locally and internationally:

A war correspondent must not bear arms. He can be shot at, but must scrupulously refrain from shooting back. He is a non-combatant, officially attached to an armed force. He is a civilian, but wears, usually, a prescribed uniform. He has no rank, but is accorded, usually, the privileges of an officer.

Farrar describes the war correspondent as an outlaw and eyewitness during World War I:

Special correspondents, press photographers, the youngest reporters on the staff, sub-editors emerging from the little dark rooms with a new excitement in eyes that had grown tired with proof correcting, passed each other on the stairs and asked for their chance. It was a chance of seeing the greatest drama in life with real properties, real corpses, real blood, real horrors with a devilish thrill in them. (Philip Gibbs, 1915, cited in Farrar 1998: 2)

Young journalists dream of becoming a foreign or war correspondent more than any other specialism in journalism. In the twenty-first century it still maintains a romanticism that negates the more mundane features of the occupation. The myths are propagated by the abundance of stories and incidents told by members of the occupation writing about themselves through memoirs and autobiographies. Most of these are colorful and amusing, occasionally offering insights into their occupational world, where they "either by circumstance or position have covered great events or interviewed the famous" (Morrison and Tumber 1988: 445).

So how do we make a normative assessment of the role of the journalist who reports on conflict. As a hero? As independent and neutral? Also, how should we account for their emotions and sensitivities? Are they embedded or independent? Are they embedded by definition, as a previous example showed? And how should we analyze ideas of patriotism, engagement, and attachment?

In contrast to ancient times, since the nineteenth century discussions on media reporting of armed conflicts have been persistently framed by the question of objectivity and the role of the war correspondent. Understanding the nature of the role of the journalist reporting conflicts requires a consideration of the question of objectivity and partisanship, questions which acquire greater significance in the light of the reporter witnessing death, atrocities, and the horror of war directly and "on site." But it also demands a long-standing discussion on the aim of journalism: What is it for? Finding out, reporting, telling the "truth," exposing, condemning, aligning with or questioning official stories, and/or giving voice to the voiceless? The figure of the war correspondent in this sense condenses the dilemmas faced by journalistic practice more generally: the relationship between objectivity and ethical responsibility, the difficult intricacies between politics and professionalism, gaining access to information but losing independence, censorship versus public condemnation. The choice between independent and therefore critical reporting or inaccurate and partial political propaganda is one that has been described in terms of supporting or not the military operation: What side are war correspondents on (Knightley 2003)?

War correspondents become trapped in the complicated relationships between the political power of governments and the media more broadly, as their role inevitably responds to the media organizations that employ them (and may cease to do so). The war correspondent's need for economic resources to work and live on the site of conflict, the difficulties of taking into account at least two sides of the war story, the need for physical protection and safety, and the compliance of some media organizations with the official narrative adopted by the government render the idea of the independent, objective, and neutral reporter a fantasy. The politics of embedded journalism, for example, brings about the formalization of an implicit relationship between the military and the press which gets officially organized and institutionalized. This has political and ethical implications for the practice of journalism not only due to censorship but also because embedding constitutes a strategic source of legitimization of war that becomes *facilitated* by the media in the eyes of the public. The war correspondent, then, is rendered a political instrument of war. The reporting of recent wars has signaled the transformation of the role of the journalist and the emergence of a new type of war correspondent: from playing a heroic role risking their lives to becoming a myth-maker at the service of propaganda.

As Knightley (2003: 547) observes:

> In the future, all media organisations wishing to report a war will be offered
> a stark ultimatum: you can either embed a correspondent with an American

or British unit and follow the rules we will set out for you, or; you can make independent arrangements to cover the war.... However, if you decide to cover the war from the enemy side and you get in our way, then we may well fire on you.

Embedded in Gulf War II

For some of the journalists who reported Gulf War II, the socialization process began some four months earlier in November 2003 when they attended one of a series of Pentagon week-long training seminars for journalists at a Marine Corps base in Quantico, Virginia. The seminar provoked the journalists into assessing their relationship with the military and even made news itself. The issue that arose was how to ensure "separation."

The media coverage of the Iraq invasion was extraordinary. War correspondents – or frontline correspondents[1] – were able to make use of a range of audiovisual aids, such as "satellite video phones, digital feed hardware, night vision goggles, and laptops" (Katovsky and Carlson 2003: xii) to report media stories: "Americans and viewers worldwide had never seen anything like the 2003 real-time coverage in Iraq" (Sylvester and Huffman 2005: 9). Yet the strategy of embedded reporters implemented in this invasion represented also an official strategy to control the flow of information in the media (Tumber and Webster 2006: 20).

While embedding provides journalists with greater safety and access, the tension between freedom of expression, objectivity, and following the rules characterizes the new era of embedded media, especially when emotional bonds, camaraderie, and identification have been established between reporters and soldiers (Katovsky and Carlson 2003: xv–xvi, Tumber and Palmer 2004). Mutual benefits are said to characterize embedding: "In the end, however, both sides agreed that in this kind of military operation, embedding worked to the mutual benefit of the media and the military" (Sylvester and Huffman 2005: 211). In their examination of the ethics of the embeds, Sylvester and Huffman make a distinction between journalists' involvement with the military and the enemy and their reporting of war events: "The embeds in general did not seem to consider such involvement unethical as long as their reporting efforts were not compromised" (2005: 214).

Whether to embed was not an easy decision for war correspondents, despite the fact that unilateral reporters were never welcomed by the armed forces. "There were inherent journalistic risks if they did, and inherent safety risks if they didn't" (Katovsky and Carlson 2003: xiv). Embeds undergo military training (weapon protection, first aid, camouflage, sanitation, and other basic military skills). Critiques leveled at the journalism of attachment include restrictions in time and space and a focus on the drama of war (Tumber and Webster 2006), no checking of information in the rush to get the story out, the mixing of emotions and facts, dismissal of objectivity, unfair reporting, stereotypes of gendered reporting, a search for moral leadership, and self-censorship (McLaughlin 2002: 166–77). Claims to objectivity are undermined in embedded reporting:

> Objectivity was feared to be the first casualty of war. In fact, the majority of the embeds said that they could not maintain objectivity. They were, after all, eating, sleeping, riding – in a couple of cases dying – with the soldiers they were accompanying.... The embeds, however, were keenly aware that they owed their lives to the soldiers surrounding them. (Sylvester and Huffman 2005: 212–13)

In this sense, embeds must be cautious of their relationship with the military forces, for "'embedded' should never mean 'in bed with'" (Page, cited in Tumber and Palmer 2004: 52).

For the journalists in the Falklands War (1982), their future was structurally entwined with that of the troops. Matters that became important to the troops also mattered to the journalists, including contact with families back home. The result was that journalists not only shared the moods of the troops through collective experience, but also began to identify with them by being part of the whole exercise.

Consequently, although some of the journalists disagreed with the decision to send the Task Force to the South Atlantic, once it seemed that conflict was inevitable, they felt an affinity with the troops, a mutual determination to see the venture through to the end. What was happening to the journalists was that their professional need to cover a story in a detached way was slowly being swamped by the very real, human need to belong, to be safe. The comradeship and closeness demonstrated by the troops, which the journalists so admired, were not just the random product that any occupational association throws up, but the response to having to work closely together, especially during military exercises, and having to solve tasks as a group. When correspondents are embedded among their own country's military, their professional values of impartiality and objectivity can look wrong or misplaced (Morrison and Tumber 1988: 130).

Martin Bell, the BBC correspondent, opened up the debate on "journalism of attachment," and the conflict in Bosnia was his landmark. Trained in a tradition that called for "objective" and "dispassionate" journalism, he came into conflict with other journalists and his editors over the journalist's position in the conflict. After leaving Bosnia, Bell tended his resignation from the BBC. In response, Bell was criticized by a senior editor of the BBC's 24-hour international news channel who argued that journalists should not give up their fundamental role of reflecting events in the world (Tumber 1997: 4).

Bell was not the only foreign correspondent working in Bosnia who changed their position. The debate in the Western media over the conflict in Bosnia tended to focus on the role of the journalist and the influence of public opinion on Western governments. Although Bell dismisses the traditional professional guidelines, he still seems to believe in the dichotomy between objective and crusading journalism. Bell disagrees with the BBC guidelines that stipulate that its reporters should be objective and dispassionate:

> I am no longer sure what "objective" means; I see nothing objective in the relationship between reporter and event, but rather a human, dynamic interaction between them. As for the "dispassionate," it is not only impossible but inappropriate to be thus neutralized – I would even say neutered – at the scene of atrocity or massacre, or most man-made calamities. (Bell 1997: 10)

At the same time however, he is not ready to give up on "objectivity," which he opposes to crusading journalism. He is careful to argue that his "journalism of attachment" is not a call for campaigning or crusading journalism, which he believes should be confined to the political and polemical literature and not in the daily diet of news:

> I am old fashioned enough to insist on the distinction between them. Besides, it is my experience that the campaigners and crusaders tend to find what they are looking for, ignoring inconvenient evidence to the contrary and the unstructured complexity of what is actually out there. (Bell 1997: 8)

Bell's position has hardly escaped criticism. Ward (1998), for example, cannot see the logic of how Bell can theoretically and clearly draw this distinction between attached journalism and crusading journalism. Ward sees Bell's position as an unsuccessful attempt to criticize objectivity, while trying to maintain most of the values of objectivity.

Bell dismisses the idea that his journalism of attachment is a desire to see the journalism of George Orwell and John Pilger take over the front line reporting of daily news. Instead he maintains that he calls for an abandonment of the dispassionate practice of the past to be replaced by

> a journalism that cares as well as knows; that is aware of its responsibilities; and will not stand neutrally between good and evil, right and wrong, the victim and the oppressor. This is not to back one side or faction or people against another; it is to make the point that we in the press, and especially television which is its most powerful division, do not stand apart from the world. (Bell 1997: 8)

In both the Falklands conflict and in Gulf War II, the journalists' adoption of military jargon, however strenuously they sought to excise it from their vocabulary, indicates how efficiently they were being assimilated. In Gulf War II the conditions for the journalists were different from those experienced during the Falklands, and the nationalities of the correspondents was not restricted as was the case during the Falklands. But other elements of the situation were very similar.

The journalist in the modern war zone faces "professional, political and personal pressures" (McLaughlin 2002: 180). War correspondents risk their lives to cover and report war events. The quality of reporting ranges from flawed, distorted, and biased to more balanced or critical accounts, influencing audiences' perceptions of the events and, in so doing, contributing to shape the reality of war. "The journalist, then, is in an impossible position: damned if he acts, damned if he doesn't" (McLaughlin 2002: 178). Modern journalists in the war zone in terms of their own consciousness face the meaning of objectivity, the tension between the private and the public, the complex relationship with the military forces, emotional and moral precepts, and the value of honesty and clarity (McLaughlin 2002).

In a speech given in November 2010, the late war correspondent Marie Colvin (2012) stated: "Our mission is to report these horrors of war with accuracy and without prejudice." However, the role of the war correspondent is not clear-cut and the circulation of the notion of "embedded journalist" during the US invasion of Iraq in 2003 has illustrated the complicated relationship between media reporting and governmental geopolitics. As part of this embedded press over 600 national and international news organization workers were attached to American military units to deliver coverage of the war (see Paul and Kim 2004, Tumber and Palmer 2004). Throughout the twentieth century, relationships between the press and the military have been marked by the tensions arising from the different goals of the press, which seeks to gain access to information in order to inform the public, and the goals of the military, which are to guarantee operational and informational security (Paul and Kim 2004).

Exploring the role of the first female reporters from a historical perspective, Sebba (1994) argued that while some women reporters were emotionally involved in their causes, concerned with issues of social justice, agitating politically for or against what they believed was right (e.g., Florence Dixie and Sheila Grant Duff), other women reporters (e.g., Elizabeth Wiskemann and Martha Gellhorn) praised objectivity, hiding their passions and emotions.

> The news media's integrity is more than just an internal matter for the journalism profession to address. News coverage does much to establish the political framework within which war is conducted. (Seib 2004: 31)

Discussing the work of journalist Chris Hedges, Seib argued that

> objectivity in war reporting is skewed from the start, distorted by boosterism that is dressed up as "patriotism," which renders war correspondents part of the machinery of war and affects the quality of wartime coverage. (Seib 2004: 31–2)

In this sense, war correspondents play a vital role in promotion and legitimation of war. Therefore "every time they write a story they have an unmeasurable but definite responsibility for what happens next" (Knightley 2003: xiii).

The Journalist as Patriot

If war correspondents are ready to risk their lives to report war events, why would they do it if not for a patriotic cause and love for one's nation? Often eccentricity, passion, career promotion, adrenaline, curiosity, madness, and a heroic spirit are mentioned. Yet patriotism has been said to be "at the heart of British journalists' culture" (Keeble 2001: 98), American citizens' pride (Tumber and Webster 2006: 53), and that which explains the American tradition "for the pen to ally itself with the sword" (Katovsky and Carlson 2003: xv). The question of loyalty to one's country is exacerbated during wartime. News organizations come to safeguard the national morale and interest during wars (Keeble 2001: 98). But patriotism can also be viewed as a partiality that challenges cosmopolitan ethical journalism (Ward 2010). Patriotism can negatively affect journalism by eroding the ethics of professional principles such as impartiality and fair reporting (Ward 2010). Drawing on his own professional experience, Ward summed up what war correspondents who "beat the patriotic drum" often feel in the front line:

> I should not embarrass Canada by reporting on mistakes in the field; I should not quote soldiers puzzled about their mission; I should do "feel good" pieces about soldiers watching hockey via satellite in warring Bosnia. (Ward 2010: 213)

Despite possible constraints for the ethical practice of journalism in forms of narrow or extreme patriotism, journalists' commitment to ethical and democratic principles can evaluate appeals to patriotism. Both moderate patriotism and democratic journalism honor similar values such as freedom of speech, critical news media, openness, transparency, and tolerance (Ward 2010). Some even place frontline reporters and military officers at a similar level in their experience of the reality of war with the subsequent psychological implications and sharing of patriotic objectives, despite stereotypical clashes of interests between secrecy and publicity (Moorcraft and Taylor 2008: ix–x).

So can journalists be patriotic under any conditions?

> Journalists can be patriots only if they are moderate, rationally constrained patriots serving their country and humanity by fulfilling their distinctive social role as critical informers of democratic citizens. They can be patriots only if they evaluate claims of patriotism according to the principles of

inclusivity, rational restraint, and public scrutiny. When journalists serve
a different form of patriotism, they violate their ethical role in an open
democratic society. (Ward 2010: 215)

In this view, patriotism in journalism can be accepted insofar as it is
inclusive, supporting all citizens; restrained and not xenophobic; and
surviving sustained public scrutiny and investigation. A global form of
moderate patriotism is then recommended for a global and democratic
form of public journalism for humanity.

Journalists often face a dilemma between their permanent responsibility
for monitoring the action of authorities and their patriotic need to support
the national armed forces, even when this may entail covering up military
inefficiency. Stories of boundary crossings between war correspondents
and soldiers between the nineteenth and early twenty-first century have
been documented, with reporters killing soldiers, being partisan and propaganda agents, arming themselves, and supporting rebels (McLaughlin
2002). In times of war, then, professional journalistic standards may
loosen moral imperatives by virtue of presenting balanced accounts on
the atrocities of war. Ironically, during wars media workers have been
traditionally seen as unpatriotic by governments, leading to censorship
and other forms of information control (Keeble 2001). The variety of perspectives often taken by war reporters range from supporting the armed
forces and depicting the enemy in negative ways, to promoting peace and
criticizing government policies and military operations.

The extent to which media present a sanitized view of war depends on
broadcasting time, varied interpretations of professional ethical standards
toward reporting the truth (however shocking it may be), and complex
historical and political factors (Keeble 2001). The patriotic spirit of war
correspondents is challenged when some of them, from a professional
commitment to reporting the truth, or emphatic feelings for the suffering
of others, or a deep affection developed for the countries covered, dare
to report from the enemy side (Moorcraft and Taylor 2008). Anger,
intimidation, and criticism is what frontline reporters receive at home after
crossing the border (Keeble 2001), quite apart from the risks of being killed
by their own country's military forces, either due to "collateral damage"
or to "shooting the messenger" operations (Moorcraft and Taylor 2008).

Safety and Legal Protection

War correspondents do not have special protection in armed conflicts
under humanitarian law, apart from that which would protect them
by virtue of their civilian status (see relevant laws and conventions:
http://www.icrc.org/ihl.nsf/full/380). In this regard, journalists and other
media professionals run a high risk of being subjected to arbitrary detention for alleged security reasons. This is where the distinction between

"war correspondents" (Article 4 A (4) of the Third Geneva Convention) and "journalists" (Article 79 of Additional Protocol I) matters. Both are recognized as civilians, but only war correspondents are entitled to prisoner-of-war status under the Geneva Convention. War correspondents are formally authorized to accompany the armed forces. By virtue of this close relationship, upon capture, they are accorded the same legal status as members of the armed forces. War correspondents thus benefit from the protections of the Third Geneva Convention as supplemented by Additional Protocol I and customary international law (International Committee of the Red Cross 2010). War correspondents constitute one category among those persons who accompany the armed forces but are not members of them. In this legal status they are entitled to protection if wounded during an armed conflict according to the Geneva Convention for the Amelioration of the Condition of the Wounded and Sick in Armed Forces in the Field and at Sea.[2] While reporters working in an embedded press system face risks equal to that of combat soldiers, this strategy is not entirely safe: The safety of those embedded in the Iraq war was greater than those who were reporting unilaterally, yet none of the latter were exempt from risk of death, as was seen in Iraq (Paul and Kim 2004, see also Tumber and Palmer 2004).

Journalists play a vital role in providing reliable information on matters of public interest, and their work can sometimes expose them to special risks of physical violence and arbitrary prosecution. These risks increase in a context where new technologies have changed the nature of armed conflicts. Tumber and Webster (2006) refer to this process as the "information war" and analyzed evidence provided by the Committee to Protect Journalists (CPJ) showing that between 1995 and 2004, 341 journalists were killed while doing their job and that the vast majority were murdered rather than killed in crossfire. The evidence also indicates that local journalists covering issues of crime, human rights violations, and corruption face the greatest threat. Other expert organizations and stakeholders have also accumulated detailed and disturbing evidence of the scale of the present threat to the physical safety of journalists and to their ability to exercise freedom of expression. The death toll of journalists in 2009 alone reached over 130. UNESCO recently announced its findings that the majority of killings of journalists take place in dangerous places that are not designated as "conflict zones" and that 80 percent of deaths in recent years are targeted assassinations.

We can distinguish between attacks on journalists that take place in time of war (or armed conflict) and those that take place outside of war and armed conflict (Noorlander 2011). During times of war/armed conflict, a different body of laws applies than at other times. The Geneva Conventions and associated documents and standards offer a degree of protection and status to journalists that clearly differentiate them from combatants. Targeting of journalists – like the targeting of humanitarian personnel or civilians, for that matter – constitutes a war crime under international humanitarian law. The UN Security Council Resolution 1738 falls into this category as well (http://www.unesco.org/new/en/communication -and-information/intergovernmental-programmes/ipdc/special-initiatives /safety-of-journalists). A large number of journalists are killed or targeted in violent attacks every year outside situations of armed conflict. Sometimes journalists are murdered without any apparent connection to their work, but often they are clearly targeted for stories they have published.[3] In the vast majority of cases, killings of journalists go unsolved in all countries where the trend is endemic. The reasons for this are complex and touch on issues of corruption and official connivance in criminal activity.

The rising toll of targeted killings of journalists causes serious concern among journalists, jurists, human rights groups, and governments. This state of affairs represents not only a persistent threat to the lives and safety of journalists targeted on account of their work, but also a dangerous and growing threat to freedom of expression in countries in different parts of the world. States are obliged under international law to respect and protect individuals exercising their right to freedom of opinion and expression, and to ensure that those rights are upheld. Those obligations also apply in times of conflict. In this regard, the International Programme for the Development of Communication (IPDC) adopted a "Decision on the Safety of Journalists and the Issue of Impunity" in March 2008, urging all member states to comply with the obligations under international law to end impunity and to prosecute those responsible for violations. As part of this decision, the Director-General of UNESCO condemned the killings of over a hundred journalists between 2008 and 2009 and requested further information about their judicial status from the member states concerned.

The Journalist as Witness

Personal commitment is often enhanced when journalists see themselves as "witnesses." With the public perceived as ignorant about world affairs, the journalist as witness has to open the public's eyes to the brutal realities of the world (Seib 2004). Journalist Robert Fisk believed that he was witnessing history when reporting from Lebanon:

> I would see with my own eyes a small part of the epic events that have shaped the Middle East since the Second World War .... I suspect that this is what journalism is about – or at least what it should be about: watching and witnessing history and then, despite the dangers and constraints and our human imperfections, recording it as honestly as we can. (Fisk 1990: x)

The role of the war correspondent is situated at the crossroads of the need to be protected and the need to gain access to the battlefront and thus become attached to the armed forces, on the one hand, and the ethical duty dictating independent reporting, on the other. The notion of "journalist as witness" (Hoskins and O'Loughlin 2010) provides a possible conceptual way out of this dilemma. It refers to the myriad ways in which war reality or "the truth of war" can be told and represented to others by those in a position to perceive it closely in times of diffused war – frontline journalists but also citizens, soldiers, NGO workers, bloggers, film-makers. Is it the journalist's role to convey "truth, accuracy, fairness, balance, authenticity" and does the mediatization of war give way to new practices of witnessing that enable alternative forms of information control (Hoskins and O'Loughlin 2010: 62). No doubt war correspondents construct the reality of war while reporting it. "The journalistic self-image – even of war correspondents – is geared more to the role model of the neutral mediator than to that of an advocate of peace journalism" (Eilders 2005: 647).

The idea of the journalist as witness presupposes the direct observation of a situation. The journalist's description may differ from government portrayals of the situation. Herein lies the role of the journalist as a hero who would report to society, disclosing lies. In "The Camera as Witness," Levac highlights the power of journalistic images. He shows how his photograph of two security service officers taking down a young Palestinian hijacker off a bus, whose skull was later crashed with a rock, came to bear witness to what actually happened and to unveil lies in the story. The photograph undermined official reports that said all of the hijackers had been shot during a rescue operation of the bus passengers (Levac 2007: 183).

Morality is at the heart of this notion – the promotion of human values. The depiction of violations of that which is human underpins the notion of the journalist as a moral witness, one which is concerned with discovering and explaining causes rather than depicting atrocities (cf. Michael Ignatieff, cited in Plaisance 2002). Bearing witness involves responsibility and commitment toward victims of war and other forms of suffering and requires the journalist to befriend them in order to represent or speak for them as a proxy (Richards and Mitchell 2011: 768). Issues of justice, engagement, and judgment, and the politics of representation are central to the role of the journalist as witness to violence and the suffering of others:

> Bearing witness as a foreign correspondent or frontline reporter involves the journalist being there and the risks associated with being there in extraordinary times of volatility, danger, and suffering. Journalists who judge the suffering of others to be injustice and who speak on behalf of these people increase their level of journalistic engagement from observation and reporting of the story to a practice of participation and making the story their own story. Bearing witness as a claim of journalistic practice involves entering into a story in which the journalist denounces the injustice experienced by those suffering. (Richards and Mitchell 2011: 769)

Yet the potential heroic role of the journalist as witness can be rapidly undermined by the emergence of forms of global surveillance facilitated by media corporations, networks, and infrastructures. There seems to be a paradox arising from the need to be in the front line to report war events and bear witness to the horror and suffering of people, on the one hand, and the fact that the very presence of war correspondents can lead to the targeting of journalists facilitated by media technologies and their surveillance capacity (Cottle 2011). In this sense, online reporting can be seen as a unique means to compare official truth claims with alternative perspectives, which are seen as more independent, subjective, interactive, and unauthorized than the former (Allan 2006).

Whether war reporting needs to provide objective or subjective accounts of the facts is a contending issue in journalism relating to broader discussions of media ethics:

> at best it bears its witness not only to how the world is but how it ought to be and might have been. It is, in the philosopher's algebra, a counterfactual business. Good journalism can only criticise what actually happened by pointing to what might have happened instead. (Inglis 2002: 83)

Truth claims cannot escape their socially constructed nature: "what counts as truth in a war zone, of course, is very much in the eye of the beholder" (Allan 2006: 109). Being witness to atrocity is neither safe, nor easy, nor desirable. The treatment of journalists as the people's witnesses or storytellers range from eagerness and admiration to incredulity and skepticism (Inglis 2002) and certainly to work dismissals, harassment, life threats, and controversy.

Witnessing and War Crimes

> By virtue of their profession, war correspondents may well find themselves among the first outside witness on the scene at war crimes. As such, they are going to need to be an informed witness, and the rest of us are going to have to become a far better informed and engaged public. (Weschler 2007: 26)

The choice not only to fulfill the journalist's moral duty to report atrocity and disclose official lies, but also to become an official witness and testify before international criminal courts, has been the subject of controversy with regard to the disclosure of confidential sources of information, press freedom, personal safety, and professional codes of conduct (Spellman 2005). Tumber (2008) formulated the ethical issues in terms of objectivity, relationship with sources, personal and industry safety, and verification of stories. In recent years, prosecution of war crimes has become widespread. The issue of international justice has been spotlighted by the recent establishment of many types of courts. The recent courts include the International Criminal Court in July 2002, the setting up of ad hoc tribunals for the former Yugoslavia in 1993, and for Rwanda in 1994;

hybrid courts for Sierra Leone in 2002 and for Cambodia in 2003; and national courts of various kinds in Kosovo, East Timor, Bosnia and Herzegovina, Croatia, Serbia, and Iraq. Some journalists willingly testified before the war crimes tribunals for Yugoslavia and Rwanda while others, particularly those employed by United States news organizations, although willing to provide information to the tribunal investigators, either tended to see the subpoena power of the tribunals as a threat to First Amendment journalistic freedoms or were specifically prevented from testifying by their news organizations (Tumber 2008, 2010). The question then arises as to whether war correspondents should be granted special protection and the right not to testify before war tribunals to safeguard their personal safety and professional integrity.

For photographers or photojournalists, the problems can become more acute even if they manage to reach the frontline. As Don McCullin (2003) reflected in an article for *The Guardian*:

> What makes a good photograph? Do you focus on the dead, like many of the photographers in these pages, or on the living? Is it still possible to speak for the Iraqis incinerated in the American ambush on the Basra road, or do you concentrate on the injured, the women and children, the civilians? Do you want to create art, or to take pictures? Some war photographers describe themselves as artists – all photographers have a leaning to be artistic – but is war the right place to indulge this inclination? There is a danger of walking through the killing fields and thinking of Goya and modern icons, of press awards or prize ceremonies at The Hague.

An analysis of the trial for war crimes committed in the former Yugoslavia in 1993 and in Rwanda in 1994 revealed the emergence of new conceptions in fighting war crimes among journalists and photojournalists (Tumber 2010). The role of the photojournalist emerged as that of a forensic journalist whose work was directed toward giving a voice to those who remain voiceless in violent confrontations. Photographs and film footage can make an impact and become powerful in holding perpetrators accountable, supplying new evidence in international criminal courts for the prosecution of ethnic cleansing crimes. Changes in photojournalists' perceptions can be understood as a result of their experiences on the ground and their interaction with a broader public, NGOs, and international organizations (Tumber 2010).

To understand the accomplishment of the dangerous tasks of war journalists, professional motivations and requirements need to be considered. Journalists in the front line have a key role in informing the public about the practices committed during the war, and they may also seek to have a direct impact on the events covered. In these practices ethical, legal, professional, and safety reasons combine together to create the complex day-to-day journalist's reality. Even though journalists may want to use their reports and recordings to help civil populations under attack, they face a series of obstacles when trying to achieve this goal. Employers preventing them from releasing information, lawyers dismissing the objectivity and legal status of the evidence, lack of resources, and the absence of minimum safety guarantees have an impact on journalists' degree of involvement when covering news related to war crimes (Tumber 2010).

The lack of response from the international community and the legal restrictions imposed on the content provided by journalists covering the Rwandan and the Balkan atrocities have produced changes in the approaches journalists and photojournalists take to war events. First, the use of images is now seen as a requirement for producing moving content and undeniable evidence of actions committed on the scene of a crime. Second, journalists have learnt that international NGOs such as Amnesty or Human Rights Watch may have the required reputation to catch the attention of the international community. Lawyers and legal authorities dismissed the value of evidence given in the international criminal tribunal for Rwanda, but Kosovo is a clear example in which journalists and international agencies advocated for a successful international intervention.

In line with this argument, there are novel ways of co-operation and proximity between journalism and human rights organizations. In order to cope with the current demands of fast interventions in war zones, NGOs advocating for human rights had to review their methodology. These new types of interventions brought human rights workers and war correspondents together. As a result of these interactions, fruitful relations for sharing legal and security advice, material resources, and key services such as transportation and translation have emerged. The journalist's need for fresh news plays a vital role in fighting war crimes. Occasionally, war correspondents are the first in documenting a crime and can supply highly valuable evidence for criminal courts and human rights organizations. Similarly, the direct contact with these organizations has provided journalists with a different sense for searching, collecting, and documenting material that can have direct implications for human rights advocacy (Tumber 2010).

Conclusion

Journalists reporting international conflicts face continuous ethical challenges in their daily work. These challenges have been discussed in relation to a range of issues: privacy, access to information, confidentiality of sources, industry codes of conduct, professionalism, and objectivity standards (Keeble 2001); telling lies and reporting stories, conflicts of interest, freedom and truth, values and principles, and the education of the emotions (Sanders 2003); and an ethical philosophy of global journalism aimed at putting conceptual order on journalistic values and beliefs and promoting a global democratic and just world (Ward 2010).

Today ethical controversies in journalism are the result of a combination of political, economic, cultural, and technological factors. Keeble (2001) identifies the following factors shaping ethical dilemmas: the fast spread of information and the existence of countless media organizations, which impose constraints on the application of general journalistic principles; the diversification and multiplicity of journalists' roles; the prevalence of technical skills over self-reflective, critical accounts concerned with ethics; the centrality of profit-making and advertising as widespread concerns; the limited scope of the journalist's individual freedom; and the need to place discussions of ethics in their broader political, cultural, and geographical context.

Journalists who cover conflict are essential contributors to the citizen's comprehension of the war. Operating in conditions of danger and discomfort, where threats to their safety are commonplace and traumatic experiences are routine, they risk death, injury, and kidnap and have to work in inhospitable locations with significant risks.

In a journey beginning with embedding in the military, traveling via the journalism of attachment, through the construction of an agenda of advocacy journalism, to appearing as a witness in a war crimes trial, the modern war correspondent is now a fully engaged journalist. Objectivity used to have a prized status within journalism. In war reporting the principle of detachment was a key element in the social construction or formation of identity. Today the idea or ethos of journalistic objectivity has evolved into one of responsible engagement – in which a moral stance is adopted and where accurate reporting demands determining responsibility. Responsible engagement, though, can be highly selective, lacking critical independence and performing a disservice to the public. The categories of objectivity, neutrality, and detachment have to be re-examined as the cultural forms of war corresponding, and the ideological framework of journalism in general, changes (see Tumber and Prentoulis 2003). War correspondents are now fully engaged, from their assignment and their stories to their appearances at The Hague.

Notes

1. The label "war correspondents" was seen by some journalists as embodying the macho type of reporter epitomized by Ernest Hemingway and they therefore preferred to be named "frontline correspondents" (see Tumber and Webster 2006, especially p. 167).
2. Geneva Conventions Act 1957 Sch. 3 art. 4 para. A(4): "persons who accompany the armed forces without actually being members of them, such as civil members of military aircraft crews, war correspondents, supply contractors, members of labour units or of services responsible for the welfare of the armed forces, provided that they have received authorisation from the armed forces which they accompany."
3. The Marlene Esperat murder in the Philippines is a good example of such a case, as is the murder of Anna Politkovskaya in Russia in 2006.

Further Reading

Readers seeking an introduction to the world of war correspondents should look no further than Phillip Knightley's *The First Casualty* (2003), a history of war reporting from the 1850s to the Kosovo war. For other general scholarly accounts see Greg McLaughlin's *The War Correspondent* (2002), Philip Seib's *Beyond the Front Lines* (2004), and Mark Pedlety's *War Stories: The Culture of Foreign Correspondents* (London: Routledge, 1995).

For a selection of journalists' personal insights of reporting on conflict see Michael Herr's *Dispatches* (New York: Knopf, 1977) about Vietnam, *War Reporting for Cowards* by Chris Ayres (London: John Murray, 2006) about Iraq, Anne Garrels's *Naked in Baghdad: The Iraq War and the Aftermath as Seen by NPR's Correspondent* (New York: Picador, 2003), Robert Fisk's *Pity the Nation* (1990) about Lebanon, *The Face of War* by Martha Gellhorn (New York: Atlantic Monthly Press, 1993), James Cameron's *Point of Departure* (Boston: Oriel Press, 1978), Seymour Hersh's *My Lai 4: A Report on the Massacre and its Aftermath* (New York: Random House,1970), Ed Vulliamy's *Seasons in Hell: Understanding Bosnia's War* (New York: Simon and Schuster, 1994), Jon Steele's *War Junkie: One Man's Addiction to the Worst Places on Earth* (London: Transworld, 2002), and photographer Don McCullin's *Unreasonable Behaviour: An Autobiography* (London: Jonathan Cape, 1990).

For influential books by media scholars on specific conflicts see Dan Hallin's *The "Uncensored War": The Media and Vietnam* (New York: Oxford University Press, 1986) and Morrison and Tumber's *Journalists at War* (1988) on the Falklands. For studies on the first Gulf War see Philip M. Taylor's *War and the Media* (Manchester: Manchester University Press, 1992), Robert Denton's *The Media and the Persian Gulf War* (Westport, CT: Praeger, 1991), Douglas Kellner's *The Persian Gulf TV War* (Boulder, CO: Westview Press, 1992), and W. Lance Bennett and David Paletz (eds.) *Taken by Storm. The Media, Public Opinion, and US Foreign Policy in the Gulf War* (Chicago: Chicago University Press, 1994). For insights into the recent Iraq war see Justin Lewis et al.'s *Shoot First and Ask Questions Later* (New York: Peter Lang, 2006), Piers Robinson et al.'s *Pockets of Resistance* (Manchester: Manchester University Press, 2010), and Tumber and Palmer's *Media at War* (2004). For information and stories about war correspondents' safety see John Owen and Chris Cramer's *Dying to Tell the Story – The Iraq War and the Media: A Tribute* (Brussels: International News Safety Institute, 2003), Roy Gutman and David Rieff's edited *Crimes of War: What the Public Should Know* (New York: Norton, 1999), and Anthony Feinstein's *Dangerous Lives* (Toronto: Thomas Allen, 2003) which examines the psychological trauma experienced by war correspondents.

References

Allan, S. 2006. *Online News: Journalism and the Internet*. Maidenhead: Open University Press.

Bell, M. 1997. "TV News: How Far Should We Go?" *British Journalism Review* March 8: 7–16.

Bellamy, C. and Holmes, R. 2001. "War Correspondents." In Richard Holmes (ed.), *The Oxford Companion to Military History*. Oxford: Oxford University Press, 971–4.

Colvin, M. 2012. Speech given at St Bride's Church, Fleet Street, London on 10 November, 2010, The Guardian, 22 February 2012, http://www.guardian.co.uk/commentisfree/2012/feb/22/marie-colvin-our-mission-is-to-speak-truth?fb=native.

Cottle, S. 2011. "Taking Global Crises in the News Seriously: Notes from the Dark Side of Globalization." *Global Media and Communication* 7(2): 77–95.

Dawes, K. 2010. "Bearing Witness: The Poet as a Journalist." *Nieman Reports*, Fall: 21–3.

Eilders, C. 2005. "Media Under Fire: Fact and Fiction in Conditions of War." *International Review of the Red Cross* 87(860): 639–48, available online at http://www.icrc.org/eng/assets/files/other/irrc_860_eilders.pdf.

Farrar, M. 1998. *News from the Front: War Correspondents on the Western Front 1914–1948*. Stroud: Sutton Publishing.

Fisk, R. 1990. *Pity the Nation: Lebanon at War*. Oxford: Oxford University Press.

Hoskins, A. and O'Loughlin, B. 2010. *War and Media: The Emergence of Diffused War*. Cambridge: Polity.

Inglis, F. 2002. *People's Witness: The Journalist in Modern Politics*. New Haven, CT: Yale University Press.

International Committee of the Red Cross. 2010. "How Does International Humanitarian Law Protect Journalists in Armed-Conflict Situations?" Interview with legal expert Robin Geiss, October 27, http://www.icrc.org/eng/resources/documents/interview/protection-journalists-interview-270710.htm.

Katovsky, B. and Carlson, T. 2003. *Embedded: The Media at War in Iraq*. Guilford: Lyons Press.

Keeble, R. 2001. *Ethics for Journalists*. New York: Routledge.

Knightley, P. 2003. *The First Casualty: The War Correspondent as Hero and Myth Maker from the Crimea to Iraq*. London: Andre Deutsch.

Levac, A. 2007. "The Camera as Witness." In R. Gutman, D. Rieff, and A. G. Dworkin (eds.), *Crimes of War: What the Public Should Know*. New York: Norton, available online at: http://www.crimesofwar.org/a-z-guide/the-camera-as-witness/.

McCullin, D. 2003. "This is War." Guardian, February 14, 2003, http://www.guardian.co.uk/world/2003/feb/14/iraq.features11.

McLaughlin, G. 2002. *The War Correspondent*. London: Pluto.

Moorcraft, P. L. and Taylor, P. M. 2008. *Shooting the Messenger: The Political Impact of War Reporting*. Washington, DC: Potomac Books.

Morrison, D. E. and Tumber, H. 1988. *Journalists at War: The Dynamics of News Reporting During the Falklands Conflict*. London: Sage.

Mowrer, S. 1943. "Bungling the News." *The Public Opinion Quarterly* 7 (1): 116–24.

Noorlander, P. 2011. "A Report to the Centre for International Media Assistance" July 20, http://cima.ned.org/publications/media-and-law-overview-legal-issues-and-challenges.

Paul, C. and Kim, J. J. 2004. *Reporters on the Battlefield: The Embedded Press System in Historical Context*. London: Royal United Services Institute.

Pease, S. J. 1942. "The Ancient War Correspondent." *The Classical Weekly* 36(6): 63–5.

Plaisance, P. L. 2002. "The Journalist as Moral Witness: Michael Ignatieff's Pluralistic Philosophy for a Global Media Culture." *Journalism* 3(2): 205–22.

Richards, A. and Mitchell, J. 2011. "Journalists as Witnesses to Violence and Suffering." In R. S. Fortner and P. M. Fackler, eds., *The Handbook of Global Communication and Media Ethics*, vol. II. Oxford: Wiley-Blackwell, 752–73.

Sanders, K. 2003. *Ethics and Journalism*. London: Sage.

Sebba, A. 1994. *Battling for News: The Rise of the Woman Reporter*. London: Sceptre.

Seib, P. 2004. *Beyond the Front Lines: How the News Media Cover a World Shaped by War*. New York: Palgrave MacMillan.

Spellman, R. L. 2005. "Journalist or Witness?: Reporters and War Crimes Tribunals." *Gazette* 67(2): 123–39.

Sylvester, J. and Huffman, S. 2005. *Reporting from the Front: The Media and the Military*. Oxford: Rowman and Littlefield.

Tumber, H. 1997. "Bystander Journalism or the Journalism of Attachment?" *INTER Media* 25(1): 4–7.

Tumber, H. 2008. "Journalists, War Crimes and International Justice." *Media War and Conflict* 1(3): 261–9.

Tumber, H. 2010. "Journalists and War Crimes." In S. Allan (ed.), *The* Routledge *Companion to News and Journalism*. London: Routledge, 533–41.

Tumber, H. and Palmer, J. 2004. *Media at War: The Iraq Crisis*. London: Sage.

Tumber, H. and Prentoulis, M. 2003. "Journalists under Fire: Subcultures, Objectivity and Emotional Literacy." In D. Thussu and D. Freedman, eds., *War and the Media*. London: Sage, 215–30.

Tumber, H. and Webster, F. 2006. *Journalists under Fire: Information War and Journalistic Practices*. London: Sage.

Ward, S. J. A. 1998. "An Answer to Martin Bell: Objectivity and Attachment in Journalism." *Harvard International Journal of Press/Politics* 3(3): 121–25.

Ward, S. J. A. 2010. *Global Journalism Ethics*. Montreal: McGill-Queen's University Press.

Weschler, L. 2007. "International Humanitarian Law: An Overview." In R. Gutman, D. Rieff, and A. G. Dworkin, eds., *Crimes of War: What the Public Should Know*. New York: Norton, 22–8.

4

Global Journalism Networks
Funding and Ethical Hurdles

Brant Houston

The year was 2001 and journalists from the US and Europe were organizing the first Global Investigative Journalism Conference to be held that spring in Copenhagen.

The Danish journalists were raising funds for the conference and were comfortable seeking and receiving money from the Danish government. The US journalists, most of whom were members of the US-based nonprofit Investigative Reporters and Editors (IRE), had a decision to make.

IRE did not take money from the US government and, in general, avoided dealing with any government money. Since its creation in 1975, IRE worried that taking such money would give the impression that the organization's activities were influenced or directed by the US government. But rather than try to impose their guidelines on their Danish colleagues, the US journalists deferred to the fundraising practices in Denmark and some other European countries where it is commonplace for journalism organizations to receive government funds for their activities. In addition, the Danish government did not expect to select any panels or speakers at the conference, nor did it attempt to exert control of the conference.

The event went on to be a success, with the participation of more than 400 journalists from 40 countries. During a second conference in 2003 the journalists from nonprofit newsrooms created the Global Investigative Journalism Network. They intended the network to be a way for journalists to keep in touch between the conferences and share stories and resources.

But with the beginning of the Global Network, so began decade-long discussions on the ethics of fundraising for conferences and investigative projects. The discussions also included maintaining journalistic credibility, based not only where funding came from, but on standards of methodology in the everyday practice of journalism.

Global Media Ethics: Problems and Perspectives, First Edition. Edited by Stephen J. A. Ward.
© 2013 Blackwell Publishing Ltd. Published 2013 by Blackwell Publishing Ltd.

The intensity of the discussion has increased over time because of the significant shift of journalism – especially in investigative reporting – from for-profit mainstream newsrooms to nonprofit newsrooms. The shift included the rise of networks of these nonprofit newsrooms – such as the Global Network – that brought together different methodologies and ethics to journalism practices and fundraising.

These shifts have thus brought new and different ethical challenges to a generation of traditional journalists used to being walled off from dealing with advertisers, who had been the primary financial supporters of their work. It also has greeted new citizen and community journalists with potential standards and ethics they often had not dealt with before.

This chapter will look at how journalists in the expanding environment of nonprofit newsrooms and networks are dealing with the ethical challenges they confront in fundraising and reporting. Among the challenges are sufficient transparency, government funding, firewalls between funders and journalists, and preventing editorial influence by funders. The chapter will also argue that these newsrooms and networks are developing commonly accepted ethical standards to ensure credibility of their work despite deep cultural, political, and economic differences. And it will review the practicalities of holding global conferences and obtaining funds to support those conferences. The review will provide an understanding of the spectrum of ethical issues while showing how a basic ethics code naturally arose and evolved, and how US journalists adapted to it.

Rise of Nonprofits and Networks

In the last three years, the migration of journalists from for-profit news organizations to nonprofit newsrooms has risen exponentially, especially in the field of investigative reporting. A US Federal Commission Communication report in 2011 stated that in the US "hundreds of nonprofit websites and blogs have arisen to provide local news" (Waldman 2011).

The Investigative Reporting Workshop at American University surveyed 75 nonprofit newsrooms that produce investigative work in 2011 and calculated that those newsrooms had $135 million in total budgets and 1,300 full-time employees. And the survey did not include public broadcasting.

In North America, the Investigative News Network was begun by nonprofit newsrooms in 2009 to promote editorial collaborations, wider distribution of the newsroom editorial content, and cost savings through the pooling of administrative resources. That network has nearly tripled in membership and now totals more than 60 newsrooms.

Another North American network, New America Media, started more than a decade ago, is composed of more than 2,000 ethnic newsrooms, both profit and nonprofit, and often deals with issues of fundraising, advocacy, and cultural differences. Many of its newsrooms have ties to other countries.

Meanwhile, the Global Network expects to double its membership from 40 organizations to 80 organizations in 2012 with member organizations from Europe, North America, Asia, South America, Australia, and Africa. Many of its organizations include those from the Investigative News Network.

Cross-cultural Standards

In this nonprofit environment, newsrooms and journalists from different countries and cultures are likely to interact more often because of the journalistic collaborations these networks engender. As a result, the questions of whether or how donations may influence the journalism become more critical. At the same time the ethics and standards of reporting become of greater importance since the collaborating newsrooms need to trust each other on the quality of reporting and methods of funding.

In North America, there is a long tradition of newsrooms having ethical guidelines set up to deal with the potential influence of money in connection with reporting. One ethical baseline is the code promulgated by the US-based Society of Professional Journalists that addresses independence and money in this section:

> Journalists should be free of obligation to any interest other than the public's right to know.

> *Journalists should:*
> - Avoid conflicts of interest, real or perceived.
> - Remain free of associations and activities that may compromise integrity or damage credibility.
> - Refuse gifts, favors, fees, free travel and special treatment, and shun secondary employment, political involvement, public office and service in community organizations if they compromise journalistic integrity.

But when moved to a global stage, the ethical guidelines become less clear and the attempt to standardize them more difficult. In some countries, such as China, the government promotes in-depth journalism while at the same time censoring stories where government leaders are criticized.

In other instances, as in Africa, journalists are paid so poorly that they routinely take "brown envelopes" of money from government leaders in exchange for covering press conferences or other stories. Eugene L. Meyer wrote in a recent report on ethics codes for the Center for International Media Assistance:

> From a Western perspective, journalism codes of ethics are an obvious benefit, akin to the preamble to the U.S. Declaration of Independence that says, "We hold these truths to be self-evident..."
> In the not-so-free world, they are not so self-evident. Nor are they always, or even often, the products of a self-regulating free and robust press. And

even when they are the products of press associations, they may represent a cultural and political compromise with a society or government that holds a more restrictive view of what journalists should and should not report.

Similarly, efforts to require government licensing or certain approved training, thereby limiting who may report, must be seen for what they are – attempts to control the dissemination of information rather than establishing ethical guidelines for journalists to follow.

The very phrase "code of ethics" means different things in different places. A code is a set of moral principles, not laws, but sometimes they are incorrectly conflated. (Meyer 2011: 4)

Furthermore, as Stephen Ward noted in *Global Journalism Ethics*, journalism ethics have been "parochial with its standards applying to particular groups" and "journalism ethics, it seems, stops at the border" (Ward 2010b: 158)

In his report, Meyer also quoted Eric Newton, senior adviser to the president of the John S. and James L. Knight Foundation, who also serves on international journalism boards, as saying the very phrase, code of ethics, "means very different things in open and closed societies." Newton said:

In an open society, it means it's voluntary. There's no administrative or legal mechanism that comes into play. It's ethics as opposed to law as opposed to policy. It can cross over the line from ethics into law if a government says, "That's unethical, therefore I'm going to put you in jail." (Newton, cited in Meyer 2011: 11)

Nonetheless, as nonprofit newsrooms and journalists from different countries and cultures network and collaborate they have increasingly worked to find – and have found – common guidelines and common definitions for credible investigative and in-depth reporting. Those goals have progressively stemmed from the fundraising questions and the desire to prevent donors from unduly influencing their journalism and undercutting their credibility.

At the same time, there is a movement both in academic and nonacademic writing to examine a global media ethics that seeks agreement on principles but is sensitive to cultural differences that may preclude criticism of government or religion (Ward 2010b, Ward and Wasserman 2010).

Funding the Conferences

The first global conference in Copenhagen had support from media companies including the Politikens Fond, Ophavsretsfonden, Dagspressens Fond, and the newspaper *Information*. Media companies have been the typical financial supporters of conferences throughout the world over past decades and IRE has relied heavily on this kind of support since its inception.

At IRE, the contributions to a conference can come in many forms. It can be the "contribution" of a media company that pays for the registration, travel, and lodging of participating journalists. This support is not considered a contribution in many other fields but just a routine training cost. A contribution also can be a generic donation for the general operations of the conference, for food and drink, for financing the attendance of journalists of color or of students, for a series of sessions on a topic (with no say on the sessions or speakers themselves) or advertising in a conference program.

IRE and other journalism training organizations eagerly seek and accept donations from journalism foundations such as the Knight Foundation (which also has extensive international programs) but it will not take federal government money directly. IRE has allowed the US State Department to finance the attendance at its annual conference of up to 20 international journalists who are participating in State Department programs in the United States.

Overall, US journalists find it difficult to conceive of routinely taking money from a government they routinely investigate. They also fear that taking government money would lead to an overreliance on it. Margaret Freivogel, an editor in a nonprofit newsroom in the US, summed up that opinion well by saying: "Government money is 'crack' and we should not go there" (Ward 2010a: 20).

The 2001 global conference funding diverged dramatically from the US standard when the organizers asked the Danish Foreign Ministry for financial support. The Ministry donated a substantial sum that allowed conference organizers to invite more than 20 speakers from Africa and other continents. The list, generated by the conference organizers, had to be accepted for funding by the Foreign Ministry but the Ministry did not offer names nor did it veto any journalism names offered. In addition, most of the funds supporting the conference's primary organizer, the Danish Institute for Computer-Assisted Reporting (DICAR), came from the European Social Fund – a fund under the European Union. The director of the now-defunct DICAR, Nils Mulvad, said the administrative burdens of obtaining and reporting on the use of the donations to the government agencies were heavy, "but they in no way wanted to have influence on the event." The Danish Foreign Ministry then made another contribution to the 2003 conference, which also was in Copenhagen.

> Looking forward I think [the] main principle is not to accept demands on speakers or panels to get a funding. On the other hand if you plan for a track [conference panel] on climate change and then get funding for that it's fine with me. Independence is the key word and securing this independence. Then we might also add some obvious things like no money from organized crime. (Mulvad, personal correspondence, 2011)

The third conference – held in Amsterdam in 2005 – also received sponsorship money from a variety of sources. The sources included several private media companies, some journalism schools, the European Journalism Center, the European Cultural Foundation, and a Netherlands government fund for a study on investigative journalism in connection with the conference. A primary conference organizer, Margo Smit, said at the 2005 Amsterdam conference that none of the sponsors and donors had any say in the program other than giving money for speaker travel and lodging. In some cases, the donors could specify a region from which the journalists should come but otherwise they could not specify their preferences.

At the next conference in Canada in 2007, a large amount of support money came from the Canadian International Development Agency to support foreign journalists' travel and lodging for the conference. Again, the organizers said the government agency had no say over the conference program and speakers. Other major amounts were given by the Canadian Broadcasting Corporation and the Open Society Foundation. The Open Society Foundation has been consistently a large contributor to the general costs of the global conference. Open Society programs sometimes are attacked in the US as promoting a liberal and progressive agenda because the Open Society was created by billionaire George Soros, who has such interests.

By the following conference in Lillehammer, Norway, in 2008, a pattern of accepting media company, foundation, and government support had emerged with no controversy. The Norway organizers received substantial support from the Norwegian Ministry of Foreign Affairs in addition to UNESCO, the Open Society Foundation, and a US antismoking foundation called Tobacco Free Kids. The Foreign Affairs money was to ensure participation from journalists in countries outside Norway.

At the next conference in Geneva, Switzerland, in 2010, the Swiss Foreign Affairs office was the biggest sponsor, but again did not influence the names of the invited or the conference panels. The lead conference organizer, broadcast journalist Jean-Philippe Ceppi, said the Swiss Federal Office for Economic Promotion was going to support the conference but only with "a condition" about a panel. Conference organizers refused that condition and did not receive the donation.

At the most recent conference in Kiev, Ukraine, in 2011, the donors broadened to the US government agency, the National Endowment for Democracy, the US Embassy, and the public–private Black Sea Trust, which is funded with foundation and government money, including funds from Germany, Romania, and the United States.

"None of our sponsors asked for influence – neither in issues discussed or names of speakers," said the lead organizer, Henrik Kaufholz, who runs the Danish journalism nonprofit SCOOP (personal correspondence, 2011). However, the participation of the US Embassy at the closing banquet in giving out a journalism award concerned some of the attending journalists. Several journalists walked out during the ceremony.

Conference Independence and Transparency

Out of these conferences, which have drawn nearly a total of 4,000 journalists from more than 80 countries, two standards have been agreed on: independence and transparency.

There has been no opposition to the standard that speakers and conference sessions be independently decided by the conference organizers. The idea that no government or business can determine the speakers or the panels has been accepted by a consensus of newsroom representatives from 40 or more countries. In addition, transparency about donors has become accepted practice. Conference organizers have disclosed all donors and published them on the conference websites and in their printed programs.

But support from the US government is not always easily accepted. Hostile reactions to the involvement of the US Embassy at the Global Investigative Journalism Network's conference in Kiev in 2011, as noted earlier, underscored deep concerns and suspicions still shared by non-US journalists about the motives of US government funders. Organizers of the conference agreed to let the US Embassy, which had supplied support for the conference, give out awards from one of their programs at the conference banquet. The decision was criticized because some foreign journalists reject any US government involvement in journalism as possible subterfuge, and US journalists are sensitive to overt State Department support.

There is a long history of distrust of US involvement and funding of journalism and the distrust became deeper when ties between US democracy programs and the US Central Intelligence Agency were disclosed in the 1980s. For example, the US State Department created the National Endowment for Democracy (NED) in the 1980s. But it soon came under scrutiny because of alleged links to the CIA. Indeed, the exposure of efforts by NED in Latin American that allegedly involved CIA funding and operatives spurred changes at NED and there have been few allegations since.

The distrust has been exacerbated in this decade by the Iraq War, renditions of suspected terrorists, US government-paid media commenting on the war without disclosing that they were being paid, and disclosures about the US government from WikiLeaks.org.

US Government and Media Funding

Ironically, NED now is one of the largest generally accepted supporters of media training and development in the world and its initiative, the Center for International Media Assistance (CIMA), has funded some of the most insightful and credible reports on international media needs, including two studies cited in this chapter.

CIMA states its mission is "to strengthen the support, raise the visibility, and improve the effectiveness of media assistance programs throughout the world." It said it does this "by providing information, building networks, conducting research, and highlighting the indispensable role independent media play in the creation and development of sustainable democracies around the world" (http://www.ned.org/about/initiatives).

In addition to NED and CIMA, The US Aid for International Development also funds several major journalism training programs such as IREX, Internews, and the International Center for Journalists. These organizations provide training globally that is widely accepted and attended by non-US journalists and has not sparked the kind of controversy prompted by the US Embassy's presence in Kiev.

But the standard of accepting support for training and money from governments does not include allowing government representatives to participate in the sessions of the global conference sessions unless they are investigators of corruption or giving a welcoming speech. As noted before, US government officials come under even more scrutiny.

Newsroom and Network Transparency

Like CIMA, many foundation and government donors also support the various networks of individual nonprofit newsrooms and the newsrooms themselves.

One prominent example of the acceptance of the intermingling of foundation and government support is the Organized Crime and Corruption Reporting Project (OCCRP). An initiative composed of several Eastern European nonprofit centers, the Project has been supported by grants from the United Nations Democracy Fund (UNDEF), the United States Agency for International Development (USAID), and the Open Society Foundations. The Project also says that specific news stories have been funded in part or done in partnership with other organizations including the Danish organization SCOOP, the Center for Public Integrity and its global reporting project, and the International Consortium of Investigative Journalists.

Because donations such as these go far beyond financing a four-day conference and instead support months and years of work, these donations and accompanying ethical issues receive more attention.

The scrutiny of the networks and nonprofits also increases because, in addition to doing their own stories, the nonprofit newsrooms and networks often serve "as coordinators and facilitators for much larger reporting and training projects," according to a 2007 CIMA report on investigative journalism and media assistance:

The more established centers have regional and international impact. The Philippine Center has done trainings across Southeast Asia and inspired the creation of a similar group in Katmandu, Nepal.

The Bosnian Center has served as the nerve center for a series of cross-border projects in Eastern Europe on the energy industry, transnational crime, and corruption. Journalists from the Romanian Center have worked as trainers in a dozen countries. SCOOP, a project of the Danish Association for Investigative Journalism, has given 150 grants to journalists in Eastern Europe and the former Soviet Union for work on stories.

The centers have proved to be a viable model for several reasons. In developing and democratizing countries, they often serve, quite literally, as centers of excellence, offering firsthand proof that top-flight reporting can be done on crime, corruption, and accountability. "The role of the Center is as a catalyst – to show that this kind of reporting is possible and to encourage others to do it," says Sheila Coronel, co-founder of the Philippine Center. (Kaplan 2007)

Greater Expectations

The nonprofit newsroom brings with it a greater expectation of transparency that goes beyond the recent trend to reveal how a story was developed. In the popular journalism book, *The Elements of Journalism*, Kovach and Rosenstiel (2007) observed that transparency of newsgathering has gained momentum and traditional newsrooms more often explain why a source is anonymous, how information is gathered and presented and how a newsroom operates. That includes posting raw data, documents, audio, and video to the web.

Over the past two decades, transparency has become a prominent principle in new media with an emphasis on bloggers and any content providers making available information about themselves and their backgrounds. In fact, transparency may be a more sophisticated way of approaching objectivity by the acknowledgement of the routine existence of personal and cultural bias.

Global nonprofit newsrooms have quickly embraced these developing ideas of transparency in newsgathering, but are deep in discussion about transparency regarding donors and revenue streams.

In the for-profit world of news, the names of advertisers are obviously public and their contribution can be measured by the size or length of the advertisement. The advertiser wants attention and publicity whether in the newspaper or on TV. Even in public broadcasting, many donors want to have their names mentioned or listed after a program. But globally, and specifically in the USA, the right of a donor to be anonymous is an accepted practice in the nonprofit field. The generally accepted "donor bill of rights" includes a passage that states the donor has a right "to be assured that information about their donation is handled with respect and with confidentiality to the extent provided by law"

(Association of Fundraising Professionals, http://www.afpnet.org/Ethics /EnforcementDetail.cfm?ItemNumber=3359).

Some donors seek privacy out of modesty or because they do not want to be solicited for other donations, and many nonprofits depend on granting anonymity to donors as a way to attract their support. Universities, where some nonprofit newsrooms are housed, routinely accept millions to tens of millions of dollars from anonymous donors. The Internal Revenue Service, the taxing agency in the USA that oversees nonprofits, follows laws that ensure donors privacy on reporting forms when made public. In fact, GuideStar, a nonprofit organization set up to increase transparency of the operations on nonprofits both in the United States and globally, never mentions the anonymity of donors as a transparency issue in a survey it did of nonprofits and their stance on transparency. The survey summed up the acceptable practices of transparency in this passage:

> For many participants, "nonprofit transparency" encompasses every aspect of an organization. As an anonymous participant said: "I think of the acronym DWYSYWD (do what you say you will do). Do the actions of the organization reflect the core values and mission it promotes? Is there genuine evidence of the agency's high regard for integrity across all core aspects of the agency – from program operation and hiring practices, to evaluation and communications as well as the financial practices (where most media attention often gravitates). Examples of evidence may include recognizing and abiding by all applicable state and federal laws, exploring appropriate accreditation opportunities, completing regular annual reports/audits and making that information readily available to funders, using independent researchers to conduct program evaluations, maintaining open lines of communication between donors and the like." (Coffman 2006)

Thus nonprofit industry guidelines actually focus more on protecting the privacy of a donor than whether they should be anonymous. Indeed, a group of new US journalism nonprofits, overseen by the Franklin Center for Government and Public Integrity, guarantees on its website that donors' anonymity will be protected.

Although in conformance with US tax law, the Franklin Center has undermined its credibility with other journalists. Its leadership is closely associated with the Republican Party and the Franklin Center's one known donor, the Sam Adams Alliance of Chicago, does not disclose its funders.

Despite the law and industry standard allowing anonymity, most non-profit newsrooms are leaning toward greater openness and disclosing all donors – or are at least all large donors. The Investigative News Network, for example, set a standard that all donors who give $1,000 or more should be disclosed by its members except under compelling circumstances and with guidelines that prevent undue influence. This mirrors a Transparency International policy about transparency in fundraising that says that all donors above one thousand Euros must be identified. This policy clearly excludes a large gift from an anonymous donor.

Without transparency of donors, global journalists can be accused of hypocrisy since they emphasize freedom of information and fight government and business secrecy. Questions can also be raised about whether there might be undue influence on coverage by secret donors who undermine the journalists' credibility.

As a result, revealing donors, at least major ones, is quickly becoming a standard. The Investigative Reporting Workshop at American University, which surveyed nonprofit newsrooms in the US in 2010 and 2011, has made transparency about donors a positive measurement of nonprofit performance. In its 2011 report it stated:

> The disclosure of donors by nonprofit news organizations seems to be improving. Of the original 60 nonprofit news publishers profiled a year ago, 47 of them or 78 percent disclosed their donors on their websites; a year later, the number of those 60 organizations disclosing their donors online has risen to 53 groups or 88 percent. This increase could be somewhat related to the adoption last January by the Investigative News Network (INN) of formal membership standards – specifically "donor transparency" for member organizations, in particular a requirement that all contributions above $1,000 be disclosed; that policy was approved by the INN Board just weeks after the release of the first Ecosystem report revealed a lack of donor transparency by several organizations. (Lewis et al. 2011)

Influence and Broad Revenue Streams

But transparency alone does not address the other deep issues that arise from donors and fundraising. A nonprofit newsroom revealing its donors does not prevent allegations of undue influence over news coverage by its donors. In fact, it may increase the allegations if there are only a few large donors.

As noted earlier, projects funded by the Open Society Foundation constantly come under attack from right-wing journalists and organization because the foundation was funded by the liberal and progressive financier George Soros. These attacks come even though there are no signs that the foundation has manipulated or influenced editorial content.

Thus journalists in a nonprofit newsroom must strive to broaden their donor base just as a traditional newspaper must strive to broaden its number of advertisers to remain financially and journalistically viable. In this way a nonprofit newsroom can partly stave off the perception that its journalism is not controlled by one or several donors.

The nonprofit newsroom also faces another different ethical hurdle in its coverage when a donor supports coverage of a particular topic such as the environment or tobacco. Most nonprofit newsrooms are relatively small and cannot (and do not intend) to cover a wide range of "beats" as the traditional community newspaper does. But to prevent the perception that they are doing coverage at the behest of a donor or group of donors, they have found they need to preselect the topics they will cover. That way, when a donation is solicited, it is solicited for a story or topic already chosen. This creates a kind of firewall against donor influence and has been a model chosen by a website, Spot.Us, which raises money to finance specific news stories. But one traditional firewall cannot be established by smaller nonprofit newsrooms: the prohibition against close contact between the journalist and the money that funds his or her newsroom.

The US public broadcaster NPR has a code of ethics that addresses underwriting, foundation grants, advertising, marketing, and promotion. It states that:

> a firewall will be maintained between NPR journalists and funders. While staff may end up talking to experts and officials who work at foundations that fund us (and their grantees), we may not discuss coverage planning with grant-making officials.

Instead, it says vice presidents for news "will assign individuals who will serve as contacts for respective divisions with funders for grant-making purposes or other communication" (http://ethics.npr.org/comparison/).

The issue of maintaining integrity has become of such interest that leaders in US public media, which include NPR and PBS, have just completed a two-year study called the "Editorial Integrity Project" (www.pmintegrity.org). The project constructed new guidelines for public media in a multimedia world, including new guidelines for donors and contributors.

This idea of a firewall is relatively easy to establish at a nonprofit newsroom that has hundreds of employees, but at a nonprofit with three to five staff members who are all journalists it is nearly impossible. In addition, foundations and donors often want to meet and talk with the journalists doing the work.

At a roundtable conference of nonprofit journalism center representatives in Wisconsin in 2010, the participants observed that the firewall between journalists and sources of revenue "is not as robust" in the new nonprofit newsrooms (Ward 2010a: 5). They said executive directors and editors often raise funds, co-ordinate coverage, and deal with donors. In some cases, representatives of foundations and major donors themselves sit on the board of directors. As Stephen Ward wrote in a conference report, "Importantly for ethics, the distance between journalist and funder in the nonprofit newsroom is reduced" (Ward 2010a: 5). Nonetheless, roundtable participants said newsrooms can create "firewalls" between the editorial process and funders. They said rules include preventing showing copy to funders or board members before publication or presentation.

Margaret Freivogel, of the *St. Louis Beacon* in Missouri, said her center's code of ethics addresses conflict of interests – reporters should not cover a story if they have a financial interest in the story or a personal relationship with the subject of the story. In addition, reporters are required to disclose all political activity and they can't report on areas in which they are active as citizens (Ward 2010a: 6).

Beyond issues of the firewall and the nonprofit newsroom is the basic vetting of a foundation or donor who will give money to the center. Government agencies usually have the cumbersome document requirements that Nils Mulvad, a Danish journalist, has noted, but those documents actually make the purpose of the donation and the obligations clear in minute detail.

Foundations also make clear their background and their intent and expectations in giving a grant and their involvement, which is usually expecting financial reports on how the money was used and performance reports on what was accomplished. It is in the area of individual donors that nonprofit newsrooms must make most clear their ethical principles such as editorial independence that ensures their credibility and integrity.

At the roundtable in Wisconsin, Charles Lewis, who founded the Center for Public Integrity and the Investigative Reporting Workshop, said centers should be suspicious of large offers of money from individual donors. He said he discovered that a funder who wanted to support the creation of another Center for Public Integrity in another country was revealed to be an arms dealer (Ward 2010a: 5).

Ethics Codes or Guidelines?

As for the overall activities of journalists, there are hundreds of journalism ethics codes globally but, as Meyer's report for CIMA pointed out, those codes differ in many ways and in some cases call for self-censorship when dealing with a country's government, cultural habits or political biases.

The report points out that Turkish journalists are working to establish a code of ethics but those journalists report in a country where there are limits on what they can report and publish, whatever their codes and the constitution may say (Meyer 2011: 13–14).

The report also notes that codes of ethics can be meaningless if applied to an environment in which low pay encourages checkbook journalism, as in Africa:

> African press codes "contain all the values you can find in the international systems, values of truth-telling, truth-seeking, balance," says Kwame Karikari, director of the Ghana-based Media Foundation for West Africa.
>
> In the non-Western world, reality intrudes. In Africa, according to Guy Berger, a South African former journalist and academic who now is UNESCO's director of freedom of expression and media development, the single most pressing problem that persists, despite being frowned upon by myriad codes of ethics, is "brown envelope" journalism – reporters accepting and sometimes soliciting bribes for coverage. In this pay-to-play

environment, condoned if not outwardly encouraged by management, whither codes of ethics?

"It's just that people are not paid good salaries for journalism, so they find ways to survive," Karikari said. (Meyer 2011: 17)

In this kind of context, following an ethics codes is nearly impossible or, at best, difficult. Nonetheless, the goal of journalistic independence from monetary influence must be recognized and steps taken to somehow achieve that goal.

The report also notes an ethics code in Tanzania that "explicitly states that media professionals 'are also expected to advance national interests, and to promote key values and behavior patterns, especially so in times of war and other crisis'" (Meyer 2011: 18). In India, it found that reporting would not necessarily specify the religion of a place of worship if it were attacked because of communal respect and restraint (Meyer 2011: 24).

This does not necessarily undermine the need for basic ethics codes, but shows that in different cultures there will not be agreement on all parts of a code. In these cases, the existence of ethics codes provides further transparency on the strengths and shortcomings of the practice of journalism in those regions. Indeed, investigative journalism newsrooms in those regions may intentionally violate the codes that call upon the journalists to report only favorable information about their countries.

Clearly, the nonprofit newsrooms, which incorporate both traditional and new digital media, will be in the forefront of finding common ground in ethical differences and debates. And in the end, it may mean that shared values should be expressed more in terms of guidelines than in formal codes that are subscribed to by professional journalism organizations.

After all, IRE, which has been in existence for more than 35 years, has never found it possible or necessary to formulate an ethics code. For example, it has members who use undercover techniques and other members who work for organizations that prohibit such techniques. So instead IRE fosters high standards through training and practice, awards, publications, and guidelines that emphasize accuracy, balance, and thoroughness of research. In this case, there are general guidelines that are not put into a formal code that is approved and voted on by a board or a membership.

So the development of global journalism ethics may be constructed in the same way. That is, journalists come up with ethical guidelines by confronting a series of difficult situations involving the influence of money. From those confrontations, journalists reach a consensus on how to maintain independence and credibility and thus create trust in their work. It may be that for some time there will continue to exist an open recognition of cultural and societal differences that ethical guidelines cannot completely address. But the recognition and discussion of differences will permit the continued move toward a more universal agreement about what global ethics should be and the reasoning behind those ethics.

Further Reading

Individuals need to reference both books and online writings to keep up with the ethical issues and challenges in the quickly changing global nonprofit journalism world.

A good base on the ethical issues is *Global Journalism Ethics* (2010) by Stephen J. A. Ward, the editor of this book. Ward thoroughly covers the philosophical issues and practical challenges in establishing a global ethics. He captures a key problem in noting that journalism ethics originally was parochial and created for "a journalism of limited reach." With journalism crossing borders instantly in the online age, those ethics do not take into account the viewpoints of different countries and cultures. *Media Ethics Beyond Borders: A Global Perspective* (2010) by Ward and Herman Wasserman offers a collection of additional viewpoints.

A cogent piece on ongoing challenges is "Media Codes of Ethics" (2011) by Eugene L. Meyer, published online by the Center for International Media Assistance. Meyer covers many of the practical problems, from cultures that differ on critical coverage of government and religion to impoverished journalists who take politicians' payments for covering the politicians' press conferences.

US journalists debating the issues of anonymous donors and transparency can be found online at "Roundtable Report: Ethics For the New Investigative Newsroom" at the Center For Journalism Ethics in Madison, WI (Ward 2010a). The journalists are founders of nonprofit investigative journalism start-ups. Suggested standards for nonprofits doing fundraising arose from the discussion.

The best view of the dramatic shift in global investigative journalism from the for-profit corporations to nonprofits centers is available in David E. Kaplan's "Global Investigative Journalism" (2007), published online by the Center for International Media Assistance. Another resource that gives historical perspective on the rise of investigative journalism nonprofits is an article I wrote for *Daedalus* on "The Future of Investigative Journalism" (which can be accessed at http://media.illinois.edu/knight/future-of-investigative-reporting).

Appendix 4.A

The Roundtable Report (Ward 2010a) provides a number of important general rules and guidelines for the ethics of nonprofit journalism. For example, the report stressed the following general rule: "The common theme of the discussions amounted to a warning for centers: No matter how complicated the issue may be, no matter how badly you need funding, do not lose sight of your fundamental commitment to good journalism – free, independent and informed reporting. First and foremost, protect your journalistic integrity."

Other guidelines from the report:

Dealing with donors

- Aim for the highest degree of transparency possible.
- Be open regarding editorial and fundraising standards.
- Disclose the ethics policy, mission statement, conflict of interest policy, and fundraising policy.
- Disclose the federal tax return and basic information about the staff, board of directors; explain how to contact the newsroom to report an error or to make a complaint.
- Vet all donors carefully; consider the multiple missions.
- Consider how accepting support from a donor or associating with another news organization may affect the integrity of your news organization.
- Develop criteria for acceptable donors; move from an initial "creepy list" to more difficult cases.
- Develop clear policies on conflicts of interest.
- Reveal the identities of all donors, and conditions attached to their donations, except in rare cases. And in those cases, explain the reasons for concealing details.
- Accept "strings" on contributions only if the conditions align with the news organization's mission.
- Refrain from giving funders undue influence over, and advance access to, news coverage.
- Publish explanations of key editorial and fundraising decisions to keep the public informed, and to solicit public comment.
- Retain editorial control. Do not relinquish legal and ethical responsibilities to funders or to the public.

Dealing with foundations and community groups

- Avoid misunderstandings with foundations and similar groups by discussing expectations and potential "outcomes."
- Avoid misunderstandings with community groups by having a dialogue on how the center's journalism can fit into the community and its needs.
- Make it clear to groups that protecting the integrity of the journalism is your first priority. Explain your journalism and your standards.

Dealing with networks

- Collaborate with other institutions, but be aware of the variety of editorial and fundraising standards of your partners.
- Within a network, seek agreements among organizations with different viewpoints on the level of tolerance for government funding, and on avoiding potential conflicts between funding and stories.

- Foster collaborations within networks and among networks to produce the highest standards possible for ensuring and protecting credibility.

References

Coffman, S. E. 2006. "What Nonprofit Transparency Means to You: October Question of the Month Results," GuideStar, http://www.guidestar.org/rxa/news/articles/2006/what-nonprofit-transparency-means-to-you.aspx.

Kaplan, D. 2007. "Global Investigative Journalism: Strategies for Support," Center for International Media Assistance, http://pdf-esmanual.com/books/21923/global_investigative_journalism__strategies_for_support.html.

Kovach, B. and Rosenstiel, T. 2007. *The Elements of Journalism*. New York: Three Rivers Press.

Lewis, C., Butts, B., and Musselwhite, K. 2011. "A Second Look: The New Journalism Ecosystem," Investigative Reporting Workshop, http://investigativereportingworkshop.org/ilab/story/second-look/.

Meyer, E. L. 2011. "Media Codes of Ethics: The Difficulty of Defining Standards," Center for International Media Assistance, http://cima.ned.org/sites/default/files/CIMA-Codes%20of%20Ethics%20-%2011-03-11_0.pdf.

Waldman, S. 2011. "The Information Needs of Communities: The Changing Media Landscape in a Broadband Age," Federal Communications Commission, http://hraunfoss.fcc.gov/edocs_public/attachmatch/DOC-307406A1.doc.

Ward, S. J. A. 2010a. "Roundtable Report: Ethics For the New Investigative Newsroom," The Center for Journalism Ethics, http://www.journalismethics.info/2010_roundtable_report_27april.pdf.

Ward, S. J. A. 2010b. *Global Journalism Ethics*. Montreal: McGill-Queen's University Press.

Ward, S. J. A. and Wasserman, H. 2010. *Media Ethics Beyond Borders. A Global Perspective*. New York: Routledge.

Part II

Media and Diverse Public Spheres

5

Contextual Ethics and Arab Mass Media

Ralph D. Berenger and Mustafa Taha

Al Jazeera is only one example of the news and information tsunami breaking over the culturally diverse mediascape of the 22-country region that converges the African, European, and Asian continents, with a combined population rivaling the United States. Technology-fueled innovations of the interconnected world, such as the Internet and mobile telephony, have tested the boundaries – and efficacy – of not only regional autocratic regimes, but of ethical practices of mostly state-owned mass media in what is known collectively as the Arab World.

This chapter focuses on media norms and values of a religion-oriented culture that shape the ethical practices of mass communicators, and argues for a better understanding of the Middle East context in which media ethics is practiced.

Contextual Ethics

The authors define contextual ethics as the audience-accepted expectation of behavior by mass media practitioners in a given set of circumstances that draw upon cues and guidance from history, cultural customs, society, politics, economics, or theology. Contextual ethics, as practiced by Middle East journalists, is more accepted and expected by news consumers who understand the culture's history, mores, adjunctive norms, and values. It is more demonstrative, more constant, and more predictable than situational ethics or moral relativism, which might also be a response to influences affecting cultural ethics, but which are more dynamic, inconsistent, and descriptively normative and unpredictable.

The authors will leave unanswered a judgment of whether other cultures practice similar contextualization – though they suspect they do – since this chapter concentrates singularly on the Middle East.

Media contextual ethics practitioners acknowledge that other ethical frameworks might exist elsewhere – and some aspects might even be worth

Global Media Ethics: Problems and Perspectives, First Edition. Edited by Stephen J. A. Ward.
© 2013 Blackwell Publishing Ltd. Published 2013 by Blackwell Publishing Ltd.

imitating, such as conduct codes and abstractions of media free from government intervention – but they are pragmatic in their application, tempered and hardened by years of oppression, punishment, and intimidation by governing authorities that have created impermeable political cultures that include mass media behavior. As the so-called Arab Spring of 2011 revealed, it was relatively simple to remove aging heads of state in Tunisia, Egypt, Libya, and Yemen, but the systems under which they held sway remain nearly intact today. Only the actors at the top changed. The fundamental templates remain.

More than geography separates East from West. An ethical media schism divides the two, both shaped by the cultural anthropology that evolved into political cultures, defined here as the accepted way things are done. Western media systems favor the individual over the state, a free marketplace of goods and ideas, egalitarianism, secularism, and the notion of representative democracy based on the principle of "one person, one vote" to elect leaders. Arab media systems operate in an environment that is paternalistic, hierarchical, communitarian, tribal, and religious, with rulers rather than leaders chosen – usually by oligarchies, blood lines, or military force – as heads of state. The ballot box is used mostly to elect parliamentarians, the majority of whom support the status quo. Free, fair, and contested presidential elections in Arab republics are rare – the first and last one was in post-Saddam Iraq in 2005. Westerners, introduced to this context, are puzzled by the way Arab media cover local news and show deference to leaders and regimes, and are confounded by the impermeable cultural rim that surround regional news gatherers and disseminators. To Middle Easterners, these practices are the norm, and they are befuddled when they see or read Western media stories critical of their own government leaders and governing political entities. If things are so bad that Western media can criticize their leaders and government that openly, they reason, then things *must really be far worse.*

Arab Media's "Special Circumstances" as Context

The Middle East is the birthplace of ancient civilizations and diverse religious movements, including the great religions of Judaism, Christianity, and Islam, and its history was written in blood as one empire conquered the other for seven millennia. With each wave of secular or religious conquest came new systems of human interaction that influenced both the dominators and the dominated (Savage 2004). As such, Middle East scholars, such as former US ambassador to Yemen, William Rugh, argue that Arab mass media constitute "special circumstances" not present in every instance in Western media (Rugh 2004: 5–14).

These special circumstances, with implications for media ethics, include a weak economic base, politicization, and cultural influences, which certainly includes the region's dominant religion, Islam.

Weak economic base

Most Western media rely on advertising sales to pay the bills. Until recently, advertising in Arab media was either the function of government agencies or large international advertising agencies who handled large multinational accounts. Street merchants simply do not see the value in advertising to neighborhood customers, and given the disparity of wealth between the oil-rich Gulf Arabs and the impoverished desert Arabs of North Africa, advertising remains a questionable base upon which most media can build. An estimated 17 percent of the region's population – about 2.6 million people – lived below $2 a day in 2010, the same as in Latin America and the Caribbean; lower than in East Asia, but higher than in Europe and Central Asia, according to the World Bank (2010). The consequences of a weak economy directly impacts the ethical health of media practitioners in the region, as journalists at times augment their meager salaries with second and third jobs with competing media, gifts and free trips, bribes and payoffs, and *wasta*, payments to managers and sources to curry favor for some future deal. Incidents of blackmail of sources by journalists or advertising representatives of businesspeople have been rumored in private, but mostly go unreported in the media. As a practice, media supported solely by advertising have yet to provide a sufficient model for media entrepreneurs to follow. Newspapers in the region aspire mostly to be national rather than local, and Arabs' reliance on oral traditions as well as religious objections in some countries to exploiting human forms, particularly females, has limited the potential of advertising (Al Jenaibi 2011: 83). Because there are few "community newspapers" serving small neighborhoods, most small merchants see no need to advertise in media products, preferring instead to rely on word of mouth advertising, in-store flyers and posters, and home-delivered handbills. What little advertising small merchants do with mass media is usually institutional.

Politicization

Rugh (2004: 5–6) asserts that Arab media have always been associated with political agendas, going back to Napoleon's introduction of newspapers in Egypt in 1798. Governments tended to control newspaper content as most continue to do so today, with varying applications of censorship and coercion. Journalists' self-censorship is widespread, and most know – or are told – the boundaries they can write about. Politically, the region has been in a state of postcolonial flux, with the "Big Man" model the most common for rulers. If they can avoid assassins, leaders tend to hang on to power and grow old in the job with little hint of successors, partly out of fear of coups but also as an insurance policy.

Official and semiofficial newspapers and government-run radio and television were the only sources of information until the satellite age and the recent emergence of privately owned newspapers and broadcast stations. Media in the Middle East are the least free among media systems in the world (Freedom House 2011). Most opposition to the regimes comes from Internet bloggers. Scores of dissident bloggers have been jailed, fined, or exiled, and the Middle East leads all regions of the world in jailing journalist-bloggers (Committee to Protect Journalists 2011). Rugh (2004: 7) points out that the common galvanizing element is the Arab World's disdain for Israel, a convenient rallying point to divert attention away from local plights. Even in Egypt, where Anwar Sadat's peace treaty in the Camp David Accord with Israel in 1978 might have sealed his fate, media routinely blame Israel for most of its own internal problems, including the Arab Spring (Reuters 2011). In a 2009 survey of journalists by the Middle East Media Guide, nearly 40 percent of the English-language print and broadcast journalists polled cited government rules in the Middle East as their greatest impediment to writing news stories (Media Source 2009: 63). Since the vast majority of media outlets in the Middle East are controlled by government directly or indirectly by loyal allies to the regimes, distinguishing political behavior from media behavior is difficult.

Even Al Jazeera, which criticizes all governments, refrains from publishing critical reports about its sponsor, the Government of Qatar (Quinn and Walters 2004, Miles 2005). That lacuna is not to be filled any time soon. In September 2011, Al Jazeera named Sheik Ahmad bin Jasem bin Muhammad Al-Thani, a member of the Qatar royal family, as the station's new managing director. He replaced the highly regarded Wadah Khanfar, who resigned amid unanswered WikiLeaks charges that he ordered changes in the network's on-air and website news coverage to appease the Bush administration (Stableford 2011).

Cultural Influence

Arab culture did not develop in a vacuum. The Middle East has been conquered, reconquered, and conquered again through the millennia by a succession of empires, each leaving behind strands of customs to be woven into a tapestry we generalize today as Arab culture. Just as the various types and forms of dominance have varied over the ages, so have cultural influences. It would be inaccurate, therefore, to say there is just one culture that impacts all or most of the region's 315 million Arabs.

As pointed out earlier, most Arab societies developed under different kinds of domination by "others." To label all customs and norms practiced by various tribes and communities as Arab culture draws perilously close to the criticisms of "Orientalism" by Edward Said (1979). Therefore, it would be more accurate to pluralize the concept as Arab cultures. Rugh (2004: 7) concludes that the Arab mass media have strong ties to these disparate and often dissimilar Arab cultures, noting that storytelling, poetry, and Arab literature predated mass media by millennia. While slowly waning in the modern Arab mass media, which mimic Western-style notions of journalistic objectivity, the importance of literature and storytelling continue as important elements in the Arab print and broadcast news products (Mellor 2005). Given the Middle East and North Africa region's estimated average high illiteracy rate of 25 percent, ranging from 3–5 percent (Israel/Palestine Territories) to 44 percent (Morocco) of the adult population depending on the country, oral traditions are vital to the transfer of culture, information and knowledge (UNdata 2012). However, any discussion of the cultural influences in the Middle East must include the impact of Islam, practiced by the overwhelming majority of residents of the Middle East. The Iqra Foundation estimates the 2012 worldwide population of Muslims at 2.1 billion, which eclipses Christianity's 1.98 billion followers. By 2030, the Islamic foundation estimates that one of three people in the world will be Muslim (Iqra Foundation 2011). The figures are much higher than those found two years earlier by the Pew Center, which set the global population of Muslims at 1.57 billion, 23 percent of the 6.8 billion world population. In the Middle East-North Africa, Pew estimates that 91.2 percent of the populations practice Islam, over a fifth of the world's Muslims (Pew Research Center 2009: 1, 29).

Islamic context of ethics and journalism

The concepts outlined by Confucius and Aristotle over two millennia ago are interwoven, but not always followed, in all three of the world's major monotheistic religions originating in the Middle East. All three affirm what Summer Sunday School pupils for centuries have known as "The Golden Rule": Behave toward others as you want them to behave to you. That basic rule is the foundation of deontological (rule-based) and teleological (outcome-based) ethics (Land and Hornaday 2006). According to Immanuel Kant ([1785] 1989), humans are all hard-wired before birth (*a priori*) with the knowledge of what is right and wrong. Kant avers that humans have a moral imperative to do right.

If the above is true, then why are there so many gray areas where media ethics appear ignored, bent, or broken to accommodate prevailing central authority, or to serve self-interests? Ethical dilemmas occur when the accepted norms of one particular culture, say the culture of journalism, rub against another set of norms, say those accepted by the prevailing society at large.

Muslims have a set of rules to follow, established by tradition and prescribed by its Holy Qur'an. Muslim journalists, who also adopt journalistic rules, standards, and practices – mostly established in the West – often find themselves in moral conflict with Islamic teachings. A moral conflict results when the two deontological sets grate against each other. These conflicts can take many forms from sensationalizing or exaggerating news, inventing stories and sources, refusing to admit and correct mistakes, using only those sources with whom the reporter or publisher agree, publishing culturally inappropriate pictures or even faked ones (*fauxtographs*) to further the regime's goals, their careers, or their ideology, rather than attempting to resolve the conflict by establishing an ethical standard to follow in the future.

Just as Christian youngsters learn Bible stories during church summer classes, and Jewish youngsters study the Torah in *yeshiva*, young Muslims might learn the tenants of Islam from the Qur'an and the Hadith in a *madrasah dīniyyah* (religious school). The *madrasah* system is often characterized in the West as training grounds for *jihad*, almost always framed in the Western media as an anti-Western, antimodernity, anti-American, and anti-Israeli confrontation. But *jihad* has multiple meanings, about which Muslims disagree, including the personal struggle between accepting what is good and what is evil.

Unlike Western societies that debate and practice separation of church and state, there is no way to separate Islam from politics in conservative Islamic thought. According to Mowlana (1993: 18), Islam is a total life system and Islamic principles are the supreme guide of conduct for all the human activities of Muslims.

Islamic principles of ethics

Even though there is no singular, accepted, or definitive discipline called Islamic ethics, there is, however, a vast body of literature pertaining to Islamic ethics in practice. According to Siddiqui (1997) one finds material on ethics in *tafsir* (Qur'anic exegesis), *kalam* (scholastic theology), and *fiqh* (jurisprudence) as well as in Sufism (mysticism). Unlike European thought and language that differentiates the Greek "ethos" from the Latin "mores," in Islam, the word most comparable to ethics is *akhlaq*, which embodies morality.

There are four important aspects of Islamic ethics emanating from the Holy Qur'an and the Hadith (the sayings and acts of Prophet Muhammad). Fazur Rahman (1983) articulated these as:

- *Iman* is the belief in the Oneness of Allah, his prophets and revealed books, the hereafter, and destiny). Although *iman* is a matter of heart, Islam encourages believers to employ reason (*aql*) and knowledge (*'ilm*) to sustain it (Qur'an 39: 9).
- *Taqwa* (piety) refers to protection and sustenance. Islam urges Muslims to guard against excessive physical, material, and moral decadence by using *taqwa* to discern right from wrong (Siddiqui 1997). Mowlana (1989: 145) argues that the believers devote their lives to liberate their soul from all things that prevent it from reaching *taqwa*.
- *Ihsan* (suitability or beauty) relates to devotion and love of Allah. Thus it functions as an inspiration for Muslim piety, particularly among Sufis (Siddiqui 1997).

- *Islam* (peace, purity, submission, and obedience) involves operational-izing *iman*, *taqwa*, and *ihsan*. Muslims "surrender themselves to God" through obedience to his will and his revelations to the prophets.

Taqiyya doctrine

The meaning of *taqiyya* is based on the Arabic word for fear, and acts as a defense mechanism to allow a Muslim to deceive others, especially nonbelievers, if they are threatened physically or spiritually. Sometimes journalists who serve brutal regimes find refuge in this Islamic doctrine as a way of easing the effects of cognitive dissonance. If Muslim journalists encounter murky ethical situations they should discern the intent of all actions, choose the lesser of two evils, ensure that the good of an action outweighs its harm, and consider whether "necessity" permits taking an unlawful action (*fiqh al-dharorah*).

When Muslim journalists encounter an ethical dilemma they cannot resolve, they can seek a *fatwa*, a legal opinion from a *mufti*. A *mufti* is a learned Muslim scholar who understands the principles of *shari'ah*. One such highly publicized *fatwa* was issued by the late Ayatollah Khomeini of Iran against writer Salman Rushdie, author of *The Satanic Verses*.

Shari'ah, Media Ethics, and Social Change

To cope with changing socioeconomic situations, Muslim journalists know they must adapt to their environments. Guided by shari'ah, Muslim journalists should use Qur'an and Hadiths as their moral compasses. But if there are no clear references in Qur'an and *sunnah* (Prophet Muhammad tradition), Islam has alternative paths. One alternative is *ijma*, which literally means "consensus." According to Siddiqui (1997), the consensus is what learned Qur'anic scholars decide on issues. In the absence of consensus, Muslims have the option of *qiyas*, which means "measuring" or comparing. In any unclear situation a Muslim can use comparable, past situations as examples and models. Utilizing this flexibility in Islam, liberal Muslim journalists can accommodate many Western media ethical concepts and practices.

The following are central, Islamic themes that influence Muslim journalists' decisions about what to cover and report.

Justice

Justice is a cornerstone of Islamic thought. Without justice, vulnerable groups (children, women, poor and elderly people) cannot be at peace with themselves or their society. The Qur'an states: "Whether it be against rich or poor ··· follow not the lust of your hearts, lest you swerve from doing justice" (Qur'an 4:135). From an Islamic perspective, journalists under repressive and corrupt regimes have a moral duty to stand up and demand reforms that benefit the *umma* (community). The concept of *umma* implies that all people are equal, and preferential status does not arise based on race, gender, or social status (Qur'an 49:13).

This strong sense of justice is at the heart of the current Middle East conflict. Palestinian Arabs consider the confiscation of properties for the creation of the State of Israel in 1948 and the forced removal of Arabs from their ancestral lands as an unjust and unforgiveable act. This sense of injustice, shared by the *umma*, fueled wars against Israel in 1948, 1967, and 1973, and skirmishes with neighboring Lebanon and Gaza ever since. The events unfolding in the Arab World in 2011 also resonated within the *umma* because in the uprisings in Tunisia, Egypt, Libya, Yemen, Bahrain, and Syria, professional and citizen journalists concentrated on stories of social and political injustices, the excesses of their rulers, and the humiliation of populaces caused by poverty, corruption, and draconian measures to quell dissenting voices. Humiliation, *New York Times* columnist Thomas L. Friedman points out, is "the single most underappreciated force in international relations," and a possible rationale for protests, insurgents, and suicide bombers. Quoting the outgoing Malaysian Prime Minister Mahathir Mohamed:

> I will not enumerate the instances of our humiliation · · · We are all Muslims. We are all oppressed. We are all being humiliated. · · · Today we, the whole Muslim [community], are treated with contempt and dishonor. · · · There is a feeling of hopelessness among the Muslim countries and their people. They feel that they can do nothing right. · · · Our only reaction is to become more and more angry. Angry people cannot think properly. (Friedman 2003)

Telling the truth

Prophet Muhammad spoke assertively of the virtue of truthfulness as a pillar of strong faith. The Prophet's message about truth is clear: Allah has no place for liars in paradise. Some Arab media practitioners replace truth with untruth or half-truths, embellishing falsehoods and fabricating news – like other unethical practitioners around the world. The motives for these actions vary. Discerning what is true in any human context and construction is often subjective and open to interpretation based on a journalist's understanding (or misunderstanding) of motivations, and historical and social contexts.

In the Arab World, truth is often determined on the "Arab Street," which was until recently the only civil society aggregate available to journalists. Following the 9/11 attacks, most Arab governments allowed public opinion surveys by internationally recognized polling organizations like Gallup, Pew, and Zogby. Social research, once suspected as a threat to Arab regimes, is now reluctantly allowed with governments' prior approval.

Exactly how this value of truth telling applies to Westernized advertising and public relations, or to distortions and falsehoods by regimes' propaganda efforts in Islamic countries, is less clear and a matter of current, intense debate (Al Janaibi 2011: 67–8).

War or peace

The Qur'an contains many contradictory verses about war and peace. Most scholars cite those peaceful and tolerant verses that live side by side with belligerent and intolerant ones. Islamic jurists (*fuqaha*) practiced *ijtihad* to decide which verses to enact into the shari'ah laws – especially the one that calls for "no coercion in religion" (Qur'an 2: 256), or the ones that urge believers to fight non-Muslims until they either convert, or at least submit, to Islam (Qur'an 8:39, 9:5, 9:29). They overcame this perplexing situation by reverting to the doctrine of abrogation (*naskh*). Abrogation maintains that verses revealed later in Prophet Muhammad's life take precedence over earlier ones, if there is a discrepancy.

Thus Muslims can argue that Islam is tolerant and can peacefully coexist with other religions "of the Book," which includes Christianity and Judaism.

Deeds speak louder than words

Consistency of what one says and what one does is a core value in Islamic ethics. To be morally legitimate, actions should have good intentions (Ayish and Sadig 1997: 108). Islamic teachings confirm the existence of moral and ethical consciousness in human beings, and encourage people to resort to their conscience for judging conduct or behavior. The influence of Islamic ethics can be greater on Muslim journalists than ethics codes adopted by their respective media organizations.

Protecting privacy and communal life

Free expression in Islam is perceived within the holistic belief in the sacredness of human life and the respect for human dignity. To protect public interest and safeguard an individual's right to honor and a good reputation, Islam sets moral constraints to muzzle defamation, incrimination, and derision.

The Qur'an instructs believers to protect and respect others, and forbids any act that may endanger others or expose their private affairs in all circumstances (Qur'an 49:11). In the same vein, God asks people to say good things about others and to refrain from suspicion and espionage (Qur'an 49:12).

In the Islamic context, a person's family life, property, and private matters are off limit to freedom of expression, and this often contradicts the training journalists receive in the West that everything in the public sphere is fair game.

Islam warns people, in the strongest terms, against "unleashing their tongues" in backbiting or tarnishing the reputations and honor of others, especially when those victimized are innocents (Qur'an 24:23). The Qur'an condemns rumor-mongering and spreading false news, particularly if the news might undermine public safety or stir fear and chaos among the people. It also encourages verification of information and veracity in news and information gathering by consulting those who are knowledgeable (Qur'an 4:83). The Scripture also warns against defaming other people and disseminating evil: "Those who love (to see) scandal published and broadcast among the believers will have a grievous penalty in this life and in the hereafter" (Qur'an 24:19).

A devotee of Islam who works for a media organization whose values might include being first with the story to beat competition (scoop mentality), serving the interests of central power (rewarding friends and punishing enemies, exaggerating the achievements of rulers, or withholding unfavorable data or news), or serving the interests of independent owners (sensationalizing stories to boost circulation and gain market share), might well come into conflict with religious ideals. Such was the case in the summer of 2001 in Cairo when the newspaper *Al-Nabaa* published color photograph stills from videotapes of a defrocked Coptic monk, Barsoum El-Muharraqi, engaging in sexual acts with several women in the fourth-century monastery of Deir Al-Muharraq, which according to Coptic Christian tradition was visited by the Holy Family in exile. The publication was seized by authorities off the newsstand, skyrocketing the cover price for that issue 40-fold, and leading to the arrest of the editor and suspension of the newspaper for several months. *Al-Nabaa* editors defended the story by saying the videotapes were part of a blackmail plot, and that the newspaper was serving the greater good by uncovering the scheme (Iviews 2001: 1). Egypt's religious authority, Al Ahzar's Grand Imam Sheikh Sayed Tantawi, however, saw it differently. Islam, he said, "opposes with all its force the publication of material that questions the integrity of others" (Iviews 2001: 1).

To clearly spell out these journalistic ideals, carefully crafted in most cases to reflect Islamic principles as well, media organizations turn to codes of ethics, the topic of a later section.

Free Religion, Speech, and Press in the Islamic Context

Although authoritarian regimes stifle free expression and discordant speech for political reasons, the potency of free expression in Islam is not diminished. Kamali (1994: 16) clarifies:

> Islam not only validates freedom of expression but it also urges Muslims not to remain silent or indifferent when expressing an opinion which is likely to serve the cause of truth, justice, or be of benefit to society.

In the Islamic context, freedom of religion and belief is a fundamental value. Thus all individuals can choose their religion without fear or compulsion (Qur'an 2:256). Support for freedom of belief is stressed in the Qur'anic revelations to the Prophet: "Say: 'The truth is from your Lord.' Let him who will, believe, and let him who will, reject (it)" (Qur'an 18:29). Freedom of religion requires a hospitable environment that discourages ridicule and blasphemy: "Do not revile those whom they call upon besides Allah, lest they out of spite revile Allah in their ignorance" (Qur'an 6:108).

Islamic freedom of expression embodies the sanctity of religion. Islam encourages people to get involved in public debate and announce their opinions without hesitation or fear of persecution, provided that these opinions uphold truthfulness and moral behavior. This touches on the important concept of *tawhid* (the supremacy and sovereignty of Allah). A person who practices *tawhid* believes that worldly life and sustenance are in the hands of God (Qur'an 51:22, 58), and that only God determines life and death (Qur'an 50:43). Consequently, such a person is expected to be more conscientious and free from control and domination. The principle of *tawhid* makes it the duty of every Muslim journalist to work for:

> the destruction of thought structures based on dualism, racialism, tribalism, and familial superiority ··· One of the dualisms, according to this principle, is the secular notion of the separation of religion and politics. (Mowlana 1989: 141–2)

The Qur'an denounces those who blindly imitate others and follow them without reasoning (Qur'an 31:21). Prophet Muhammad instructs Muslims:

> Let none of you be turned into a tail (*imm'ah*): that is a person who does good work or embarks upon evil only when he sees others doing the same. But make up your minds. Let everyone join others in good deeds and avoid participation in evil conduct. (Translated by Kamali 1994: 53)

Prophet Muhammad urged the *umma* to speak out and be engaged: "He who remains silent about truth is a dumb devil" and "the best form of *jihad* is to utter a word of truth to a tyrannical ruler" (Kamali 1994: 51). This directive is in tandem with the scriptural principle of "commanding to the right (*ma'ruf*) and prohibiting from the wrong (*munkar*)," which represents the pillar of Islamic social responsibility. Social responsibility requires Islamic media to follow Islamic principles and encourages audiences to follow suit (Mowlana 1989: 142).

In Islam, *shurra* (consultation) is the basis of good governance. A prerequisite for *shurra* is the right to get accurate and authentic information to make informed judgment. Those who gather and disseminate information should verify its authenticity before transmitting it to the *umma*. Veracity is the keystone of Islamic thought and necessitates personal and social responsibility as well as accountability.

Freedom of expression in Islam emphasizes human dignity and serving the common good. Media practitioners, as well as the public, should not misuse this freedom to inflict damage on others. However, when there is no point in speaking, silence becomes a virtue. Prophet Muhammed says: "It is indicative of piety for a Muslim to remain silent in regards to matters which do not concern him" (Kamali 1994: 122). Yet denouncing an evil in public is encouraged if this public denunciation corrects wrongdoing or establishes communal justice.

Egypt, the Middle East's largest Muslim country of over 80 million people, has freedom of speech and press guaranteed by Article 6 of the constitution, as government-paid journalists would be quick to point out. But difficult times required suspension of such trouble-making ideals as free assembly, press, and speech until the "emergency" was over. This refers to Law 162 of 1958, popularly known at the Emergency Law, which suspended constitutional protections for citizens and journalists, legalized censorship, and suspended civil liberties – often at whim. The law has been on the books since 1958 and has been renewed every year since – except for 18 months in the 1980s – and had been rigorously enforced after the 1967 Six Day War with Israel and the 1983 assassination of President Anwar Sadat (Kassem 1999: 57–8, Williams 2006). Law 162 is still in effect, though slight modifications were proposed by military rulers in September 2011 to mollify Arab Spring protesters.

The turn of the twenty-first century, however, signaled something transformative on the horizon for a young population growing up with Western media products advertised on television, cell phones, computers, and social network sites like YouTube, Facebook, and Twitter. Exposed to the freedoms of the West and the harsh realities of autocratic rule by aging leaders, something was about to change (Berenger 2006: 219). Mass media were also coming of age in the region, partly forced by competition with Western media that were making inroads with bilingual audiences in the Middle East.

Codes of Ethics: Providing Professional Journalism Context

Many news organizations in the Middle East have codes of ethics that outline what is expected good behavior for journalists. Not only are these codes "Islamic-friendly," but they comply with press laws enacted in each country. Often they contain lofty ideals that superficially seem like ethic codes in Western media: values of truth telling, honesty, transparency, fairness, and resistance to propaganda. How well the Middle East media's practice reflects the ideals in their codes of ethics is often in the eye of the beholder.

In many ways, Western and Middle Eastern media ethics practices differ, according to Kai Hafez (2002: 225–6). Regional factors such as culture, religion, and politics play a vital role in determining what is ethical and what is not. Youssef Ibrahim, a *Wall Street Journal* foreign correspondent, referred to these as "fundamental, common denominators" (Robison 2005: 2). Because of these factors, Middle Eastern audiences readily can identify unethical media missteps made by international media organizations who "parachute" in journalists to cover fast-breaking news stories, but lack the cultural sensitivity, context, and knowledge that local journalists possess. The most common faux pas is to group all Arabs into one category and assume that all Arabs are Muslims. Another misstep is to assume that all Arabs think and act alike on all matters, or share the same norms and values.

Middle East audiences vary widely in what they believe and who they believe in, and there are few ethical standards that could be accepted by all media practitioners in the region. Nart Bouran, head of news at Abu Dhabi Television, is clear on that point: "There are universal things: you can't lie, you can't make things up. These are things that all journalists learn no matter where they are from" (Robison 2005: 2).

The Dubai-based Al Arabiya TV channel is a part of the Saudi-owned MBC group and is considered to be Al Jazeera's main competitor in the Middle East. Al Arabiya's assistant general manager, Saleh Nagm, who had worked for several years with BBC, told Robison (2005: 4–5) that there are more similarities than differences between media in the Arab World and the West: "You have to see the whole scope of Arab media and then judge upon it." Nagm said that in theory, the principles of media ethics are universal. Practice, however, depends on other factors, including local politics, economics, and culture. In another words, ethical practices must take *context* into account.

Gift-giving or bribes?

Some culturally accepted journalistic practices in the Middle East would be considered egregiously unethical in the West. An example of such inconsistency of media ethics between the East and West is the treatment of "gifts" to and from journalists. In the United States, codes of ethics generally forbid journalists receiving or giving gifts. Some US media operations even draw the line over receiving as much as a cup of coffee from a source. In the Middle East, and especially in the Arab World, gift-giving is expected normative behavior. It is considered proper etiquette to offer guests, including journalists working on a story, coffee or a soft drink or a small gift, and it is good manners for the guest or journalist to accept them. Giving gifts, the value of which depends of the status of the giver, is commonplace, and the practice is culturally accepted and even expected. The line could be drawn over the issue of *wasta* (a form of tribute given in anticipation of some future favor, usually a gift or another favor). Robison cites an example of a promotional event in Doha where briefcases, filled with promotional trinkets and advertising novelties, were delivered as perks to each news correspondent's room. The briefcases delivered to Arab journalists also contained envelopes filled with cash (Robison 2005: 2–3). Little wonder poorly paid Arab journalists lobby their news executives to allow them to cover all-expense-paid promotional events around the Middle East.

Protocol news

A characteristic of state-run media is "protocol news" – the praise of a country's leader, no matter what the leader actually does. Broadcast stations can be counted on to lead most news broadcasts with a story about the comings, goings, and doings of the country's chief executive, and newspapers nearly always run a flattering picture of the leader or his family on the front page. It's not uncommon to see, hear, or read a lead story about the country's leader extending birthday wishes to another, or seeing pictures of them sitting in throne-like chairs to meet visiting dignitaries. Egypt's state-owned *Al Ahram*, the largest newspaper in the Arab World with a daily circulation of around 600,000, went a step farther in September 2010 when the newspaper Photoshopped an official White House picture of regional leaders at a White House conference, headed by President Barack Obama. To show their president's importance in world affairs, editors cut and spliced Mubarak out of the group of Middle East leaders, headed by President Obama, to make it appear that Mubarak was leading the delegation rather than trailing it in the original picture (Adams 2011). The manipulated photograph was spotted by an Egyptian blogger Wael Khali, who blew the whistle on the ruse.

According to *Al Masry Al Youm*, an independent newspaper in Cairo, *Al Ahram*'s editor-in-chief Osama Saraya defended the photograph, saying:

> the expressionist photo is ⋯ a brief, live and true expression of the prominent stance of President Mubarak in the Palestinian issue, his unique role in leading it before Washington or any other. (*Al Masry Al Youm* 2010)

Al Jazeera's Ethical Dilemmas in Context

With the emergence of Al Jazeera, the region's most prominent news outlet, a new era for journalism began, with a new emphasis on codes of ethics that prescribe journalistic behavior. Al Jazeera's current code was adopted in July 2004 as a way to enhance its credibility with viewers. Berenger (2006: 212–13) speculates that the next battle for audiences between competing media in the Middle East might well be over which media outlet is perceived by audiences as the most credible. Codes of ethics, like mission statements, can help readers, viewers, or users to understand the ethical goals of a news organization. According to Robison (2005: 3), Al Jazeera's code of conduct was intended to convey an "Arab view of world affairs." The code consists of 10 rules, each directed at the network's

journalists   (http://www.aljazeera.com/iwantaje/201052121352560224
.html). One line of Al Jazeera's ethics code reads: "Endeavour to get to
the truth and declare it in our dispatches, programs and news bulletins
in a manner which leaves no doubt about its validity and accuracy."
Another reads: "Distinguish between news material, opinion and analysis
to avoid the pitfalls of speculation and propaganda."

Perhaps implied in Western codes of ethics is an inherent distrust of
government and those who govern at all levels. Such distrust, alluded to
in Alexis de Tocqueville's *Democracy in America* (2000) over 260 years
ago, inculcates US society and the media that reflect it. Left alone from the
intrigues of European monarchs and self-interested patricians, America's
political system developed differently and independently from Europe at
a time when the autocratic Ottoman Empire was shaping the Middle
East's sociopolitical cultures. Mass media grew up in the context of the
new world ideology; Middle Eastern media, slower to start and grow,
followed the prevailing ideologies of the region, completely autocratic
and authoritarian. These differences are reflected in today's various media
laws and codes in the Middle East region.

Ahmed Al Skeikh, who joined Al Jazeera after working with the BBC
and BBC Arabia, said the BBC and Al Jazeera follow different codes of
ethics. Al Sheikh said that early staffers at BBC Arabia were sent directly
from the network's head offices and followed the same codes of ethics
established there. A Jordanian journalist, who worked for Reuters and the
Associated Press, said he prefers working for Western media because they
are "better than their Arab counterparts at defining and teaching the norms
of the profession" (Robison 2005: 3, 4). The journalist added that one of
the things he learned during his experience with Western news agencies
was the importance of not taking sides on any given issue, especially in the
Middle East. Middle East journalists often find alien the idea of neutrality,
as Al Jazeera's management is quick to point out. Neutrality cannot exist
when reporting from a certain regional perspective. Nor, in the case of
Arab international media, is neutrality the point.

The Sami Al-Hajj incident

In its short history, Al Jazeera has been at Ground Zero in the battle
over contextual ethics. The celebrated case of Sami Al-Hajj, a Sudanese
reporter arrested by Afghani troops in 2001 as an "enemy combatant" and
eventually detained for seven years at Guantanamo Bay's prison facility in
Cuba, is but one example. Al-Hajj maintained he was only doing his job in
covering the war in Afghanistan, but American and Pakistani authorities
claimed he was a conduit for information to the Taliban and Al Qaeda.
Al-Hajj was classified as an "enemy combatant" whose "access to senior
terrorist leaders demonstrates his probable connections to the al-Qaida
network and other militant jihadist organizations." The US government
considered his extensive travels in Taliban strongholds and access to

Taliban and Al Qaeda leaders as probable cause for his detention. He was represented as "a member of al-Qaida who is an expert in logistics with direct ties to al-Qaida leadership" (Mutter 2011).

After the publication by WikiLeaks.org of previously classified documents, the case against Al-Hajj was revealed as circumstantial at best. Following his release in May 2008 he filed a lawsuit with the international court saying he was falsely imprisoned. Nothing has come of the lawsuit and Al-Hajj continues today as an Al Jazeera reporter on human rights (Fouché 2009).

Whether Al-Hajj passed information from one Al Qaeda cell to another might never be known or even adjudicated, but Western and Pakistani intelligence officers were sufficiently suspicious of his actions to detain him. His ease of travel between Talibani and Al Qaeda forces, and the flavor of his reporting for Al Jazeera, certainly indicated his acceptance by the warring factions, perhaps because he was reporting news from an Arab context, which Al Jazeera itself promotes.

The University of Sana'a incident

While Al Jazeera is considered by viewers as the most credible Arabic news channel in the Middle East, the station was recently accused of inciting the Arab public against their governments during the uprisings in Egypt, Libya, Yemen, and Syria. On March 20, 2011, Al Jazeera aired a video outside the University of Sana'a that showed the killing of 52 protesters. Yemini government officials accused Al Jazeera of fabricating the report and video. An information ministry source told the *Yemen Observer*:

> Al Jazeera screened this video on Wednesday and alleged that it was shot recently in Yemen. It reported that this was footage of the Yemeni Central Security forces torturing Yemeni protesters. (Al-Kibsi, 2011)

According to the *Observer* article, Al Jazeera confessed during live air time that the video was screened due to a technical error. The *Observer* later reported on behalf of the information minister that those videos were also fabricated: "activists revealed that the same video was posted on the Web site YouTube on March 13. The video depicted a rural area and not Sana'a" (Al-Kibsi 2011).

This incident might have been more than mere sloppy reporting. Remembering the Islamic values of truth-telling and a Muslim's obligation to speak out against injustices, the incident should be placed in context. The Yemeni government did use oppressive force to subdue a demonstration, which Al Jazeera cameramen detailed. But where did this incident occur and when? The practice of using file footage of previous disturbances to visually illustrate another event – once widely practiced by Western journalists when they could not get to a location fast enough to record the actuality – is now generally deemed unethical in the West, and increasingly so in Arab countries as well. Al Jazeera obviously wanted to show what was happening in Sana'a, but it did not have visuals from that scene. An explanatory slide saying this was file footage of an earlier event might have lessened the charge of fabrication. Arab media still have a learning curve to overcome.

The Samir Kuntar incident

In 2008, criticisms of Al Jazeera arose as the station aired footage of Lebanese civilians celebrating the release of Lebanese Druze Samir Kuntar, who had spent 29 years in an Israeli prison for killing five Israelis. On July 19, 2008, Al Jazeera covered celebrations honoring Kuntar's release. Ghassan bin Jiddo, head of the station's Beirut office, called Kuntar a "pan-Arab hero" and threw him a birthday party. Bin Jiddo wished Kuntar a happy birthday, a cake was brought in and a band played patriotic music. Bin Jiddo then showed pictures of Kuntar in a military uniform and another one that was taken on the day of his release. The two pictures were printed on the birthday cake (http://www.youtube.com/watch?v=oFWVkSU3ic4).

Israel's Government Press Office (GPO) threatened to ban the network unless steps were taken to prevent similar incidents from happening again. Just days later, Al Jazeera's General Director Wadah Khanfar wrote in an open letter that the content of the program "violated [the station's] Code of Ethics," and that he regarded "these violations as very serious." He said that he had taken measures to ensure against a similar incident occurring (Stern 2008).

Khanfar's letter was published in Israel's daily *Ha'aretz*. The Israeli newspaper added that Al Jazeera apologized for airing the footage, which the station denied it did. Al Jazeera's lawyer demanded that *Ha'aretz* apologize for publishing "false information about the Arabic news station's apology." The lawyer said that Khanfar wrote a press release that *explained* the station's position on the situation but did not apologize to the public. The lawyer denied any allegations that the GPO had ever requested an apology from Al Jazeera (Bannoura 2008). Reuters published an article on August 7, 2008 which quoted the head of Israel's GPO saying, "We are not looking for an apology · · · but for a serious investigation which will be brought to our attention in a professional way" (Landau 2008).

Three years later, Khanfar, who was credited with putting Al Jazeera on the world media map, resigned his position following WikiLeaks' disclosure of cables alleging that he altered coverage of Iraqi news in 2005 to appease the US State Department (*Global Post* 2011).

These examples demonstrate the difficulty of overwriting professional codes of conduct, refined in the West, on the cultural contextual template of what Arab journalists perceive and believe is proper, if not commendable, behavior. To celebrate the release of a convicted murderer with a birthday cake would never be done in the West, but given the Palestinian–Israeli context, apparently no one at Al Jazeera thought it was beyond the pale to honor a man who Arab journalists felt was a heroic figure in the long-festering conflict against a greater injustice than loss of lives. Khanfar's tortured response nearly three weeks after the broadcast speaks to the ethical dilemma context caused in this case.

Conclusion

This chapter advances the premise that media ethics in the Middle East must be viewed in the context of what societal members consider normative behavior for media organization to practice. The authors question whether a model of universal media ethics is possible, in part because norms and values vary too much between cultures based on specific historical antecedents, socialization, and ideologies; and in part because religion (Islam) provides the moral underpinning for journalists' expected behavior. The Western tradition – based on Judeo-Christian concepts and philosophical principles derived from ancient Greek thinkers – often differs prescriptively from Middle East traditions and behavioral expectations. In many ways Rudyard Kipling's century-old observation in "The Ballad of East and West" that "East is East and West is West, and never the twain shall meet" is appropriate, although Western modernity concepts are modifying many traditional beliefs and practices in the Middle East. A Western concept in origin, journalism bridges that East–West divide. However, many Western journalistic practices are anathema to Middle East cultural traditions that are more oriented toward community over the individual interests; and culturally responsible and authority-deferential speech over the "public's right to know" and the commodification of information. Journalistic values of truthfulness, fairness, and unbiased reporting free from government interference constantly rub against cultural traditions in the Middle East, resulting in ethical dilemmas for journalists.

Islamic media ethics is a work in progress.

Further Reading

Readers are advised to consult the following three books:

Mamoun Fandy's *(Un)Civil War of Words: Media and Politics in the Arab World* (London: Praeger Security International, 2007) is written by a journalist working within the structures of Arab media. Fandy has witnessed Arab journalistic practices from the inside at Al Jazeera and Al Arabiya channels. He analyzes the relationship between Middle East media organizations and governments. The Western public–private media dichotomy is not useful, Fandy says, to understanding how Arab media function. Owners and editors use their media outlets to push political ideas more directly than Western media do, and working as a journalist in this environment can be more of a blood sport than a profession. Arab media shape and are shaped by the region's historical and political contexts, and the author concludes that media are seldom part of what Western scholars call "civil society." Two generations of Middle East Arabs have been cultivated by anti-Western, Soviet-style propaganda to hold visceral, negative views of the West. Fandy suggests the West should stop competing with Arab media in the Middle East for the hearts and minds of the Arab Street, and concentrate instead on helping local civil society groups that further democracy in the region.

Arab Media: Globalization and Emerging Media Industries by Noha Mellor, Mohammed I. Ayish, Nabil Dajani, and Khalid Rinnawi (Cambridge: Polity, 2011) is an authoritative introduction to the emerging Arab media industries in the context of globalization and its impacts. It focuses on publishing, press, broadcasting, cinema, and new media in the Arab World, and discusses the regulation and economics of these industries. The authors argue that the emergence of international Arab mass media has changed the politics, technology, and newsroom cultures of international media. The book gives a contemporary overview of the characteristics of Arab media, from serving as propaganda vehicles for regimes, to acting as profit-oriented enterprises while continuing to deal with state interventions and self-censorship.

Mahjoob Zweiri and Emma C. Murphy's edited volume *The New Arab Media: Technology, Image and Perception* (Reading: Ithaca Press, 2011) introduces and analyzes some of the important issues surrounding the new media revolution in the Middle East by examining the "Janus-like" faces of new media: their roles in projecting Arab society internally as well as internationally. The book's nine chapters look at the impact of Al-Jazeera, implementation of the Internet in the region, use of the media for diplomacy and propaganda, image culture, use of the Internet by religious diasporas, ICTs and the Arab public sphere, the influence of satellite TV on Arab public opinion, and the explosion of local radio stations in Jordan.

References

Adams, P. 2011. "Egypt Crisis: *Al-Ahram's* Own Revolution in Cairo," BBC News, 18 February, http://www.bbc.co.uk/news/world-middle-east -12498705, accessed June 5, 2011.

Al Janaibi, B. 2011 "The Changing Representation of the Arab Woman in Middle East Advertising and Media." *Global Media Journal-Arabian Edition* 1(2): 67–88, available at http://gmj-me.com/gmj_custom_files/ volume1_issue2 /articles_in_english/volume1-issue2-article-67-88.pdf, accessed November 30, 2011.

Al-Kibsi, M. 2011. "Al Jazeera Shows Iraqi Videos to Fabricate News about Yemen." *Yemen Observer*, March 26, available at http://www.yobserver.com /front-page/10021008.html, accessed November 30, 2011.

Al Masry Al Youm. 2010. "Fake Mubarak Photo Continues to Provoke Reactions," September 17, http://www.almasryalyoum.com/en/node/131585, accessed August 15, 2011.

Ayish, M. and Sadig, H. B. 1997. "The Arab-Islamic Heritage in Communication Ethics." In C. Christians and M. Traber, eds., *Communication Ethics and Universal Values*. Thousand Oaks, CA: Sage: 105–27.

Bannoura, S. 2008. "Al Jazeera Demands an Israeli Apology." International Middle East Media Center, August 19. http://www.imemc.org/article/56608 ?print_page=true, accessed October 5, 2011.

Berenger, R. D. 2006. "Media in the Middle East and North Africa." In T. L. McPhail, ed., *Global Communication: Theories, Stakeholders and Trend*, 2nd ed. Oxford: Blackwell, 192–225.

Committee to Protect Journalists. 2011 "Imprisonments Jump Worldwide, and Iran is the Worst." http://www.cpj.org/reports/2011/12/journalist -imprisonments-jump-worldwide-and-iran-i.php, accessed December 8, 2011.

Fouché, G. 2009. "Al-Jazeera Journalist Imprisoned in Guantánamo Bay to Sue George Bush." *Guardian*, July 17, http://www.guardian.co.uk/media /2009/jul/17/guantanamo-bay-al-jazeera, accessed December 3, 2011

Freedom House. 2011. "Freedom in the World: Middle East and North Africa." http://www.freedomhouse.org/sites/default/files/inline_images /TableofIndependentCountriesFIW2011.pdf, accessed November 12, 2011.

Friedman, T. L. 2003. "The Humiliation Factor." *New York Times*, November 9. http://www.nytimes.com/2003/11/09/opinion/the-humiliation-factor .html, accessed November 13, 2011.

Global Post. 2011. "Al Jazeera News Director, Wadah Khanfar, Resigns After WikiLeaks Disclosure," September 20. http://www.globalpost.com/dispatch /news/regions/middle-east/iraq/110920/al-jazeera-wadah-khanfar-resigns, accessed January 5, 2012.

Hafez, K. 2002. "Journalism Ethics Revisited: A Comparison of Ethics Codes in Europe, North Africa, the Middle East, and Muslim Asia." *Political Communication* 19: 225–50.

Iqra Foundation. 2011. "Muslim Population in the World," December 8. http:// www.islamicpopulation.com/world_general.html, accessed November 12, 2011.

Iviews staff. 2001. "Sex, Church Ties and Video Tape: The Controversy Over Egypt's Tabloid Press." Iviews.Com., June 22. http://www.iviews.com /articles/Articles.asp?ref=IV0106-1440, accessed June 30, 2011

Kamali, M. H. 1994. *Freedom of Expression in Islam*. Kuala Lumpur: Berita Publishing.

Kant, I. [1785] 1989. *Foundation of the Metaphysics of Morals*, 2nd edn. New York: Prentice Hall.

Kassem, M. 1999. *In the Guise of Democracy: Governance in Contemporary Egypt*. New York: Ithaca Press.

Land, M. and Hornaday, B. 2006. *Contemporary Media Ethics*. Spokane, WA: Marquette Books.

Landau, A. 2008. "Al Jazeera Says Prisoner 'Party' Breached Code of Ethics," Reuters, August 7. http://www.reuters.com/article/2008/08/07 /idUSL7107412.

Media Source. 2009. "Insight/Media Source: 2009 Journalist Survey." *Middle East Media Guide*. http://www.middleeastmediaguide.com/downloads /mejournalistsurvey2009.pdf, accessed November 30, 2011.

Mellor, N. 2005. *The Making of Arab News*. Lanham, MD: Rowman and Littlefield.

Miles, H. 2005. *Al Jazeera: The Inside Story of the Arab News Channel That is Challenging the West*. New York: Grove Press.

Mowlana, H. 1989. "Communication, Ethics, and Islamic Tradition." In T. W. Cooper, ed., *Communication Ethics and Global Change*. White Plains, NY: Longman, 137–46.

Mowlana, H. 1993. "The New Global Order and Cultural Ecology." *Media, Culture and Society* 15(1): 9–27.

Mutter, P. 2011. "The War Against Al Jazeera and Sami Al-Hajj." *Foreign Policy in Focus*, June 1. http://www.fpif.org/articles/the_war_against_al_jazeera _and_sami_al-hajj, accessed August 12, 2011.

Pew Research Center. 2009. "Mapping the World's Muslim Population: A Report on the Size and Distribution of the World's Muslim Population," October. http://www.pewforum.org/Muslim/Mapping-the-Global-Muslim -Population(2).aspx, accessed December 2, 2011.

Quinn, S. and Walters, T. 2004. "Al Jazeera: A Broadcaster Causing Ripples in Stagnant Media Pool." In R. D. Berenger, ed., *Global Media Go to War: Role of Entertainment and News During the 2003 Iraq War*. Spokane, WA: Marquette Books, 57–72.

Rahman, F. 1983. "Some Key Ethical Concepts of the Qur'an." *The Journal of Religious Ethics II*: 170–85.

Reuters. 2011. "Cairo: Protestors Try to Demolish Wall at Israeli Embassy." *Jerusalem Post*, September 9. http://www.jpost.com/MiddleEast/Article.aspx ?id=237365, accessed October 30, 2011.

Robison, G. 2005. "Universal ethics?" US Center on Public Diplomacy, Middle East Media Project, April. http://uscpublicdiplomacy.org/pdfs/Robison _-_Universal_Apr05.pdf, accessed November 8, 2011.

Rugh, W. A. 2004. *Arab Mass Media: Newspapers, Radio and Television in Arab Politics*. Westport, CT: Praeger.

Said, E. W. 1979. *Orientalism*. New York: Vintage Books.

Savage, T. M. 2004. "Europe and Islam: Crescent Waxing, Cultures Clashing." *The Washington Quarterly* 27(3): 25–50.

Siddiqui, A. 1997. "Ethics in Islam: Key Concepts and Contemporary Challenges." *Journal of Moral Education* 26(4): 423–31

Stableford, D. 2011. "Al Jazeera Director Resigns Amid Scandal; WikiLeaks Cable Reveals He Met with U.S. Intelligence, Agreed to Remove 'Disturbing' Content." The Cutline Weblog, September 20. http://news.yahoo.com /blogs/cutline/al-jazeera-director-resigns-amid-scandal-,wikileaks-cable- 202032780.html, accessed November 2, 2011.

Stern, Y. 2008. "Al-Jazeera Apologizes for 'Unethical' Coverage of Kuntar Release." *Haaretz*, June 8, http://www.haaretz.com/news/al-jazeera -apologizes-for-unethical-coverage-of-kuntar-release-1.251249.

Tocqueville, A. 2000. *Democracy in America*. Chicago: University of Chicago Press.

Undata. 2012. "The State of the World's Children." http://data.un.org/Data .aspx?d=SOWC&f=inID%3A74, accessed September 14, 2012.

Williams, D. 2006. "Egypt Extends 25-year-old Emergency Law," *The Washington Post*, May 1. http://www.washingtonpost.com/wp-dyn/content/article /2006/04/30/AR2006043001039.html, accessed November 12, 2011.

World Bank. 2010 "Recent Trends of Poverty in the Middle East and North Africa," February. http://www.worldbank.org/en/news/2010/02/19/recent -trends-poverty-middle-east-north-africa, accessed November 18, 2011.

6

From Journalism Ethics to an Ethics of Citizenship
Evidence from Colombia

Hernando Rojas and Tim Macafee

The field of journalism ethics receives continued scholarly attention, in no small part because of the critical relationship that exists between news and civic (and democratic) outcomes. Journalism ethics has traditionally been conceptualized as a "species of applied ethics that examines what journalists and news organizations should do, given their role in society" (Ward, 2009: 295). To be sure, defining and meeting ethical journalistic standards has not been a simple task, given the multifaceted nature of an enterprise that includes journalistic behavior, but also organizational and system level constraints.

Stephen Ward (2009: 297) encapsulates the evolution of the field of journalism ethics from the invention of an ethical discourse for journalism during the seventeenth century, through a "public ethics" narrative reinforcing the public sphere during the Enlightenment, to a liberal theory of the press during the nineteenth century – one that evolves to a professional ethics of objectivity in the twentieth century and that is currently under assault from different viewpoints.

Critics suggest enlarging journalism ethics' conceptual base, through the development of a new robust theoretical basis (Ward 2011b: 738), as well as by acknowledging and consequently developing "mixed media" ethics that take into account emergent media platforms. This chapter seeks to contribute to the latter by examining journalism's performance in an understudied context (Colombia), assessing trust on traditional media as well as media's trustworthiness, contrasting traditional media's impact on democratic practices with emerging media, and concluding by theorizing on the emergence of new form of public that realigns journalism ethics within a broader context of citizenship ethic.

Most studies of journalism ethics have focused on the global "North" with some exceptions that have sought to compare press performance

Global Media Ethics: Problems and Perspectives, First Edition. Edited by Stephen J. A. Ward.
© 2013 Blackwell Publishing Ltd. Published 2013 by Blackwell Publishing Ltd.

in different parts of the world (e.g., Freedom House Indexes), as well as how certain journalist's attitudes compare with those of the United States (Weaver 1996: 83). While these studies are certainly important, they assume a universal relationship between media and democracy, one that is better established empirically within specific contexts.

The Colombian Context

For most of Colombia's independent life, violence has played a key role as a conflict resolution mechanism, despite the nation's formal democratic structure. Wars between centralist and federalists, and then between liberals and conservatives, characterized most of the nineteenth century as well as the first half of the twentieth century. In the context of the Cold War, the confrontations between liberals and conservatives subsided, while a new confrontation with communist guerillas brewed. This as yet unresolved conflict was fueled with money from illegal drugs and further developed as new armed actors, representing drug barons and traditional rural elites, emerged as right-wing paramilitary groups.

In the last decade of the twentieth century, traditional political elites facing both international pressure and increasing displacement by drug barons engaged in a frontal war against drug trafficking that has been somewhat successful. This "war against drugs," with important involvement from the United Sates, coupled with a shift in the center of gravity in the drug business to Mexico, led to an important stabilization of Colombia at the turn of the century.

As the concern over drugs receded, political elites once again turned their attention to communist guerrillas. A failed peace process with FARC, Colombia's oldest and most important guerrilla group, influenced the presidential elections in 2002. Then Alvaro Uribe, a right-wing politician who promised that guerrillas would be defeated with force, was elected president (and subsequently re-elected for a second four-year term in 2006).

During Uribe's two terms in office, a process of negotiations with right-wing paramilitary groups was enacted and a strong military offensive against guerilla groups undertaken. These parallel processes served to reduce the operational capabilities of left-wing guerrillas and reduced the threat of right-wing paramilitary groups. Despite Uribe's popularity, which contributed to the election of a member of his political party – Juan Manuel Santos – as President in 2010, various scandals involving corruption in government contracts, human rights violations, and illegal monitoring of opposition parties remain a challenge to the political system.

Colombia's political system can be characterized as a formal democracy in which regular elections are held. A traditional conservative–liberal party divide evolved into a multiparty system with certain parties representing the right (supporting free trade, agrarian interests and a strong military, e.g., Partido de la U, Conservative Party), others representing the political center (seeking social reforms, e.g., Partido Liberal, Partido Verde), and others the left (proposing a wider role for government, protecting Colombian production and land redistribution, e.g., Polo Democratico Alternativo).

In the midst of the political turmoil that has characterized the turn of the century, urban geographies have emerged as a political alternative to Colombia's violence cycles. Since 1992 a series of local governments have emphasized political accountability, cultural innovations on citizenship, and the physical transformation of the cities that have changed the political game (Muñoz et al. 2003). With decreasing violence and the increasing importance of public opinion in the political process, Colombia can be examined today as a case study of how societies can choose to resolve their political conflicts through inclusion rather than exclusion, through dialogue rather than through force. We argue that the success of this process is clearly tied to journalism and its capacity to promote citizenship.

Colombia's media system is largely deregulated. It comprises a weak public system (limited funding, limited production capacity, and small audience shares) and a vibrant private system. Leading television news channels, daily newspapers, radio stations and web outlets are private advertising-based enterprises. With clear partisan allegiances during most of the twentieth century, today the press in Colombia is independent from political parties, relatively independent from government, and heavily tied to big business interests. Colombia's media system has been described as a market-based press with a "weak legacy of media pluralism" (Waisbord 2008: 3). In this informational context, radio continues to play an important role, but by and large two private television channels (RCN and Caracol) are the main sources of information for most people in the country. Newspapers and magazines, despite having smaller audiences, are highly influential in setting the media agenda and have emerged as the most important news providers online.

While there are still important digital divides and inequalities regarding new communication technologies, particularly in rural areas, by 2010 already 55 percent of urbanites (that constitute 75% of the country's population) had Internet access, and 81 percent owned a cell phone (Rojas et al. 2011). The use of new communication technologies for informational purposes is on the rise with 61 percent of those with access using it to get the news online, and 19 percent participating in online forums and reading blogs with a news and politics orientation (Rojas et al. 2011). Traditional news media enterprises are the prevalent source of news online, but, as is happening in other parts of the world, emerging actors, including bloggers, citizens, and NGOs, now share this discursive space. A good example of these emerging outlets in Colombia is *La Silla Vacia* (http://www.lasillavacia.com/), an online news and analysis site in which professional journalists, formerly attached to traditional media, report, comment, and foster debate about ongoing political issues.

Trusting Journalists

In traditional accounts of journalism ethics, journalists have an ethical duty to provide the public with credible news and analysis (Ward 2005), which in turn allows individuals to make informed decisions on their political preferences, making representative democracy possible. While journalist associations have for the most part dismissed audience evaluation and feedback as criteria to assess the ethical norms that guide the quality of their work (Ward and Wasserman 2010: 279), it seems logical that if citizens do not trust media, the impact of the information generated by journalists will be of limited value. Thus promoting democracy, one of the central ethical obligation of journalists (Kovach and Rosenstiel 2007), would remain unfulfilled. This issue is only amplified with the deliberative turn in accounts of democratic functioning (Delli Carpini, Cook and Jacobs 2004), and the emergent responsibilities of media in such a system. Understanding that trust in media is necessary for journalism to accomplish its democratic function, we turn to examining trust in media in the Colombian context.

Our research suggests that despite the limited pluralism of media that we alluded to in our introductory remarks, media in Colombia are one of the institutions in which people tend to trust. Based on probability sample surveys of over 1,000 respondents that represent the general population of the country, we have monitored trust in Colombia over the past years. Our results show that with the exception of trust in church and in others, media are more trusted than government, the judiciary, Congress, or political parties (see Figure 6.1). For a more detailed analyses of the evolution of trust in Colombia, as well as methodological details of the surveys on which this data is based, see Rojas and Pérez 2009, Rojas, Perez, and Gil de Zúñiga, 2010, Rojas et al. 2011).

Having established that Colombians tend to trust media, it seems appropriate to disentangle what type of trust is important for democratic functioning. Idealist notions of trust conceptualize it as a virtue that is cognitive and emotional, and oriented by normative orientations. Trust then implies an attitude of optimism toward the goodwill and competence of the other in specific domains of interaction (Jones 1996). Braithwaite, (1998) has identified two sets of trust norms: One is based on security values that operate for exchange situations and that are highly cognitive, and built on factors such as perceived competence and consistency (e.g., trusting a business partner based on past business interactions). The other refers to communal trust norms and is based on harmony values (e.g., trusting others despite not having interacted directly with them).

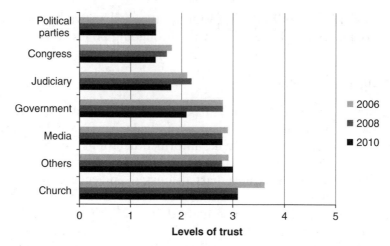

Figure 6.1   Social, Institutional and Media Trust in Colombia

The consequences attributed to trust, or the lack thereof, depend on basic assumptions of what trust implies. We can view trust from a utilitarian perspective, based on theories of purposive action according to which individuals have interests and goals and act reasonably when their action is fit to attain such goals as maximizing their utility (Coleman 1990). Under this logic, trust becomes an expectation that others will fulfill their commitments because it is in their best interest to do so. Building on this notion, Hardin (2002: 1) defines trust as encapsulated interest:

> I trust you because it is in your interest to take my interests in the relevant matter seriously ··· You value the continuation of our relationship, and you therefore have your own interests in taking my own interests into account. That is, you encapsulate my interests in your own interest.

In notions of trust as encapsulated interest, trust is not inherently normative (Hardin 2002) but is rather a relation between specific parties and particular actions. It is mostly a cognitive phenomenon, involving risk to the truster. This risk is a function of the trustworthiness of the trustee. This notion of trust as encapsulated interest seems particularly relevant for journalism ethical concerns, since it would be only through making citizens' interests their interest that journalists would fulfill their democratic obligations. Now journalists might think that this is what they traditionally do, but one has to wonder whether it is plausible for any institution to know what people need without letting people speak for themselves, and construct these needs as part of a community conversation. Historically, news organizations have not been active in cultivating audience participation in their operations, limiting such interactions to letters to the editor and call-in shows. However, with the rise of new interactive media, coupled with declining trust in media (at least in some parts of the West), news media have been forced to start taking audience trust and participation in the process of news production more seriously by using, for example, Facebook, Twitter, online chats, and citizen polls – the whole movement of what today is called "participatory journalism" (Singer et al. 2011).

A normative orientation of trust – that is, seeing value in trust because it reduces transaction costs without inquiring about the suitability of that trust – might result in more efficient social relations among citizens, but not necessarily more democratic ones. Trusting media acritically, or not trusting it when it deserves trust, dissipates the critical link between citizenship and journalism that is required for democracies to work. This leads us to pose the question of whether mainstream media in Colombia are worthy of the public's trust.[1]

A Journalist's Trustworthiness

In order to answer this question, and as part of a larger comparative research project, we conducted in 2010 a content analysis of the three most important news outlets in Colombia (*El Tiempo*, the leading print publication in the country, and RCN and Caracol, the two leading television stations). While our results are not representative of Colombian media as a whole, they are a systematic attempt to assess the trustworthiness of the elite news outlets in the country, by looking at a series of quality indicators (for a detailed methodological account on the content analyses in which the following section is based see Mazorra 2011).

While establishing that the "quality" of news is no simple matter, we employ five indicators that shed light on this phenomenon: (1) average number of sources used per story; (2) diversity of news sources (professional background, gender, and minority status); (3) whether the news story provides the social and political context in which it develops; (4) whether the social consequences of the information are made explicit; and (5) whether the public policy implications of the information are present.

In terms of sources our research indicates an average of 1.3 sources per news item, an extremely low number if news media are thought to present multiple perspectives on issues (it is worth pointing out that print media do a little better than television with an average of 1.6 sources). In terms of the nature of these sources, our research also points to the presence of important inequalities: marked preference for official sources, underrepresentation of females, and the invisibility of ethnic minorities as sources of news (see Figure 6.2).

With respect to the type of sources that are more prevalent in the news, it is clear that government officials and administrators prevail, while citizens tend to appear seldom, and when they do it is often as victims of crime (see Figure 6.3).

In addition to sources, we were interested in establishing whether news reports provide the social and political context in which they take place, as

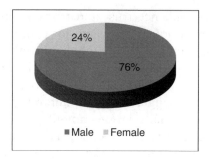
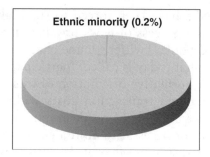

Figure 6.2   News Sources in Colombian Media

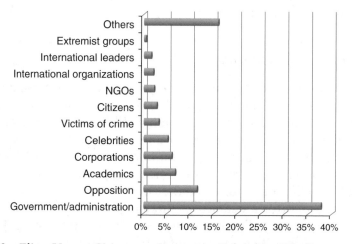

Figure 6.3   Elites Versus Citizens as Sources in Colombian Media

well as whether the social consequences and public policy implications of the information are present. Our findings, reported in Figure 6.4, suggest that overall the coverage tends not to provide contextual information and is mostly episodic in nature (Iyengar 1991).

Based on these results, we argue that mainstream media has advanced significantly in terms of independence and watchdog journalistic roles. For example, during 2008 and 2009 the news media investigated and exposed the execution of civilians that were being framed as enemy combatants by the Colombian armed forces to demonstrate their "effectiveness" in the war against guerrilla groups. However, there is ample room for improvement. It would appear that the incorporation of multiple viewpoints, and particularly citizen voices, as part of their routine coverage is a requirement for the future.

Bearing in mind the limitations of mainstream journalism in Colombia, it is plausible to wonder if news consumption in Colombia plays a similar role with respect to democratic integration as it does in more consolidated democracies. A robust tradition of literature suggests that informational

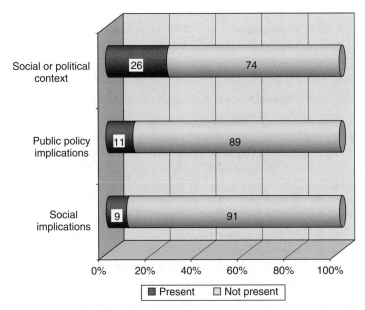

Figure 6.4   News "Quality" in Colombia

uses of media are positively associated with diverse democratic participatory behaviors (see, e.g., Shah et al. 2001).

Journalism and Civic Engagement

In order to explore the relationship between news consumption and civic engagement we analyzed the impact of newspaper use and television news on 17 behaviors including a wide range of activities such as voting, attending rallies, volunteering, working for community projects, and donating money to civic and political causes (for a detailed description of these behaviors and their prevalence in the Colombian context see Rojas et al. 2011). To test these relationships we created a participation additive index that ranges from 0 to 17 (that is, from not having done any of the behaviors to having engaged in all of them) and employed a regression model that controls for demographic variables. The aim of the index was to examine the influence of traditional media consumption on participation (see Figure 6.5).

Not surprisingly, we find a modest direct relationship between newspaper use and civic participation and no significant relationship between television news use and participation. Furthermore, these variables contribute little to the overall explanation of participation (only 4% of the variance in participation is explained). Based on the content analysis regarding the quality of news explained above, it makes sense that newspapers would be relatively more closely related to civic engagement than

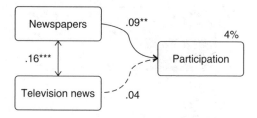

Model controls for education, age, gender, and income. Sample size
1,058; significance levels p = **<.01; ***<.001

Figure 6.5   News as an Antecedent of Democratic Participation

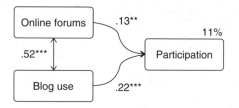

Model controls for education, age, gender, and income.
Sample size 577; significance levels p = **<.01; ***<.001

Figure 6.6   New Media as an Antecedent of Democratic Participation

television, but also that the important limitations of news overall would hinder their contribution to democratic engagement.[2]

Having examined the effects of traditional news on civic participation we turn our attention to emerging media and how they may contribute to these civic outcomes. In order to compare the effects of traditional news with emerging media forms in which citizen participation is more prevalent (conceptualized as a fifth state by Christians et al. 2009), we tested a similar model to the one described above. Instead, however, we examined the impact of blog consumption (Gil de Zúñiga, Puig-i-Abril, and Rojas, 2009) as well as presence in online forums as antecedents of engagement (see Figure 6.6).[3]

The comparison with our previous model (traditional media) is striking on multiple levels. In the first place, in the online domain the relationship between different modes (blogs and forums) is much closer than for traditional media, in which the relationship between TV news use and newspapers was also positive but weaker. Second, the relationships between information and participation are significantly stronger than for traditional media, and third, and most importantly, the amount of variance in participation levels that is explained by this model increases substantially (from 4% for traditional media to 11% for the new media).

We interpret these findings as robust support for the notion that informational uses of new communication technologies result in increased

participation in the civic domain. Our results suggest the relative importance of emerging sources of information as antecedents of participatory
behavior. In countries such as Colombia, in which the availability of
diverse viewpoints in traditional media is limited, the blogosphere and
online forums are part of a broader emerging networked public sphere
(Friedland, Hove, and Rojas 2006). They are alternative information
providers, vis-à-vis traditional media, which contribute to democratic
practices.

Citizenship Ethics

Emerging information and sense-making environments incorporate distributed participation in the making, distribution, and interpretation
processes of news from nonprofessional contributors. The incorporation of citizen's media content into the news poses important challenges to
the quality control of news and to the norms that have been traditionally
used to evaluate stories (Ward, 2011a: 14). One way to confront these
challenges is to extend traditional notions of journalistic professionalism
to emerging media actors and expect that bloggers, for example, adhere
to the "sacred" rules of the profession (see, e.g., Gil de Zúñiga et al.
2011). Another avenue is to "open" journalism ethical concerns to all
citizens, expecting that this broader discussion will incorporate citizen
values and expectations of media, ultimately reinvigorating professional
standards (Ward and Wasserman 2010: 276). Alternatively, as we contend
in this chapter, we should make the broader ethics of citizenship central
to journalism ethics.

Embracing a citizen ethic as a cornerstone of journalism practice is of
course not an either–or proposition. Instead it is about placing traditional
professional concerns alongside the concerns of citizenship. It is about
the "opening up (of) civic space outside of the state and the market
to consider the kinds of habit and characters we need to run the good
society" (Bunting 2010: 6). This embracing of citizenship entails a move
from media-centric concerns to public-centric concerns. That is, how can
journalists and citizens work to enable discursive public places?

While one could contend that this has always been a central concern of journalists, this movement from a journalism ethic to a citizen
ethic entails a move from focusing almost exclusively on the process
of journalism to focusing also on its outcomes. This is of course not a
new idea: It inspired the public journalism movement of the late twentieth century (Friedland 2003). However, with technological change and
energized citizenship mobilization around information (in production,
dissemination, and interpretation) these traditional relationships need
reconceptualization.

Advocating that journalism takes on an ethics of citizenship in a globalizing world naturally raises the question of what type of citizenship is

being considered. While citizenship has traditionally been understood as a relationship to a state, and journalists have worked in an era of national citizenships, these relationships are also in flux. As the consequences of political actions are increasingly less geographically contained, journalists, and the norms governing the profession, are ill equipped to deal with competing demands for attention, framing, and mobilization around global issues.

Historically, the concept of citizenship appears as a demarcation between urban communities based on equality that contrast with traditional rural hierarchies. This concept of equality, initially applied to very limited groups, became, with the French revolution, an ethical requirement of political functioning (Giesen and Eder 2001).

A journalism ethic that embraces citizenship will thus be at the service of political equality among social actors, a proposition that requires a fundamental expansion of the journalistic role to embrace citizenship construction, rather than assuming citizens as existing outside the realm of journalistic activity.

Notions of citizenship pose fundamental challenges to journalism ethics in multiple domains, but we will highlight three: (1) the need to expand its focus from relations with government to relations with corporations, as more everyday life activities are co-ordinated via market mechanisms; (2) the need to expand its scope from the local to the global, as more system-level activities are no longer located at the local or even national level; and, (3) the need to recognize emerging publics, as networks become a privileged social structure.

While traditional journalism remains focused on government activities, increasingly the locus of political activities shifts toward civic engagement and political consumerism. Fully examining the implications of these shifts exceeds the possibilities of this chapter, but it is important to point out that traditional media routines are ill equipped to deal with these changes.

Furthermore, the journalistic craft continues to be closely aligned with the national political structures under which it developed, despite the globalization of media conglomerates and the fact that issues are increasingly global in nature. This poses another fundamental challenge to journalism ethics: how to cover "foreign affairs" in a globalized world. A clear example of this issue can be seen in coverage of war, in which journalists can easily embrace a national perspective as embedded reporters, despite their international audiences and global responsibilities (see Reese 2010).

Maintaining journalistic practices that are nationally bound does not enhance journalism's capacity to make sense of a world that is increasingly integrated by global market forces. Thus, to maintain its sense-making capacity, journalism will need to fully embrace the global, adopt a networked form that goes beyond professional actors, and center its ethical dilemmas alongside the dilemmas of global citizenship. If it fails to do so, as the Colombian case illustrates, citizens will seek alternative forms of integration.

Emerging Publics

As part of the process of change, we have observed the emergence of new forms of publics made possible by new technology (Wojcieszak and Rojas 2011). The underlying idea is that in a similar way in which print made possible the emergence of geographically dispersed and large publics infused with common information and enthusiasm (Tarde 1969), in the early twenty-first century new communication platforms (including discussion forums and blogs, but also social networking sites and microblogging platforms such as Twitter) make possible a new type of public, one that revolves around people's social connections.

Debates concerning macro-level publics have usually centered on their potential for achieving rational solutions to collective problems, with two issues dominating scholarly thinking in this area: (1) scale, and (2) the juxtaposition of mass and interpersonal forces. The problem of large-scale social groups has led to different ideas of how publics can be sustained: ranging from mass publics sustained by media (Page 1996) to notions of small-scale publics brought together to represent the larger public as in deliberative polls (Fishkin 1995), or citizen juries (Gastil et al 2008), to ideas of issue publics, that is, segments of the population who care deeply about particular issues (Kim 2009).

In all these conceptualizations media play a critical role as information providers. However, as mentioned above, new communication technologies have made possible a different type of public, one that is not issue-based, although it is permeated by issues; one that does not have a mass scope, yet its size, dispersion, and origin go beyond traditional notions of interpersonal interactions; and one that may not be representative of the population at large, but instead is constituted by the cumulative social interactions of individuals as they traverse different facets of life. In sum: egocentric publics.

This idea of egocentric publics builds on network studies that no longer defined community as a spatially bounded membership of one solidarity or kinship group, but instead reformulated the nature of community to one of multiple limited memberships in many types of "personal community" (Wellman 1988) This is possible by looking at the type of relationships – a personal community or network of ties – instead of a spatial clustering of potential relations.

Egocentric publics are based on social networks, but rather than highlighting the access to resources that personal communities provide, we emphasize the communicative potential of our social relations. In particular, we have asserted that communication technologies enable the emergence of a meso-level public for the ego (e.g., through blogs and online forums), one that is broader than a personal community and thus theoretically less dense and more heterogeneous, one that is not issue

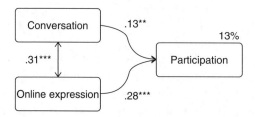

Model controls for education, age, gender, and income.
Sample size 577; significance levels p = **<.01; ***<.001

Figure 6.7   Expression as an Antecedent of Democratic Participation

or geographically fragmented, yet is permeated by issues and geography, and one that we can engage with more loosely that traditional publics. Our previous work (Wojcieszak and Rojas 2011) shows that engaging one's egocentric public online decreased political extremism, and while the mechanism by which it does so remains an open question, we argue that it is the increased heterogeneity of our social relations (a byproduct of network size, geographical dispersion, and time displacement) that has this moderating effect.

Following our previous analyses, we turn to examine whether these egocentric publics may contribute to democratic engagement, or if instead, face-to-face social relations maintain a privileged status as predictors of political activity. To do so we replicate our previous analyses but using online expression and face-to-face political conversations to predict participation. Our analysis (see Figure 6.7) suggests that online expression to our egocentric publics is positively related to civic engagement (see also Rojas and Puig-i-Abril 2009); furthermore, the impact of online expression is larger than that of face-to-face political conversation.

These results suggest to us a final challenge for journalism ethics. Traditionally journalists have been concerned with a public, or rather The Public, but increasingly networks of communication make possible the emergence of multiple publics, including the egocentric publics that we have discussed. Failure to recognize these emerging publics, or the inability to incorporate their resources and needs as part of a broader media ecology, will compromise journalism's service to democratic goals.

Understanding the importance of contextual forces, we are convinced that the trustworthiness of journalists, the increasing importance of emerging information outlets, and the importance of online expressive practices in publics that are in a process of reconfiguration are not a singularity of the Colombian case. We conclude by pointing out that circling the wagons around professional standards will not solve the issues faced by journalists in the twenty-first century; instead we propose embracing a notion of citizen ethics to guide media practitioners and journalism ethicists as they strive to take the interests of others as their own.

Notes

1. We are aware that trust in media is multifaceted and not only depends on the journalism craft per se, as the hostile media phenomenon literature makes blatantly obvious. Citizens may also display a "hostile" attitude toward media and perceive bias even when there is none. However, examining other sources of media trust, or distrust, go beyond the scope of this chapter. For a review of the hostile media literature see, for example, Vraga, Tully, and Rojas (2009).
2. We understand that all the positive effects of news on participation are not direct, but also indirect, through, for example, gains in political knowledge and political efficacy. However, for the purposes of our argument here we are limiting our model to the comparison of direct effects.
3. In this analysis only those with Internet access are considered.

Further Reading

A good place to start understanding the Latin American media system is Silvio Waisbord's *The Press and the Public Sphere in Contemporary Latin America* (2008). Readers who are interested in the Colombian context may wish to explore the trilogy on communication and politics published by the Universidad Externado de Colombia that includes Rojas and Pérez, (2009), Rojas et al., (2010), and Rojas et al., (2011).

For an in-depth theorization on trust and the distinction between trust and trustworthiness we recommend Russell Hardin's *Trust and Trustworthiness* (2002).

The role of news consumption as a precursor of citizen engagement is fairly well established in the communication literature. However, readers from other disciplines interested in this literature can investigate Jack McLeod's notion of communication mediation (e.g., Shah et al. 2001). Finally, for some of the emergent claims made in this chapter, we suggest considering Magdalena Wojcieszak and Hernando Rojas's (2011) article on egocentric publics, Stephen Reese (2010) on journalism under globalization pressures, and Bernhard Giesen and Klaus Eder (2001) on citizenship.

References

Braithwaite, V. 1998. "Communal and Exchange Trust Norms: Their Value Base and Relevance to Institutional Trust." In V. Braithwaite and M. Levi, eds., *Trust and Governance*. New York: Russell Sage Foundation, 9–27.

Bunting, M. 2010. "Fanning the Flames of Vital Debate." In *Citizen Ethics in a Time of Crisis*, http://www.citizenethics.org.uk/docs/EthicsTemplateDoc.pdf.

Christians, C. G., Glasser, T. L., McQuail, D., Nordenstreng, K., and White, R. A. 2009. *Normative Theories of the Press*. Urbana: University of Illinois Press.

Coleman, J. S. 1990. *Foundations of Social Theory*. Cambridge, MA: Harvard University Press.

Delli Carpini, M. X., Cook, F. L., and Jacobs, L. R. 2004. "Public Deliberation, Discursive Participation and Citizen Engagement: A Review of the Empirical Literature." *Annual Review of Political Science* 7: 315–44.

Fishkin, J. S. 1995. *The Voice of the People: Public Opinion and Democracy*. New Haven, CT: Yale University Press.

Friedland, L. 2003. *Public Journalism: Past and Future*. Dayton, OH: Kettering Foundation.

Friedland, L., Hove, T., and Rojas, H. 2006. "The Networked Public Sphere." *Javnost – The Public* 13: 5–26.

Gastil, J., Black, L., Deess, E. P, and Leighter, J. 2008. "From Group Member to Democratic Citizen: How Deliberating with Fellow Jurors Reshapes Civic Attitudes." *Human Communication Research* 34: 137–69.

Giesen, B. and Eder, K. 2001. "European Citizenship: An Avenue for the Social Integration of Europe." In K. Eder and B. Giesen, eds., *European Citizenship Between National Legacies and Postnational Projects*. Oxford: Oxford University Press, 1–13.

Gil de Zúñiga, H., Lewis, C., Willard-Hinsely, A., Valenzuela, S., Lee, J. K., and Baresch, B. 2011. "Blogging as a Journalistic Practice: A Model Linking Perception, Motivation, and Behavior." *Journalism: Theory, Practice and Criticism* 12: 586–606.

Gil de Zúñiga, H., Puig-Abril, E., and Rojas, H. 2009. "Weblogs, Traditional Sources Online and Political Participation: An Assessment of How the Internet is Changing the Political Environment." *New Media and Society* 11: 553–74.

Hardin, R. 2002. *Trust and Trustworthiness*. New York: Russell Sage Foundation.

Iyengar, S. 1991. *Is Anyone Responsible? How Television Frames Political Issues*. Chicago: University of Chicago Press.

Jones, K. 1996. "Trust as an Affective Attitude." *Ethics* 107: 4–25.

Kim, Y. M. 2009. "Issue Publics in the New Information Environment: Selectivity, Domain-specificity, and Extremity." *Communication Research* 36: 254–84.

Kovach, B. and Rosenstiel, T. 2007. *The Elements of Journalism: What Newspeople Should Know and The Public Should Expect*. New York: Random House.

Mazorra, D. 2011. "El Contenido de las Noticias en Colombia." In H. Rojas, M. Orozco, H. Gil de Zúñiga, and M. Wojcieszak, eds., *Comunicación y Ciudadanía*. Bogotá: Universidad Externado de Colombia Press, 277–92.

Muñoz, J., Arturo, J., Bromberg, P., and Moncada, R. 2003. *Refelexiones Sobre Cultura Ciudadana en Bogotá*. Bogota: Observatorio de Cultura Urbana.

Page, B. I. 1996. *Who Deliberates? Mass Media in Modern Democracy*. Chicago: University of Chicago Press.

Reese, S. 2010. "Journalism and Globalization." *Sociology Compass* 4: 344–53.

Rojas, H., Orozco, M., Gil de Zúñiga, H., and Wojcieszak, M. 2011. *Comunicación y Ciudadanía*. Bogotá: Universidad Externado de Colombia Press.

Rojas, H. and Pérez, I. 2009. *Comunicación y Participación Política*. Bogotá: Universidad Externado de Colombia Press.

Rojas, H., Pérez, I., and Gil de Zúñiga, H. 2010. *Comunicación y Comunidad*. Bogotá: Universidad Externado de Colombia Press.

Rojas, H. and Puig-i-Abril, E. 2009. "Mobilizers Mobilized: Information, Expression, Mobilization and Participation in the Digital Age." *Journal of Computer Mediated Communication* 14: 902–27.

Shah, D. V., McLeod, J. M., and Yoon, S. H. 2001. "Communication, Context and Community: An Exploration of Print, Broadcast and Internet Influences." *Communication Research* 28: 464–506.

Singer, J. B, Hermida, A., Domingo, D., Heinonen, A., Paulussen, S., Quandt, T., Reich, Z., and Vujnovic, M. 2011. "Participatory Journalism: Guarding Open Gates at Online Newspapers." Malden, MA: Wiley-Blackwell.

Tarde, G. 1969. *On Communication and Social Influence*. Chicago: University of Chicago Press.

Vraga, E., Tully, M., and Rojas, H. 2009. "Reducing Hostile Media Perceptions: Can News Media Literacy Reduce Perceptions of Bias?" *Newspaper Research Journal* 30: 68–81.

Waisbord, S. 2008. *The Press and the Public Sphere in Contemporary Latin America*. Cambridge, MA: Harvard University Press.

Ward, S. J. A. 2005. "Philosophical Foundations for Global Journalism Ethics." *Journal of Mass Media Ethics* 20(1): 3–21.

Ward, S. J. A. 2009. "Journalism Ethics." In K. Wahl-Jorgensen and T. Hanitzsch, eds., *The Handbook of Journalism Studies*. New York: Routledge, 259–309.

Ward, S. J. A. 2011a. *Ethics and the Media: An Introduction*. Cambridge: Cambridge University Press.

Ward, S. J. A. 2011b. "Ethical Flourishing as Aim of Global Media Ethics." *Journalism Studies* 12: 738–46.

Ward, S. J. A. and Wasserman, H. 2010. "Towards an Open Ethics: Implications of New Media Platforms for Global Ethics Discourse." *Journal of Media Ethics* 25: 275–92.

Weaver, D. 1996. "Journalists in Comparative Perspective: Backgrounds and Professionalism." *Javnost – The Public* 3: 83–91.

Wellman, B. 1988. "The Community Question Re-evaluated." In M. P. Smith, ed., *Power, Community and the City*. New Brunswick, NJ: Transaction, 81–107.

Wojcieszak, M. and Rojas, H. 2011. "Egocentric Publics and Political Extremity: How Communication Technologies Enable New Publics That Discourage Political Extremity." *The International Journal of Press Politics* 16: 488–507.

7

Media Ethics in a New Democracy
South African Perspectives on Freedom, Dignity, and Citizenship

Herman Wasserman

What role should the media play in a new democracy? What are the ethical duties owed by a media to a citizenry that has only recently emerged from centuries of colonialism and apartheid? How should the media orientate itself toward a society that is considered the most unequal in the world?

These are the questions the South African media have been grappling with since the democratization process in the country started in 1990 with the release of Nelson Mandela and the unbanning of the liberation movements. The first democratic elections in 1994 ushered in a new era of transparency and freedom, welcomed by a media that had to endure a repressive array of restrictive laws under apartheid. The new, negotiated constitution adopted in 1996 safeguarded the right to freedom of expression, alongside the right to human dignity. In the years to follow it became clear that these two rights were sometimes in tension. While the media have stood firm on the right to freedom of expression, especially in the light of increasing clashes and tensions with the government and the ruling party, critics have accused the media of not having contributed enough to the restoration of citizens' right to human dignity and the healing of South African society.

At the same time as having had to orientate itself toward a new democratic landscape, the South African media at the end of apartheid also re-entered the global arena after years of economic sanctions and political isolation. This meant that South African media felt the impact of globalization very directly, as local media companies were bought up by international interests: The Irish Independent News and Media group took over and consolidated a number of English-language newspapers shortly after democratization, local media enterprises extended their reach into other parts of Africa and indeed the world, and hybrid forms of media emerged in the country as a result of the coming together of global formats

Global Media Ethics: Problems and Perspectives, First Edition. Edited by Stephen J. A. Ward.
© 2013 Blackwell Publishing Ltd. Published 2013 by Blackwell Publishing Ltd.

and local content (an example of this is the rise of tabloid newspapers, see Wasserman 2010a, to which we will return later).

The South African case is instructive for debates about global media ethics, citizenship and democracy in an era of accelerated globalization of the media industry. This chapter will therefore discuss South African media ethics against the background of theories of democratization and debates about global media ethics. The first section will locate South African media ethics in the literature around new democracies and "transitology." The following section will highlight shifts in procedural media ethics that have occurred in South Africa after democracy, and contrast these shifts with contesting normative propositions for substantive media ethics in the postapartheid era. The chapter concludes with suggestions for future development of media ethics in South Africa.

Media Ethics in a New Democracy

As has been the case in other "new democracies" such as those emerging in Central Europe after the end of the Cold War, as well as in other African countries after the end of colonialism, the South African media after apartheid found itself in a new environment in which it had to define its roles and responsibilities in new ways. The opening up of a democratic public sphere, the intensified impact of globalization with the end of the country's isolation, and the redefinition of civil society in relation to a now legitimate state (cf. Murphy 2007: 2 for similar processes in other new democracies), had profound implications for the way that the South African media conceived of its role in normative terms. One of the key debates in the literature of "transitology" is to what extent democratization brought about complete transformation of these erstwhile authoritarian states, or merely resulted in the repositioning of partnerships between elites (Sparks 2008, 2009, Splichal 1992). Critics have pointed out that in the South African case the political system was transformed radically, with citizenship rights now extended to all South Africans, but that the "narrowest practical definition of democracy" was used to justify an "elite transition" from apartheid to neoliberalism (Bond 2000: 1). On this view, the political system was radically reformed, but economic policies adopted after apartheid still favored elites and continued to marginalize the poor majority of South Africans, for whom economic justice is still evasive. As far as the media is concerned, critics point to the fact that the media have largely been supporting this economic arrangement, and have presented a view of reality from a vantage point in the middle-class suburbs (Friedman 2011). From this suburban perspective, media freedom is an important right in the new democracy, but there is less interest in the basic economic rights – and the associated human dignity – of those citizens for whom life in the postapartheid democracy is still a struggle for survival.

When assessing the development of media ethics in South Africa in the post-apartheid era, the tension between the newly acquired democratic right to freedom of expression and the imperative on the media to contribute to the restoration of the right to dignity, remains at the centre of debates about media ethics. A distinction therefore has to be made between the normative contestations around *substantive ethics* and the shifts in the *procedural* media ethical landscape in postapartheid South Africa. While the progress made on media ethical *procedures* have been most visible, there is not yet agreement about the *substantive* issues of the media's role in constituting the "good life for purposes of human flourishing" (Caldwell 2011: 61) in the postapartheid sphere. The distinction between procedural and substantive ethics can be summed up by looking at the criteria for an action to be judged as ethical. In procedural ethics, an action is considered ethical if the process followed certain "rules" closely. In substantive ethics, the "(substantive) conclusion matters more than how (that is, the procedures) one reaches it" (Caldwell 2011: 61). Examples of procedural ethics would be the deontological ethics of Immanuel Kant, where the rational process of identifying and adhering to a specific *duty* would qualify an action as ethical, or dialogical ethics, where the outcomes of ethical deliberation are assumed to be good as long as that deliberation took the form of dialogue (Caldwell 2011: 60–1). In contrast, substantive ethics are concerned with the concrete content of the ethical decisions reached, more than the process that was followed. Amartya Sen makes a similar distinction in his discussion of justice (Sen 2009), which is applied to the Indian media by Shakuntala Rao in her contribution to this volume. Sen contrasts the procedural form of justice in early Indian jurisprudence, *niti*, with the substantive form, *nyaya*. Whereas the first concept is concerned with the rules and processes that make justice possible, the latter form considers how the rules of justice affect people's everyday lives. As Rao discusses in more detail, the procedural *niti* for Sen is located in the "transcendental institutions" that deliver justice through rules and regulations, whereas *nyaya* refers to the kind of world, the type of society that we want to see emerge from these institutions and their rules. Sen criticizes John Rawls for his "transcendental institutionalism," which Sen sees as an idealistic approach to a perfectly just society, whereas his own comparative approach acknowledges that sometimes a choice needs to be made between various alternative forms of justice that are sometimes in tension.

To apply Sen's distinction between *niti* and *nyaya*, or between procedural and substantive ethics to the postapartheid South African democracy, one can compare the democratic institutions and processes (e.g., the courts, the free press, the five-yearly ballot) with the outcomes of these democratic processes and institutions in everyday life – for example, the extent to which all citizens have the opportunity to make their voices heard in democratic debates, or the extent to which the everyday lived experiences of the majority of South Africans have improved. Heller (2009), in his comparison between South African and Indian democracy, makes the distinction between the "status" of citizenship and the "practice" of citizenship. The former refers to the legalistic, nominal rights to inclusion into the democratic polity that all South Africans have come to enjoy when formal democracy arrived in the country in 1994. The latter refers to the extent to which all South Africans have a voice in the public sphere and the opportunity to impact on decision-making processes that determine the quality of their daily lives.

As far as the South African media and its role in postapartheid democracy is concerned, different approaches to the end of "a better life for all," to borrow the ruling African National Congress (ANC)'s slogan, can be noted. On the level of procedural ethics, much emphasis has fallen on refining the procedures and institutions of regulation (through a Broadcasting Complaints Commission) and self-regulation, under a Press Council. Of late the debates about the effectiveness of these forms of regulation have been heightened, and at times heated. While some disagreement exists about the best procedures and institutions that would ensure an accountable, ethical media, these debates are underpinned by a deeper, unresolved question about what the desired substantive outcomes of ethical institutions and procedures should be. This substantive question is a normative one: What role should the media play in a transitional, developmental democracy such as South Africa? What exactly is the contribution from the media toward this democracy that these procedures and institutions are meant to facilitate? The separation between procedural and substantive ethics is therefore not absolute: Procedural ethics implicitly assume certain normative substantive goods to exist, whereas substantive ethics needs to be expressed in procedural terms in order to become articulate and intelligible (Caldwell 2011: 65–6).

The changes and current debates occurring on these two levels of ethics in the South African media context will be discussed below.

Procedural Shifts

Although the procedural and the substantive in media ethics cannot be completely separated – Caldwell (2011: 66) draws on the work of Charles Taylor to critique this separation as rooted in the Cartesian duality between thinking (epistemology) and being (ontology) – a tension between these different modes of engaging with ethical questions can be noted when we look at media ethics in South Africa as a transitional democracy. In the South African context, the shift from a highly legalized environment under apartheid, to a self-regulatory media ethical environment after apartheid, meant that significant attention had to be paid to the processes and systems to ensure effective self-regulation. Debates about media ethics in recent years have consequently been dominated by questions regarding regulation (i.e., procedural questions) that have often obscured the more substantive questions of what the outcome or result should be of the media's contribution to the "good life" in postapartheid South Africa. In other words, where debates have often been very heated around whether the media should be self-regulated, coregulated, or submit to statutory oversight, the question of what exactly an ethical media should do to deepen democracy did not often progress beyond common-sense notions of media as a "pillar of democracy," a "defender of the public interest," or the "fourth estate of government."

As a result, an impasse has developed between the procedural and substantive aspects of postapartheid media ethics. Let us deal with the procedural aspects first. Since the beginning of the democratization process, much effort has been put into constructing a formalist ethical system (Christians 2010: 173) for South African media that could be aligned with the values of the new democracy, such as transparency and accountability. The apartheid system of oppressive laws regulating the media made way for a system of self-regulation, with at its center a Press Council, adjudicating public complaints with reference to ethical codes befitting the new democratic era (see Kumwenda 2011 for an overview of these developments). A statutory body with stronger fines than the press self-regulatory system, the Broadcasting Complaints Commission, was formed to adjudicate complaints against broadcasters.

These regulatory systems were underpinned by media ethical codes that were in themselves products of globalization, or, more precisely, "glocalization" (Wasserman and Rao 2008). They drew inspiration from international codes, mostly from the UK and the US, but adapted them for a local setting, through for instance an emphasis on preventing racism in reporting. The re-entry of South Africa into a globalized media landscape subjected it to the same line of questioning that has characterized debates in global media ethics recently, namely: To what extent can media ethics be universalized across borders and countries? (For viewpoints on how this complex debate impacts on media ethics in Africa and South Africa in particular, see *Ecquid Novi* 2008, Ward and Wasserman 2010a, *Journalism Studies* 2011).

The procedural ethics of the press in South Africa were put under pressure in the debates around press freedom over the past few years (see Wasserman and Solomon 2012, *Ecquid Novi* 2011).

The relationship between journalists and the ANC-led government has been marked by tension throughout the postapartheid era, as both parties negotiated the rules and responsibilities of the media in a new democracy, but especially so during the last five years. In 2011 a Protection of State Information Bill was passed by Parliament amid ongoing threats by ruling party to establish a statutory media appeals tribunal with harsher sanctions against offending journalists than the current self-regulatory system allows for.

The tribunal proposal has been seen as a sign of the sensitivity of politicians in the ruling party to the increasingly adversarial reporting by the media of corruption, mismanagement, and nondelivery by the democratic government. The proposal also flows from mounting criticism by the ANC of the self-regulatory South African Press Council and Press Ombudsman. In these criticisms, human dignity as an ethical value enshrined in the Constitution as a countervailing force to the right to freedom of expression, has often been taken to imply that media should not invade the privacy of politicians or portray them in a bad light.

Self-regulatory systems are often criticized for not being powerful or proactive enough when dealing with ethical transgressions, because they are seen to represent a professional clique and therefore are inevitably biased in favor of journalists or the media industry (see Ward and Wasserman 2010b for criticisms against the British Press Complaints Commission and a contrast between their professional ethics and a more "open" ethics made possible by new media technologies). The South African Press Council has received similar criticisms, although these criticisms were arguably more politically loaded than has been the case in, for instance, Britain. While the South African Press Council has been criticized for not imposing strong enough sanctions, the alternative proposal of a statutory media tribunal has come from the ruling ANC party. Accusations of bias in favor of the media industry are also frequently underpinned by sweeping political economy critiques that see journalists as serving a media industry owned and controlled by whites. A recent example was an attack on a black newspaper editor for being an "agent for white capitalists" (IOL 2011). In the face of threats that a media tribunal might be established, the Press Council in 2011 embarked on a nationwide series of public hearings in an attempt to improve its system of self-regulation. In response, the ANC undertook to give the Press Council some leeway and the opportunity to improve. One of the results of this consultative process was a revised press code and constitution for the Press Council, although it remains to be seen whether these adjustments will be adequate to ward off the dangers of statutory regulation. The media industry (represented by the South African Editors' Forum and Print Media SA) initiated a Press Freedom Commission (PFC) that investigated aspects of the current self-regulation process and made recommendations to improve it (the Commission's report with recommendations can be found at http://www.pressfreedomcomm.org/report-of-recommendations).

In *procedural* terms, South African media ethics after apartheid have therefore made great strides in setting up systems that facilitate the "right" rational moral reasoning, although the criticisms against these processes have reflected a more deep-seated difference of opinion about the *substantive* ethical principles that should guide the "good life for purposes of human flourishing" (Caldwell 2011: 61) in postapartheid

South Africa. The ethics of the relationship between media, citizenship, social justice, and the deepening of democracy have therefore up until now largely been addressed in terms of *procedures*, but there has been less agreement on what the *substantive outcome* of these procedures should be and what the *material effects* of ethical media practice on the everyday life of citizens in postapartheid South Africa should be (Caldwell 2011: 61). The emphasis on the mechanisms and codes of media ethics in South Africa has focused so much on "doing no harm," that the question of what the "doing of good" would be has been neglected (cf. Caldwell 2011: 73). Media freedom has been insisted upon as an intrinsic good, but in most cases the debates have been about how to achieve a negative freedom – a media unfettered from constraints – rather than an engagement about positive freedoms – what the media should commit itself to be doing. This is not to expect that consensus about the substantive outcomes of an ethical media in a "new" democracy would be easily reached. There is "thin" political agreement on the constitutional values of human dignity, equality, and freedom, but disagreement on what exactly those values mean in everyday media practice. Not only have government and the media often clashed around differential interpretations of the relationship between these values (e.g., how freedom of the media weighs up against its perceived responsibilities), but also among journalists these values often take on different iterations (see Wasserman 2010b). There is often an assumed relationship between procedures and these core constitutional values, for instance the PFC's claim that press freedom in accordance with an agreed regulatory regime would enhance "our democracy which is founded on human dignity, the achievement of equality and the advancement of human rights and freedoms" (http://www.politicsweb.co.za/politicsweb /view/politicsweb/en/page71656?oid=294997&sn=Detail).

But these norms and values, and how they would impact on democratic life in South Africa, have been contested and interpreted in different ways by different stakeholders in the mediated communication process. The shifts in the ethical procedures in postapartheid South Africa did not therefore guarantee agreement about the substantive outcomes of these deliberations. Let us now turn to the debates about these concrete outcomes, as envisaged in contested normative positions.

Substantive Debates

Regardless of one's assessment of the extent to which the democratization of South Africa constituted radical transformation or "elite continuity" (Sparks 2008), it is evident that the South African media have become both a site and an agent for change (cf. Teer-Tomaselli and Tomaselli 2001: 123) in the new democracy. Through providing a platform for debates and representation of a wider variety of perspectives than were ever possible under apartheid, the media became an *agent* for change (however limited this role proved to be). But perhaps even more significant from the point of view of media ethics, was the fact that the media also was the *site* of much change in terms of its practices, procedures, and normative frameworks. The changes taking place on the procedural level of media ethics have been the most visible, notably in the establishment of a self-regulatory system for the press and the drawing up of press codes. There is, however, still little agreement and a general lack of debate about the substantial outcomes of these ethical procedures, that is, what the central values are that these procedures should be underpinned by and how they relate to the media's role in a new democracy. For some participants in the debate about what the South African media should be doing to ensure human flourishing for all citizens in the democratic South Africa, the substantive outcome of ethical journalism would be a government that is accountable to its citizens, which requires a vigilant, "watchdog" type of journalism to speak on behalf of citizens. On this view, the media can and should be adversarial toward the government in order to achieve this accountability, as this is their duty in terms of the right to freedom of speech.

An opposing view is that adversarial journalism may contribute to the widening of social rifts by setting up an "us and them" discourse. A hostile, attack-dog journalism directed at a legitimately elected, democratic government seeking to establish trust in democratic institutions after centuries of colonialism and apartheid, might, on this view, be read as insulting to those who still see the ruling party as the movement of liberation. These critics argue that the media should be more sensitive in their reporting, show more respect for the dignity of news subjects, and adopt a more humane approach to journalism (see Duncan 2011 and Grootes 2011 for two opposing points of view in this regard). The substantive outcome of this approach would be measured relationally, for example, greater social cohesion, even if the media might have to sacrifice some of its power to keep the government on its toes.

The notion of dignity as an ethical concept can be problematic. The protection of an individual's dignity can become a spurious defense to avoid the media's unearthing of corruption and wrongdoing, as in the case of the "insult laws" in place in many African countries that are meant to protect politicians' dignity from "insults" by the media. Berger (2007: 141) indicates how these laws regularly result in harassment of journalists in Africa. A recent uproar over an art work that depicts president Jacob Zuma with his genitals exposed, in a parody on an iconic poster of Lenin, again illustrated how the notion of "human dignity" can still be used in the service of political power, but also point to unfinished business with regards to racial reconciliation in South Africa (Smith 2012, Friedman 2012). However, it has also been argued (Christians and Nordenstreng 2004: 21) that human dignity can be seen as a universal "protonorm" (alongside truth telling and nonmalfeasance) that spans media cultures globally. As far as the South African media is concerned, the ethical value of the protection of human dignity is especially pertinent given the country's history of systemic racism and the denial of the right to dignity for the majority of the country's citizens. While democratization has restored the legal and political rights to citizenship denied to the majority under apartheid, the continued exclusions from economic equality and the realization of social empowerment have resulted in a widespread experience of marginalization from the public sphere (Von Lieres 2005: 23). While South Africans are nominally rights-bearing citizens who are all equal in the eyes of the law and at the ballot box, the on-going social inequalities inherited from apartheid are still mirrored in the struggles of the majority of the country's citizens to gain access to the public sphere and set media agendas. Former president Nelson Mandela was one of the first critics to question the South African media's privileging of sectional rather than national interests as a result of its political economy (Mandela 1994). More than a decade and a half into democracy, critics (e.g. Friedman 2011) are still pointing out that while the South African media are vigorous in defending their democratic freedoms, the commercial media are still biased toward the middle class and not doing enough to overcome the exclusions of the past.

In South Africa, as has been noted in other new democracies as well, conflicts have arisen about the extent to which the media should act as a watchdog of the new democratic government, or whether in fact an adversarial or antagonistic media would undermine the fragile trust put in the new government (Voltmer 2006: 4). Debates in South Africa after apartheid have often resonated with arguments elsewhere in the developing world that envisaged a supportive role for the media that would help the postcolonial/postapartheid government obtain its developmental goals. In a highly unequal society like South Africa, where the scars of racism and oppression are still visible everywhere, it may be argued that an adversarial, watchdog media ethic could polarize society even further. The defense that adversarial journalism protects the public interest is weakened by the question as to which public and what interests are represented in such a stratified society. Indeed, the question can be asked: Which public, which citizens, whose interests are being represented in the post-apartheid media (Wasserman and De Beer 2005, 2006)?

As an alternative to the liberal-democratic notion of "watchdog journalism," this argument is in favor of "guide dog journalism" (Gurevitch and Blumler 2004: 338, McQuail 2005: 178). In South Africa, other alternative frameworks to the liberal-democratic one, such as an indigenized/African ethics, have also been proposed and will be discussed below. As has been the case elsewhere, the South African media have resisted demands for more supportive or collaborative roles. The contestation around normative models has therefore been intense at times, sometimes leading to head-on conflicts.

These conflicts, which will be discussed in more detail below, can be summed up by seeing them as representing a tension between two central media ethical concepts – freedom and responsibility, or, in terms of the South African Constitution that enshrines the new democratic values, the tension between the human rights of freedom of expression and the right to human dignity. In the normative debates that ensued after the arrival of democracy, the South African media usually defended their freedom vigorously, while critics have argued that this freedom should be tempered by a responsibility toward a transformation of society and a more active striving toward reinstating the dignity of subaltern communities. Media ethical traditions in the West have also sought to balance freedom with responsibility. This is perhaps best represented in the social responsibility framework, which has gained global traction (Christians and Nordenstreng 2004). But this tradition has generally sought to minimize harm by restraining freedom where it infringes on dignity (e.g., racist stereotyping). South African press codes also contain these types of limitations within the social responsibility framework. The point is, however, that these limitations are seen in terms of negative liberties (what the press should not do) rather than in terms of substantive goals to actively strive for, as contributions to the transformation of postapartheid society. The assumption seems to be that as long as the press is free, and avoids doing harm, it would automatically contribute to the deepening of democracy, hold government accountable, and give a voice to the public. However, what that deepening would entail, which issues are put on the agenda for governmental accountability, and who "the public" is in a highly unequal and socially polarized country, is not self-evident.

Although the American-inspired social responsibility model has been globalized to a significant extent (Christians and Nordenstreng 2004), it has been noted that normative concepts central to liberal-democratic ethical frameworks have been interpreted or negotiated in significantly different ways, especially in regions of the Global South (Wasserman 2006, Wasserman and Rao 2008). For instance, interviews with journalists in South Africa and Namibia, two "new democracies" in Africa (Wasserman 2010b), have brought to light how concepts such as "freedom" and "responsibility" are contested rather than self-evident. The notion of media responsibility is sometimes used as a pretext for the protection of powerful interests, so as to say that a "responsible" media would not insult political leaders or invade their privacy. Similarly, the "responsibility" of African media to promote "African values" can also be employed in essentialistic ways to dismiss critics of the government as racist, colonialist, or sell-outs to the West.

The South African case is a good example of how normative theories are linked to their social, political, and historical contexts. Theories are ways of understanding the world, and these understandings are based on lived experiences within specific contexts.

In the South African context, normative theories have largely been developed in response to the country's apartheid history. Under apartheid, the media in South Africa were polarized into broadly two camps – those who opposed apartheid and those who were loyal to the government. In both these camps a spectrum of positions could be discerned. The English-language commercial press adhered to the liberal-democratic monitorial role of the press (in the terminology used by Christians et al. 2009), as a "watchdog" to point out the human rights abuses of the apartheid system. Because most of these newspapers were linked to mining capital and therefore capitalist in orientation, their critique was more limited than the alternative or underground press, who assumed a more radical, adversarial position. The Afrikaans-language press (with the exception of some Afrikaans alternative papers) by and large supported the ruling Afrikaner Nationalist Party by playing a collaborative role.

With the advent of democracy, the South African media had to consider which of these roles it wanted to adopt. As Berger (2008: 1) points out, the renegotiation of a journalistic paradigm in this era posed a particular conundrum to journalists who had supported the struggle for democracy: Should they continue supporting the liberation movements now that they had formed the new government (even if the movement itself had increasingly become riven with internal divisions), or should they continue in the adversarial mode which characterized the liberal and radical media's stance toward the state under the previous dispensation? The broad consensus among the mainstream commercial media was the latter,[1] coupled with an increasingly commercialized orientation, while the public service broadcaster, the South African Broadcasting Corporation (SABC), has increasingly come under fire for what is seen as its uncritical support for the government. The various positions taken in these debates include a development journalism framework, in which a greater collaborative role for the media was proposed as a way to support nation-building after the racial conflict during apartheid. Another position was that tradition and "indigenous values," such as the African concept of *Ubuntu* (i.e., the African communitarian philosophy that emphasizes interdependency, deriving from the saying "a person is a person through other persons," or "I am because you are") would see a less individualistic approach to media responsibility and ethics (Christians 2004, Wasserman and De Beer 2004). However, this claim has been criticized for its romanticism and essentialism, as well as its perceived inability to provide surveillance of and resistance to power (see Fourie 2008, Tomaselli 2003). There has also been a discourse of "professionalism," underpinned by liberal-democratic values and the normative framework of social responsibility, which resonates with global narratives of media freedom, journalistic professionalism, and democratic participation.

The latter position is informed by Habermasian notions of rational debate in an open, diverse public sphere where critique is a feature of a vibrant democracy (Tomaselli 2009: 17). The interventionist strategies of "media development," driven by NGOs and funding bodies in the North with an aim of capacitating media in the South, can be seen as part of this trend (Berger 2010).

Although these positions can be seen to represent the key positions in the ongoing normative debates (see Wasserman 2011 for more discussion of the various approaches), they are by no means clearly defined or settled. Constant negotiation and overlap between them can be noted. While the procedural ethical arrangements in the South African media landscape continue to be challenged, as noted above, there is all but clarity about what the substantive outcomes of these procedures should be and which of the normative frameworks highlighted above, or which combination of them, should take precedence. The situation is made even more complex by the continued development of media genres and platforms, as a result of the shifting patterns of media consumption and the accelerated globalization of available formats. An example of such a development was the highly controversial emergence of new tabloid newspapers on the market. The format of these papers was modeled on the UK's "red top" tabloids (e.g., the *Sun*) but their content was highly localized – another example, in other words, of the glocalization of South African media. Their content showed a penchant for gossip and sleaze, but their focus was highly localized communities of the poor and the working class who still, after more than a decade of democracy, remained marginalized by the mainstream press. Their approach to politics was not in the dominant "watchdog" mode of attacks on government, but rather through the telling of seemingly mundane – if sensationalized – stories of the precariousness of everyday life in the black and "colored" townships.

These stories told of frustration with the nondelivery of basic services like water and electricity or the struggle to gain access to government bureaucracies, the devastation wreaked by drugs and gangs, the crime and violence that terrorize poor communities (although the mainstream media usually report it as an assault on the middle class), and the indignity of poverty. The stories were not written in the rational, distanced way mostly found in the elite press. The topless women on page three of some tabloids (not all, and in some cases canceled as a result of reader feedback), stories on the supernatural, and the sensationalist tone and colloquial language were indications that professional standards were not being adhered to, that media were "dumbing down" under foreign influences and the desire by big media houses to make a profit. And while there was much that could be faulted on the level of procedural/formalistic ethics (stories about the creatures of superstition can't be verified, gossipy stories often only had one source, privacy was often invaded, etc.), a case could be made for the way in which these tabloids did force the journalistic community in the country to reflect on their substantial ethical values. The challenge these tabloids posed to the mainstream was that, although they seemed to flout the formalist ethics of fact-checking, balance, and social mores, it could be argued that in some ways they contributed more effectively to substantive ethical outcomes such as participation, inclusion, pluralism, and truth telling about hitherto excluded and marginalized citizens than the mainstream media did. What this shows is that while popular media (like in this case the tabloids) may stray outside the procedural/ formalistic tenets of the press codes, their unruly, emotive stories that validate the daily struggles of their readers may in fact have a more direct impact on the everyday life of their readers than the elite press, with its adherence to the tenets of procedural ethics. In the heated debates about the new tabloid papers (see Wasserman 2010a for a historicization and contextualization of these debates) a tension between procedural and substantive ethics was therefore brought to the fore which would require a much deeper and sustained engagement with media ethics than merely repairing the current self-regulatory system or choosing between contesting normative frameworks.

Conclusion: Challenges Ahead

In conclusion, I suggest one approach that could be followed to regenerate this ethical conversation.

As made clear by the preceding discussion, the media ethics landscape in South Africa has been a terrain of much debate since the democratization of the country. Procedural ethics, in the form of press codes and self-regulatory systems, have been set up to align with the new democratic values of transparency and accountability. However, in substantive terms, there is still much negotiation, contestation, and disagreement about what the role of the media in postapartheid society should look like, how media should contribute to the deepening of democracy, and how media could contribute to the overcoming of continued marginalization of a large part of its citizenry.

Debates around the role of the media in a transitional society have frequently resulted in open conflict between the media and the state. Most often the central roles envisaged for the media have been reduced to the liberal-democratic "watchdog" or "Fourth Estate" monitorial paradigm versus a collaborative developmental one. The normative frameworks in dispute have, however, largely been deductive in nature, derived from media systems theory developed in the Global North. Attempts to critique and "Africanize" these inherited Northern frameworks have in turn frequently lapsed into essentialist identity politics. The result has been a normative impasse with media ethics being seen largely in formalistic terms, as a strategic ritual to protect an existing corporatist media paradigm on the one hand, and crude political economic critiques and attempts to co-opt the media into political power projects on the other.

The development of new media technologies and the globalization of media, with the resultant fragmentation of audiences and bewildering diversity of perspectives, could lead one to argue that normative frameworks for the media are out of sync with the globalized media culture within which we live. This line of questioning forms part of a particularly productive area of research in recent years in the area of global media ethics.

These challenges and disputes should not be used to justify a move toward a position that is somehow "beyond" normativity, or as an excuse not to engage with moral questions. Instead, what is needed is an approach to media ethics that would not seek to impose ethical concepts and values "from above," as they have been inherited from normative frameworks elsewhere, on the assumption that their meanings are self-evidently applicable to the South African context. Nor should the refinement of a procedural system of self-regulation, however important such a process might be, be seen as a sufficient response to the contestations around media ethics in South Africa as an example of a posttransition new democracy. In transitional contexts, where various stakeholders are still getting to grips with their roles and responsibilities and where democratic institutions, including the media, are still in the process of being established and democratic processes strengthened, allowance should be made for the ongoing negotiations of ethical concepts and values. For this reason, an approach to media ethics rooted in specific contexts, based on the particular lived experience of media producers and consumers, is appropriate.

Such an approach could be called a cultural approach to normative media ethics, as it seeks to engage with the shifting, open-ended dynamics of how media are engaged with within the specificities of everyday lived experience. This approach should not be confused with a *culturalist* approach that rejects foreign influences on media ethics as imperialist and uncritically celebrates romantic notions of "indigenous culture" or "authenticity." By a cultural approach is meant not the reductionist and essentialist views of belonging and the right to speak that have often marred Afrocentric normative approaches, but an ethics rooted in actually existing media practices and everyday lived experiences of audiences.

A cultural approach instead would recognize that people's everyday engagement with media is influenced by local histories, social identities, and material contexts as well as global flows and contraflows. The meaning that emerges from these encounters with media, and the content that is subsequently given to notions such as "freedom," "responsibility," and "dignity," are therefore also bound to shift in relation to changing contextual factors and citizens' experience of life in the new democracy.

Such a normative approach to media will resemble an ethics of care, in which media practitioners immerse themselves in the life-worlds of citizens to listen to everyday experience and suspend their own assumptions in order to engage in relationships with communities. In turn, political actors and media consumers will engage in dialogue with media practitioners to seek agreement about the substantive outcomes of ethical frameworks and procedures.

A cultural approach to media ethics will benefit from the notion of narrative ethics, where media's role is not only to act as watchdog on behalf of a vaguely articulated public interest nor to represent "the people," but to listen to the stories of everyday life that articulate democratic politics as experienced by citizens. This does not mean that the often very courageous investigative and adversarial journalism that serves to expose many instances of corruption, abuse of political power, and cronyism in democratic South Africa, does not have a place in the ethical ecology. There is a danger that a more communitarian approach to journalism in a socially fragmented country could lead journalists to become partisan with regard to group interests instead of engaging these interests critically. However, there is still much work to do by postapartheid journalism to listen to the everyday stories of the marginalized and the poor that often find themselves outside of the scope of media attention, however closely those media may adhere to formal ethical codes.

Especially in a highly unequal country such as South Africa, still scarred by histories of polarization and subordination, the notion of "the public interest" is highly problematic, and a compassionate ethics of listening to subaltern publics can contribute to a healing of historical scars, reduce suspicion of the media, and enhance journalists' (as a social elite) understanding of life as lived in communities whose experiences may differ vastly from theirs.

Instead of relying solely on proceduralist media ethics based on social contract thinking and rational deliberation between interlocutors around ethical concepts, a narrative approach would seek to understand how ethical concepts are interpreted, applied, and given meaning within specific, concrete, lived contexts. Such an approach would be rooted in an ethnographic understanding of morality, that is, the realization that "morality is rooted in everyday experience and gains multiple levels of complexity" (Christians 2010: 178). The narrative approach would eschew the notion, based in Enlightenment thinking, that a global social contract for media ethics may be arrived at via arguments about the authority and validity of ethical rules and concepts in a rational and deliberative way. In a postmodern, fragmented global society, getting moral agents to participate in, let alone agree on, a formalist set of norms for global media, is a mistake. Following MacIntyre, Christians (2010: 179) argues for a perspective on media ethics rooted in "the way humans actually experience life and how they interpret it, that is, in narrative." Moral action arises out of "our life narratives lived out in a historical context" (Christians 2010: 179), and so a "shift from principle to story, from formal logic to community formation, is appealing" (2010: 180). Christians links to James Carey's notion of "communication as culture" to explain how narrative provides a path to moral understanding:

> Narratives are linguistic forms through which we argue, persuade, display convictions, and establish our identity. They contain in a nutshell the meaning of our theories and beliefs. We tell stories to one another about our values and concerns, and our aspirations. (Christians 2010: 181)

For a cultural approach to normative ethics to succeed, it would have to be rooted in cultural studies approaches to media and draw on its methodologies, such as ethnography and discourse analysis of everyday experiences and stories of the ordinary. In as much as media would still be seen to fulfill a monitorial and mobilizing role, these functions will emerge from the "bottom up" via an embeddedness in everyday lived experiences.

Such an approach could reinvigorate normative frameworks instead of pitting them against each other in a politically loaded ethical zero-sum game. Instead of imposing media ethical concepts on the media and their publics, the relationship should be reversed so that everyday experiences of media practitioners and citizen-consumers invest ethical concepts with meaning.

Through such a bottom-up, lived approach to media ethics, facilitated by a media that seeks to listen to the narratives of citizens' everyday life instead of rushing to speak on their behalf, the questions posed at the beginning of this chapter – What role should the media play in a new democracy? What are the ethical duties owed by a media to its citizenry? How should the media orientate itself towards an unequal society? – should be answered by journalists and their publics in a relational manner. The procedures of media ethics, like self-regulation and codes, should then become spaces where narratives may be told and listened to, instead of rules and regulations to police the media or legitimate their actions. If formalist media ethical processes could mean something in a new democracy such as South Africa – and perhaps this would also be true of other transitional, postconflict, or postauthoritarian societies elsewhere in the world – it would be to facilitate compassionate relationships rather than fierce oppositions.

Note

1. A recent example of the ironies that occur when the watchdog paradigm is coupled with commercial interests was when the Independent News and Media group decided to run a supplement celebrating the centenary of the ANC. In what was clearly a commercially inspired move by a newspaper group who routinely does not shy away from attacks on the ANC-led government, calls were made to advertisers to buy space in the supplement. When the opposition party the Democratic Alliance was approached to buy an advertisement, they objected to the Press Ombudsman, saying that the

supplement constituted political bias and was therefore in contravention of the Press Code. See Wasserman and Jacobs (2011).

Further Reading

To understand the debates in South African media ethics, one first has to get a sense of the shifts that have occurred within the country's media after apartheid. The following sources all attempt to provide overviews of the broad contours of postapartheid media and the transformation occurring in this environment: A. Olorunnisola and K. Tomaselli's edited volume, *The Political Economy of Transformation of the South African Media* (Creskill, NJ: Hampton Press, 2001); A. Hadland, E. Louw, S. Sesanti, and H. Wasserman's collection, *Power, Politics and Identity in South African Media* (Cape Town: HSRC Press, 2008); and H. H. Wasserman and S. Jacobs's *Shifting Selves: Post-Apartheid Essays on Mass Media, Culture and Identity* (Cape Town: Kwela Books, 2003). The academic journals *Ecquid Novi: African Journalism Studies*, *Communicatio*, and *Critical Arts* also, from time to time, feature articles on media ethics against this background.

For a discussion about African media ethics as distinct from Western media ethics, F. Kasoma's 1994 work *Journalism Ethics in Africa* (Nairobi: ACCE, 1994) is seminal. See also F. Banda's 2009 critique and appraisal "Kasoma's Afriethics: A Reappraisal," in the *International Communication Gazette* 71(4): 227–42.

For specific discussions of media ethics in South Africa, N. Hyde-Clarke's collection *Communication and Media Ethics in South Africa* (Cape Town: Juta, 2011) provides a good overview of current debates. Three good textbooks that look at media ethics case studies from South African perspectives are: L. Oosthuizen, *Media Ethics in the South African Context* (Cape Town: Juta, 2002); R. J. Lansdowne, *Media Ethics: An Introduction to Responsible Journalism* (Cape Town: Oxford University Press, 2002); and F. Kruger, *Black, White and Grey* (Cape Town: Double Storey, 2004).

References

Berger, G. 2007. *Media Legislation in Africa: A Comparative Legal Survey.* Grahamstown, SA: School of Journalism and Media Studies/UNESCO.

Berger, G. 2008. "A Paradigm in Process: What the Scapegoating of Vusi Mona Signalled about South African Journalism." *Communicatio* 34(1): 1–20.

Berger, G. 2010. "Problematizing 'Media Development' as a Bandwagon Gets Rolling." *International Communication Gazette* 72(7): 547–65

Bond, P. 2000. *Elite Transition: From Apartheid to Neoliberalism in South Africa.* London: Pluto Press.

Caldwell, M. 2011. "Between Proceduralism and Substantialism in Communication Ethics." In N. Hyde-Clarke, ed., *Communication and Media Ethics in South Africa.* Cape Town: Juta, 58–75.

Christians, C. G. 2004. "Ubuntu and Communitarianism in Media Ethics." *Ecquid Novi* 25(2): 235–56.

Christians, C. G. 2010. "Communication Ethics in Postnarrative terms." In L. Steiner and C. G. Christians, eds., *Key Concepts in Critical Cultural Studies*. Urbana: University of Illinois Press, 173–86.

Christians, C. G., Glasser, T. L, McQuail, D., Nordenstreng, K., and White, R. A. 2009. *Normative Theories of the Media*. Urbana: University of Illinois Press.

Christians, C. G. and Nordenstreng, K. 2004. "Social Responsibility Worldwide." *Journal of Mass Media Ethics* 19(1): 3–28.

Duncan, J. 2011. 'Spitting in the Faces of the Poor. *The Media*. January: 19.

Ecquid Novi: African Journalism Studies. 2008. Special issue on Africa and the Search for Global Media Ethics, 29(2).

Ecquid Novi: African Journalism Studies. 2011. Special issue on Press Freedom in Africa, 32(2).

Fourie, P. J. 2008. "Ubuntuism as a Framework for South African Media Practice and Performance: Can it Work?" *Communicatio* 34(1): 53–79.

Friedman, S. 2011. "Whose Freedom? South Africa's Press, Middle-Class Bias and the Threat of Control." *Ecquid Novi: African Journalism Studies* 32(2): 106–21.

Friedman, S. 2012. "Spear Row Can Get Us to Face Our Real Problem," *Business Day*. http://www.bdlive.co.za/articles/2012/05/30/steven-friedman-spear -row-can-get-us-to-face-our-real-problem, accessed September 3, 2012.

Grootes, S. 2011. "Stop Humiliating People." *The Media*. January: 18.

Gurevitch, M. and Blumler, J. G. 2004. "State of the Art of Comparative Political Communication Research: Poised for Maturity?" In F. Esser and B. Pfetsch, eds., *Comparing Political Communication*. Cambridge: Cambridge University Press, 325–43.

Heller, P. 2009. "Democratic Deepening in India and South Africa." *Journal of Asian and African Studies* 44: 123–49.

IOL (Independent Online). 2011. "Miyeni Column Halted Amid Furore," *IOL News*, August 1, 2011. http://www.iol.co.za/news/south-africa/miyeni -column-halted-amid-furore-1.1109941, accessed December 11, 2011.

Journalism Studies. 2011. Special issue on Explorations in Global Media Ethics. 12(6).

Kumwenda, O. 2011. "Press Councils and the Democratic Political Landscape in South Africa." In C. Hyde-Clarke, ed., *Communication and Media Ethics in South Africa*. Cape Town: Juta, 117–35.

Mandela, N. 1994. "Address to the International Press Institute, Cape Town, February 14," http://www.sahistory.org.za/pages/people/special%20projects /mandela/speeches/1990s/1994/1994_international_press_institute.htm, accessed December 5, 2011 .

McQuail, D. 2005. *McQuail's Mass Communication Theory*. London: Sage.

Murphy, P. D. 2007. *Negotiating Democracy: Media Transformations in Emerging Democracies*. Albany, NY: SUNY Press.

Sen, A. 2009. *The Idea of Justice*. Cambridge, MA: Harvard University Press.

Smith, D. 2012. "Jacob Zuma Painting Vandalised in South African Gallery," *Guardian*. http://www.guardian.co.uk/world/2012/may/22/jacob-zuma -painting-vandalised-gallery?INTCMP=ILCNETTXT3487, accessed June 3, 2012.

Sparks, C. 2008. "Media Systems in Transition: Poland, Russia, China." *Chinese Journal of Communication* 1(1): 7–24.

Sparks, C. 2009. "South African Media in Transition." *Journal of African Media Studies* 1(2): 195–220.

Splichal, S. 1992. "Media Privatization and Democratization in Central-Eastern Europe." *International Communication Gazette* 49(1–2): 3–22.

Teer-Tomaselli, R. and Tomaselli, K. G. 2001. "Transformation, Nation-Building and the South African Media, 1993–1999." In K. Tomaselli and H. Dunn, eds., *Media, Democracy and Renewal in Southern Africa*. Colorado Springs, CO: International Academic Publishers, 123–80.

Tomaselli, K. G. 2003. "'Our Culture' vs. 'Foreign Culture': An Essay on Ontological and Professional Issues in African Journalism." *Gazette* 65(6): 427–41.

Tomaselli, K. G. 2009. "Repositioning African Media Studies: Thoughts and Provocations." *Journal of African Media Studies* 1(1): 9–21.

Voltmer, K. 2006. "The Mass Media and the Dynamics of Political Communication in Processes of Democratization." In K. Voltmer, ed., *Mass Media and Political Communication in New Democracies*. London: Routledge, 1–20.

Von Lieres, B. 2005. "Culture and the Limits of Liberalism: Marginalisation and Citizenship in Post-apartheid South Africa." In S. Robins, ed., *Limits to Liberation After Apartheid: Citizenship, Governance and Culture*. Oxford: James Currey, 22–32.

Ward, S. J. A. and Wasserman, H. 2010a. *Media Ethics Beyond Borders*. New York: Routledge.

Ward, S. J. A. and Wasserman, H. 2010b. "Towards an Open Ethics: Implications of New Media Platforms for Global Ethics Discourse." *Journal of Mass Media Ethics* 25(4): 275–92.

Wasserman, H. 2006. "Globalised Values and Postcolonial Responses: South African Perspectives on Normative Media Ethics." *The International Communication Gazette* 68(1): 71–91.

Wasserman, H. 2010a. *Tabloid Journalism in South Africa: True Story!* Bloomington: Indiana University Press.

Wasserman, H. 2010b. "Freedom's Just Another Word? Perspectives on Media Freedom and Responsibility in South Africa and Namibia." *International Communication Gazette* 72(7): 567–88.

Wasserman, H. 2011. "Towards a Global Journalism Ethics Via Local Narratives: Southern African Perspectives." *Journalism Studies* 12(6): 791–803.

Wasserman, H. and De Beer, A. S. 2004. "Covering HIV/Aids: Towards a Heuristic Comparison Between Communitarian and Utilitarian Ethics." *Communicatio* 30(2): 84–98.

Wasserman, H. and De Beer, A. S. 2005. "Which Public? Whose Interest? The South African Media and its Role during the First Ten Years of Democracy." *Critical Arts* 19(1&2): 36–51.

Wasserman, H. and De Beer, A. S. 2006. "Conflicts of Interest? Debating the Media's Role in Post-Apartheid South Africa." In K. Voltmer, ed., *Mass Media and Political Communication in New Democracies*. London: Routledge, 59–75.

Wasserman, H. and Jacobs, S. 2011. "Commercialism, Zille, Political Reporting and Independent Newspapers," *The Media Online*, December 9. http://themediaonline.co.za/2011/12/commercialism-zille-political-reporting -and-independent-newspapers/, accessed December 12, 2011.

Wasserman, H. and Rao, S. 2008. "The Glocalization of Journalism Ethics." *Journalism: Theory, Practice, Criticism* 9(2): 163–81.

Wasserman, H. and Solomon, M. 2012. "Outcry and Protest as South Africa Passes New 'Secrecy Bill'." The World Today, January: 24–7.

8

Democratization by Boilerplate
National Media, International Norms, and Sovereign Nation Building in Postwar Liberia

Jo Ellen Fair

"The Love of Liberty Brought Us Here," for 160 years Liberia's national motto, recalls a founding discourse that remains the core of the official rhetoric of the government of Liberia today. Imperfect, even deeply flawed because the vast majority of Liberians descend not at all from the freed slaves and captives responsible for the country's creation in 1847, the motto serves because there is nothing to replace it. All states require rallying cries, and liberty is too noble and attractive a symbol to discard for a principle so rarified as historical accuracy.

"To prepare for peace, we must prepare for war," said an American media trainer, age approximately 28, at a June 2011 workshop for media professionals in Liberia's capital, Monrovia. International teams of democratization and free press experts were readying Liberian journalists to report professionally and responsibly on the country's national elections, which had been scheduled for later that year. These would be Liberia's second elections since a horrific 14 years of civil war tore the country apart between 1989 and 2003. Earnest, well-meaning, well-educated, and intelligent, staffers and contract employees of American and European human rights, democratization, and free press NGOs flooded Monrovia training centers in 2011 with misplaced bromides such as this, too familiar and principled sounding to discard for a set of realities so complex as a unique national history.

In this chapter I explore the interplay of national history, the growth industry of international democratization and free press advocacy, and the question of sovereignty during the postconflict reconstruction of once-failed states. I am concerned in particular with the creation of media narratives of democracy and democratization in fragile states highly dependent on outside help. My case is Liberia, where the national press and communications culture lost its bearings and its purpose during a prolonged period of national disintegration, and where international experts rushed in when the peace had been secured to bolster media in the name of reconstruction, democratization, and good governance. In essence, then, this chapter is about the ethical tensions between an international democratization advocacy machine that has appeared in the world over the last several decades, in particular its public relations and media wing, and the rights, obligations, and long-term advantages of the people of a nation writing their own history and future in their own idiom.

The chapter is organized in three parts: (1) a brief history of Liberia with a particular focus on the recurring, politically difficult, and quintessentially Liberian question of *belonging*; (2) an introduction to free press advocacy and training by outsiders in states embarking on "democratization," especially in states like Liberia recovering from serious conflict and disintegration; and (3) an account of democratization discourse-making in Liberia from 2009 to 2011. This last part explores the tensions that inhered and the distortions that emerged when shell-shocked, poverty-stricken local media professionals confronted confident, professional internationalists to create together, out of a mix of materials – local and global – a set of stories about the past and future intended to set the nation straight on a course of political improvements aimed at an authentically Liberian version of the universally admired condition called democracy.

Those Who Belong Create the Nation: Short History of Belonging in Liberia

Any brief telling of Liberian history – and probably this is true of any country – will ultimately be unjust. Concision requires omissions and simplifications that no specialist and no Liberian could entirely countenance. Yet historical understandings are necessary for any exploration of national narrative building today. Thus I begin with the story of the creation of Liberia and the problems that arise when a nation's founding myths and its lived realities sharply diverge.

What is now the Republic of Liberia was once a philanthropic endeavor of the American Colonization Society (ACS) intended to repatriate freeborn and manumitted Africans by establishing a sanctuary in Africa for "free people of color" (Moran 2006: 53–73, Tellewoyan 2006: 87–125). The earliest settlement of repatriated ex-American slaves occurred in 1821, near the site of present-day Monrovia, after ACS officials apparently convinced representatives (a problematic category, of course) of the Dei, Bassa, and Gola peoples to cede some of their lands. Soon, settlements of repatriates and recaptives (Africans who had been on board impounded slaving ships), dotted the coastline. In 1847, the repatriates and recaptives and their descendents declared independence from the ACS, demarcated the territory of a state, and pronounced the existence of the Republic of Liberia. This population – former slaves and their descendents – over time became known in Liberia as "Americo-Liberians," "Congoes," or "settlers."[1]

To consolidate the state and its control over land, this group expanded inland from the coast during the nineteenth and twentieth centuries, into territory already occupied by 16 or more indigenous ethnolinguistic groups, all of them organized and governed in one way or another by their own leaders. Sometimes via conquest and sometimes via co-operation and the incorporation of indigenes into a polity that formally blurred distinctions between settlers and others, the Liberian government gradually over a century or more established rule over all of the Liberian interior (Guannu 2000: 77–88, Sawyer 2005: 1–22, Tellewoyan 2006: 276–364).

From 1879, the True Whig Party, a replica of the by then defunct Whig party of the United States, dominated Liberian political life and state power. In the twentieth century the party and the state were personified by two particularly powerful presidents, William Tubman (1944–71) and William Tolbert (1971–80). Both Tubman and Tolbert espoused views and designed policies meant to promote greater respect for indigenous groups and their absorption into the formal economy and the Liberian state. Under Tubman and Tolbert, Liberia's privileged elites – composed mainly of the descendents of the nineteenth-century settlers and recaptives, "acceptable" (i.e., assimilated) indigenes, and educated immigrants from other parts of West Africa – were more and more able to live the dream of urban, modern life. However, despite a rhetoric of inclusion and gestures that did benefit some previously disadvantaged persons, Liberia's twentieth-century governments were, on the whole, unable or unwilling to redress the century of inequities and the fundamental lack of opportunity for advancement that bore heavily on the great majority of interior, indigenous people.

Out of this dynamic of modern versus traditional and urban versus rural came a pervasive, incessant, binary national system of labeling. Liberians were either civilized (*kwi*) or uncivilized (country). This binary largely replaced rhetorically the old, nineteenth-century settler–indigene ethnic divide, but functionally it replicated it. Ethnic differences had melted a bit, but mainly they had been redefined as differences of class. Loyalty to the True Whig Party or identification with it became something of a class marker, essential to one's maintenance of *kwi* or "civilized" status. There was little room in the party for the great majority of Liberians who were *country*, though leaders did effectively patronize these populations when politically necessary. Thus was Liberia's oligarchy built on a foundation of ethnicity, class, aspiration, resentment, and fear (Burrowes 1989, Guannu 2000, Moran 2006).

On April 12, 1980, Master Sergeant Samuel K. Doe, who was not from the elite (he portrayed himself as the champion of indigenous Liberians), seized power in a bloody coup, murdered President Tolbert and most of his cabinet members, and launched Liberia toward a late-twentieth and early-twenty-first century history of sustained political violence. Doe won a rigged presidential election in 1985, but his policies, politics, and governing capacity as president proved no less disturbing and erratic than they had been before this assumption of the quasi-legitimacy of a quasi-elected presidency. In 1989, a rebel army led by ex-Doe ally Charles Taylor crossed into Liberia from Ivory Coast, seeking to overthrow Doe's government. Liberia's First Civil War ensued, propelled in the first instance by Taylor's ruthless individual will to power, but quickly joined by a multiplicity of competing and shifting interests, including rebel armies sometimes indistinguishable from thuggish bands, the Liberian national army, and irregulars loyal to Doe. All parties were guilty of terrible wartime excesses. President Doe was brutally murdered by soldiers led by Prince Yormie Johnson in September 1990. Fighting continued until 1996, when a ceasefire and disarmament brokered by outside parties took effect. This war claimed more than two hundred thousand lives and displaced a million others.

Charles Taylor won a 1997 presidential election, but peace was fragile. Many Liberians questioned the moral suitability and legitimacy of leadership by a former brutal rebel. Dissidents formed militias in the north and across Liberia's borders in Guinea and Sierra Leone, and war erupted again in 1999. Liberia's Second Civil War was more broadly regional and transnational than the first had been. The government of Guinea overtly supported the main anti-Taylor militia (Liberians United for Reconciliation and Democracy or LURD), which was also allied in the early years with dissident groups in Sierra Leone. A variety of regular and irregular forces loyal to President Taylor fought back and forth against rebel groups and their allies in Liberia, Guinea, and Sierra Leone from 1999 to 2003, sometimes expanding Taylor's control into neighboring countries (by 2002 Taylor was effectively leading the rebel opposition to Sierra Leone's government), sometimes shrinking back to the extent that Taylor controlled only a fraction of Liberia.[2] In July 2003, with Monrovia and the government close to falling to the rebels, a ceasefire was declared. ECOWAS (the Economic Community of West African States), Nigeria, Ghana, the United States, and the United Nations co-operated to hold the peace and negotiate the Accra Comprehensive Peace Agreement in August. Taylor resigned, and a National Transitional Government was installed in Monrovia, which held titular power until the 2005 elections of a Senate, a House of Representatives, and President Ellen Johnson Sirleaf. President Sirleaf's government, supported by UN peacekeepers, gradually extended its authority over previously rebel-held territories across the country and now has tenuous control over the whole of a largely peaceful Liberia.[3]

Questions of belonging animate Liberia's history. The motto "The Love of Liberty Brought Us Here" dates from a time when Americo-Liberians could blithely, even innocently, exclude from consideration the peoples they found when they arrived, despite their being the country's vast majority. Later, as the state struggled with the moral or at least political imperative of inclusion, it elected to retain the motto but ingeniously reinterpreted it. It was said again and again during the Tubman and Tolbert periods that Liberia's indigenes *also* came for liberty, traveling not geographically but morally. They had come for liberty in the sense of arriving at voluntary union with the Liberian state and at recognition of the superiority of the civilization that the state proffered. Civilization – *kwi* – was liberation from the hold of primitive tradition. Or so said the state (Brown 1982, Kulah 1999: 76–85, Moran 2006: 77–100).

By the mid-twentieth century, a less metaphorical variant of this rhetoric of inclusion also could be heard: Liberia's indigenous groups, it was said, were themselves relative newcomers, driven to safe haven in Liberia before the nineteenth century by unrest, slave raiding, and war in surrounding territories (d'Azevedo 1969: 1–22, Konneh 1996, Kulah 1999: 105–12). By this logic, tortured and incorrect, all Liberians could be said to have descended from persons who had come to Liberia – literally migrated into the national territory – for liberty.

During the civil war years, 1989–96 and 1997–2003, combatants accused their rivals and enemies habitually of not being true Liberians but interlopers originally from other places: Sierra Leone, Guinea, Ivory Coast, and the United States (Ellis 2007: 31–74, Konneh 1996, Levitt 2005: 205–42). The porosity of West African borders, cultural continuities transcending national boundaries, and the spillover of the Liberian civil wars into neighboring countries rendered some of these charges credible, but of main interest here is that *belonging* was so quick to be challenged, and so fragile.

Belonging fractured in other ways during the civil war years. A multiplicity of militias, including child brigades, all commanded loyalty on the part of their members. Even those who were not combatants, not members of a militia, occasionally needed to affirm fealty or temporary loyalty to whatever band seemed ascendant in the region. The jumble of loyalties felt during a long, shifting, multifactional civil war – some passionate, such as the camaraderie of fellow combatants, some feigned or contingent, such as supplication for survival – challenged, damaged, and arguably destroyed the normal monopoly or near-monopoly of the state on political allegiance, on political belonging and its symbols. During the war years it was more important than ever to *belong*, but instead of stressing their identification with the nation, citizens threw their immediate, first-order loyalty to fellow partisans or to shifting casts of local protectors, all the while accusing *others* of not belonging to Liberia.

Quite apart from Liberia's unique political history – settlement and domination by ex-American slaves and their descendants, one-party rule, uneasy relations between elites and others, and eventual civil war – one central *economic* reality in twentieth- and twenty-first-century Liberia impinges sharply on the question of belonging. The formal economy of the country through most of the twentieth century was dominated by a single non-Liberian (indeed, American) firm: Firestone Rubber. Under the terms of a 99-year lease signed in 1926, Firestone's Liberian plantations cover nearly one-quarter of the total surface area of the nation, and the company's labor practices are troubling. The rubber produced by Firestone is destined for export, as is most of the output of Liberia's other main industrial crop, oil palm (oil palm plantations were mostly owned by wealthy Liberians). Even today, land tenure laws make it such that only a fraction of Liberia's citizens are in a position to own land, even to own their own small farms. "To whom does Liberia belong?" has throughout the nation's history been a question that has reverberated in the realm of the economy at least as strongly as in the affairs of the state. How firmly can one belong to a country whose economy seems in so many regards to belong to others? Managing the uncertainties of belonging, including the huge question of differential access to natural resources, especially land, is the great challenge of Liberia's postcivil war government. It is deeply entwined with all other aspects of national rebuilding, including, as we shall see, development of media that speak to, for, and among Liberians.

Democratization, Postconflict Reconstruction, and Free Press Advocacy

Like most states emerging from a prolonged period of political contortion, turmoil, or war, Liberia teeters on the edge of functionality. Its people are understandably uncertain about the future; they wonder what they should do. Their own government and the international community (the governments of transitional states unfailingly echo the international consensus) increasingly give a simple answer: Embrace liberal democracy! Belong to the community of democratic states. Join the free and the proud. The new Liberia, in other words, is said by the international community to need good governance, rule of law, open markets, modern infrastructure, and civil society (Collier 2007, Hayman 2011, Weiss 2000). Furthermore, according to this rhetoric – the rhetoric of the United Nations, the US government, the European Union, foundations of all stripes, and countless nongovernmental organizations – Liberia equally needs to open the gates of reasoned public debate through the media, for democracy cannot function without the free exchange of political ideas. This is the formula of international state building everywhere. A healthy press system is said to contribute to robust public debate within a hardy civil society, which in turn reinforces good governance and fortifies democracy.

The free press movement that swept into Liberia when civil war ended in 2003 had arrived in much of the rest of Africa 10 years earlier, on the winds of 1990s structural adjustment and post-Cold War political reform and democratization. Media liberalization elsewhere in Africa during this earlier period was seen as essential groundwork in the broader effort to create forward-looking constitutions, representative government, multiparty elections, and the legitimate rule of law. A main element tended to be the abolition of newspaper licensing laws to open the way for private, commercial, competitive print journalism. Broadcast media privatization and deregulation did the same for radio and television. State-owned media outlets of all kinds were cut loose. In African country after African country these reforms had many of their intended consequences. Newspapers, radio, and television boomed in Africa in the 1990s. New newspapers – often scrappy and poorly printed – filled kiosks from Accra to Niamey to Bamako. New radio stations up and down the dial filled national airwaves with a mix of local favorites, rap, country, and lots of talk. Telenovelas imported from Latin America, games shows, then reality shows from the United States and Britain, Bollywood and Nollywood movies, as well as endless politically oriented local public affairs shows, streamed into living rooms, storefronts, bars, and restaurants where Africans gathered for television. All of this was happening during a time when dictators were giving up power, becoming converted democrats, becoming apparent advocates of the new neoliberal realities and the media freedoms that undergirded them.

Not all was perfect in the new liberalized African mediascape of the 1990s and early 2000s. The relationship between press and government was evolving, and not all of the experiments that ensued were ethically defensible or forward-looking (Banda 2010, Diedong 2008, Fair and Gadzekpo 2011). Old lines of tension between government and press sometimes resurfaced with new twists. Privatized media now could be wooed and seduced by politicians and office-holders promising further reforms and favors in return for positive coverage (Fair 2008, Gadzekpo 2007, Nyamnjoh 2005). Nonetheless, a reasonable case can be made that media liberalization in most African countries beginning in the 1990s was on balance a success, an important contributor to political improvements and the creation of freer societies by the turn of the century (AfroBarometer 2003, Ogbondah 2003, Ogundimu 2003, Wahl-Jorgensen and Cole 2008).

Liberia simply missed all of this. The nation was at war with itself. In the midst of civil war, what was at stake in Liberia was not good governance or the freedoms of expression necessary for democracy, but rather survival. Journalists and their news organizations were under mortal threat (Press 2009, T. Kamara, publisher and editor of *The New Democrat* and S. Peabody, editor of *The Daily Observer*, in interview with the author, Monrovia, July 2009).[4] Rebel leader, then president, Charles Taylor regularly used harassment, surveillance, detention, and torture to silence journalists all through the 1990s and early 2000s, and had media houses that were critical of him closed, vandalized, or burned down (Freedom

House 2004, Press 2009, K. Best, publisher of *The Daily Observer* and A. W. Kekuleh, station manager of *Radio Veritas*, in interview with author, Monrovia, July 2009). When Taylor ran for the presidency in 1997, at least three-quarters of Liberians eligible to vote cast their ballot for him (Ellis 2007: 109, Harris 1999, Reno 1999: 79–111). It was hard not to vote for a man whose campaign slogan was "He killed my Pa; he killed my Ma; I will vote for him," a man who had taken personal possession of Liberia's only nationwide radio station and employed it unsparingly to promote his cause (Freedom House 2004: 330–33, Human Rights Watch 2003: 47–54). The 1997 election signaled that warlord politics reigned in Liberia. The press and the people were utterly cowed. When the country slid back into civil war in 1999, self-censorship borne of intimidation and violence largely immobilized Liberia's remaining vestigial press.

With the negotiated peace in 2003, help rushed in. The United Nations, the governments of Western countries, foundations, and multitudes of nongovernmental organizations were prepared to help secure Liberia's peace, reconcile society, and rebuild the state. Democratization and its accoutrements of a free press, an independent judiciary, rule of law, an educated public, an open economy, strong state institutions, a robust civil society, and respect for human rights were the developments and core values that would ensure peace and tranquility in Liberia, as everywhere, according to the international convention. Human decency and the global order required conformity to universally recognized twenty-first-century norms (Barnett and Finnemore 2004, Collier 2009).

The list of organizations active in trying to revitalize media and the press in Liberia between 2003 and 2011 is impressive but also disturbing, considering that the sector (print, radio, and television) that these organizations had come to help was, by 2003, after 14 years of war, tiny. There were sometimes more outside media experts on the ground in Liberia than there were Liberian media professionals of any kind. Outside groups active in media reconstruction in Liberia during this period included the United Nations Mission in Liberia (UNMIL), the United Nations Educational, Scientific, and Cultural Organization (UNESCO), the United Nations Development Program (UNDP), the United States Agency for International Development (USAID), the International Freedom of Expression Exchange, the International Federation of Journalists, the World Association of Newspapers, International Media Support, Journalists for Human Rights, the International Center for Transitional Justice, the Open Society-Media Network Program, the Radio Netherlands Training Center, the Alexia Foundation for World Peace and Understanding, the Norwegian Human Rights Foundation, the National Endowment for Democracy, Article 19, Freedom House, the Center for International Media Ethics, Humanity United, Canadian Journalists for Free Expression, Goldman Sachs Corporate Engagement, the International Coalition for the Responsibility to Protect, the Hirondelle Foundation, Free Voice, the Media Legal Defense Initiative, the BBC Trust, Search for Common Ground, the International Research Exchange (IREX), Ushahidi, and several North American and European universities.

African groups also participated in efforts to rebuild Liberia's media. They included the Economic Community of West African States, the Panos Institute of West Africa, the Media Foundation for West Africa, the West African Journalists Association, the Open Society Institute for West Africa, the International Press Center, Media Rights Agenda, African Elections Project, and the International Institute for Information and Communication Technologies.

These lists, by no means exhaustive, demonstrate the overwhelming consensus in the international community that a working, independent press builds and maintains states, and that fragile, postconflict states in particular have much to gain from rapid media development. Such a list also hints at desperation. The international community needed to do *something* in Liberia to bolster the odds of peace and stability, and developing the press – providing journalism training courses or funding Liberian media NGOs to promote press professionalization – seemed a noble and manageable endeavor. But this international scheme of good intent required something substantial, even something heroic, from Liberia's depleted, war-weary press. Liberian media had been tasked with telling the nation's hardest stories, stories whose meanings and whose endings were far from evident even to Liberia's few remaining clear-sighted observers. In a country where former warlords and confessed killers were serving in the House and Senate as elected representatives of the people, where shell shock, fear of militias, fear of children, and fear of venturing outside zones protected by UNMIL soldiers were part of people's day-to-day realities, what stories could a national press tell, particularly such a depleted press? The questions facing Liberia's media – what happened in the past, how to reconcile the past with the present, and how to construct a postconflict Liberia predicated on newly trumpeted universal values of democracy when even prewar Liberia was, at best, as a nation, a work in progress – were probably too great to be solved by anyone.

International Experts, Liberian Media, and National Discourse Making

Into the near vacuum of the postwar working Liberian media streamed the international organizations listed above. And others. The kind of help they proffered was varied, including infrastructure, equipment, publishing, production, and training. International consultants and Liberia's vestigial media profession became counterparts, even teammates, in a campaign to explain the past and create a public discourse about Liberia's future, with the ultimate aim of constructing a democratic Liberia according to conventional global norms. What accounts about Liberia's history, the war, belonging, nation, and future came out of these efforts, and what has been their impact on the media profession and Liberia's democracy? This section explores these questions along three exemplary lines, selected because they allow us to consider, in turn, media content, creation of this content, and the reflections of Liberian media professionals on what has transpired. Specifically, the section looks first at Monrovia's media streetscape in the 2009–11 period: its official billboards, signage, and wall paintings – messages that give us an idea how global and local media actors, often working in consort with governmental and transgovernmental agencies, envisioned Liberia's past, present, and possible futures in official and quasi-official pronouncements. It then considers the content of internationally sponsored media training sessions, what transpired as international experts attempted to help Liberian professionals reconstruct their profession and create a national media culture and coherent media messaging true to Liberia's history but focused on a peaceful democratic future. Finally, this section considers how Liberian journalists and other media professionals responded to the descent on Monrovia of international funding for media development and teams of international media experts – what they thought about the trainings and new directions for media advocated by outsiders.

Monrovia's media streetscape, 2009–11

Liberia was overwhelmingly rural before the civil wars, but more than 40 percent of all Liberians now live in or around Monrovia. The city overflows with displaced country Liberians who came for safety during the war and stayed. Monrovia was not designed for these masses. In any case, the city is still half destroyed, only partly rebuilt. Buildings gutted by war stand between new towers. On the hill just below the grand Ducor Hotel, once the five-star symbol of Liberia's progress, now an empty shell, squatters have constructed shanties next to weed-infested tennis courts where the elite once played. In one direction is a splendid panorama of West Point, a slum; in another, a view of one of Liberia's proudest monuments, a sculpture honoring the country's Americo-Liberian settlers. Around the hotel and the monument, ex-child soldiers, high on glue and other substances, extort guide fees (i.e., protection money) from visitors. All of Monrovia has a feel of trauma and permanent damage.

When the international community arrived after the civil wars to help install democracy, the rule of law, free markets, and a functioning media system, it wished to signal that it would stay as long as needed. It also began conveying, via pictures and words, the conditions to which the Liberian people, as citizens of the democratizing world, needed to aspire. Hortative billboards, signs, and wall paintings crowd Monrovia's main roads, dominating public spaces. The signs are not so much informational as prescriptive. They presume to define for Liberians the central issues that should be animating Liberian political life. They propose a working set of attitudes and conduct, conceived by the international community, agreed to by the state, which redefine Liberia and aspire to direct Liberia's postconflict democratic transition. These messages legitimize and enforce the authority of the state while also seeming, curiously, to be about managing the state, corralling it into conformity with international norms (Shapiro 2004: 48–9, Ferguson 2006: 1–23).

"Liberia is my identity," "Dignity for the people," "Rewrite the future," "Say yes to children, give them a future," "Help people help themselves," "Know your constitution, promote the rule of law," "Act against violence," "Rescue our people," "Healthy environment, happy people," "Truth for reconciliation," "Be that positive agent of change and pay your taxes," "Let's build a culture of transparency, accountability, and integrity for sustainable development," "Liberia is all we have, say no to violence," "Join us on the new team Liberia," "Help develop a new Liberia," "Build Mama Liberia," and "Liberia will rise again!" Even the much-feared Armed Forces of Liberia (AFL) are rehabilitated in a series of billboards paid for by the US-Liberian agency responsible for security reform. These show, in one instance, young men and women in uniform, with the caption, "A new army, a new Liberia." In another a soldier stands proudly with his wife and children beside him: "Upholding family values, join the new AFL." In yet another, soldiers proudly carry the Liberian Lone Star flag as they march in tight formation in front of St Peter's Lutheran Church, where the AFL slaughtered six hundred Liberians in 1990: "Salute to our beloved Liberia, follow me."

The international community's support for President Ellen Johnson Sirleaf is highly evident in Monrovia's streetscape. One large painted mural in Mamba Point, near the US Embassy, recalls one of Sirleaf's proudest accomplishments, restoring a portion of Monrovia's electrical grid soon after the 2005 elections. The left of the mural shows the city before the election, students studying and doctors operating in near dark. At the center of the picture, Sirleaf plugs in an outlet. On the right, postelection Liberians are studying and working indoors and others are celebrating outside under streetlights. Past, present, and future meld in these public images. The new Liberia, vaguely a product of a glossed-over national history but fundamentally forward looking, is an entity about which citizens should primarily feel pride and the sense of a bright future.

Trust us, join us, see this vision of the Liberia to which you belong: These are the sentiments. Yet this Liberia is "sponsored by," or in some cases "provided by" – these are the actual phrases used in signage – UNMIL, an American foundation, USAID, an international human rights organization, or the European Community. The overlay without irony of nationalist pride and international authorship is nothing short of astonishing. While some Liberian professionals surely were involved in the selection of images and creation of these messages, the hands of internationals are everywhere, to the point that nearly all signboards in Monrovia perversely challenge the sovereignty and the spirit of democracy that they were erected to undergird.

Whom this signage actually was intended to reach is strangely unclear. Only about 42 percent of Liberians are literate (though reading skills were not necessarily required for comprehension of the entire didactic cityscape). One sensed on Monrovia streets from 2009 to 2011 that some signs were intended by international actors not so much to accomplish their stated aims as to publicize their own efforts to one another, to mark what they were contributing toward building a new Liberia. Omnipresent, these streetside messages were a most visible public expression of Liberia's desperation, its seriously wounded indigenous public media capacity, and the international community's agenda for reforming the nation in a manner consistent with global norms (Douzinas 2007, Ferguson 2006, Shapiro 2004).

Monrovia's streetscape – its public signage – was emblematic of the state of Liberia's media in general during the years after the war. Deferential to internationalists (UNMIL Radio – entirely a United Nations Mission in Liberia enterprise – was by far the most important radio station in Liberia as late as 2010), deeply reliant on outside help, hewing exhaustedly to an upbeat but false-seeming democratization and national-pride boilerplate, the Liberian media as a whole during this period seemed a shell, supported logistically and with rhetorical assistance from the international community, but not entirely authentic because behind it were abstractions such as democratization and progress more than a sense of the will of the citizenry of the land.

Training Liberia's depleted corps of media professionals

As the war period came to an end in 2003, Liberia's depleted media corps began to reassemble. Publishing and broadcasting, corrupted but not entirely stopped during the war, resumed, re-energized. Immediate international help, especially financial help, was a factor in the re-establishment of newspapers and radio stations in Monrovia after 2003, but local media professionals, especially newspaper journalists, showed considerable courage and initiative during this period, taking risks to recreate a free press in a place where continued respect for press freedom was by no means a sure thing. The success rate of newspapers in the early years was low, but new ones kept appearing to replace those that had folded. Private radio stations, mostly featuring music and talk, boomed (though, as noted, none rivaled UNMIL Radio for professionalism and authority). Yet as the 2005 elections approached, the first since Liberians elected warlord Charles Taylor under duress in 1997, political leaders harshly criticized Liberia's emerging media for its unprofessionalism and tendency to sensationalist coverage.

In light of this criticism and fear in the international community that not enough had been done to bring Liberian print and broadcast journalism up to acceptable standards, Monrovia's multitude of international media-focused organizations redoubled their efforts in 2005, often with new infusions of funding from abroad. Liberal democracy's powerful orthodoxy about media was now ascendant in Monrovia: A free press fosters public debate and transparency of government. In return, a legitimately elected government protects free expression. But the orthodoxy had a twist, common in states that are rebuilding from tragedy: In the eyes of the state and its advocates, a truly professional free press in a transitional society will do nothing that would jeopardize the essential task of national rebuilding.

The irony inherent in this conflation of professionalism and dependability was not lost on Liberian media professionals. In general, however, as international media groups began their professionalization push in 2005, the Liberia media community played along, accepting the role they had been assigned as trainees in writing news and developing media to rebuild the nation along democratic lines. Internationally sponsored training sessions proliferated in Monrovia for Liberian editors, writers, broadcasters, and media managers. The sessions covered all imaginable grounds, including grammar, story organization, writing techniques, story gathering, relations with government, and building an advertising base.

Many international media organizations developing training sessions for Liberian media professionals preferred to work through the Press Union of Liberia (PUL), established in 1964 and dedicated to advocating for press freedom and protecting journalists from unlawful government intrusions. Other international groups elected to fund and work with local media NGOs such as the Center for Media Studies and Peace Building; the Liberia Media Initiative for Peace, Democracy, and Development; and the Liberian Media Center. All of these local NGOs – there were many more like them – had as their mission to professionalize journalism by improving standards of reporting, thereby promoting democracy and national reconstruction.

Liberian media professionals – especially journalists – knew their problems and shortcomings. They could reel them off and delve into deep detail: lack of reporting and writing skills; lack of technology; lack of time and resources, especially for in-depth work; low pay; low status; bribery; blackmail; necessary self-censorship; owners and editors demanding stories that supported their financial or economic interests; and intimidation and harassment by the government and private sector powerbrokers. Managing editors and owners, too, had long lists of concerns about the practice of journalism in Liberia: young, inexperienced reporters lacking analytic skills and historical knowledge; pressure from the government, the private sector, and international organizations to buy news coverage; refusal of major advertisers such as the government or international organizations to pay their advertising bills as a way of expressing displeasure; unannounced tax audits by the government; the barring of some reporters from official, public government functions; licensing; the constant threat of prosecution for libel; lack of access to public documents; reporters' reliance on anonymous sources (which makes story verification out of the question); competition with the online diaspora press for news, advertising revenue, and social respect; and a close-knit government class and social networks that make reporting stories that are critical or challenging to those in power virtually impossible.[5]

These problems run deep. They are foundational matters of national history, Liberian culture, a ruined economy, and a dysfunctional state. They are the core of the problem of creating a workable free press in Liberia. Unfortunately, they cannot be workshopped away. They are not amenable to the training solution that the international community felt equipped to provide. So trainings happened – this is where a great deal of the international free-press money went because training is one tangible and hard-to-fault action the international community can take – but the training concentrated not at all on the problems every Liberian journalist knew stood between them and a serviceable media culture – those listed above – but rather, overwhelmingly, on the third- and fourth-tier questions and problems that an international contractor might capably workshop. So Liberian journalists and other media personnel were prepared to go along with trainings inspired by the international community's fears and injunctions about media professionalism and democracy, but, ironically, the trainings that ensued were likelier to feature lessons on grammar and praise for democracy in the abstract than they were to address the issues that stood between journalists and good work in the Liberian context.

"Skills deficit" is the term international free press organizations most often apply to Liberia's press (Randall and Pulano 2008, UNESCO/UNDP 2005, IREX 2009, Truth and Reconciliation Commission 2009, International Media Support 2007). In the run-up to key national events such as the Truth and Reconciliation Commission (TRC) hearings and final report (2009) and the long election season (2010–11), Liberian journalists could (and some did) attend trainings just about every week. The president had opined publicly that she thought reporters preferred sensationalism to sensitization, or education, because rumors and lies are easier to produce than truth (IFEX 2006), and this rebuke was seen as license and incentive for improving skills in any way possible. Attending journalist trainings became de rigueur during these years – even though three-quarters of Liberians said they trusted the news media already and thought they kept a watchful eye on government (InterMedia 2008, AfroBarometer 2009b).

We may take it as a given that international training involves the transmission of values, norms, and practices from one culture to another. There is nothing inherently wrong with such transmissions, but each receiving media culture is particular and unique. It is irresponsible to assume that a workshop developed for media coverage of elections in Ghana, Benin, or Nigeria will work as well in Liberia, especially given Liberia's recent history. Off-the-shelf platitudes about accuracy, responsibility, and impartiality may resonate in societies that have not been decimated by war, but state failure of the kind Liberians experienced changes every-day life and trust; it diminishes the willingness of people to respond to exhortations by authorities. The international community's preferred time frame for transformation also limits the effectiveness of these exhorta-tions because it typically is unrealistically short (AfroBarometer 2009a, Bertelsmann Stiftung 2010).

Training for election reporting became especially widespread in 2010 and 2011. Guidelines for election coverage were generated by international and national teams and printed up. The Press Union of Liberia updated its code of conduct for election reporting (Press Union of Liberia 2010, International Institute for ICT Journalism 2011). Journalists were told in trainings and generally agreed that as much as possible it would be best to refrain from overt partisanship, and from interest- or party-driven (and financed) coverage. To that end, Liberian news organizations agreed after much public debate that they would not endorse presidential or legislative candidates. But it seemed from three workshops I attended that no one had informed the international trainers of these developments.

The Arab Spring was still fresh, and these well-credentialed international media professionals enthused about the power of the media to bring about revolutionary change, take down politicians, and challenge the status quo. "Evil prevails because good people choose to do nothing. You have to have courage when you report your elections," one trainer told journalists. Another urged, "Don't let these politicians win. You have to expose them, go after them, investigate, every chance you have." But in a country where just eight years ago courage to expose political leaders likely would have landed the journalist in prison or much worse, these calls, meant to inspire, rang very hollow. In one workshop, journalists couldn't have missed the Assistant Minister of Information shaking his head "no," as the trainer described the various ways a journalist might go "undercover" to investigate a politician or business leader.

The rhetoric of free press and its practice in Liberia don't always match: Liberian journalists can still get into trouble – sued, fired, harassed, jailed – for criticizing a member of government, taking an unflattering photo, or refusing *cato*, a word derived from the French *cadeau* for gift IFEX 2011, Leaf and Schmall 2011, Schmall 2011, Center for Media Studies and Peace Building 2008, AllAfrica 2011). In the trainings I observed, the Liberian journalists sat stony silent. Undeterred, trainers would arrive at their inevitable denouement: that in liberal democracies news organizations endorse candidates for election and that this is the right course for Liberians, too. The idea of always endorsing a candidate finally did provoke a response: "We've agreed not to do that here," "Our democracy isn't mature enough," "We have to try our best to not be partisan for the good of the country," "We don't want to fall back into violence." In one session a young journalist asked: "How do you stay independent when endorsing a candidate?" His concern likely was that politicians would use money and/or power to seal endorsements. Another expressed discomfort over telling Liberians what to think or how to vote in a time when the war was too fresh and democracy too fragile: "Sometimes you can go too far under the guise of news." The trainer's response was to explain that endorsements were just part of a news organization's responsibility in "real" democracies: "Papers are part of the body politic, part of democracy, so of course you can say who the better candidate is. Your audience doesn't have to agree." These exchanges seemed frustrating for trainers and trainees. While ideas about grammar rules and sentence structure might harmlessly flow from one culture to another, the principles of liberal democracy developed in the West could not be transferred or translated directly into the experience, knowledge, and professional habits of Liberian journalists.

Liberian responses

A venerable editor, a man whose newspaper was torched during the war years, leans forward across his desk and folds his hands:

> There are so many international mantras: first DDR [disarmament, demobilization, and reintegration], then peace building, then national reconciliation, good governance, rule of law, democracy. Are we doing state building now or is it capacity? I can't keep up. (interview #5, May 27, 2011)

He said he refuses to send his reporters to trainings. "They go; they're bored; they collect a per diem, and have a free lunch. I train my reporters inside this newsroom. Liberia is too much of an NGO paradise." Many of the young reporters I interviewed said while they benefited from hands-on workshops where trainers showed them how to use new software or social media, they also felt that the trainings introduced a hodgepodge of ideas with little opportunity for practice. As one Liberian trainer said, "We want them to develop expertise. Yet all the time we're on to the next hot issue the NGO sees Liberians as needing to address" (interview #21, May 27, 2011). Journalists are frustrated by what they can identify as the prefabricated imprint of the international community. As one woman with several years of radio experience said:

> I want to learn. I keep on coming. But most of these is much talk about what you people like to talk about, all this democracy, democracy when Liberians just want no more fighting, plenty to eat, and jobs. (interview #12, May 23, 2011)

On a Sunday afternoon, three senior reporters, one from radio, one from television, and one from print, hastily assemble some 30 of their colleagues in one of their homes with a promise of cold Fantas and Club beers. I was there as a guest and observer, the only foreigner. Intended as a mentoring session for less experienced journalists, the meeting focused on preparing for the upcoming elections and reporting on them. One of the hosts, serving as moderator, begins:

> Liberia has had a troubled history. It is now time to cut loose of your religion, what county you were born, whether you are a city boy or country. We are all Liberians. Our people tend to believe what journalists say because they are poor and [had] no book [education]. We as professionals must be professional. Liberia first. (interview #3, May 22, 2011)

Sitting in a circle passing a microphone around so all can hear over the din of neighborhood kids, traffic, and music, journalists ask each other about personal safety, how to refuse bribes, how to deal with editors' or owners' "advice" on story angles, how to report on sensitive topics such as government corruption or the perception of it, how to get sources to talk on-the-record or protect the confidentiality of others, and how to negotiate political sensitivities so they will not be barred from press conferences or other official events. They discuss the likelihood of election-related violence and whether Liberia could become another Rwanda or Kenya. They ask each other about the major parties' platforms and the authority of the National Election Commission. They agree that they will not endorse political candidates, but they also try to work through reconciling a national identity – being Liberian – with the competing social, economic, political, and cultural loyalties that tug at them. Summing up the complexities, one female reporter concludes: "We are hearing from government, PUL, editors, and NGOs always telling us how to do our work. Being a journalist is one of the hardest jobs to do" (interview #19, May 22, 2011).

Conclusion

This kind of locally organized meeting, small-scale as it was, signals a strong desire on the part of Liberian journalists to work toward professionalization in a Liberian way for the good of the nation. It also signals a capacity for co-operating without the agendas or inducements of outsiders. As one of the meeting's organizer's exclaimed,

> No banking method tonight! We didn't just pour into their heads how they ought to be doing their reporting. We had a real dialogue. I know what happened here tonight may not change how my colleagues are covering the elections, but we recognized for ourselves our common challenges. (interview #4, May 22, 2011)

There are many common challenges, of course. They include continued bribery, sensationalism, partisanship, and growing tension among the press, government, and opposition parties. But there is a central challenge, too, to Liberia's democracy: finding a national narrative that binds Liberians. It seemed far likelier to participants in this meeting that workable solutions to these challenges might come out of spontaneous local gatherings of journalists than out of high-cost affairs (often extremely high-cost affairs – international experts are expensive to haul across oceans) organized by non-Liberian well-wishers.

Democratization transplanted may build a state, but it does not necessarily build a nation to which people feel they belong. Liberal democracy rests on the principle that citizens owe allegiance to a state that guarantees them equal rights and freedoms. But what happens when citizenship and rights become so intensely divisive that the nation falls apart, as happened in Liberia? What happens when citizens are no longer certain they belong? Belonging – diverse, contested, unsettled – does not fit comfortably into an international schema of postconflict reconstruction that is based on structuring a democracy. Belonging is a more fundamental matter than creating rules for governing the state. Democracy, with its high value on individual autonomy and responsibility, may even hinder the development of a sense of belonging, which is more tied up in group loyalties than individual responsibilities. Herein lies the conundrum of Liberia's journalists. They have been charged by government and the international community with helping to build a new Liberia, but they know too well the fractured fragility of their society. To what should they try to be loyal – truth or a set of hopes whose workability in Liberia is an open question?

Imported schemes for the promotion and protection of a free press as a bulwark of democracy in Liberia are unlikely to be sufficient to keep Liberia's hard-working but underresourced media professionals in Liberia and engaged. There may be a place in postconflict states for international organizations intent on helping journalists and the journalistic ethos and mission prosper, but workshops and conferences devoted to high principles of journalism in the West and "how the press works in successful democracies" are of limited value. Stepping out of the way while Liberian journalists help themselves, as in the meeting described above, may not satisfy the impulse to assist, but in many situations it may be the wisest course.

Another possibility suggests itself: Solid news reporting *by* international media organizations *from* a fragile nation can inspire confidence on the part of local journalists that the travails of their nation matter to the world, and that their stories have value. For the cost of a media development workshop or creation of yet another externally supported media advocacy office in Monrovia, an international organization could underwrite a handful of international journalists filing stories from the fragile nation, even jointly reported with local colleagues. Reporting by outsiders on a country such as postconflict Liberia models Western practices and ideals rather than clumsily trying to instill them. And when working international reporters get things wrong (as happens), civil society led by local journalists will criticize their work, not – as after a workshop – collect their per diem and go home. All in all, this kind of intervention by media advocacy groups would foster a healthier dynamic than their didactic work does now, a dynamic that is truer to the spirit of the journalism enterprise.

Liberians elected Ellen Johnson Sirleaf in November 2011 to a second presidential term. The elections – emblematic of Liberia's democratic coming of age – were fraught. International observers judged them free and fair, but the primary opposition party boycotted the second round of voting. Three Liberians died in election-related violence. The government closed two radio and one television station citing public safety concerns. The democratization boilerplate leaves little rhetorical space for imperfection and even less for failure. One of the journalists who attended the Sunday meeting back in May emailed after these events to say that he had received threats for his coverage. "Election, can't debate? . . . I am considering having to leave Liberia" (interview #2, October 22, 2011).

Notes

1. Burrowes (1989) provides important criticism of Western scholarship that perpetuates a binary that situates Americo-Liberians as oppressors and indigenes as victims. Burrowes suggests that this binary reduces Liberian political history to a morality play between oppressors and victims, a play narrated by (white) Americans and Europeans.
2. The Hague's Special Court for Sierra Leone found Charles Taylor guilty on 11 counts of aiding and abetting crimes against humanity and war crimes on April 26, 2012. In May 2012 he was sentenced to 50 years in prison.
3. For accounts of the civil wars, see, Ellis 2007, Daniel 1992, Huband 2001: 137–58, Levitt 2005, Reno 1999, Utas 2003, Waugh 2011, Williams 2006, and Youboty 2004.
4. Burrowes (2004) provides an excellent history of government-press relations in Liberia up to 1970. Many of the tensions, direct manipulation, and overt threats he identifies are relevant beyond 1970. Yet his history also shows at times a vibrant, independent press.
5. I interviewed 42 journalists, editors, publishers, programmers, and station managers. These interviews usually lasted an hour, sometimes several. Most often we met in newsrooms but sometimes a second or third time at some other public place such as a teashop or public building. Interviews were open-ended discussions of journalism as a profession in Liberia. Because of concerns expressed by many of the journalists I talked with, I identify them by interview number. Only when citing a historical incident, well-recorded, do I name them, and with their permission. I do not identify journalists' news organizations or trainers and groups that held workshops.

Further Reading

Readers who seek an introduction to the country of Liberia might start with Ayodeji Olukoju's *Culture and Customs of Liberia* (Westport, CT: Greenwood Press, 2006). For those interested in the Liberian media specifically, Carl Patrick Burrowes's 2004 book and Robert Press's 2009 article are good starting points, demonstrating the complex relationship historically and contemporarily of the press to various institutions of power.

But the practice of journalism never operates in a vacuum. As everywhere, Liberian journalists are cultural actors and the news organizations they work for are institutions embedded in the history, politics, and economics of the country. Many accounts of Liberia's civil wars by Western journalists cast the violence simplistically, relying on the well-worn stereotype of African conflicts as "tribal." Both Stephen Ellis's *The Mask of Anarchy* (2007) and Mary Moran's *Liberia: The Violence of Democracy* (2006) challenge readers to understand Liberia's tumultuous history outside of that framework. Last, the final report of Liberia's Truth and Reconciliation Commission, available online (http://trcofliberia .org/reports/final-report), is an important, though politically charged, document, which includes chapters on the media.

References

AfroBarometer. 2003. "Freedom of Speech, Media Exposure, and the Defense of a Free Press in Africa," *Afrobarometer Briefing Paper No. 7*, http://www.afrobarometer.org/publications/afrobarometer-briefing-papers /196-bp-7, accessed May 16, 2010.

AfroBarometer. 2009a. "Are Democratic Citizens Emerging in Africa?" *Afrobarometer Briefing Paper No. 70*, http://www.afrobarometer.org/publications /afrobarometer-briefing-papers/264-bp-70, accessed May 16, 2010.

AfroBarometer. 2009b. "Popular Opinions on Democracy in Liberia, 2008," Afrobarometer *Briefing Paper No. 73*, http://www.afrobarometer.org /publications/afrobarometer-briefing-papers/267-bp-73, accessed May 16, 2010.

AllAfrica. 2011."Weah on Anti-Media War Path," http://allafrica.com/stories /201110070844.html, accessed October 7, 2011.

Banda, F. 2010. "Negotiating Journalism Ethics in Zambia: Toward a 'Glocal' Ethics." In S. J. A. Ward and H. Wasserman, eds., *Media Ethics Beyond Borders: A Global Perspective*. New York: Routledge, 124–41.

Barnett, M. and Finnemore, M. 2004. *Rules for the World: International Organizations in Global Politics*. Ithaca, NY: Cornell University Press.

Bertelsmann Stiftung. 2010. *Transformation Index 2010: Political Management in International Comparison*. Gütersloh, Germany: Bertelsmann Foundation.

Brown, D. 1982. "On the Category of 'Civilized' in Liberia and Elsewhere." *Journal of Modern African Studies* 20: 287–303.

Burrowes, C. P. 1989. *The Americo-Liberian Ruling Class and Other Myths: A Critique of Political Science in the Liberian Context*. Occasional Paper 3. Institute of African and African-American Affairs. Philadelphia, PN: Temple University Press.

Burrowes, C. P. 2004. *Power and Press Freedom in Liberia, 1830–1970: The Impact of Globalization and Civil Society on Media-Government Relations*. Trenton, NJ: Africa World Press.

Center for Media Studies and Peace Building. 2008. "Triumph of Impunity: Attacks on Freedom of Expression in Liberia," http://www.ifex.org /download/en/AttacksVol2CEMESPLiberia.pdf, accessed September 5, 2012.

Collier, P. 2007. *The Bottom Billion: Why the Poorest Countries Are Failing and What Can Be Done About It*. New York: Oxford University Press.

Collier, P. 2009. *Wars, Guns, and Votes: Democracy in Dangerous Places*. New York: Harper Perennial.

Daniel, A. 1992. *Monrovia Mon Amour: A Visit to Liberia*. London: John Murray.

d'Azevedo, W. 1969. "A Tribal Reaction to Nationalism, Part 1." *Liberian Studies Journal* 1: 1–22.

Diedong, A. 2008. "Establishing Journalistic Standards in the Ghanaian Press." *African Communication Research* 1: 206–32.

Douzinas, C. 2007. "The Many Faces of Humanitarianism." *Parrhesia* 2: 1–28.

Ellis, S. 2007. *The Mask of Anarchy: The Destruction of Liberia and the Religious Dimension of an African Civil War*. New York: New York University Press.

Fair, J. E. 2008. "Soft Control of the Press: Dubious Normalcy in Ghana." *Dissent*, Spring, 39–42.

Fair, J. E. and Gadzekpo, A. 2011. "Reconciling a Nation: Ghanaian Journalists and the Reporting of Human Rights." In B. Musa and J. K. Domatob, eds., *Communication, Culture, and Human Rights in Africa*. Lanham, MD: Rowman and Littlefield, 51–68.

Ferguson, J. 2006. *Global Shadows: Africa in the Neoliberal World Order*. Durham, NC: Duke University Press.

Freedom House. 2004. *Freedom in the World 2004: The Annual Survey of Political Rights and Civil Liberties*. Lanham, MD: Rowman and Littlefield.

Gadzekpo, A. 2007. "Fifty Years of the Media's Struggle for Democracy in Ghana: Legacies and Encumbrances." *Ghana Studies* 10: 89–106.

Guannu, J. S. 2000. *A Short History of the First Liberian Republic: A Sequel to Liberian History up to 1847*, 2nd edn. Monrovia: Republic of Liberia.

Harris, D. 1999. 'From "Warlord" to 'Democratic' President: How Charles Taylor Won the 1997 Liberian Elections.' *Journal of Modern African Studies* 37: 431–55.

Hayman, R. 2011. "Fund Fraud? Donors and Democracy in Rwanda." In S. Straus and L. Waldorf, eds., *Remaking Rwanda: State Building and Human Rights After Mass Violence*. Madison: University of Wisconsin Press, 118–31.

Huband, M. 2001. *The Skull Beneath the Skin: Africa After the Cold War*. Boulder, CO: Westview Press.

Human Rights Watch. 2003. "World Report: Liberia." New York: Human Rights Watch.

IFEX. 2006. "President Attacks Journalists' Ethics in Recent Speech, Calls for Media Reform," http://www.ifex.org/liberia/2006/09/04/president_attacks_journalists_ethics/, accessed March 3, 2011.

IFEX. 2011. "Alerts – Liberia." 2011. IFEX. http://www.ifex.org/liberia/alerts/, accessed November 12, 2011.

InterMedia. 2008. "Liberia: Public Opinion on News," http://www.audiencescapes.org/country-profiles/liberia/public-opinion-news/public-opinion-news-483, accessed March 5, 2010.

International Institute for ICT Journalism. 2011. "Guidelines for Reporting Elections in Liberia," www.africanelections.org/LIBERIA%20MEDIA%20GUIDE.pdf, accessed September 5, 2012.

International Media Support. 2009. "Strengthening Liberia's Media," 2007. http://www.i-m-s.dk/files/publications/Liberia_webfinal%201202-2007.pdf, accessed July 10, 2009.

IREX. 2009. "Liberia: Media Sustainability Index," http://www.irex.org/resource /liberia-media-sustainability-index-msi, accessed August 3, 2010.

Konneh, A. 1996. "Citizenship at the Margins: Status, Ambiguity, and the Mandigo of Liberia." *African Studies Review* 39: 141–54.

Kulah, A. F. 1999. *Liberia Will Rise Again: Reflections on the Liberian Civil Crisis*. Nashville, TN: Abingdon Press.

Leaf, A. and Schmall, E. 2011. "In Liberia, Silencing Press Critics Through Libel Lawsuits." Committee to Protect Journalists., http://cpj.org/blog/2011/07/in -liberia-silencing-press-critics-through-libel-l.php, accessed October 19, 2011.

Levitt, J. 2005. *The Evolution of Deadly Conflict in Liberia: From 'Paternaltari- anism' to State Collapse*. Durham, NC: Carolina Academic Press.

Moran, M. 2006. *Liberia: The Violence of Democracy*. Philadelphia, PN: University of Pennsylvania Press.

Nyamnjoh, F. B. 2005. *Africa's Media: Democracy and the Politics of Belonging*. London: Zed Books.

Ogbondah, C. 2003. "Media Laws in Political Transition." In G. Hyden, M. Leslie, and F. Ogundimu, eds., *Media and Democracy in Africa*. New Brunswick, NJ: Transaction Press, 55–80.

Ogundimu, F. 2003. "Media and Democracy in Twenty-first Century Africa." In G. Hyden, M. Leslie, and F. Ogundimu, eds., *Media and Democracy in Africa*. New Brunswick, NJ: Transaction Press, 207–38.

Press, R. M. 2009. "Candles in the Wind: Resisting Repression in Liberia (1979–2003)." *Africa Today* 55: 2–19.

Press Union of Liberia (PUL). 2010. "Election Coverage Code of Conduct." Monrovia: PUL.

Randall, L. and Pulano, C. R. 2008. "A Review of Media Coverage of the Truth and Reconciliation Process in Liberia." Monrovia: Liberia Media Center and International Center for Transitional Justice.

Reno, W. 1999. *Warlord Politics and African States*. Boulder, CO: Lynne Rienner.

Sawyer, A. 2005. *Beyond Plunder: Toward Democratic Governance in Liberia*. Boulder, CO: Lynne Rienner.

Schmall, E. 2011. "Paying Off: The Problem of Bribes in the Liberian Press." *Columbia Journalism Review*, http://www.cjr.org/currents/paying_off_1 .php, accessed July 12, 2011.

Shapiro, M. 2004. *Methods and Nations*. London: Routledge.

Tellewoyan, J. 2006. *The Years the Locusts Have Eaten: Liberia 1816–2004*. Bloomington, IN: Xlibris.

Truth and Reconciliation Commission. 2009. "Media and Outreach in the TRC Process." Truth and Reconciliation Report, Appendices, Vol. 3, http:// trcofliberia.org/resources/reports/final/volume-three-6_layout-1.pdf, accessed May 5, 2010.

UNESCO/UNDP. 2005. "Liberia Media Development Program: Governance and Rule of Law," http://unesdoc.unesco.org/images/0019/001915/191530e.pdf, accessed August 3, 2010.

Utas, M. 2003. *Sweet Battlefields: Youth and the Liberian Civil War*. Uppsala, Sweden: Uppsala University Dissertations in Cultural Anthropology.

Wahl-Jorgensen, K. and Cole, B. 2008. "Newspapers in Sierra Leone: A Case Study of Conditions for Print Journalism in a Post-conflict Society." *Ecquid Novi* 29: 1–20.

Waugh, C. 2011. *Charles Taylor and Liberia: Ambition and Atrocity in Africa's Lone Star State*. London: Zed.

Weiss, T. G. 2000. "Governance, Good Governance, and Global Governance: Conceptual and Actual Challenges." *Third World Quarterly* 21: 795–814.

Williams, G. 2006. *Liberia: The Heart of Darkness*. Bloomington, IN: Trafford Publishing.

Youboty, J. 2004. *A Nation in Terror: The True Story of the Liberian Civil War*. Philadelphia, PN: Parkside Impressions Enterprises.

Part III

Global Issues

9

The Role of Global Media in Telling the Climate Change Story

Sharon Dunwoody and Magda Konieczna

Covering a global story as important, complex, and messy as climate change is no easy job, and mass media the world over are both praised and taken to task for their efforts. The issue has become vividly politicized in some countries (the United States is perhaps the best example); couple that fact with the scientific uncertainties embedded in scientists' best efforts to model the climate of the future and you have a recipe for controversy and for ethical dilemmas. This chapter will first make a brief argument on behalf of the reality of a changing climate at the global level, will recognize the nonetheless contentious nature of the issue, then will suggest that media organizations have an ethical responsibility to cover these types of issues with a keen level of sensitivity to audience, to evidence, and to the global scale of the problem and its likely solutions.

First, permit a comment about terminology. The terms "climate change" and "global warming" are often used interchangeably, and we will do that in this chapter. Terms such as these become heavily loaded during controversies, so we cannot control the reader's reaction to them. We would urge our readers to equate the terms with a newer phrase, "climate disruption," that is gaining some currency and that, we feel, more accurately represents what is now happening to Earth's thin atmospheric layers.

How Solid Is the Science?

We will be brief here because the evidence for increasing climate disruption worldwide, as well as for human activities as driving forces for these disruptions, is well established. Those with a deep understanding of these physical processes gather periodically under the banner of the Intergovernmental Panel on Climate Change (IPCC), the leading international body for the assessment of climate change, to evaluate the available data. Over the course of four assessments since 1990, the IPCC's conclusions have only strengthened. In the latest report, scientists assert that "warming

Global Media Ethics: Problems and Perspectives, First Edition. Edited by Stephen J. A. Ward.
© 2013 Blackwell Publishing Ltd. Published 2013 by Blackwell Publishing Ltd.

of the climate system is unequivocal" (IPCC 2007: 2) and, further, that "it is *likely* [emphasis in the original] that there has been significant anthropogenic warming over the past 50 years" (IPCC 2007: 5). A recent survey of climate scientists in the United States indicates that respondents are nearly unanimous in their belief that global warming is under way (Farnsworth and Lichter 2012).

Put more simply, the weight of evidence – a term we will discuss later in this chapter – strongly suggests that temperatures are increasing on a global scale and at a faster rate than normal, and that human activity is contributing substantially to that process.

The IPCC is now beginning work on the next iteration of its periodic evaluations. The Fifth Assessment Report, with a 2014 completion date, has more than 800 scientists on board and a rigorous schedule of analytical meetings on its docket. In an acknowledgment of the confidence scientists now have in their conclusions about the inevitability of warming and consequent climate disruptions, the fifth assessment will put greater emphasis on assessing the socioeconomic impacts of those changes, as well as on both mitigation and adaptation options for countries around the world.

So Why All the Debate?

It is hard to find a complex scientific issue around which so many experts have coalesced in agreement on both the nature of the problem and its causes. Why, then, are countries such as the United States embroiled in arguments about these very matters? Why have efforts to create global policies in order to slow down and eventually stabilize the warming and consequent damage been so unsuccessful? (By way of example, recall the 2009 gathering of countries in Copenhagen, Denmark, where efforts to hammer out a global agreement on limiting emissions failed spectacularly. We offer some analyses of media coverage of that event later in the chapter.) Among the many possible reasons, we will explore three here: the challenge of dealing with uncertainty; the disembodied nature of this particular risk, at least for the developed world; and the power of ideology as a decision-making heuristic.

Humans do not cope well with uncertainty

Although we seem to have a visceral understanding of probability – for example, we know that our recently purchased lottery ticket is probably not a winner and that a 20 percent chance of rain means that we likely can make it through a day of errands without an umbrella – uncertainty makes us uncomfortable. Not only do we have a difficult time accurately deciphering uncertainty "language" (Budescu, Broomell, and Por 2009), but psychologists argue that we will go to great lengths to reduce the uncertainty that we do perceive. Communication scholars have built entire research programs around the ways in which we gather and evaluate information to minimize uncertainty (Berger and Calabrese 1975, Berger 1986).

Uncertainty is centrally involved in the concept of risk, and it appears to be a major actor in fueling controversy. Lay individuals experience uncertainty as a form of "not knowing" (Powell et al. 2007), and a lack of knowledge about a risk is a classic invitation to downplay or ignore that risk. Additionally, in a recent report examining the communication of uncertainty in climate change, the US Climate Change Science Program noted that high levels of uncertainty permit – and, indeed, may even force – individuals to make sense of a risk within the framework of their own, personal value systems (Morgan et al. 2009). The inevitable variance in those value systems leads to divergent risk beliefs, and those differences, in turn, promote the use of uncertainty as a rhetorical tool in disagreements (Heazle 2010). When it comes to climate change, for instance, those skeptical of a human contribution to warming often argue that the uncertainties of the science are too great to recommend policy responses while those convinced of a human contribution counter that the uncertainties are manageable and should not short-circuit action to lower emissions.

If it doesn't affect me personally, why should I care?

It can be hard enough to get people to agree on the nature of risks that may affect them personally. What happens when a risk appears to be a problem for others but not for oneself? This is the case with global warming in many developed societies. Leiserowitz (2006) asked Americans to react to the term "global warming" by describing the first picture that came into their heads. Participants overwhelmingly responded with images of melting icebergs and polar bears. Such images do, in fact, reflect important stakeholders in the climate change process, but they also mean that Americans tend to view global warming as a distant problem, as one that does not affect them directly. Since we already underestimate our personal likelihood of coming to harm from virtually all risks (Weinstein 1980, 1989), convincing us that global warming is serious enough to require immediate and substantive policy attention is a formidable job, indeed.

Ideology as a heuristic device

Another byproduct of confronting a risk that we don't believe affects us is that we anticipate little gain from learning about that risk. Learning is a labor-intensive process, and we engage in it only when we have a direct and pressing need (and sometimes not even then). Things that probably won't affect us can be safely ignored, and studies over the years have demonstrated that, for Americans at least, our understanding of climate warming processes is modest, indeed (Bostrom et al. 1994, Leiserowitz and Smith 2011).

In that low-knowledge environment, when confronted with the need to make a decision, we typically default to the use of rules of thumb, experience-based strategies that require little time and effort (Gigerenzer and Todd 1999). Such heuristic decision making is commonplace: When we have a medical problem, the recommendations of a physician (an expert) are usually good enough. Seeing an issue discussed repeatedly on TV talk shows (redundancy) is often enough to convince us that the issue is important. We may use a friend's reaction to a truth claim (someone like us) as a good-enough guide for our own reaction to that same claim.

When it comes to global warming, scientists hope that lay audiences will default to scientific expertise as their heuristic of choice. Many do, of course, but others employ a different rule of thumb altogether: political ideology. The best predictor of one's position on climate change in the United States, in fact, is partisan affiliation, with liberals professing beliefs in the reality and seriousness of climate repercussions and conservatives expressing skepticism (Dunlap and McCright 2008). Those partisan differences are not just applicable to the United States; one recent survey has unearthed them in Canada as well (Borick, Lachapelle, and Rabe 2011). But regardless of where they occur, such politicization virtually guarantees divergent viewpoints and heated exchanges.

The questions posed by this chapter, then, are these: What constitutes ethical work for a journalist engaged in covering an issue of global portent about which experts agree but for which lay audiences perceive considerable disagreement? What processes are ethically demanded of journalism as it confronts changes at a global scale that – if not mitigated in some way – will have serious socioeconomic consequences for people worldwide, with particular damage to populations who have the fewest resources and who will be least resilient? And for an issue that is truly global in scope, can journalism – that most local of occupations – play a role in constructing deliberative communities in which problems can be articulated and policies considered?

We will consider these questions through the lens of three topical arenas: the importance of understanding the audience for global warming narratives, ethical dimensions of journalists' efforts to evaluate truth claims, and the challenge for journalists of managing the tensions between local and global imperatives in their stories.

Understanding the Audience

Despite the obvious centrality of "the average Joe or Joan" to journalism, the true audiences for their products are often things of mystery to journalists. Although professing to write for people just like their moms or their next-door neighbors, journalists' most important audiences over the decades have been their editors and their sources. Science journalists in particular have had to tread carefully. They often must cajole editors into letting them cover developments that are highly complex and that look boring. And their scientific sources will scrutinize their stories closely, looking for the smallest error, the missed coauthor, the overambitious adjective. In decades past, unhappy scientists often thought nothing of calling the journalist's boss to complain that they had been "burned" by a reporter's story or of cutting the reporter off from future interactions.

While editors and sources still constitute important reference nodes, the twenty-first century has thrown a science journalist's *real* audience back into the mix; they make up an eclectic brew of individuals with substantial information needs but little scientific expertise and little time to spend on journalistic narratives. As users of traditional journalism products dwindle, media organizations are working desperately to decipher the wants and needs of those waning numbers of subscribers. They are also wrestling with the fact that people who come to their narratives often do so via social media rather than from the front page, and in a much more active stance. These are individuals whom Rosen calls "the people formerly known as the audience" (Rosen 2006), and they exercise increasing amounts of control over their own exposure to and processing of science news.

An ethical focus on the audience for climate change coverage, we argue, must be sensitive to what individuals know about the issue and, particularly, to the belief systems through which they will filter global warming stories. We take up those two dimensions below.

What do lay audiences understand about climate change?

Most of the data we have about knowledge comes from surveys of Americans. And one major source of those surveys is the Yale Project on Climate Change, which has been querying Americans about global warming knowledge, beliefs, and behaviors for a number of years. We reference some of that program's work here.

A majority of Americans believes that global warming is happening, and nearly half (47%) believe that the warming is caused by human activity. However, uncertainty about the issue remains high, so high, in fact, that more than a third of Americans say that, given new information, they could easily change their minds about the issue (Leiserowitz and Smith 2011). Indeed, more than half of a recent national sample indicated they would need "a lot" or at least "some" additional information in order to form firm opinions.

Such volatility suggests that most people invest little time in learning about global warming, and the Yale data corroborate that. Fewer than half of Americans surveyed said that they had given global warming much thought recently, with attention to the issue declining since measurements began in 2008. Not surprisingly, most felt that the issue was not very important to them personally.

Media coverage of climate change can influence learning, albeit modestly (Zhao et al. 2011), and we make the argument here that maintaining ongoing coverage over time is an ethically sound response to a complicated issue such as this. Media narratives serve an important signaling function in society, both for lay audiences and for policy makers. But if coverage is driven primarily by large-scale events or crises, the result will be a wildly uneven volume of stories over time that encourages audiences to overvalue the importance of an issue in the "up" times while undervaluing it in the "down" times. Science communication scholar Max Boykoff has been tracking the volume of climate change newspaper coverage around the world since 2004. As his graph at http://sciencepolicy.colorado .edu/media_coverage/ shows, with the notable exception of both South America and Africa, where global warming coverage is negligible, media coverage worldwide has ebbed and flowed, driven primarily by events (such as the 2009 conference in Copenhagen, the high point on the graph). Event-driven coverage is classic and time-honored journalistic behavior, of course, but we urge professional colleagues to consider the interpretive cost to audiences of the resulting roller-coaster ride. If society needs to maintain a sustained focus on such large-scale issues as climate change, then more continuous, thematic coverage would facilitate that goal.

Collisions between beliefs and information can be fatal (to the message)

Journalists are well aware that readers/viewers are not blank slates. Far from it, audience members bring a bevy of beliefs about the world to any narrative, and we now have good evidence that those beliefs serve as effective filters. How you interpret the narratives that you encounter in the media depends quite a lot on what you already believe to be true.

Yale legal scholar Dan Kahan and colleagues argue that these beliefs stem from something they call "cultural cognitions," which they define as "the tendency of individuals to fit their perceptions of risk and related factual beliefs to their shared moral evaluations of putatively dangerous activities" (Kahan, Jenkins-Smith, and Braman 2011: 148). We spend a lifetime building understandings of our world, and some of those beliefs become very robust. One person may embrace fundamental religious tenets, another a liberal political philosophy, and yet another a world view that sees Homo sapiens as sharing – not dominating – the Earth. In all cases, novel information will be filtered through these belief screens in a way that aligns the message with those values (Dunwoody 2007).

It is this process that explains the wildly divergent reactions of conservatives and liberals to climate change information in the United States where, in a 2011 survey, majorities of Democrats (78%), Independents (71%), and even Republicans (53%) indicated they believe global warming is happening compared to only 34 percent of Tea Party members, a radically conservative subgroup (Leiserowitz et al. 2011a). Certainly, ideologically diverse audiences now have access to ideologically diverse media channels and sources, so conservatives, for example, can limit their exposure to climate change information to that provided by conservative outlets such as Fox News. But scholars note that our processing of messages is so closely tied to our beliefs that, even when our preferred channels go "rogue" and present us with more balanced information (as Fox often does in its news programs), we will perceive the story as supporting our beliefs (Baum and Gussin 2007). Some scholars suggest that these filters are so deeply rooted as to be even more fundamental than political ideology. Feinberg and Willer (2011), for example, have gathered experimental evidence that people's basic psychological assumptions about whether the world is a just and stable place or, conversely, whether it is a venal, unpredictable one can influence their reaction to messages; those on the "just and stable" side in the study responded to information about the potentially dire consequences of global warming with increased skepticism about whether climate change is actually taking place (perhaps viewing the apocalyptic information as a threat to their values), while those with a more critical view of the world's social structure found the possibility of a global warming calamity to be entirely plausible.

Journalists are not necessarily trying to persuade, but they do hope that their messages will be ingested and interpreted in ways consonant with the meanings that they embed in those narratives. Thus ethical coverage of an issue such as climate change must be cognizant of audience filtering systems. A small number of strategies exist that try to work around these filters by addressing them directly. For example, Rowan (1999) recommends something called a "transformative explanation," which first acknowledges the logic of a person's existing belief but then, before proposing a new one more consonant with the evidence at hand, demonstrates through examples that the original belief is flawed.

Another strategy, note Zhao et al. (2011), is to emphasize the science of climate change more than its political dimensions. Stories that focus on the politics of the issue are much more likely to emphasize controversy, and audiences respond to the presence of controversy with either bewilderment or by defaulting to their filters. It appears that readers or viewers are more likely to acknowledge the validity of scientific evidence and thus may be more likely to "believe" messages that include descriptions of scientific processes and findings.

The Challenge of Addressing Truth Claims

When scientists disagree about what's true, a journalist's ethical responsibility, we argue, does not stop at accurately capturing a subset of opinions on the matter (an act referred to by many as "objectivity" and/or "balance") but, rather, should include sharing with audiences where the weight of evidence lies along that continuum of truth claims. That is, the reporter needs to go beyond description in order to grapple with analysis. This requires at least a minimal familiarity with norms of evidence, as well as an ability to capture the spread of opinions across communities of expertise.

While all this may sound obvious to some readers, it is difficult for journalists to accomplish. Norms in some countries encourage journalists to engage in active analysis of what they see and hear, but in others, norms limit reporters in ways that, while facilitating reporters' ability to work with sources and editors, can harm the quality and usefulness of resulting stories. In this section, we tackle this issue first by identifying a couple of the normative challenges with which journalists cope, secondly by briefly describing the kinds of interpretive damage these norms can wreak on narratives, and finally by suggesting a strategy for dealing with the problem, something we call "weight-of-evidence" reporting.

Normative challenges

One of journalism's biggest problems is that it cannot easily declare what's true, especially when truth is contested. Although tasked with ferreting out "truth," journalists are often prevented from doing so by an array of factors. For one thing, journalistic work proceeds at a pace that subverts the typical journalist's efforts to learn enough about any one topic to be able to distinguish among truth claims. For another, truth itself is a murky phenomenon that can morph over time. Finally, audiences in many cultures assign a clear but limited role to their reporters: that of transmitter. If journalists appear to be stepping out of that role to judge the claims of a source, they will often be castigated, not just by audiences but also by editors and peers.

Two norms have provided journalists with ways to override this truth-telling conundrum: objectivity and balance. These two terms come bearing a variety of meanings. Scholars of journalism account for a number of those definitions, many far more expansive than the ones we employ in this chapter (see, eg, Mindich 2000, Ward 2005, Maras 2012). Here, we hew to a set of understandings that have emerged from our ongoing interactions with science and environmental journalists. In that practical domain, we have found, objectivity demands that, if you cannot declare some truth claims to be more valid than others, then you can at least capture those claims accurately. This emphasis on careful replication of a source's meaning engages both reporter and source in a consideration of the goodness of fit between source message and journalistic rendition. That evaluation is a worthy process, as a poor fit is synonymous with sloppy journalism. But a focus on accuracy leaves validity – whether what the source said was actually true – unexplored.

Scientists aid and abet an emphasis on objectivity by conflating accuracy with truth-telling. The scientific community typically ranks accuracy as its highest priority when evaluating science stories, but it is important to remember that the operationalization of "accuracy" in almost all instances is a judgment about the degree of alignment between the scientist's message and the way in which the journalist represents that message in a story (Dunwoody 1982).

Balance, although related to objectivity, focuses on capturing some representation of the array of competing truth claims. It demands: If you cannot declare some truth claims to be more valid than others, then at the very least reproduce the array of possible claims in your story. The goal of such a narrative is to allow readers/viewers to detect the variance and to explore for themselves the possibility that one or more claims are "more right" than others. Put another way, journalists are saying to their readers: "The truth is in here somewhere" but leaves the challenge of determining what's true up to the reader or viewer.

One common criticism of this practice-centered notion of balance is that it encourages journalists to opt for voices at the extreme ends of the truth continuum. That is, a global warming story may contain someone who declares the data to be inconclusive and the problem to be a nonstarter for the country, as well as someone else who argues that the evidence is clear and the problem both serious and imminent. Theoretically, one way to illustrate the spread of viewpoints on an issue is, indeed, to capture the views sitting in the two tails of the distribution. But while that variance may be a meaning intended by the reporter, the audience could interpret the narrative much more simply: that there are two legitimate positions on climate change, one intensely skeptical and the other intensely supportive of the phenomenon.

Both objectivity and balance make sense as surrogates for truth-telling, and they have the benefit of keeping relationships between reporter and sources amiable, as, again, the emphasis is on maximizing the goodness of fit between what sources say and what journalists present in their narratives. But both norms also have significant downsides for the audience.

One downside is that an objective story can be a false one. Some years ago, when a self-described geologist predicted a 50–50 chance of a severe earthquake with an epicenter at New Madrid, MO, journalists rushed to publicize the information. Although no earthquake occurred – a result that actual geologists had predicted – thousands of folks emptied grocery store shelves and left home in anticipation of the disaster. Journalists may have accurately captured the predictions of the so-called geologist, but those predictions were not true.

A balanced story can lead audiences to an equally erroneous conclusion. Confronted with a narrative that, by giving equal space to an array of truth claims seems to declare them all to be legitimate, audience members are likely to conclude that no single viewpoint has a lock on the truth (Corbett and Durfee 2004). For many issues – climate change among them – this conclusion is wrong.

Another downside of balance is that different types of evidence can be arrayed in ways that make them seem comparable to audiences when, in fact, they are not. For example, in recent court cases pitting intelligent design advocates against evolutionary biologists and school teachers over whether religious beliefs belong in science classrooms, the balanced coverage of local media may have encouraged audiences to believe that there really was a "scientific" controversy over the validity of evolutionary theory (Rosenhouse and Branch 2006). Nothing could be further from the truth, of course; these cases embroil their participants in ideological – not scientific – disagreements.

Climate change coverage in American mass media has foundered on the two norms of objectivity and balance for many years (Boykoff and Boykoff 2007), although recent stories increasingly assume, consonant with the IPCC reports, that climate disruption is real and that humans are contributing to the warming process. Given the ubiquity of media coverage that portrays a variety of climate change viewpoints as potentially legitimate, however, it should come as no surprise that, at a time when scientists are nearly unanimous in their agreement that warming is underway with a strong human footprint attached to it, Americans still feel that scientists are divided on the issue (Leiserowitz et al. 2011b).

Weight-of-evidence reporting

Holding journalists responsible for adjudicating truth claims is unrealistic, for a host of reasons articulated earlier in this chapter. We propose, instead, a "weight-of-evidence" approach in which society would hold journalists ethically responsible for sharing with audiences not just the variance in truth claims on an issue but – importantly – where the experts fall along that continuum of claims. Put another way, a weight-of-evidence approach would make it clear that there is disagreement about what's true with respect to global warming but then would share with the audience where the experts place themselves in that contested space.

Some scientists object to including the voices of scientific mavericks in stories, arguing that minority points of view are unlikely to be proven correct and that their inclusion would only sow confusion among readers/ viewers. But we think there are good reasons to retain these voices. Differing voices are out there, and audiences need to be aware that what the scientific majority defines as "true" is indeed contested, however marginally. At a more pragmatic level, though, when audiences perceive an issue to be controversial – whether or not that characterization is warranted – the presence of only a single truth claim in a story presents a credibility problem. Readers/viewers expect to see an array of viewpoints, and the presence of only one – even if it is the most likely one – will make them suspicious of the motives of the reporter.

Still, determining how experts array themselves in contested space is not always easy. Specialty reporters tend to have a head start, as they have committed years to working in the area and thus can more quickly determine possible variance in expert opinion. But general reporters or those who parachute into an issue are at a disadvantage. Years of experience on the beat is likely an important predictor of useful weight-of-evidence narratives, as it is of quality journalism generally.

But even good weight-of-evidence stories can leave reporters open to charges of bias. While journalists are not making truth claims themselves, the reporter is often making it clear to readers/viewers that some truth claims are being judged as less valid than others. Sources who find themselves so "demeaned" may fight back. For example, an international controversy about whether silicone breast implants can cause health problems in women pitted scientists and interest groups against one another for years in the 1980s and 1990s. Legal claims multiplied and the maker of the implants, Dow Chemical, was driven to bankruptcy by the episode. As systematic evidence became available, *New York Times* science reporter Gina Kolata wrote a number of front-page, weight-of-evidence stories indicating that the studies could find no link between the implants and the health claims made by those who believed they had been harmed by the implants. Kolata was criticized by interest groups and even by other journalists, who accused her of being an "apologist for corporate science" (Dowie 1998: 18).

Managing the Tension Between Global and Local

Climate change is a global phenomenon that requires a global policy response. It is the paradigmatic example of an issue that affects people all over the world (Brossard, Shanahan, and McComas 2004) because it influences the "transnational commons," that is, resources that are shared by people around the world and are not controlled by any single government (Hannerz 1996). Climate change crosses borders, which contributes to making it what Eide and Kunelius call "a historically unforeseen challenge to global governance and regulation" (Eide and Kunelius 2010: 12). These scholars argue that, despite widespread concern over a variety of global problems, the world has, thus far, faced few issues requiring a globally negotiated response and that climate change is a serious contender for precisely such status (Eide and Kunelius 2010).

The inherently global nature of climate change puts it in conflict with journalism, which naturally emphasizes the local. Localization in journalism is often played out as a focus on how global issues influence the local, or an effort to frame global issues as being affected by a national history and politics (Eide and Kunelius 2010). Sociologists of news production (Gans 1979, Tuchman 1978) found long ago that couching news in familiar narratives makes the information more palatable to audiences. As far back as 1979, Herbert Gans wrote that foreign reporters focus on issues relevant to American interests and present these issues using themes common in domestic coverage (Gans 1979). If anything, recent trends in journalism, for instance a growing focus on the hyperlocal as an attempt by American media to find a sustainable business model in the face of an erosion of money in journalism, have exacerbated the pattern of localization by adopting as narrow a focus as possible, generally on a particular geographic area (Kurpius, Metzgar, and Rowley 2010). This trend is pushed by grant-making agencies, many of which see hyperlocal journalism as the cure to journalism's financial woes (Metzgar, Kurpius, and Rowley 2011).

Some scholars argue that the global risk from processes such as climate change is so large that people need to reach across borders and accept the notion of planetary threat, and that acceptance can lead to the creation of a set of common values that, in turn, can give rise to political action (Beck 2005). The world is becoming increasingly globalized, and this globalizing tendency is increasingly mediated through communication flows. Because of journalists' profound influence on these flows, some scholars of international media argue that journalists have a responsibility to present issues such as climate change along with their global contexts, making it clear that people the world over are in this fix together. This idea comes from the tradition of global journalism, which is a type of journalism that attempts to explain how issues around the world are intertwined (Ward 2010) and how the economic, political, social, and ecological overlap (Berglez 2008). This kind of journalism best lends itself to news coverage that is increasingly "deterritorialized" (Berglez 2008: 845), that is, based on complex flows of information across borders. People who advocate this view of journalism believe it can build a more inclusive world. "Journalism at its best contributes to social transparency, which is at the heart of the globalization optimists' hopes for democracy" (Reese 2010: 345).

Certainly, emphasizing the relevance of the global to the local is a key part of doing good journalism; a disaffected journalism that appears to pertain only to a distant demographic or to a deterritorialized audience is disengaging. Journalists must instead strive for a middle ground, a way to present issues as having global causes and solutions while making clear how they affect the local.

> Media maintain both global and culturally specific orientations – such as by casting far-away events in frameworks that render these events comprehensible, appealing and relevant to domestic audiences; and second, by constructing the meanings of these events in ways that are compatible with the culture and the dominant ideology of societies they serve. (Gurevitch, Levy, and Roeh 1991: 206)

In this way a responsible, locally focused story privileges neither the local nor the global at the expense of all else; instead, it uses the local to introduce, explain the importance of, contextualize, and explain a global issue or trend.

An analysis of the reporting on the 2009 United Nations Climate Change Conference, held in Copenhagen in November of that year, can help shed light on how the local can either complement or hinder the global in climate change reporting. The conference was particularly interesting given the urgency of the rhetoric that surrounded it and the fact that the meeting ultimately failed to forge a global policy response to our changing climate. A study of climate change reporting on two television networks in each of Canada and the United States (Konieczna et al. 2011) found two very different attitudes toward the global nature of climate change. Contrary to past findings (Wittebols 1996, Spears, Seydegart, and Zulinov 2010), Canadian reporting was found to be much more locally focused than US reporting. This means that the Canadian programs used more local sources and that they used more "local framing," while US programs used a larger number of global sources, as well as more global framing, even in situations in which sources were largely from the United States.

In this study, "global framing" was characterized as a focus on how issues around the world are intertwined (Ward 2010) and as an effort to employ a global outlook to demonstrate how economic, political, social, and ecological issues around the world overlap. Globally framed stories may be laden with the notion that "each human being has equal moral worth and that equal moral worth generates certain moral responsibilities that have universal scope" (Brock and Brighouse 2005: 4).

"Local framing" was used to mean reporting grounded in a national outlook (Berglez 2008). It was identified as being present in stories that focused on issues from a culturally bound point of view (Ruigrok and van Atteveldt 2007), that is, from within the country featured in the coverage.

An example or two will help illustrate this point. A Canadian story about Amazon deforestation, for instance, did not mention that the destruction causes global problems or that slowing it would contribute to a global solution to climate change (Konieczna et al. 2011: 16). This is an example of a situation in which a journalist missed the opportunity to provide global framing, even though it made sense for the story. In contrast, an American story about a debate between politicians Sarah Palin and Al Gore – an obviously domestic story – was framed globally in the reporter's introduction: "Former Governor Palin's op-ed is just one more example of how politics at home will impact what the United States can accomplish here in Copenhagen" (Konieczna et al. 2011: 19). This is an example of how a naturally domestic story was globally framed by American television journalists.

Both of these examples come from extremes: the localization of a truly global story, and the overglobalization of a largely local story. Instead, a responsible global climate journalism runs down the middle, localizing where possible but never failing to tie to global causes and solutions when appropriate.

Conclusion

In an article proposing philosophical foundations for an ethics of global journalism, Ward laid out three foundational principles: (1) Journalists have a responsibility to provide credible news and analysis; (2) Journalists must make sure that the provision of such news and analysis serves public needs and does no harm to audiences; and (3) The audience for journalistic work is all of humanity, not just an interested or potently powerful subset (Ward 2009).

We believe the arguments presented in this chapter are consonant with those principles. High quality coverage of climate change will take as its mission the challenge of informing the broadest possible audience; will approach truth claims analytically, not just descriptively; and will draft narratives that allow audiences to understand impacts at both local and global levels. More specifically, we are led to recommend the following approaches.

Care deeply about reaching not just the science-committed audience but also the audience member who is neither interested in nor alarmed by the possible repercussions of climate change. We acknowledge that some beliefs are so robust as to be impermeable to counter-information, so there are some audience segments that will be unreachable. But studies of public perceptions and understanding of global warming suggest that great swaths of the audience know little about the topic. These individuals can be reached by skilled storytelling that emphasizes explanation and by ongoing coverage that, by its presence alone, reinforces for audiences the salience of the issue.

Emphasize the science of climate change even in stories dominated by policy concerns. Our analysis of the Copenhagen conference stories unearthed a pattern quite common to journalistic work: the tendency to categorize information in ways that encourage inclusion of some details in stories to the exclusion of others. The Copenhagen meeting sought to forge global policies to limit human emissions, and journalists covered the conference faithfully in that topical way. Their stories focused almost exclusively on policy matters, recording the behaviors of countries at the meeting, tracking the comings and goings of president and premiers, and monitoring the activities of protesters. The science of climate change was missing in action. Zhao and colleagues (2011) found that attention to science/environmental information was strongly positively related to individuals' perceptions that global warming is happening through human agency, while attention to political news was negatively related to those beliefs. This suggests that stories focusing exclusively on the political aspects of climate change may increase public skepticism while those that include information about the science may be less likely to do so. Stories about the important policy aspects of this issue would benefit from inclusion of science information. One interesting addition to global warming policy stories would be information about the science of decision making itself. Researchers can now speak to a variety of interesting and sometimes counterintuitive patterns that might help readers/viewers better understand the difficulties of establishing climate change policies at a global level.

Explanation of concepts and processes in stories will be critical to public understanding of climate change. As we noted above, most people know little about the issue, and they will rely on journalistic products, among other avenues, to learn. Journalists do include explanation in their narratives, but they (as is the case for most writers) do not attend carefully to the strengths and weaknesses of various explanatory strategies. As a result, explanatory efforts often fail for a variety of reasons. Sterman (2011) notes that the "mental models" of climate change processes already held by audience members are simplistic and often wrong, and he encourages communicators to think creatively about ways of explaining complex systems. Such strategies might include carefully chosen images, attention to story frames, ways to offer comparisons, and – quite possible in new communication channels – interactive representations of climate change information. Journalists are fond of insisting that their goal is to inform, not to educate. But if the goal of ethically responsible journalism is to help audiences understand *enough* about a complex issue to develop stable opinions and guides to action, then journalists must opt into explanatory strategies that work.

Supplement journalistic definitions of "news" to include long-running, thematic coverage. Central to much of journalism is the importance of monitoring the environment (broadly speaking) in order to respond, in real time, when things happen. Journalistic beats are themselves predicated on that episodic expectation; media organizations station journalists where events and decisions are likely to occur. But the tendency of audiences to use media messages as arbiters of what is important suggests that long-running issues that deserve to remain "front of mind" should be treated more thematically. Those issues might themselves be turned into beats, for example, with journalists assigned to probe the nooks and crannies of ongoing processes in search of information that furthers public and policy deliberations. Well-heeled media organizations already do this when, for example, they assign individual reporters to cover a presidential candidate for the duration of his or her campaign; editors expect coverage of stump speeches and other events but also invite more analytic efforts, all in service to keeping an important issue on the public agenda. It may be time to consider this strategy on behalf of a larger group of issues.

Respect skepticism, but use a weight-of-evidence approach to represent divergent points of view on climate change. It is important for journalists to share with their readers/viewers the existence of divergent truth claims.

But it is just as important for those stories to help audience members select among the claims. Failure to provide this kind of assistance is a recipe for audience misunderstanding of the issue, something that is clearly not in a journalist's best interests. The best way to help audiences, we think, is to indicate how experts aggregate along the truth continuum. The reporter can make clear that this part of the narrative is informational, not prescriptive, and readers/viewers have the freedom to use that information as they please.

Strike an appropriate balance between a local and a global focus. As stated above, the strong local focus of much of the reporting on the Copenhagen climate change conference is inappropriate in that it could make it difficult for audience members to understand the global nature of the problem. At the same time, an overly global focus can make issues and problems seem distant. Using a local focus to lead the reader into a story and to lend currency, and then following with an explanation that focuses on global impacts, may strike an appropriate balance.

Despite growing pessimism among scientists and policy analysts about the likelihood that humans can change their policies and behaviors quickly enough and on a large enough scale to slow warming and the disruptions that it is already causing, many peoples of the world are indeed alarmed about climate change and seeking ways to intervene. Some countries – the United States is a particular case in point – are reluctant participants and, because of their global dominance, are stalling efforts to both reduce emissions and – perversely – adapt to changes. It is not the job of journalism to persuade us to care about global warming, but it is the ethical responsibility of journalism *to give us the option of caring* by keeping the issue on the public agenda, by helping us learn about what is going wrong and how to fix it, and by never letting us forget that we global residents are in this together.

Further Reading

The Yale Project on Climate Change Communication (http://environment.yale.edu /climate/) provides the most regularly updated effort to track public perceptions of climate change, albeit among American adults. Yale scholar Anthony Leiserowitz has also produced a useful cross-cultural look at public opinion in "International Public Opinion on Climate Change" in collaboration with Gallup World Poll (http://environment.yale.edu/climate/research/literacy-on-climate-change-/). Readers looking for further analysis of how journalists constructed the Copenhagen and Bali climate change summits could start with Eide and Kunelius (2010).

Those interested in the question of whether it makes sense to expect a worldwide journalistic ethics can turn to Ward's *Global Journalism Ethics*. (2010), Additionally, Berglez (2008) offers a definition and historical context for the concept of global journalism, and Gurevitch, Levy and Roeh (1991), as well as Reese (2010), connect the concept to the issue of globalization.

References

Baum, M. A. and Gussin, P. 2007. "In the Eye of the Beholder: How Information Shortcuts Shape Individual Perceptions of Bias in the Media." *Quarterly Journal of Political Science* 3: 1–31.

Beck, U. 2005. *Power in the Global Age: A New Global Political Economy.* Malden, MA: Polity.

Berger, C. R. 1986. "Uncertain Outcome Values in Predicted Relationships: Uncertainty Reduction Theory Then and Now." *Human Communication Research* 13(1): 34–8.

Berger, C. R. and Calabrese, R. J. 1975. "Some Exploration in Initial Interaction and Beyond: Toward a Developmental Theory of Communication." *Human Communication Research* 1: 99–112.

Berglez, P. 2008. "What is Global Journalism? Theoretical and Empirical Conceptualizations." *Journalism Studies* 9(6): 845–58.

Borick, C., Lachapelle, É., and Rabe, B. 2011. *Climate Compared: Public Opinion on Climate Change in the United States & Canada.* Key Findings Report. National Survey of American Public Opinion on Climate Change and Public Policy Forum–Sustainable Prosperity Survey of Canadian Public Opinion on Climate Change. Ann Arbor: University of Michigan.

Bostrom, A., Morgan, M. G., Fischhoff, B., and Read, D. 1994. "What Do People Know About Global Climate Change? 1. Mental Models." *Risk Analysis* 14(6): 959–70.

Boykoff, M. T. and Boykoff, J. M. 2007. "Climate Change and Journalistic Norms: A Case-Study of US Mass-Media Coverage." *Geoforum* 38: 1190–1204.

Brock, G. and Brighouse, H. Eds. 2005. *The Political Philosophy of Cosmopolitanism.* Cambridge: Cambridge University Press.

Brossard, D., Shanahan J., and McComas, K. 2004. "Are Issue-Cycles Culturally Constructed? A Comparison of French and American Coverage of Global Climate Change." *Mass Communication and Society* 7(3): 359–77.

Budescu, D. V., Broomell, S., and Por, H. 2009. "Improving Communication of Uncertainty in the Reports of the Intergovernmental Panel on Climate Change." *Psychological Science* 20(3): 299–308.

Corbett, J. B. and Durfee, J. L. 2004. "Testing Public (Un)Certainty of Science: Media Representations of Global Warming." *Science Communication* 26(2): 129–51.

Dowie, M. 1998. "What's Wrong with the *New York Times's* Science Reporting?" *The Nation,* July 6.

Dunlap, R. E. and McCright, A. M. 2008. "A Widening Gap: Republication and Democratic Views on Climate Change." *Environment* 50(5): 27–35.

Dunwoody, S. 1982. "A Question of Accuracy." *IEEE Transactions on Professional Communication* PC-25(4): 196–9.

Dunwoody, S. 2007. "The Challenge of Trying to Make a Difference Using Media Messages." In S. Moser and L. Dilling, eds., *Creating a Climate for Change.* Cambridge, MA: Cambridge University Press, 89–104.

Eide, E. and Kunelius, R. 2010. "Domesticating Global Moments: A Transnational Study on the Coverage of the Bali and Copenhagen Climate Summits."

In E. Eide, R. Kunelius, and V. Kumpu, eds., *Global Climate, Local Journalisms: A Transnational Study of How Media Make Sense of Climate Summits*. Freiburg, Germany: Projektverlag, 11–50.

Farnsworth, S. J. and Lichter, S. R. 2012. "The Structure of Scientific Opinion on Climate Change." *International Journal of Public Opinion Research* 24(1): 93–103.

Feinberg, M. and Willer, R. 2011. "Apocalypse Soon? Dire Messages Reduce Belief in Global Warming by Contradicting Just-World Beliefs." *Psychological Science* 22(1): 34–8.

Gans, H. J. 1979. *Deciding What's News: A Study of CBS Evening News, NBC Nightly News, Newsweek, and Time*. New York: Random House.

Gigerenzer, G. and Todd, P. M. 1999. *Simple Heuristics That Make Us Smart*. New York: Oxford University Press.

Gurevitch, M., Levy, M. R., and Roeh, I. 1991. "The Global Newsroom: Convergences and Diversities in the Globalization of Television News." In P. Dahlgren and C. Sparks, eds., *Communication and Citizenship: Journalism and the Public Sphere*. London: Routledge, 195–216.

Hannerz, U. 1996. *Transnational Connections: Culture, People, Places*. London: Routledge.

Heazle, M. 2010. *Uncertainty in Policy Making: Values and Evidence in Complex Decisions*. London: Routledge.

IPCC. 2007. *Climate Change 2007: Synthesis Report*. Fourth Assessment Report of the Intergovernmental Panel on Climate Change. Geneva, Switzerland: Intergovernmental Panel on Climate Change. http://www.ipcc.ch /publications_and_data/publications_ipcc_fourth_assessment_report _synthesis_report.htm.

Kahan, D. M., Jenkins-Smith, H., and Braman, D. 2011. "Cultural Cognition of Scientific Consensus." *Journal of Risk Research* 14(2): 147–74.

Konieczna, M., Mattis, K., Liang X., Tsai, J., and Dunwoody, S. 2011. "Global Public Sphere in Decision-Making Moments: An Examination of Canadian and American Television Coverage of the 2009 United Nations Framework Convention on Climate Change in Copenhagen." Presentation, Annual Convention of the Midwest Association for Public Opinion Research, Chicago, IL, November 18–20, http://www.mapor.org/2011_papers/4b2Konieczna.pdf, accessed September 6, 2012.

Kurpius, D., Metzgar, E. T., and Rowley, K. 2010. "Sustaining Hyperlocal Media: In Search of Funding Models." *Journalism Studies* 11(3): 359–76.

Leiserowitz, A. 2006. "Climate Change Risk Perception and Policy Preferences: The Role of Affect, Imagery, and Values." *Climatic Change* 77: 45–72.

Leiserowitz, A., Maibach E., Roser-Renouf, C., and Hmielowski, J. D. 2011a. *Politics and Global Warming: Democrats, Republicans, Independents, and the Tea Party*. Yale Project on Climate Change Communication. New Haven, CT: Yale University and George Mason University. http://environment .yale.edu/climate/files/PoliticsGlobalWarming2011.pdf, accessed March 2, 2012.

Leiserowitz, A., Maibach, E., Roser-Renouf, C., and Smith, N. 2011b. *Climate Change in the American Mind: Americans' Global Warming Beliefs and Attitudes in May 2011*. Yale Project on Climate Change Communication.

New Haven, CT: Yale University and George Mason University. http://environment.yale.edu/climate/files/ClimateBeliefsMay2011.pdf, accessed March 2, 2012.

Leiserowitz, A. and Smith, N. 2011. *Knowledge of Climate Change Across Global Warming's Six Americas*. Yale Project on Climate Change Communication. New Haven, CT: Yale University. http://environment.yale.edu/climate/files/Knowledge_Across_Six_Americas.pdf, accessed March 2, 2012.

Maras, S. 2012. *Objectivity in Journalism*. Cambridge: Polity.

Metzgar, E. T., Kurpius, D. D., and Rowley, K. M. 2011. "Defining Hyperlocal Media: Proposing a Framework for Discussion." *New Media and Society* 13(5): 772–87.

Mindich, D. T. Z. 2000. *Just the Facts: How "Objectivity" Came to Define American Journalism*. New York: NYU Press.

Morgan, M. G., Dowlatabadi, H., Henrion M., Keith, D., Lempert, R., McBride, S., Small, M., and Wilbanks, T. 2009. *Best Practice Approaches for Characterizing, Communicating, and Incorporating Scientific Uncertainty in Climate Decision Making*. Washington, DC: Climate Change Science Program and the Subcommittee on Global Change Research. National Oceanic and Atmospheric Administration.

Powell, M., Dunwoody, S., Griffin, R., and Neuwirth, K. 2007. "Exploring Lay Uncertainty About an Environmental Health Risk." *Public Understanding of Science* 16: 323–43.

Reese, S. D. 2010. "Journalism and Globalization." *Sociology Compass* 4(6): 344–53.

Rosen, J. 2006. "The People Formerly Known as the Audience." *PressThink*. http://archive.pressthink.org/2006/06/27/ppl_frmr.html.

Rosenhouse, J. and Branch, G. 2006. "Media Coverage of 'Intelligent Design'." *Bioscience* 56(3): 247–52.

Rowan, K. E. 1999. "Effective Explanation of Complex and Uncertain Science." In . M. Friedman, S. Dunwoody, and C. L. Rogers, eds., *Communicating Uncertainty: Media Coverage of New and Controversial Science*. Mahwah, NJ: Lawrence Erlbaum, 202–23.

Ruigrok, N. and van Atteveldt, W. 2007. "Global Angling with a Local Angle: How U.S., British, and Dutch Newspapers Frame Global and Local Terrorist Attacks." *The International Journal of Press/Politics* 12(1): 68–90.

Spears, G., Seydegart, K., and Zulinov, P. 2010. "The News Balance Report." Erin Research Inc. http://www.cbc.ca/news/pdf/news-balance-eng-oct1b.pdf.

Sterman, J. D. 2011. "Communicating Climate Change Risks in a Skeptical World." *Climatic Change* 108: 811–26.

Tuchman, G. 1978. *Making News*. New York: Free Press.

Ward, S. J. A. 2005. *The Invention of Journalism Ethics: The Path to Objectivity and Beyond*. Montreal: McGill-Queen's University Press.

Ward, S. J. A. 2009. "Philosophical Foundations for Global Journalism Ethics." *Journal of Mass Media Ethics* 20(1): 3–21.

Ward, S. J. A. 2010. *Global Journalism Ethics*. Montreal: McGill-Queen's University Press.

Weinstein, N. D. 1980. "Unrealistic Optimism About Future Life Events." *Journal of Personality and Social Psychology* 39(5): 806–20.

Weinstein, N. D. 1989. "Optimistic Biases About Personal Risks." *Science* 246: 1232–3.

Wittebols, J. H. 1996. "News from the Noninstitutional World: U.S. and Canadian Television News Coverage of Social Protest." *Political Communication* 13: 345–61.

Zhao, X., Leiserowitz, A. A., Maibach, E. M., and Roser-Renouf, C. 2011. "Attention to Science/Environment News Positively Predicts and Attention to Political News Negatively Predicts Global Warming Risk Perceptions and Policy Support." *Journal of Communication* 61(4): 713–31.

10

Ethics of Global Disaster Reporting

Journalistic Witnessing and Objectivity

Karin Wahl-Jorgensen and Mervi Pantti

It is through the media that most of us encounter disasters and bear witness to suffering around the world. In recent years we have witnessed a series of large-scale disasters, including the Indian Ocean tsunami in 2004, Hurricane Katrina in 2005, the cyclone in Burma and the Sichuan earthquake in China in 2008, followed by devastating earthquakes in Haiti in 2010 and Japan in 2011, and the tsunami and nuclear meltdown at Fukushima. All have caused unforeseen loss of human life, intense social disruption, and economic damage. The total number of natural disasters over the last two decades has quadrupled and during the same period more people have become affected by them (Oxfam International 2007). When mediated, disasters have the capacity to mobilize solidarities both within and beyond national borders. Media reports play a crucial role because they can position us as a global moral community and signal normative emotional and ethical responses on the part of both journalists and audiences.

In a globalized world, disasters and crises have also become more mobile, crossing geographical boundaries and reverberating around the world. The witnessing of journalists is centrally connected to media technology: "being there" as eyewitnesses gives journalists the authority to tell their stories (Zelizer 1998, 2007). Such acts of bearing witness have taken on new forms and channels as communication technologies, including mobile telephony, the Internet, and social media, have entered the daily communications mix and both interpenetrate with mainstream media and provide overlapping and alternative communication channels. Relating to these developments, new questions have arisen about the role of social media and citizen participation in circulating and constructing meanings of disasters and defining public knowledge, emotion, and action in global, national, and local contexts. For example, the Asian tsunami in

Global Media Ethics: Problems and Perspectives, First Edition. Edited by Stephen J. A. Ward.
© 2013 Blackwell Publishing Ltd. Published 2013 by Blackwell Publishing Ltd.

2004 showed how "ordinary people" may have an increasingly important role to play in disaster coverage by providing immediate information and dramatic eyewitness images and accounts. The exponential increase in mobile telephony around the world in recent years played a key part in the relief efforts following the Haiti earthquake in 2010, alerting rescuers to the location of buried victims and communicating disaster relief services and raising money for relief efforts from donors around the world.

Crises, including natural disasters, war, political conflicts, provide useful lenses for investigating journalistic routines and practices (Allan and Zelizer 2004). This chapter explores some of the complexities of the ethical implications of changing practices of disaster reporting in a world where disasters are not only becoming more frequent but also more prominent in signaling processes of globalization. As Beck (2000: 15) argues:

> The underlying basis here is an understanding that the central human worries are "world" problems, and not only because in their origins and consequences they have outgrown the national schema of politics. They are also "world" problems in their very concreteness, in their very location here and now in this town, or this political organization.

Global problems require global solutions, and journalistic practices play a crucial role in both enabling and limiting particular outcomes. Here, questions of ethics are central. Ethics pertains to the "analysis, evaluation and promotion of what constitutes correct conduct and virtuous character in light of the best available principles" and in the context of a consideration of journalism's public roles and responsibilities (Ward 2008: 139, Ward 2009: 295–6). The field of journalism ethics, which examines the obligations surrounding the behavior and practices of journalists and journalism, is a dynamic and ever-changing field that is particularly challenged by the advent of globalization. This is illustrated strikingly in disaster reporting, where, as we will argue, despite the continued importance of the nation-state as the central interpretive framework, globalization and new technologies have opened up for new models and understandings of the role of journalists.

With respect to disaster reporting, debates on journalism ethics have historically focused on issues such as how to avoid "bad" journalistic behavior, particularly in relation to the invasion of the privacy of victims (e.g., Ewart 2003), and the representation of graphic images of death and suffering (e.g., Sanders 2003: 104, Ward 2009: 297). It has tended to examine cases where individual journalists and news organizations have violated codes of ethics and set aside concern for victims and families in their pursuit of sensational stories (Sanders 2003: 96) or, on the other hand, to provide guidance for journalists setting out to report on disaster and trauma. For example, the Dart Center for Conflict and Trauma has issued guidelines for journalists covering tragedy, and instructs, among other things, as follows:

> Avoid unneeded gory details about the victims' deaths. After the Oklahoma City bombing, certain reporters chose not to reveal that body parts were dangling from the trees near the federal building. Ask yourself whether the images are pertinent or will do unnecessary harm to certain members of your readership or broadcast audience. (Dart Center 2003: 3)

Such debates highlight the very real and high-stakes situations that journalists face in covering disaster and tragedy, and dramatize the tension between the ethical principle of avoiding harm and the commercial imperative that drives news operation.

Moving beyond these conventional areas of debates there is a relatively new and fertile area of research on disaster reporting which, although it only rarely explicitly discusses ethics (e.g., Chouliaraki and Orgad 2011, Tester 2001), is centrally concerned with the moral conduct of journalists and how it impinges on audience reactions. This research takes as its vantage point the context of globalization in examining the reporting of disasters around the world. It focuses on the role of compassion in disaster reporting which represents the suffering of distant others (e.g., Boltanski 1999, Chouliaraki 2006). The role of disaster reporting in engendering compassion and, relatedly, a cosmopolitan sensibility, turns on a particular understanding of journalistic practice. This is one which sees the journalist as actively involved in shaping and constructing the meaning of particular events in relation to understandings of the ethical responsibilities of the global community, nations, and individual citizens/audience members. Such an understanding is at odds with the conventional understanding of the detached and "objective" journalist, and signals a concurrent shift in the understanding of the role of emotion in journalistic practice. At the same time, it is strongly tied to and informed by emerging calls for a more cosmopolitan approach to journalism ethics: As Ward (e.g., 2005, 2008) has argued, the globalization of news media requires a radical rethinking of the principles and standards of journalism ethics which has traditionally been quite "parochial" in its approach. He and others have suggested that the adoption of a cosmopolitan attitude enables an enlargement of perspectives and an opening up to understanding the predicament of distant others through the cultivation of compassion.

In this chapter, we wish to focus on emerging ethical questions around the journalistic cultivation of compassion and cosmopolitanism in the context of swift and profound changes wrought by globalization and new media technologies. We suggest that disasters and their reporting have profound ethical implications, not just in terms of understandings of the role of journalists in society and, relatedly, questions of journalistic conduct, but also in terms of how journalists and the texts they produce position audiences in ways that encourage particular modes of thinking and acting in relation to the suffering of distant others. We argue that while the negotiation of objectivity and detachment/engagement in covering stories is central to the everyday ethical labor of journalists, the concept of "bearing witness" to disaster calls these categories into question. We then consider how the forms of compassion that might be cultivated as a result of disaster coverage are not evenly distributed, but rather parceled out according to a geopolitically inflected "calculus of death," where the nation-state and its interests remain at the forefront despite the realities of globalization. Finally, we turn to the question of how new media technologies may be challenging orthodoxies of disaster reporting in opening up new forums for amateur contributions, broadening the global public sphere but also raising difficult ethical questions.

Journalistic Witnessing as Emotional Labor

The role of journalists in bearing witness to suffering is central to the ethical dilemmas of disaster reporting. Journalists' witnessing creates the ethical and sociopolitical conditions under which we respond to distant suffering and global injustices (Kurasawa 2007, Peters 2001). Journalists are engaged in the labor of bearing witness by being present on the scene of suffering (see Allan and Zelizer 2004, Peters 2001). The physical significance of "being there" is no less important in the present-day media landscape that permits technologically facilitated connectivity and proximity. Journalists on the ground in disasters – who experience the suffering and destruction on the behalf of audiences and victims – communicate their knowledge of the event, and at times also the emotional impact it has on them as individuals. Through their personal testimonies, they turn audiences into witnesses as well (cf. Ashuri and Pinchevski 2009).

Yet the issue of what it means to bear witness in an ethical manner is by no means straightforward because it invites questions pertaining to the epistemology of journalism: Does bearing witness mean that journalists tell stories of disastrous events in a detached, impartial, and objective manner to convey the factual "truth"? Or does it entail a commitment to generating an understanding of the suffering which enables audiences to experience, and empathize with, the pain of others? Should journalists foster new moral and emotional bonds with distant others? Should they motivate the public to take action? Should journalists take on the role of moral educators (e.g., Seib 2002, Chouliaraki 2008)?

On the one hand, providing truthful accounts can be seen as an end in itself in journalists' witnessing (Richards 2010). For instance, Leff (2010) argued that "journalists' moral responsibility isn't to elicit a particular reaction or outcome; their responsibility is to bring home the truth." Truth, then, means raw "fact," objectivity, and neutrality. Indeed, such a perspective is compatible with conventional understandings of journalism ethics, underpinned by the ideal of objectivity as a cornerstone of the journalistic profession (e.g., Schudson and Anderson 2009). To observers such as Ward (e.g., 2005, 2008, 2010) questions of journalistic ethics have historically been intrinsically and foundationally tied to the ideal of objectivity, at least as conceived in Western, liberal democratic understandings of the role of the press (cf. also McNair 2011). Along those lines, journalism has been heavily invested in its claims to be a "facts-centered discursive practice" (Chalaby 1998). This conception places at center stage the conventional ideal of the journalist as an impartial and distanced observer whose main aim is to gather information for audiences/citizens, packaged in a garb of neutrality as "news from nowhere" (Epstein 1973). Yet the grounding of journalism ethics in the ideal of objectivity has emerged from a relatively parochial and narrow-minded understanding of the responsibilities of journalism (Ward 2008), and observers are now beginning to call for alternative understandings that take into consideration the consequences of globalization. Such understandings are often described with the label of "global journalism" (e.g., Berglez 2008, Ward 2008) and suggest that new realities – but also new intellectual resources – open up for a reconsideration of practices of objectivity and the cultivation of cosmopolitanism.

Clearly, the established normative ideal that journalists should provide the public with impartial testimony is called into question in the discussion of cosmopolitanism and global compassion. Journalists have an important role in the development of "cosmopolitan empathy" (Beck 2006: 7) in that their testimonies can help to bring a global tragedy home, shape opinion, and contribute to humanitarian action. The ability to imagine distant others' suffering (and the available horizons of moral action) is seen as the basis of global compassion (e.g., Sznaider 1998: 123, Boltanski 2000, Seaton 2005: 265).

The world's neglected humanitarian emergencies have made it clear that the cultivation of cosmopolitan imagination and empathy is not a simple achievement. We have argued elsewhere that it requires the cultivation of both emotional and rational capacities among audiences (Pantti, Wahl-Jorgensen, and Cottle 2012). Hence, journalists' testimonial labor is not only rational but also emotional: It is about knowing and caring (cf. Bell 1998). As such, drawing up a binary distinction between emotional expression and detached objectivity may be a spurious and unhelpful exercise. In recent ethical assessments of disaster coverage, journalists' witnessing of crises have been connected to some degree of emotional engagement. As Howard Tumber and Marina Prentoulis (2003: 227) have observed, there is a general call today for a more "human" reporting that departs from an old style "founded on a 'macho' attitude that prohibited any display of emotion," For instance, Ward (2010), in commenting on the Haitian earthquake coverage, argued that in disaster reporting the emotional and the objective dimensions of journalism should converge into what he calls a "humanistic journalism":

> A journalism of disasters is not a journalism of Olympian detachment. It is not a journalism fixated on stimulating the emotions of audiences. It is a humanistic journalism that combines reason and emotion. Humanistic journalists bring empathy to bear on the victims of tragedy – an empathy informed by facts and critical analysis.

In this view journalists are motivated by their own emotions and *do something* by generating empathy for the victims through their empathetic *and* informed analysis. However, "stimulating the emotions of audiences" arises here as a problem for responsible journalism. Disaster reporting increasingly permits or even requires that stories of disasters move beyond the "bare facts," give voice to the victims, and deploy affective ways of humanizing the suffering to resonate with audiences. Among other things, the Dart Center for Conflict and Trauma guide to coverage of tragedies advises the following:

> Focus on the person's life. Find out what made the person special: personality, beliefs, environment (surroundings, hobbies, family and friends), and likes and dislikes. Treat the person's life as carefully as a photographer does in framing a portrait . . . .
>   Use pertinent details that help describe victims as they lived or provide images of their lives. Example: "Johnny loved to play the guitar in the evening to entertain his family, but it also helped him escape the stress of his job as a sheriff's deputy." . . .
>   Use quotes and anecdotes from the victim's relatives and friends to describe the person's life. Especially those that tell how the person had overcome obstacles. Seek current photos of the victim (but always return them as soon as possible). This way, you know what the person looked like in life. (Dart Center 2003: 6)

Despite the growing emphasis on telling stories of tragedy and disaster that humanize victims and generate compassion among audiences demonstrated in this statement, journalists frequently resist the idea that they should display their *own* emotions or act as "emotional educators" who instruct audiences on how they should feel (Pantti 2010, Pantti et al. 2012). Echoing journalism's traditional normative claim of objectivity and neutrality, the primary role journalists ascribe to themselves is that of the uninvolved witness: The task of a journalist is to "register" emotions of those involved in disasters, not to actively incite or manage public emotions. There is a conundrum in these professional and academic statements: Journalists want audiences to care, while at the same time rejecting the idea that they have set out intentionally and deliberately to do so, as that would imply they have crossed the line of journalistic professionalism and its demarcations of impartiality, detachment, and objectivity. These tensions regarding the hopes to elicit compassionate responses on the one hand, and remaining faithful to industry-based and professional expectations of emotionally detached journalism on the other, are exemplified in the following statement, by a senior journalist who has covered a range of global disasters:

> It's a very fine line. It's a very difficult one to walk, I think. Because on the one hand, you do want to be impartial and I don't want to tell you to feel desperately sorry for those people in Christchurch or for those people that were on the beach in Thailand when the tsunami hit on their honeymoon, or whatever the story is for that family in Eritrea that has had everything decimated. But at the same time, you want people to really care, because, you know, life is not a rehearsal and you should care. While you're complaining because your McDonald's is a bit too hot, there are people dying that could be saved by the £2 you spent on that coffee. (BBC editor/reporter cited in Pantti et al. 2012: 105)

Moreover, while journalists and news organizations see emotion as a legitimate part of disaster narratives – expressed for example in the testimonies of victims and eyewitnesses or embedded in emotionally engaging images and sounds – they tend to share the view that journalists should not bring their own emotional responses into their reporting (Pantti 2010). This raises important ethical questions about what happens when journalists bear witness to their *own* experiences, rather than providing accounts of the suffering they have observed: Could such practices actually contribute to convicting "the conscience of the observer" (Peters 2001: 713)? Do emotional expression and physical signs of emotions (such as the reporter's voice trembling with anger) add to the authenticity of the report and thereby to the moral force of witnessing? The normative distinction between giving a channel to the emotions of people affected by a tragedy on the one hand, and making journalists' own feelings visible on the other is drawn up clearly in BBC correspondent David Loyn's (2003) plea for objective journalism:

> This [objective] approach is not dispassionate. It can be hugely passionate, requiring emotional engagement and human imagination. But it is not about my passion, how I feel. The viewer or listener does not want to know how I feel, but how people feel on the ground.

In recent years, the discussion about a shift toward a more emotional and engaged disaster reporting has intensified. For instance, CNN International's managing director Chris Cramer suggested that the Asian tsunami changed how journalists report the news:

> What has been different about much of the reporting, particularly on TV, has been that the emotional attachment between reporter and victim has been obvious. Gone is the professional, some might say artificial, detachment...

> Now, for the first time, media professionals are starting to tell us how they
> feel about some stories. And it will probably make them better journalists.
> (Cited in Lyall 2005)

It seems that the emotional involvement of the journalist has become
more acceptable, or even expected in certain situations. What has changed
is that new media platforms and forums representing different expressive
styles facilitate professional and nonprofessional journalists' emotional
involvement in their stories. Journalists, then, seem to find increased
cultural license and media opportunity to reflect on their own emotional turmoil and the dilemmas of witnessing traumatic disasters. Carmit
Wiesslitz and Tamar Ashuri (2011) argued that online journalism has
fostered the emergence of a new journalistic model which they call "the
moral journalist"; unlike the "objective" journalist who is supposed to
remain outside of events, "moral journalists" (who are, however, typically
nonprofessional) presents their personal experiences as they witness the
suffering and pain of others with the aim of changing the witnessed reality.
Personal accounts and emotional confessions circulate in online and traditional media where journalists proclaim not only to care about the stories
they are reporting on, especially when embedded in the disaster zone and
confronting human tragedy, but also give vent to their own emotions in
doing so (Pantti et al. 2012).

With the growing awareness that reporters are subjected to traumatiza-
tion when witnessing the suffering of others, it has become easier to see
journalists as vulnerable human beings who respond emotionally like the
rest of us (Beam and Spratt 2009, Rentschler 2009). Along those lines, the
Dart Center for Conflict and Trauma has reflected, in a variety of reports
and statements, on the emerging recognition that journalists, caught up in
traumatic events, are themselves subject to the posttraumatic stress that is
widely seen to affect victims, emergency workers, and anyone else close to
the disaster (Dart Center 2003). If anything, the demands of conventional
practices of objectivity may make it more difficult for journalists to recover
from their exposure to trauma:

> Journalists who cover any "blood-and-guts" beat often build a needed and
> appropriate professional wall between themselves and the survivors and
> other witnesses they interview. But after reporters talk with people who
> have suffered great loss, the same wall may impede the need of journalists
> to react to their own exposure to tragedy. (Dart Center 2003: 3)

In the emerging "human" culture of reporting, becoming emotionally
involved in a story is not automatically deemed unprofessional, but is
rather viewed as an inescapable reality of journalistic work. As journalism
educators Tom Rosenstiel and Bill Kovach (2005) noted in their comment
on the surge of emotional expression among US journalists who covered
Hurricane Katrina in 2005, journalists "are in essence our surrogate

observers. It would have been odd, even distressing to most, if reporters had reacted like journalistic robots to the devastation in the Gulf Coast." One much discussed example where a journalist "crossed the line" from the position of the distant observer was BBC reporter Ben Brown's interview in Aceh in Indonesia with a woman who had lost her husband and four children in the 2004 Boxing Day tsunami. A neutral interview turned into an awkward act of comforting as Brown put his arm around the bereaved woman, who was weeping and clinging to him. The appeal of this footage was described by a managing editor for CNN, Nick Wrenn: "The Ben Brown incident really brought it home to me – just the raw emotion of it. And it is an emotional experience, and I think sometimes you have to engage. To me that was one of the most powerful packages that I saw out of all the broadcasters" (Dart Center 2005).

Despite the increased cultural license to display and elicit emotions, most journalists continue to subscribe to ideals of objectivity as conventionally understood, in terms of impartiality and detachment. At the same time, they nonetheless concede that not only do they care but they want their news reports to help audiences to care as well, pointing to the need for an understanding of objectivity that allows for a journalism which has the capacity to articulate and enable affective engagements. The question of how such an understanding may translate into practice remains open and contested: There is no normative consensus over what emotions journalists ought to display, and when and how, but the issues around journalists' emotional expression that are typically discussed include the situational appropriateness and authenticity of emotional responses, the "right amount" of emotion for the situation (not too much, or too little of it), and the motivation behind the display of emotion (Pantti 2010).

What can we say about the advantages of a more emotionally oriented approach to reporting? A more emotionally engaged approach has been seen to help generate a new moral imagination when bearing witness to human suffering. It has been argued that journalists should learn to care more about their stories and "allow themselves to feel the anguish of what it's like to be a victim" to be able to help people to see injustice and suffering *as something that must be addressed* instead of offering them comfort or excitement (Santos 2009: 39). As Willis (2003: 129) claimed:

> readers and viewers become more engaged in a story if they feel the reporter cares about the story, the people in it, and cares enough about the reader or viewer to write a story evidencing that care.

There is, then, a recognition that a journalism ethics for a globalized world in which disasters are increasingly frequent and prominent should not be predicated on a strict view of journalists as impartial, detached, and distant observers, but rather as people who are able to put themselves in victims' shoes – to empathize with their predicament – and might thereby build compassion and solidarity in audiences.

Journalism, Disaster, and Geopolitics: Limits of Compassion

At the same time, however, we would also suggest that the cosmopolitan imagination – and hence the possibilities for the cultivation of compassion – is restricted by the nationally and geopolitically inflected narratives of disasters (Chouliaraki 2006). This means that the opportunities for more compassionate ways of reporting, and hence new understandings of journalistic ethics, are not evenly distributed but are instead profoundly informed by global power relations, or by what we might call the "geopolitics of disaster coverage." By this term we mean to emphasize that under conditions of globalization, where the media have become an arena for the ongoing reinforcement and contestation of global power relations, disaster coverage and the audience reactions it constructs are heavily influenced by geopolitics at the levels of ideology and journalistic practice. As such, this term enables us to understand the subtle ways in which disaster coverage is inherently informed by politics, rather than considering the journalists' social obligations first and foremost, as it always points to the nation-state (Billig 1995) and its role within dynamic global power relations. As Chouliaraki (2006: 22) argues, the relationship between spectators and the distant victims of disasters reflect the global distribution of power: "it is always 'audiences in North America or Western Europe [that] react to knowledge of atrocities in East Timor, Uganda, or Guatemala,' rather than the other way round." Geopolitics plays a role at the level of journalistic practice because it informs the allocation of resources and the prioritization of particular stories over others. When disasters make the news, it is often not merely the result of any objective measure of the "seriousness" of the disaster, as indicated by the loss of life, but of *where* the disaster happened and *who* it affects (see also Mody 2010). This, in turn, has profound consequences for how audiences understand the world and the people who inhabit it. Coverage of disasters is informed by concerns about "compassion fatigue" or the public's limited attention to major global crises, including disease, famine, war, and death, caused by what critics such as Susan Moeller (1999) have identified as irresponsibly event-oriented, sensationalist, and short-termist media coverage which exhausts audiences in its relentless and unending parade of death and horror.

A 1995 large-scale content analysis by the Pew Research Center for the People and the Press concluded that "the way the media covers international news may be doing little to change the American public's indifference to concerns about world events and foreign policy" (Pew Research Center 1995: 1). The study highlighted features of international coverage which have been consistently documented by scholars: News organizations tend to prioritize domestic news, or news that has a clear domestic "angle"; they cover different regions according to their perceived importance and focus on dramatic, violent, and conflictual stories. They therefore fundamentally construct "The Foreign" as a place of violence, conflict, danger, and spectacle, and disaster coverage is no exception. Although the report identified what its authors saw as distinctive features of American international coverage, such as an emphasis on unbiased and objective reporting, the nation-centered orientation of international news that it identified reflects a broader set of long-standing journalistic practices which cut across geographical boundaries and arise on the basis of a complex combination of ideological causes and professional routines that structure understandings of what counts as "newsworthy"

These power relations also pervade the reporting of disaster, demonstrating "glaring differences that reflect global hierarchies of place and human life" (Joye 2009: 45). The global hierarchy of suffering invests more significance in the disasters and traumatic events that claim Euro-American victims, while suffering outside the West is routinely minimized or ignored. This practice, in turn, normalizes and perpetuates global inequalities. For example, Joye (2010) found that Flemish television news devoted about 50 percent of their disaster coverage to European disasters, even though they only accounted for a total of 11.4 percent of all disasters that occurred over the period studied. On the basis of this geopolitical hierarchization, Joye argued that proximity, understood as a meta-concept covering "cultural affinity, historical links, geographical distance, trade or economic relations as well as psychological or emotional distance" (2010: 588) can be seen as a powerful predictor of disaster coverage. Indeed, measures of proximity in this broader and more politicized sense matter because journalists, in selecting what stories to cover, make predictions about the affective response of the audience and hence construct and delimit the cultivation of compassion and cosmopolitanism.

In the case of the 2011 earthquake in Japan and the subsequent tsunami, much of the media's attention quickly turned to the disaster's consequences for the global economy, shaken by the long-standing financial crisis as well as by upheaval in the Middle East. This coverage highlighted the geopolitical significance of Japan. Media reports emphasized the interconnectedness of the global economy, as everything from the sale of smartphones to the production of cars was affected by the earthquake. The shocks of the earthquake, in other words, were felt as shocks to the global economy, as automotive factories around the world had to shut down and the stock markets reeled. For example, a commentary in the British quality newspaper, the *Daily Telegraph*, published three days after the earthquake and tsunami struck, opened by suggesting that:

Amid the scale of the human catastrophe, any consideration of the economic consequences of the Japanese earthquake might seem faintly distasteful if not even perverse. Yet any disaster on this scale also has the capacity for extreme long-term economic damage and Japan is going to require careful management over the months ahead.

It then considered in detail the financial consequences of the disaster in a global context:

> The immediate impact will almost certainly be to push Japan back into technical recession.
>
> Fortunately, the area most directly affected is quite sparsely populated by Japanese standards and in economic terms not particularly important. The region hit by the Kobe earthquake in 1995 was in this regard of considerably more consequence.
>
> Nonetheless, the effect of the quake has been to bring economic activity to a grinding halt, rather in the way September 11, a comparatively localised event, managed to create a temporary hiatus across the entire US economy....
>
> All the same, the history of such disasters is that after a brief lull, economic activity tends to bounce back, boosted by heavy spending on renewal.

After this assessment, which, among other things, reassuringly stated the relative unimportance of the affected region and could be viewed, by the admission of its author, as both distasteful and perverse, the article concluded as follows:

> What can be said with certainty is that the world economy needed another disaster like a hole in the head. The best that can be said for this one is that unlike most economic disasters, at least it wasn't man-made. (Warner 2011)

This piece was not unique in its callousness, but instead was symptomatic of a larger trend of focusing attention away from the scale of human suffering and hence the cultivation of compassion, and toward questions of the impact of the disaster on global and national economies. The scale of this coverage was unprecedented. A Nexis UK search showed that in the two weeks following the earthquake and tsunami, there were a total of 1,454 articles on the global economic consequences of the disaster in major world newspapers. Though the case of the Japanese earthquake and tsunami was unusual precisely because of Japan's central importance to the global economy, it also forcefully demonstrated the geopolitical logic of disaster reporting which means that the extent to which disaster reporting might cultivate an ethics of compassion depends largely on *where* the disaster happens and *who* suffers its consequences.

In other words, if there is no such thing as "news from nowhere" (Epstein 1973), discourses ostensibly generating a cosmopolitan sensibility are rarely politically innocent. If respect for the "rights of others" (Benhabib 2004) is central to cosmopolitanism, the geopoliticized nature of discourses on disaster means that some victims have more rights than others, insofar as their representation is more likely to give rise to audience compassion and hence action and intervention. This demonstrates that questions of ethics in disaster reporting need to be linked to an analysis of power relations – not just between individuals, but also between nation-states – and the ways in which they determine the extent to which journalists foster an ethics of compassion (cf. also Moeller 1999). Thinkers have long recognized that compassion and solidarity are created through individualized storytelling which enables audiences to put themselves in someone else's shoes. Hannah Arendt (1968: 104) thus suggested that storytelling about individual lives are able to connect up to larger issues of the common good by penetrating "the meaning of what otherwise would remain an unbearable sequence of sheer happenings." As the narrator in Graham Greene's classic novel, *The Quiet American*, observed, "suffering is not increased by numbers, one body can contain all the suffering the world can feel" (cited in Benthall 1993: 196).

Nevertheless, the politics of pity (Boltanski 1999: 3–19) generated out of stories about distant sufferers tends to be crafted out of a stock of geopoliticized discourses, often with a postcolonial tint. Rather than challenging global power relations, it might reinforce notions of the superiority of Western nations. Such a narrative does not invite compassion in the sense of a genuine recognition of the fundamental rights of distant others (cf. Benhabib 2004). Indeed, the French philosopher Jacques Rancière has been critical of claims around cosmopolitan regimes, under which he fears that human rights become the rights of victims (cf. Fine 2007: 80) or "of those unable to enact any rights or even any claim in their name, so that eventually their rights had to be upheld by others" (Rancière 2004: 298). To Rancière, such representations work to justify humanitarian military intervention, in itself a project predicated on the naturalization of particularly Western normative regimes, and seen by critics as underwriting neocolonial projects.

However, Chouliaraki (2006) has suggested that rather than assuming the best we can achieve is a politics of pity, we need to carefully distinguish between different types of disaster coverage and the forms of emotional response that they elicit to better understand the ethical implications of the spectatorial positions constructed. To this end, she has proposed a typology of three different forms of news of suffering, what she calls "adventure," "emergency," and "ecstatic" news. Adventure news is "news of suffering without pity," characterized by brief, factual reports represented by a "void of agency" because of the absence of any human actors from the story. As a result, "there is no possibility of human contact between the other and the spectator." By contrast, emergency news is "news of suffering with pity," which represents victims as individuals who can be helped by the action of distant others. Finally, ecstatic news, exemplified by coverage after the September 11 attacks, brings the sufferers as close to the spectators as possible, opening up a space for identification (Chouliaraki 2006: 10–11). On the basis of her analysis of these three types of news, Chouliaraki concludes that news of suffering "reserves the spectators' capacity to connect for those who are like 'us' while blocking this same capacity for the largest majority of world sufferings – those experienced

by distant 'others'" (2006: 181). The suffering of those who are proximate and similar in a geopolitical sense, in other words, is far more likely
to attract ecstatic news coverage. It seems, then, that there is a scope
for disaster reporting to open up for a cosmopolitan imagination – one
which is premised on a form of journalistic witnessing which allows
audiences to empathize with the suffering of distant others. Nonetheless,
the possibilities for the cultivation of cosmopolitanism are inhibited by
structural features of disaster reporting – as, indeed, of journalism more
broadly – namely those of the apparently inevitable grounding in the
nation-state, and the structuring role of geopolitical power relations. This
form of parochialism may, however, be under challenge by the emergence
of new media technologies which generate new modes of witnessing and
broaden the range of witnesses from professional journalists to a larger
global public sphere which draws on both amateur and professional voices.

Nonprofessional Eyewitnesses

One of the most significant changes in recent years in disaster reporting –
and in media witnessing in general – is the proliferation of "citizen journalism." With new visual-driven communication technologies enabling new
opportunities for documenting and distributing information across the
globe, ordinary people are playing an increasingly active role in the labor
of bearing witness to distant suffering and in disaster response in general.
As Frosh and Pinchevski (2009: 300) argue, crises or disasters today are
not only something that audiences "see" in the media as the ultimate witnesses of tragic events but something "they are increasingly socialized to
create" as the most important producers of mediated testimonies. Images,
in particular, have become a vital part of nonjournalists' witnessing,
and a powerful – but problematic – source for professional journalism
(Andén-Papadopoulos and Pantti 2011). It can be argued that the camera
phone has become an essential tool in the current destabilization of the
border between professional journalism and "citizen journalists."
    The citizen witnessing is intrinsically a transnational phenomenon as
eyewitness accounts are increasingly being addressed to a global public
via social networking sites or transnational media channels. Today's
eyewitnesses are themselves capable of creating and distributing media
content without mediators functioning as gatekeepers, determining who
qualifies as a witness and counterbalancing the eyewitness' subjective
position through its truth-telling rituals and ethical rules (Ashuri and
Pinchevski 2009: 139, Thomas 2009: 101, Zelizer 2007: 421). In addition,
citizen photographs are particularly effective in appealing to viewers'
emotions, and can be propelled by the international news media into
global media events. At this juncture, citizen eyewitness' ability to have
an influence on public discussion seems be greater than ever before.

Amateur photographs and video typically enter mainstream news in situations when the news event is unexpected or sudden (as was the case with the 2004 tsunami), or when journalists' access to the scene has been inhibited (as happened for example with the postelection protests in Iran in 2009 and also during the Arab Spring uprisings in 2011 and 2012). Thus the importance of citizen images of breaking news events arises from the fact that they provide instant and "raw" eye-witness accounts of unfolding events (Pantti and Bakker 2009). By doing so they help to establish journalism's own claims to authority which allow news organizations and journalists to present their accounts of reality as truthful and relevant (Zelizer 2007). The 2004 tsunami coverage has often been identified as the decisive moment not only in adopting a more emotionally engaged reporting style but also in the use of citizens' eyewitness imagery in professional news coverage (Riegert et al. 2010, Zelizer 2010: 244–66). The video footage and photos of the tsunami which circulated in the mainstream media was, in Barbie Zelizer's words, "close-up, grounded in real time, personal, genuine, explicit, and terrifying" (2010: 249).

Citizen imagery is often credited with providing crisis reporting with a new kind of closeness, that is, a heightened sense of emotional identification through the "raw," immediate, and subjective testimonials of ordinary people struggling to bear witness to the scene around them. Images taken by involved citizens promise to eradicate barriers of physical and social distance between spectators and sufferers seen in the media (see e.g., Chouliaraki 2008). At the same time, they raise several ethical questions for professional journalism. To start with, the physical presence of "being there" does not guarantee responsible reporting (see Silverstone 2006) and some observers have asked whether new visual technologies might in fact contribute to the creation of "citizen paparazzi" rather than "citizen journalists" (Glaser 2005). The much appreciated "aura of authenticity" of citizen images arises from the fact that the pictures are generated by individuals involved in the events rather than journalists as "detached observers" (Pantti and Bakker 2009, Williams, Wahl-Jorgensen, and Wardle 2011). However, as Ashuri and Pinchevski (2009: 140) write, involvement may come with the annihilation of perspective. The moral foundation of witnessing that includes recording significant events, revealing conditions of injustice, and creating empathy towards sufferers does not necessarily hold in a situation where every participant can become an eyewitness. As Mette Mortensen writes, sometimes "being there" and being able to snap pictures seems to be a sufficient motive for an eyewitness:

> Much contemporary eyewitnessing appears to be an extension of the mundane habit of visually documenting our lives, that is, when passers-by photograph a fire or a traffic accident with their mobile phones. (Mortensen 2011: 72)

While the work of bearing witness is greatly enhanced by the existence of global public spaces where eyewitnesses' accounts of distant suffering can be widely disseminated and responded to, the challenges of structural inequality remain largely unchanged. There is no guarantee that citizen witnessing will narrow the distance between the interests of "people like us" and the suffering of distant others. It appears that the citizen witnessing is no less connected to geopolitical power relations and to the cultural attribution of meaning and significance to disasters than mainstream media representations. That some disasters remain forgotten and some voices are silenced is seen in some recent studies. In her study on BBC convergent news of the Haiti earthquake, Chouliaraki (2010) asserted that the boundary between the "silent sufferer" and the "speaking Westerner" is not necessarily disappearing with the new media technologies and online platforms that have allowed for the proliferation of ordinary voices, as the vast majority of nonjournalist testimonial messages come from NGOs and other Westerners indirectly affected by the disasters.

The "who" and "why" questions of citizen testimonials are central when we think about responsible journalism. The problem of establishing who produced a particular photograph or video clip (and why, when, and where) as well as their typically graphic nature renders the journalistic value of nonjournalists' images complex. Either way, such images raise specific ethical issues that the mainstream media must deal with before it can publish or broadcast them to avoid jeopardizing the core journalistic value of truth-telling. Professional journalists in different European countries distinguish themselves from the citizen journalists or amateurs by referring to their editorial judgment (what is relevant, accurate, and "good") and commitment to ethical codes and practices such as verification (Pantti and Bakker 2009). In today's networked media environment, however, acts of publishing are not simply about truth-telling and revealing new information, but also about making ethical statements. For example, by publishing (or deciding not to publish) images from nonprofessional photographers which are already available in the public domain, news organizations make a claim about their ethics. Interviews with Finnish broadcast and print journalists point to the fact that most of the amateur imagery they receive through international news organizations is too graphic to show to a general public, or it can be shown only by using various distancing techniques (such as using black and white images) or identifying it as disturbing content (see Becker 2011). As Karin Becker writes, journalists have long developed strategies to incorporate pictures produced outside journalism's editorial control into the professional discourse:

> In order to include the aura of "truth" embedded in the private picture's apparent closeness and lack of control, journalism must frame the picture within its own agenda of news, including the ethical considerations that entail. (Becker 2011: 38)

In a new situation where professional newsmakers are competing with nonprofessional photographers, it is increasingly difficult to assert any collective ethical standard in producing and publishing images. However, establishing general principles for the use of nonjournalist imagery of disasters is a crucial task for global journalism ethics given the increasing power of amateur visuals to define global publics, frame significant events, and shape news production (Pantti and Andén-Papadopoulos 2011). Codes of ethics, which have traditionally neglected visual reporting, were largely written before the explosion of digital photography and especially camera phones and, as a study of US journalism ethics codes shows, they do not provide a sufficient framework for dealing with issues of authenticity or how to handle graphic images across media platforms (Keith, Schwalbe, and Silcock 2006). News organizations face a constant need to make decisions about whether or not to show violent images, which ones to use and why, where to show them (on broadcast news bulletin or online news) and how to present them, for example whether they should be digitally edited to reduce their horror factor, and how they should be captioned and contextualized (Perlmutter and Hatley 2004). While these decision-making dilemmas prompted by images of death and violence are far from new, the fact that graphic, newsworthy images are today "everywhere" makes established media organizations' decisions more important – and difficult. It has been suggested that for news organizations wishing to appear respectable, the figure of the amateur provides "an ethical bumper" for presenting graphic images:

> The amateur, willing to point his or her camera at anything, shoulders the ethical responsibility of producing such footage. Meanwhile, the network can frame such footage with multiple declaimers about its "disturbing content," while simultaneously reaping the benefits of presenting a more graphic picture of a given event. (Bridge and Sjøvaag 2009)

John Taylor (1998) writes that journalists' codes of ethics have traditionally restricted them from displaying dead bodies, dying people, and bloody details of a violent event. In practice, as we have discussed above, there is a well-documented hierarchization of death and violence which means that graphic imagery is usually reserved to those deaths that are not perceived to be literally or culturally close in geopolitical terms. The proliferation of amateur and activist imagery that does not adhere to the standards of "good taste and decency" governing mainstream news media, together with a global reach of today's journalism, makes this a question global media ethics needs to address.

Conclusion: Cosmopolitanism and Crisis Reporting

In this chapter, we have explored key ethical issues surrounding the coverage of disasters in a globalized environment characterized by swift technological change. We have suggested that one key development wrought in part by globalization is the emergence of a new lens through which to view the ethics of disaster reporting: one which does not necessarily show journalists as distanced, impartial, and detached observers first and foremost, but rather as witnesses to the suffering of distant others who are able to paint vivid and compelling pictures of the experience on the ground so as to cultivate compassion in audiences. This conception challenges conventional understandings of journalism ethics as tied to objectivity, but also opens up for broader conceptions of the roles and responsibilities of journalists. To be more specific, our consideration of disaster reporting suggests that a more normatively desirable and practicable model of objectivity incorporates an understanding of journalism as a discourse which often has affective registers and consequences and may open up for the cultivation of compassion. Nonetheless, we have also argued that openings for compassion and cosmopolitanism are not evenly distributed, but profoundly determined by what we have referred to as the geopolitics of disaster reporting. It means that victims in geopolitically proximate countries and regions are more likely to be represented in compassionate ways, and also that the construction of suffering is informed by concerns about the health of a globalized economy, as in the case of the 2011 Japanese earthquake. This suggests that any consideration of how to articulate and realize a journalistic ethics of compassion cannot be ignorant of global power relations. However, we have also argued that even if the "home nation" remains at the forefront, a space remains for the cultivation of cosmopolitan sensibilities based on the forging of emotional connection. Along those lines, a just ethical approach would be one that takes for granted the moral duty of considering *all* human experiences of loss, suffering, and death as equally worthy of compassion, and makes this explicit in the training of journalists, the writing of codes of ethics, as well as in newsroom practices and procedures.

Finally, we suggested that the increasing use of amateur imagery in disasters creates new ways of sharing information about disaster which might heighten emotional involvement. This development also raises new ethical questions around the responsibility of nonprofessional journalists which need to be addressed urgently. It seems, then, that globalization and new media technologies have destabilized categories long taken for granted in discussions of journalism ethics – particularly those of objectivity and professionalism. If anything, recent developments remind us that the truth claims on which journalism and its ethics rest are always fraught, contingent, and open to contestation.

Further Reading

Several books are useful for those who wish to know more about global disaster reporting. Our recent coauthored volume with Simon Cottle, *Disasters and the*

Media (2012), examines several of the themes explored in this chapter, looking at the reporting of disaster through the lenses of globalization, new technology, and emotion. Taking a broader scope, Simon Cottle offers a deep analysis of how global crises become constructed and contested in the contemporary news media in *Global Crisis Reporting: Journalism in the Global Age* (Maidenhead: Open University Press, 2009). For individuals interested in how news media construct death and grief, we suggest Folker Hanusch's historical overview *Representing Death in the News: Journalism, Media and Mortality* (Basingstoke: Palgrave Macmillan, 2010) and Carolyn Kitch's and Janice Hume's *Journalism in a Culture of Grief* (New York: Routledge, 2007) – both of which include considerations of the ethical implications of such coverage.

Much has been written about emotions and ethics in philosophy and political theory, though rarely in relation to global issues. Virginia Held explains the relevance of a "care ethics" to political, social, and global questions in *The Ethics of Care* (Oxford: Oxford University Press, 2006). Fiona Robinson develops a critical ethics of care that attends to the global relations of dependency and vulnerability in *Globalizing Care: Ethics, Feminist Theory, and International Relations* (Boulder, CO: Westview Press, 1999).

For readers interested in visual ethics and the role of images in disasters and war, we would suggest Susan Sontag's *Regarding the Pain of Others* (New York: Picador, 2004), Judith Butler's *Frames of War: When is Life Grievable?* (London: Verso, 2009) and *Cloning Terror: The War of Images, 9/11 to the Present* by William J. Thomas Mitchell (Chicago: University of Chicago Press, 2010).

References

Allan, S. and Zelizer, B. 2004. "Rules of Engagement: Journalism and War." In S. Allan and B. Zelizer, eds., *Reporting War: Journalism in Wartime*. London: Routledge, 3–22.

Andén-Papadopoulos, K. and Pantti, M., Eds. 2011. *Amateur Images and Global News*. Bristol: Intellect Books.

Arendt, H. 1968. *Men in Dark Times*. New York: Harcourt Brace Jovanovich.

Ashuri, T. and Pinchevski, A. 2009. "Witnessing as a Field." In P. Frosh and A. Pinchevski, eds., *Media Witnessing: Testimony in the Age of Mass Communication*. Basingstoke: Palgrave Macmillan, 133–57.

Beam, R. and Spratt, M. 2009. "Managing Vulnerability: Job Satisfaction, Morale and Journalists' Reactions to Violence and Trauma." *Journalism Practice* 3(4): 421–38.

Beck, U. 2000. *World Risk Society*. Cambridge: Polity Press.

Beck, U. 2006. *Cosmopolitan Vision*. Cambridge: Polity Press.

Becker, K. 2011. "Looking Back: Ethics and Aesthetics of Non-Professional Photography." In K. Andén-Papadopoulos and M. Pantti, eds., *Amateur Images and Global News*. Bristol: Intellect Books, 23–40.

Bell, M. 1998. "The Journalism of Attachment." In M. Kieran, ed., *Media Ethics*. London: Routledge, 15–22.

Benhabib, S. 2004. *The Rights of Others: Aliens, Residents, and Citizens*. Cambridge: Cambridge University Press.

Benthall, J. 1993. *Disasters, Relief and the Media*. London: I. B. Tauris.

Berglez, P. 2008. "What is Global Journalism? Theoretical and Empirical Conceptualisations." *Journalism Studies*, 9(6): 845–58.

Billig, M. 1995. *Banal Nationalism*. London, England: Sage.

Boltanski, L. 1999. *Distant Suffering: Morality, Media and Politics*. Cambridge: Cambridge University Press.

Boltanski, L. 2000. "The Legitimacy of Humanitarian Actions and their Media Representation: The Case of France." *Ethical Perspectives* 7(1): 3–16.

Bridge, J. and Sjøvaag, H. 2009. "Amateur Images in the Professional News Stream." Paper delivered at *ICA*, Keywords in Communication, 59th Annual Conference of the International Communication Association, Chicago.

Chalaby, J. 1998. *The Invention of Journalism*. Basingstoke: Macmillan.

Chouliaraki, L. 2006. *The Spectatorship of Suffering*. London: Sage.

Chouliaraki, L. 2008. "The Media as Moral Education: Mediation and Action." *Media, Culture & Society* 30(6): 831–52.

Chouliaraki, L. 2010. "Witnessing in Post-television News: Towards a New Moral Imagination." *Critical Discourse Studies* 7(4): 305–19.

Chouliaraki, L. and Orgad, S. 2011. "Proper Distance: Mediation, Ethics, Otherness." *International Journal of Cultural Studies* 14(4): 341–5.

Dart Center for Conflict and Trauma. 2003. "Tragedy and Journalists: A Guide for More Effective Coverage," http://dartcenter.org/files/en_tnj_0.pdf, accessed January 6, 2012.

Dart Center for Conflict and Trauma. 2005. "Covering the Tsunami: A Frontline Discussion," http://dartcenter.org/content/covering-tsunami-0, accessed October 6, 2011.

Epstein, E. J. 1973. *News from Nowhere*. New York: Vintage Press.

Ewart, J. 2003. "Prudence not Prurience: A Framework for Journalists Reporting Disasters." Paper delivered at ANZCA02 conference, Bond University, Queensland.

Fine, R. 2007. *Cosmopolitanism*. London: Routledge.

Frosh, P. and Pinchevski, A. 2009. "Crisis-Readiness and Media Witnessing." *The Communication Review* 12(3): 295–304.

Glaser, M. 2005. "Did London Bombings Turn Citizen Journalists into Citizen Paparazzi?" OJR: The Online Journalism Review, July 12, http://www.ojr.org/ojr/stories/050712glaser/

Joye, S. 2009. "The Hierarchy of Global Suffering: A Critical Discourse Analysis of Television News Reporting on Foreign Natural Disasters." *Journal of International Communication* 15(2): 45–61.

Joye, S. 2010. "News Media and the (De)construction of Risk: How Flemish Newspapers Select and Cover International Disasters." *Catalan Journal of Communication* 2(2): 253–66.

Keith, S., Schwalbe, C. B., and Silcock, B. W. 2006. "Images in Ethics Codes in an Era of Violence and Tragedy." *Journal of Mass Media Ethics* 21(4): 245–64.

Kurasawa, F. 2007. *The Work of Global Justice: Human Rights as Practices*. Cambridge: Cambridge University Press.

Leff, D. R. 2010. "In Defense of Appealing to Emotions in Media Coverage of Catastrophe," http://virtualmentor.ama-assn.org/2010/09/msoc1-1009.html.

Loyn, D. 2003. "Witnessing the Truth." OpenDemocracy, February 20, http://www.opendemocracy.net/media-journalismwar/article_993.jsp

Lyall, K. 2005. "The Emotional Toll of Disaster Reporting." Dart Center for Journalism and Trauma, http://dartcenter.org/content/emotional-toll-disaster-reporting-0.

McNair, B. 2011. *An Introduction to Political Communication*, 5th edn. London: Routledge.

Mody, B. 2010. *The Geopolitics of Representation in Foreign News: Explaining Darfur.* Lexington, KY: Lexington Books.

Moeller, S. 1999. *Compassion Fatigue: How the Media Sell Disease, Famine, War and Death.* London: Routledge.

Mortensen, M. 2011. "The Eyewitness in the Digital Age." In K. Andén-Papadopoulos and M. Pantti, eds., *Amateur Images and Global News.* Bristol: Intellect Books, 63–75.

Oxfam International. 2007. "Climate Alarm: Disasters Increase as Climate Change Bites," Briefing Paper No. 108, http://policy-practice.oxfam.org.uk/publications/climate-alarm-disasters-increase-as-climate-change-bites-114103.

Pantti, M. 2010. "The Value of Emotion: An Examination of Television Journalists' Notions on Emotionality." *European Journal of Communication* 25(2): 168–81.

Pantti, M. and Andén-Papadopoulos, K. 2011. "Transparency and Trustworthiness: Strategies for Incorporating Amateur Photography into News Discourse." In K. Andén-Papadopoulos and M. Pantti, eds., *Amateur Images and Global News.* Bristol: Intellect Books, 97–112.

Pantti, M. and Bakker, P. 2009. "Misfortunes, Sunsets and Memories: Non-Professional Images in Dutch News Media." *International Journal of Cultural Studies* 12(5): 471–89.

Pantti, M., Wahl-Jorgensen, K., and Cottle, S. 2012. *Disasters and the Media.* New York: Peter Lang.

Perlmutter, D. and Hatley, L. 2004. "Images of Horror from Fallujah: 'The Transparency of Angst and Indecision about the Fallujah Images Have Been Good for Journalism'." *Nieman Reports* 22, http://www.nieman.harvard.edu/reports/article/100834/Images-of-Horror-From-Fallujah.aspx.

Peters, J. D. 2001. "Witnessing." *Media, Culture and Society* 23(6): 707–27.

Pew Research Center for the People and the Press. 1995. "A Content Analysis: International News Coverage Fits Public's Ameri-Centric Mood," http://www.people-press.org/files/legacy-pdf/19951031.pdf.

Rancière, J. 2004. "Who is the Subject of the Rights of Man?" *The South Atlantic Quarterly* 103(2/3): 297–310.

Rentschler, C. 2009. "From Danger to Trauma: Affective Labor and the Journalistic Discourse on Witnessing." In P. Frosh and A. Pinchevski, eds., *Media Witnessing: Testimony in the Age of Mass Communication.* Basingstoke: Palgrave Macmillan, 158–81.

Richards, A. 2010. "Bearing Witness: An Analysis of the Reporting and the Reception of News about Distant Suffering in the Light of John Howard Yoder's Work on Witness." PhD thesis, University of Edinburgh.

Riegert, K., Hellman, M., Robertson, A., and Mral, B. Eds. 2010. *Transnational and National Media in Global Crisis: The Indian Ocean Tsunami*. New York: Hampton Press.

Rosenstiel, T., and Kovach, B. 2005. "Media Anger Management." *The Washington Post*, October 2, http://www.journalism.org/node/138.

Sanders, K. 2003. *Ethics and Journalism*. London: Sage.

Santos, J. 2009. *Daring to Feel: Violence, the News Media, and their Emotions*. Lanham, MD: Lexington Books.

Schudson, M. and Anderson, C. 2009. "Objectivity, Professionalism and Truth Seeking in Journalism." In K. Wahl-Jorgensen and T. Hanitzsch, eds., *The Handbook of Journalism Studies*. London: Routledge, 88–101.

Seaton, J. 2005. *Carnage and the Media: The Making and Breaking of News About Violence*. London: Penguin.

Seib, P. 2002. *The Global Journalist: News and Conscience in a World of Conflict*. Lanham, MD: Rowman and Littlefield.

Silverstone, R. 2006. *Media and Morality: On the Rise of Mediapolis*. Cambridge: Polity.

Sznaider, N. 1998. "The Sociology of Compassion: A Study in the Sociology of Morals." *Cultural Values* 2(1): 117–39.

Taylor, J. 1998. *Body Horror: Photojournalism, Catastrophe, and War*. Manchester: Manchester University Press.

Tester, K. 2001. *Compassion, Morality, and the Media*. Buckingham: Open University Press.

Thomas, G. 2009. "Witness as a Cultural Form of Communication: Historical Roots, Structural Dynamics and Current Appearances." In P. Frosh and A. Pinchevski, eds., *Media Witnessing: Testimony in the Age of Mass Communication*. Basingstoke: Palgrave Macmillan, 88–111.

Tumber, H. and Prentoulis, M. 2003. "Journalists under Fire: Subcultures, Objectivity and Emotional Literacy." In D. Thussu and D. Freedman, eds., *War and the Media: Reporting Conflict 24/7*. London: Sage, 215–30.

Ward, S. J. A. 2005. "Philosophical Foundations for Global Journalism Ethics." *Journal of Mass Media Ethics* 20(1): 3–21.

Ward, S. J. A. 2008. "Global Journalism Ethics: Widening the Conceptual Base." *Global Media Journal* 1(1): 137–49.

Ward, S. J. A. 2009. "Journalism Ethics." In K. Wahl-Jorgensen and T. Hanitzsch, eds., *The Handbook of Journalism Studies*. London: Routledge, 295–309.

Ward, S. 2010. "Emotion in Reporting: Use and Abuse," Center for Journalism Ethics, October 14, 2010, http://ethics.journalism.wisc.edu/2010/10/14/ethics-center-co-authors-report-on-nonprofit-journalism-10/.

Warner, J. 2011. "Tragedy Might be Final Straw for Fragile Confidence," *Telegraph*, March 14, 2011. http://www.telegraph.co.uk/news/worldnews/asia/japan/8379812/Tragedy-might-be-final-straw-for-fragile-confidence.html.

Wiesslitz, C. and Ashuri, T. 2011. "'Moral Journalists': The Emergence of New Intermediaries of News in an Age of Digital Media." *Journalism* 12(8): 1035–51.

Williams, A., Wahl-Jorgensen, K., and Wardle, C. 2011. "'More Real and Less Packaged': Audience Discourses on Amateur News Content and Their Effects on Journalism Practice." In K. Andén-Papadopoulos and M. Pantti, eds., *Amateur Images and Global News*. Bristol: Intellect Books, 193–207.

Willis, J. 2003. *The Human Journalist: Reporters' Perspectives and Emotions.* Westport, CT: Praeger.

Zelizer, B. 1998. *Remembering to Forget: Holocaust Memory through the Camera's Eye.* Chicago: University of Chicago Press.

Zelizer, B. 2007. "On 'Having Been There': 'Eyewitnessing' as a Journalistic Key Word." *Critical Studies in Media Communication* 24(5): 408–28.

Zelizer, B. 2010. *About to Die: How News Images Move the Public.* Oxford: Oxford University Press.

11

Affective Expertise
The Journalism Ethics of Celebrity Sourcing

Katherine M. Bell

The summer 2011 cover story in the upbeat business magazine *Fast Company* details actor Matt Damon and his efforts to bring clean water to poor villages around the world. The piece features Damon and "water expert" Gary White and their partnership in founding Water.org, which helps local people secure funding to drill for and pipe in fresh water. The headline reads: "Can Matt Damon Bring Clean Water to Africa" (McGirt 2011). It is accompanied by a two-photo series, one image of Damon standing in front of what looks to be a round porthole window, the other a longer shot of an unidentified girl in the Dogon region of Mali collecting dirty water from a mud hole. The window provides an orange-gold spherical halo behind the actor. It is a none-too-subtle echo of a stained-glass portrait of Jesus. Overlaid on the Damon photo is the upper-case caption "CAN THIS MAN," followed by the caption "SAVE THIS GIRL?" over the girl's photo.

What follows is a glowing news account of Damon and his work with White and the organization. Damon himself does not express hubris about his philanthropic work. The notion that he is out to "save" these poor, distant villages comes out in the journalism. The author, senior writer Ellen McGirt, and editors create the metaphorical equation between Damon's philanthropy and divine intervention through the headline, the photos, the captions, and the piece itself.

This story offers a memorable example of a theme that runs through journalism about celebrities and their social causes. News stories, particularly about distant locales, frequently hit an emotional register that borrows from ideas of Christian charity and the importance of good works. But here, as with other examples, we read that Damon "is more than just the pretty face of Water.org. He has turned himself into a development expert." Thus the actor who, as a famous person, has a

Global Media Ethics: Problems and Perspectives, First Edition. Edited by Stephen J. A. Ward.
© 2013 Blackwell Publishing Ltd. Published 2013 by Blackwell Publishing Ltd.

well of affective power on which to draw, is also styled rhetorically as someone with the credentials of the more traditional journalistic source. The bifurcated pictorial image of salvation and need is a vivid shortcut to the problem that needs fixing.

In recent decades, activism by entertainment celebrities has burgeoned into a media staple, an industry in its own right. Bono started the Product Red campaign as a commercial funding response to poverty and AIDS in Africa. George Clooney spends his "celebrity credit card" working to avert human rights abuses in Sudan (Diehl 2010). Oprah Winfrey built a school for girls in South Africa. Angelina Jolie and Madonna have both adopted babies from the African continent and taken up philanthropic activities. Alicia Keys started the Keep a Child Alive charity to help people affected by HIV in Africa. The list goes on. It seems every celebrity has, indeed *must* have, a cause. As John Street notes:

> When Bono... is granted an audience with the Pope or is invited to spend time with the U.S. President in the White House, it certainly *seems* as if the worlds of politics and popular culture are almost inseparable. (Street 2006: 359)

The celebrity activist's distinct voice on the political stage is one that journalism cannot ignore.

Celebrity activism and philanthropy raise questions about how credibility and expertise are derived in the media, and how they negotiate the tensions between the rational and detached, the basis of news norms, and the spectacular, which is embedded in the political economy of mainstream news. Celebrity is part of a turn in cultural authority regarding expertise. The media's role in ordaining what constitutes news (and therefore knowledge) is bound up with the merging of news and entertainment, and with the proliferation of lifestyle media and social media. News, in whatever form, can originate from outside big media, though it is still vital to the production of original journalism. This reality alters traditional definitions of news and of sources. And different media forms are blended in the public mind (Baym 2001). Genres as different as the nightly news, entertainment gossip websites, and popular satire programs all play a role in public life and increasingly in mainstream news.

In the midst of this convergence the mainstream news media, always in search of a sound bite to help cut through the weeds of complex social policy, have the socially conscious celebrity as a go-to quotable source. The rich and famous are now in the stable of official sources that are the legitimizing foundation of news. They pronounce on issues ranging from animal rights to voting, from the environment to poverty, and they come in every political stripe. Anderson Cooper of CNN interviews not only pundits, politicians and policy wonks about major issues of the day, he has been known to ask Roseanne Barr and Ted Nugent (representing liberal and conservative views respectively), and Joan Rivers about their views on government policy.[1] *New York Times* columnist Nicholas Kristof has written extensively about Sudan through the eyes of George Clooney. NBC anchor Brian Williams traveled to Africa with Bono to make his work the focal point of stories about poverty and AIDS. The line between news and popular culture is flattening out, and the famous source is an aspect of this turn.

Celebrity, then, is a site where we can examine how mainstream news adheres to its traditional norms as it also embraces spectacle and the "cool" factor that encroaches on – and pays for – the production of so-called "serious" news. It is a good place to explore how the media deploy the celebrity as eyewitness and expert source, and as a mediator between the blended spheres of citizenship and consumption. It is not that an affective turn, as exemplified by the celebrity spokesperson, is inherently negative. The affective, after all, is a form of knowledge that has been delegitimized and suppressed in modernity. But given the emotional power of celebrities, their work as brands and commodities in the culture industries, and the media's need for a simple narrative, journalism frequently reaches for stock myths, such as that of superhuman salvation, to tell stories of celebrity engagement with social issues.

Here I discuss the ethical implications that arise from celebritized expertise as a mode of cultural authority in North American journalism. I look at the historical context of the "authoritative voice" in mainstream media culture and problematize the missionary or savior theme that typifies much news coverage of celebrity work in Africa. These representations have deep implications for the global politics of race, class, and gender and for our understanding of the power relations of globalization generally. Ultimately, I argue, a journalistic turn to the famous source signals neither a media culture in decline nor a wholesale democratization of public life. Not all celebrity good works are equal, nor is the journalism about them. However, all publicity about celebrity involvement has deep implications for the ethics of representation on a global level.

Celebrity as Cultural Authority

The celebrity is a "voice above others," as P. David Marshall says (1997: x). Famous people have an instantaneous platform for their views and self-publicity. As a social phenomenon, we can think of celebrity as a discourse, a commodity, a lifestyle, a social category, a system of mediation, a source of power, and means of containment. Celebrities as individuals serve as both role models and cautionary tales about the perils of excess (Marshall 1997, Turner 2004). They are products of a triangulated relationship with the culture industries and the audience or public. They are constructed on uniqueness and distance, and on the fantastical notion that we can somehow be part of their private lives via the media (Dyer 1986).

Walter Benjamin called this relationship the "cult" of the movie star, an "aura" of transcendence created by the culture industry to establish emotional links with the audience (Benjamin 2006: 254). Fans and audience members relate to fame and to famous individuals based upon a dynamic emotional, parasocial connection that must be continually reproduced. Stars

> enact ways of making sense of the experience of being a person in a particular kind of social production (capitalism), with its particular organization of life into public and private spheres. (Dyer 1986: 17)

As an organizing force for the affective domain of society (Marshall 1997), celebrity is an important site of identity construction and social-political influence. We derive our subjectivities and allegiances in part from celebrity, or at least the lifestyles conjured for us by its ubiquity in Western life. Fame is not only an aspiration for some; it offers a template for performing everyday life.

One of the great paradoxes of celebrity is that it is based upon the valorization of the individual but its power lies in collective embrace. It symbolizes uniqueness and communality, the rarified and the ordinary. These contradictions make celebrity a valuable conduit between the culture industries and audiences. Celebrities provide journalism with a source of views and knowledge that fulfill many conflicting requirements, for example that news appear "objective" as it also spins a compelling tale of human existence.

Although they trade on uniqueness, entertainment celebrities must be reproducible within the culture industries of film, television, music, and the like. They must be different enough to appear unique but conformist enough not to be deemed subversive (Braudy 1986: 5–8). The media do not warm to "cage-rattling" celebrities such as Sean Penn or Jane Fonda, who are deemed overly political and difficult (Hollar 2007). They are part of the machinery of cultural production and there are expectations about their compliance with its norms. In Marxian terms, celebrities are congealed labor, as Dyer says. They are used in conjunction with production labor to make cultural commodities. They are drivers of consumer capitalism who promote all manner of products and services, either directly endorsing consumer brands or as "thought leaders" in the production of lifestyle that drives the economy of wealthy societies.

As brands, celebrities give emotional resonance to the cold, hard exchange relationship of the marketplace (Lury 2004: 87–92). Brands are a creation of the advertising industry to help make similar products stand out and have meaning beyond their use value. Famous people animate an affective relationship with commodities and consumer culture, whether they are promoting their own creative projects, a consumer product such as makeup or athletic wear, or a cause such as poverty, animal rights, or the environment. Significantly for journalism, their endorsements in all of these areas cross over and multiply their cultural authority in terms of salience and perceived legitimacy in the public mind.

In the language of critical discourse analysis, such brand crossing can be thought of as recontextualization, where a celebrity's meaning and power can be reappropriated in new situations outside of their specialty as actors, musicians, or other creative producers. Celebrity can be appropriated by journalism and by the famous, and taken up by an audience in a selective manner (Chouliaraki and Fairclough, 1999: 118). This recontextualization conceals some of the contradictions inherent in the fact that celebrity is once and for all a commodity and an exchange relationship. Recontextualization enables the construction of celebrity as expert and philanthropist uncritically, even as this production first and foremost bolsters the brand.

Todd Gitlin found precisely how celebrity cultural authority could be adapted and recontextualized for multiple social contexts in his foundational study of the 1960s antiwar movement in the United States. It continually regenerates itself via media publicity: "After a point, celebrity can be parlayed – by celebrity and the media – into more celebrity: it is like money or a credit rating" (Gitlin, 1980: 147). This transferability is partly what gives a movie star the authority to speak on complex social issues outside of his or her specialty. The celebrity brand is the perfect vehicle through which to integrate commerce and citizenship, pop culture and the public sphere.

Celebrities have long used their brand capital for charitable aims. Danny Kaye was the first UNICEF ambassador in the 1950s. Audrey Hepburn was well known for her work in that capacity in the 1980s and early 1990s. Now there is an entire industry built up around matching celebrities with social causes, and journalism is part of that machinery. The website Look to the Stars, for example (http://www.looktothestars.org/), watches these connections and reports on celebrity doings in philanthropy. People can and do make a career out of helping famous people manage their charitable personas and matching charities with big "names" (Holson 2010). The reasons for this phenomenon are myriad, and related to the political economy of media, ranging from increased exposure through new media and new avenues of old media (such as the news-format entertainment program). The celebrity charity industry is not unrelated to the spectacle of media events created around famous people in the news. It is part of the "integrated news spectacle," a convergence of social and institutional forces and technologies in the current moment (Compton 2004). The look, feel, and content of news have changed over time, and it has become heavily celebritized.

In terms of social engagement, the well-known figure can provide a kind of shorthand for our own beliefs. Such figures embody politics and pleasure and are signifiers of our own desired lifestyle. As affective leaders, they can inspire fans' deeper knowledge and commitment on social issues, or can stand in entirely for our own engagement. It is too simple to suggest that people blindly follow celebrities. Celebrities fulfill a need for simplified and generalized knowledge for the public (Richey and Ponte 2011). They speak not as traditional credentialed experts, but as themselves, using their brand to draw both fans and leaders with economic and political power. Indeed their access to institutional power is half the equation.

The journalist's role in this calculus of legitimacy is not simply as one who translates it, but also as one who produces it. Contemporary news in North America and some other parts of the developed world derives its authority in part by using expert sources to untether the reporter from the contested substance of the story. There is credibility in detachment. Sourcing is part of the "objectivity" paradigm of news and the use of sources is historically linked to the professionalization of journalism dating back to the nineteenth century. It is tied as well to the professionalization of expertise in the sciences and social sciences, and to the rise of liberal democracy. Importantly, a journalist's own legitimacy can, in turn, be enhanced through access to sources, including the famous and fabulous.

Journalism and Legitimacy

Journalism history records that the newspaper's move toward political neutrality was an economic imperative and part of a drive toward professionalization in the late nineteenth and early twentieth centuries. Scholars trace the North American roots of journalistic objectivity at least back to the US penny press of the 1830s (Schudson 1978: 12–60, Schiller 1981: 47–75) and, as Stephen Ward's work suggests, into antiquity (Ward 2004). Political parties did not fund the upstart publishers of one-cent newspapers of the 1800s, unlike their more expensive partisan predecessors. They were commercial products and they needed to appear impartial in order to attract advertisers and readers. As early as 1867, US journalism guides were essentially promoting a form of objectivity as a methodology (Mirando 2001). Many of the prescribed traits of contemporary news began to appear during that time: a detachment from party politics, an emphasis on producing news as fact, the use of expert sources, and a spare writing style (Mindich 1998, 2005).

As the commercial press burgeoned, so did concerns about its power and methods. The attendant scrutiny about its practices brought codified statements of ethics that included the imperative of objectivity (Ward 2004: 204–13). The fully formed performance of journalistic objectivity emerged only at the end of World War I, however. Michael Schudson (1978) has suggested that it was entrenched as a practice in the wake of a press outmaneuvered by a government war propaganda machine, and by a growing professional public relations industry. In short, news media professionals needed neutrality as a vocational stance in order to position themselves in the marketplace and in the public mind.

At the same time, commercial journalism has relied on the power of storytelling. News must be detached and yet tap into the current of human emotion that animates all of our lives. As *Washington Post* journalist and author E. J. Dionne says, media people are expected to be hard-hitting yet unbiased, a check on power yet neutral, analytical yet dispassionate (1996: 232–62). Good journalism is asked to do all of these competing tasks. Sometimes the balance tips, as with the era of yellow journalism, McCarthyism, or the more recent *News of the World* phone-hacking scandal, where spectacle triumphs and all sense of proportion is cast aside.

In this recipe for producing news, the rational, credentialed expert has been differentiated from the so-called "real person" source or eyewitness, an everyday person who breathes immediacy and humanity into the cold, hard facts of an issue or event. The credentialed expert is a child of the Enlightenment, along with liberal democracy, scientism, statistical tracking, and the rise of professionalism. The complex, rationalized world of modernity presented a conundrum for expertise as democracy flourished. It asked more of citizens, and in a sense democracy and expertise are at odds in the kinds of knowledge they foster – generalized versus specialized. As Stephen Turner writes:

> One assumption of meaningful discussion is some degree of mutual comprehension. But in the case of expert knowledge, there is very often no such comprehension and no corresponding ability to judge what is being said and who is saying it, and consequently no possibility of genuine "discussion." (Turner 2003: 12)

Journalism is expected to provide a bridge between expert knowledge and the citizen as it also aims to entertain.

Even Walter Lippmann, a journalist and early media commentator, found liberal democracy unrealistic in its expectation that average citizens be "omnicompetent," able to express a considered opinion on every issue (Lippmann 1965). His highly nonpopulist answer to this dilemma was the "disinterested expert" who would essentially translate complicated ideas to compensate for this perceived lack of knowledge in the citizenry. He said the press could not be expected to place its fourth-estate role above its economic imperative as a moneymaking venture (Lippmann 1965: 203). Furthermore, he felt that citizens are essentially lazy and therefore susceptible to the "manufacture of consent" by the elite (p. 158). Those in power well know, he argued, that building consensus is not about rational agreement on issues of the day but about finding symbols onto which people can latch their beliefs (p. 132). In other words, he believed that citizens' engagement was mainly *affective* and therefore knowledge must be simplified.

This is an enduring function of objectivity as it was fashioned starting in the nineteenth century. Expertise built upon the Enlightenment notion of a detached "view from nowhere" (Nagel 1986) is woven into the fabric of public consciousness even as it is demonstrated to be a social construct. Today, it is not uncommon to hear people speak colloquially of a news report not being "objective," an assessment that often means the critic disagrees with the dominant thrust of the reporting. Still, the pursuit of "unbiased," value-free knowledge remains valorized as a way to translate ideas and codify opinion.

Yet the contemporary understanding that objectivity is synonymous with the purely factual, the scientific, and "the cold-blooded restraint of the emotions," as Lorraine Daston puts it (Daston 1992: 598), is relatively new. What has been called "aperspectival" objectivity was essentially deployed as a communication tool for validating expert scientific knowledge beginning in the mid-nineteenth century. It bridged that tension between specialized and generalized knowledge inherent in liberal democracy described by Turner (2003) above. It was part of a codification of scientific life. Aperspectival objectivity is at least partially about ease of communication (Daston 1992). The need for public accessibility trumps depth and complexity.

The privileging of cold, hard facts as a superior model for journalism was part of the professionalization of news, a legitimizing effort with roots in the depoliticization of science and social science. Reform-minded social scientists sought to ameliorate the harsh effects of industrialization for the working class in the mid-1800s, but a movement toward academic professionalism and neutrality subsumed them (Furner 1975, Ross 1991). A professional scientific academy sought recognition as a source of disinterested guidance to society's leaders. Humanitarian objectives were discredited and receded to the background in the late 1800s (Smith 1994: 19–24). Mark Smith suggests that objectivity was a tool that served to place scientists in the position of having their knowledge "unavailable to, but accepted by, lay persons" (p. 19).

Journalism followed the "depoliticized" path, and with many of the same criticisms. Critical scholars have argued that the paradigm of objectivity or "balance," as it is often called in newsrooms, supports neoliberal interests and a military-industrial complex,[2] while discrediting feminist, civil rights and countercultural movements in the mass media. Within the frame of objectivity, voices outside of the realm of official sources have been deemed less credible, or even unworthy (see Gans 1979, Gitlin 1980, Hallin 1986). As journalists interview and quote officials partly to deflect allegations of bias, performing the "strategic ritual" of objectivity, they privilege powerful elite sources of knowledge (Tuchman 1972). They plumb the ranks of the academy, politics, the military, think tanks, and lobby groups for people sanctioned as "legitimate" spokespeople to explain and opine about the issues of the day as the news defines them. They use "real life" or eyewitness sources in tandem with the credentialed experts to fashion a journalism that is defensible as being unbiased and compelling as a story that resonates on a human level.

Yet the new media landscape of news and opinion has pushed the guarded boundary that distinguishes *news* from *not news* as traditionally defined. This shift has implications for how sources are derived and presented. Delli Carpini and Williams (2001) argue that US journalism actually surrendered its gatekeeping function during the Clinton–Lewinski sex scandal. It was a watershed moment when alternative media, comedians, and other commentators got ahead of the story. Journalists began interviewing each other with increasing frequency, and online media built the story hour by hour. Mainstream news people found they were no longer setting the agenda and they began to adapt "by increasingly mimicking the form and substance of its new media competitors" (Delli Carpini and Williams, 2001: 174). Now there are many platforms and genres for publicity, and new forms of journalism that do not adhere to the professional norms discussed above, though the use of "expert" sources remains a cornerstone even of more explicitly opinion-centered genres of journalism, and for good reason. Experts bring legitimacy as much as they bring knowledge.

Entertainment celebrities have the dual role of being elite sources of ideas and knowledge, but also populist figures with persuasive power. They occupy a terrain that is both rarefied and ordinary. They are expert and eyewitness. Celebrity begins to alter the nature of cultural authority. One of journalism's roles has been to translate expert knowledge for the public, but the political economy of the media has helped create the celebrity expert as part of its economic imperative. They fulfill the dual roles of providing legitimacy and bringing the "real person" element that is so important to narrating a good story. They are a good bet for readership, ratings, and clicks.

We see a flattening out of what counts as expertise, what counts as journalism, and what counts as politics and social engagement. Journalism, celebrity, and politics all cross and converge. Not only are celebrities experts, they appear as journalists and politicians in some instances. Celebrities run for office. Politcos become journalists. There is a performative "restyling of politics" (Corner and Pels 2003: 16) in the mashup of entertainment, social-political life, and journalism, for, in fact, many journalists are famous. Such fluidity, a sort of vocational crossing, brings new modalities of authority built up more explicitly on emotion and steeped in the cult of fame.

Flattening out suggests the potential to open the media landscape to counterdiscourses from symbolically annihilated groups. Yet journalism's uptake of celebrity in the context I elaborate below can produce simplified media narratives that belie the privilege and inherent commercial nature of celebrity as a discourse. It sets the stage for a branded performance of personal expertise that maintains much of the ideological force of so-called disinterested knowledge discussed earlier. After all, the norms of news such as source selection and interviewing, some of which are performed as well in entertainment and lifestyle media genres, are still in place, functioning to bring about legitimacy. But the players are celebritized, with all of the attendant glitz and affective power that goes beyond that of a traditional news source.

At issue here is a central concern of cultural studies: the politics of representation, specifically of what knowledge is valued, who gets to speak, who is discredited or silenced. These questions are at the heart of the representational ethics of how and by whom issues such as AIDS and poverty in Africa, and a host of other social problems, are taken up (or not taken up) in the mass media. Valorized knowledge is bound up with power and with representations of race, gender, class, sexuality, and the processes of globalization. The links between lay and expert knowledge are complicated in the digital media era. Certainly what counts as knowledge or truth is more fragmented in the celebritized mediascape, for better and for worse.

Below is a reading of how this flattening out and celebritization of expertise plays out in the production of ideas and representations of Africa and Africans in the Western imagination. Journalism's use of celebrity sources as experts, in these cases, essentially produces Africa as an exotic, albeit sickly, locale that is in need of saving. This media characterization produces a neocolonial power dynamic that reinscribes stereotypes dating back centuries but retooled for the globalized media-economic landscape.

The Mission: News and the Narrative of Salvation

In the *Fast Company* cover story, Damon is a cultural authority of transcendent proportions, starting with the images. His picture is a close-up, looking directly at the camera with the halo effect behind him. The girl is shot from above in an almost animalistic pose as she stoops to collect water. The camera angle looking down on her, combined with the pose, creates the imagery of one who is less than human. Visually the bifurcated image connotes dichotomization, with Damon as the polar opposite of the young girl, rhetorically, socially, and materially.[3] In the photo caption he is a "water warrior," who eschews fancy galas in favor of digital fundraising and hands-on action. The warrior label suggests one who is dispatched to use physical force to save the day when talk has failed, a kind of Superman figure.

In the story itself, McGirt (2011) characterizes Damon as self-effacing, an unpretentious person who "lives a quiet life for a celebrity of his stature." Humility, combined with extra-human power, is embodied in Jesus, the Christian tradition's savior. We learn that in the developing world Damon goes unrecognized from his day job as an "international heartthrob." People in distant countries are apparently unaware that they are in the presence of Hollywood royalty. The story juxtaposes this anonymity with the instant recognition he receives as he goes to pick his child up from school in Manhattan. He retains his middle-class sensibility and is ordinary in spite of his extraordinary life, McGirt reports.

Yet, as this story would have it, Damon is a redeemer of distant Others. While the piece is about how the organization Water.org helps people secure financing for their own self-identified and initiated water projects, the magazine offers its target audience of Western readers a Matt Damon who is the hope for salvation of poor people far away. Such a characterization is deeply entwined in the Western colonial project. Christianity was the "civilizing" instrument of the colonizing powers in Africa and elsewhere. The colonial zeitgeist of moral superiority was the mandate for bringing both capitalism and Christianity to the "dark" places of the earth in the nineteenth century. It justified the exploitation of the continent's human and natural resources. While celebrities operating in Africa may not see their mission as religious or divinely inspired, journalism's deployment of this narrative echoes an imperialism that asserts white and divine salvation.

It must be said that celebrities at times invoke religious themes themselves, which could influence their prominence in news accounts. Bono's Product Red campaign creates publicity materials around a slogan called the Lazarus Effect, a biblical reference to Jesus's power to undo death. The Lazarus effect refers to the story in John's Gospel (chapter 11) where Jesus demonstrates his divine powers by bringing his follower back from the dead. Product Red has used the slogan to draw a simplified link between the lifesaving impact of antiretroviral drugs for HIV patients and their campaign. Just "two pills a day," purchased with money raised through Western consumers buying designated "Red" products from iconic brands such as Apple, Converse, and Starbucks, can save a person infected with HIV.

The name of Madonna's charity, Raising Malawi, suggests the lifting up of a helpless people, or literally raising children. Her organization's school curriculum created for children is based loosely on a popularized version of the Kabbalah teachings of the Jewish tradition, which represents her personal spiritual leanings. The website for her charity is replete with stories and photos depicting the pop diva amid throngs of adoring black people.

The infantilizing of people in the colonies and of Africans and African-American slaves has been a racial discourse dating back centuries (see Burton 1994, Hall 1997, Said [1978] 2003). It was essential to producing the moral and intellectual superiority of white colonizers who believed that the exotic, primitive Others had to be civilized into the European ideals of work and family. As these examples suggest, this problematic narrative retains social force in contemporary media accounts of life in Africa. They prompt a perception of a homogeneous continent that is desperately poor, sick, and tribal.

At times journalism does take up the tough questions of power, privilege, and representation regarding celebrity in distant locales. For example, *New York Magazine* published a lengthy examination of Madonna's charity in the wake of missing funds, its abandonment of plans to build a promised school, and the firing of employees (Grigoriadis 2011). The piece includes a picture of Madonna as Mary, with her adopted Malawian son David representing the infant Jesus. The headline reads: "Our Lady of Malawi." The online publication *Spiked* has published numerous critiques of celebrity involvement in Africa that take up the imperialist themes, including a piece that describes the trend as a "crusade" (Hume 2005) and one with the headline "Live Aid: the White Pop Star's Burden" (Rothschild 2010). A piece on Madonna's charity in the culture and entertainment site Jezebel was headlined "The White (Wo)man's Burden," also denoting the neocolonial ethos of the pop icon's project (Peterson 2009).

Yet journalism produces a plethora of "salvation" themes. One distinction is that critical journalism seldom involves an interview with the celebrity. Interviews with celebrities, a much bigger audience draw, tend not to broach difficult topics such as celebrity adoption, or the commodification that goes with a cause-marketing effort like Product RED. The celebrity is ultimately beholden to no one for his or her role in this powerful discourse of salvation. Celebrities are sometimes asked about such criticisms in general terms, but seldom about specific critiques directed at them.

One notable exception is a November 2006 interview on BBC2's *Newsnight* when the presenter Kirsty Wark asked Madonna direct questions about the controversy surrounding her adoption of David. It had been surrounded by criticism that she appeared to pull strings in the Malawi judicial system and that David still had a father and other living relatives who were torn about losing him. Madonna granted that rare interview to deny her critics' claims that she had received special treatment from the judicial system. And she specifically used her access to media to do so.

Feature stories that do interview celebrities tend to be much more uncritical, touting their everyday qualities as philanthropes. In 2007, in an *NBC Nightly News* series of reports from Africa on a junket organized by Bono, Brian Williams explained that the Irish rock star is treated as a head of state by African officials but his fame is unknown to the people he visits on the ground. A February 2011 story about George Clooney in *Newsweek* magazine noted the Spartan accommodation he keeps while in Sudan (Avlon 2011). In 2009 Madonna told a CNN interviewer that she was happily toiling in anonymity in Malawi until the press showed up (Cho 2009).

This apparent anonymity serves a number of purposes. It goes some way to detaching the excesses of fame from the juxtaposing relentless poverty and invisibility of the people enduring unspeakable hardship. This tamping down of fame and fortune activates a form of legitimacy that comes from being a source on the ground. It creates rhetorical distance between the celebrity as brand and celebrity as expert or eyewitness, helping to construct the humility and selflessness that is needed if we are to think of Matt Damon, or any celebrity, as someone who can "save" Africa with humility.

Yet celebrities are also set up as credentialed experts. News accounts frequently reassure the audience that the famous person is in it for the long haul and he or she is highly schooled in the problems and potential solutions. As mentioned, McGirt touts Damon as a "development expert," a move toward constructing him in the realm of the credentialed official source as he retains his powerfully branded cultural authority of celebrity. An article in *Time* magazine quoted US Treasury secretary Paul O'Neill as saying Bono knows his stuff around poverty, AIDS, and debt (Tyrangiel 2002). An article in the *Guardian* quoted from former UK prime minister Tony Blair's memoir a passage where he stated that Bono could be prime minister (Michaels 2010). Stories about the work of actors from Sean Penn in Haiti to George Clooney in Africa make a point of affirming the celebrity's deep commitment and knowledge, again by quoting a politician or other authority figure that the audience is likely to recognize (Heller 2011). The celebrity leverages the expertise of already sanctioned news sources and they can leverage the fame and affective power of the famous spokesperson.

Some celebrities formally partner with recognized experts. This resolves any question of legitimacy for journalistic purposes. As mentioned, Matt Damon works with Gary White, a trained engineer who has worked for years on water issues and is a recognized name in the world of aid work and microfinance. George Clooney, who has cofounded the Not on Our Watch project and initiated the Satellite Sentinel project to monitor and deter conflict between North and South Sudan, works with John Prendergast, a well-known figure in the aid and development world. Prendergast is a founder of the Enough Project, dedicated to ending genocide and crimes against humanity. The two men frequently appear together for interviews about the political and humanitarian conditions in Darfur and Sudan generally. Clooney defers to Prendergast, an activist who has worked from within the halls of power for the US State Department, and from outside as the driving force behind numerous human rights campaigns.

The signaling of instant credibility sets the stage for a compelling portrayal of a celebrity response of superhuman proportions against an intractable problem on behalf of the needy, and one that has no politics. The celebrity credit card, as Clooney calls it, is gold. It brings much favorable coverage. From a representational perspective, the journalistic narrative of celebrity savior is also producing the subjectivities of the people who are to benefit from aid. As the examples above suggest, those being "saved" are frequently backgrounded and abstracted by the celebrity, who is ultimately the centerpiece of the news coverage. The casting of a musician or actor as spokesperson for invisible Others invariably boosts that person's brand, while the people at the heart of the project remain largely nameless, as is the girl at the mud hole. While Bono has tried to suggest that his celebrity is not the issue, and that journalism's role is to make people stand up off the page and walk, it is ultimately the celebrity who is the focal point of news accounts.

To be sure there is benefit that comes of celebrity intervention. Famous people bring media salience to problems that are otherwise not on the radar for the media, often because they are not being raised by any of the usual sources, such as government leaders. These are not winning issues for politicians. Sometimes significant material aid flows from celebrity endorsement. Bono's Red campaign for example raised $180 million, as of 2011. Yet if this benefit comes at the cost of discourses that perpetuate the very global imbalance that is the problem, then there are both ethical and political-economic consequences.

This contradictory power relation is perhaps most visible in the deployment of motherhood, a powerful theme in twenty-first-century celebrity philanthropy and an example of how celebritized expertise operates globally. In 2006, CNN's Anderson Cooper produced a special edition of his nightly *AC 360* cable news program called "Angelina Jolie: Her Mission and Motherhood," about the actor's work as a goodwill ambassador for the United Nations High Commission on Refugees. The interview was billed as being devoted to the world's 15 million refugees. It came just days after Jolie gave birth to her daughter Shiloh, with actor Brad Pitt, in a hospital in Namibia. The title of the two-hour special invokes the missionary theme explicitly, and in the context of the powerful, heavily celebritized discourse of motherhood. These are two racially charged historical tropes vis-à-vis Africa and other formerly colonized places.

Jolie is one of the most high-profile mothers and celebrity philanthropists with links to the African continent. Both she and Madonna are mothers of their own biological children and of babies adopted from the developing world. The children are an aspect of Jolie's Hollywood makeover from her youth as a goth wild child to a philanthropist and working mother of six. Three of her children with Pitt are adopted, from Cambodia (Maddox), Ethiopia (Zahara), and Vietnam (Pax). Shiloh was their first biological child, born in Namibia in 2006 amid a media spectacle and criticism about the resources the small country expended on ensuring the privacy and security of the famous couple (see O'Neill 2006).

Jolie and Pitt have chosen to parent publicly, gaining a measure of control over the paparazzi who track their every move. The interview Jolie bestowed on Cooper was an exclusive for CNN. It was an entertainment-style encounter. Cooper, who gained a reputation during Hurricane Katrina as someone who asked pointed questions about the plight of the dispossessed,[4] did not delve into the challenging questions associated with Jolie's childbirth. It is an aspect of the story that raises tough questions about race and class privilege. Neither did Cooper ask broader questions about the complex issue of international adoptions generally, though the interview implicitly frames adoption as one answer to the problems of poverty, the AIDS pandemic, and displacement.

The interview is laden with discussion about Jolie as a mother, as one might expect given the timing. She and Cooper entwine discussion of her work as a UN goodwill ambassador with her motherhood to create a form of highly personal affective expertise on the topics of refugees, war, poverty and aid. In doing so they – and Cooper specifically as the journalist – reinscribe racial stereotypes of people in Africa, and elsewhere in the developing world, as passive victims who manage to maintain a sunny approach to life. The special, which includes reports from CNN correspondents, is very much about Jolie as a mother as well as about her journey to the cause of celebrity emissary, and her impressions of the situation on the ground in refugee camps. She is both expert and eyewitness on the topics of refugees and motherhood, and she deftly blends the two.

For example, she invokes her persona as a mother to answer larger questions about the conditions on the ground. She takes her personal anxieties that her adopted daughter could be sick and uses them to elaborate a larger point and make the poverty "real" for people:

> COOPER: One in four children in Niger dies before the age 5, which to me, I still cannot wrap my mind around. It's hard – I always try to figure out, how do you make that real for people here? You know, how do you make that a reality? Is it something you have figured out a way to make real for people?
> JOLIE: No. I don't think so. I mean, I'd like to – I certainly know with my children, maybe – I mean, people – a lot of people ask me about my daughter Zahara who is an AIDS orphan, and she – because we couldn't hide her from the press. People knew how sick she was when she came home. And so maybe in some way, she's been hopefully a positive example of what just basic care and food can do to a child. (Cooper 2006)

She goes on to say that her own child was not HIV positive and what a relief it was. She explains how it feels (guilty) to take just one child for adoption when so many are in need. The exchange culminates in the two agreeing that it is important to "do what you can." This is stated not as a plea to viewers exactly, but as a personal credo for the privileged. It is an individualistic answer to the larger structural question of childhood poverty and illness that Cooper raised. It is a skilful merger of the public and private that is well suited to journalism's need for a compelling narrative to animate a complex question. She explicitly makes the political "real" via her own personal experience as a mother.

Cooper injects his own perspective, based on experience working as a journalist in areas of devastation and conflict. He framed one question thus:

> Do you go through phases? I mean, when I first went to Somalia in the early '90s during the famine, I remember being overwhelmed. And then I felt like I was going through phases, the more wars I would go to, of anger, and then confusion... (Cooper 2006)

At another he mentions his favorable views of the organization Doctors Without Borders. Early on he lauds the fact that Jolie gives one third of her income to charity. Clearly this entertainment-genre interview is not under the rubric of journalistic objectivity, and yet it is being performed as such, with the ostensible subject the serious issue of stateless peoples. It is a potent media event.

Other female celebrities have deployed their maternal selves as a form of expertise in their philanthropic causes. Model Christy Turlington cites being a mother as her reason for getting involved in Bono's Product Red campaign. Madonna inserts the phrase "as a mother" into her media explanation of how and why the plight of Malawian children resonates with her, and to explain the desire to take all of the children home (Cho 2009). Even childless Oprah Winfrey has invoked motherhood to speak of the girls who attend her exclusive school in South Africa. When abuse allegations against the school's dorm matron surfaced, a shaken Winfrey told Fox News in November 2007: "I am a mama bear when it comes to protecting my children. These girls are like my children."

This is not a critique of experiential ways of knowing, including motherhood. As many feminist scholars have pointed out, the structural separation of the public and private realms is historically bound up with women's oppression. The barrier between the professional and domestic, the rational and irrational, is the division between the masculine and feminine, the visible and invisible, and even work and not work (cf. Fraser 1992, Warner 2002). To insist that the private and affective have no place in the public realm is to accept a dichotomy that has marginalized what is categorized as the feminine. It places the rational and solemn on the one side and the emotional and frivolous on the other, as many scholars have argued. And it devalues female subjectivity. Mainstream news, with its roots in modernity's scientism and rationality, is a party to that representation of gender.

Yet here ideal motherhood is celebritized, *white* motherhood. It reinscribes a form of privilege with strong neocolonial implications for the ethics of representation. One pointed example is how Jolie is able, in the context of the 2006 Cooper interview, to state unproblematically that she and Pitt are in the process of deciding the race, gender, and nationality of their next adoptive child. The decision, she says, is "going to be the balance of what would be best for Mad and for Z right now." It is an astonishing moment that has the unfortunate ring of someone speaking about selecting a family pet. The interview has given her carte blanche to make such a remark, and Cooper leaves unchallenged the enormous privilege contained within it.

These media representations are presented in the context of the flattening out of expertise and the recontextualization of fame in the converged genres of news, entertainment, and lifestyle. Jolie's expert motherhood is activated by white privilege and the legitimacy accorded her as a "credentialed" UNHCR celebrity diplomat. In a sense she has a diplomatic passport to pronounce on all things related to women and children, to speak for those perceived to be voiceless. She claims, intentionally or not, the privilege of white femininity and its presumption to speak for motherhood, as many feminist scholars have argued.[5] Cooper enables her privilege by giving her a pass.

From a news perspective Jolie fulfills multiple imperatives – eyewitness, expert source, and recognizable name. These attributes satisfy the broadcast media's need for serious content and audience numbers. She is a "get" in broadcast parlance. Cooper's own legitimacy as a journalist lends credence to Jolie's project, and she brings prestige to him as a journalist. Her 2006 interview brought visibility to a struggling cable news network. The Cooper interview drew more than 1.3 million viewers, according to the Associated Press, amid some criticism that CNN had sullied itself as a purveyor of hard news and that it managed to make even a celebrity interview boring (USA Today, 2006).

Conclusion

The problematic depictions that emerge from coverage of Africa are but one example of how the celebritization of knowledge and cultural authority has implications that resonate globally. The crossover of celebrity as news source brings a recontextualized use of fame that serves to boost the cultural authority and brand of the spokesperson as it satisfies the conflicting needs and mandates of the media in an environment where news, entertainment, and lifestyle are one. The format and performance of the news in the cases described above adheres to norms of mainstream news, including the use of credentialed experts. But the celebrity serves as the eyewitness and "human interest" source as well, and one with enormous affective power and a following.

This is not a wholesale rejection of celebrity involvement in social issues. Some celebrities have had a significant impact on problems to which they have turned their resources and lent their name. With rich countries' intransigence and broken promises on global issues, it is understandable that people with fame and material means want to help. Given journalism's weakness at raising difficult issues that are not circulating in the halls of power, celebrity can provide a window on problems such as poverty, malnutrition, genocide, and disease that are not winning issues for political leaders at home.

Yet a media narrative that sets up a Hollywood star as the divine answer to those vexing questions is ultimately fueling the hegemonic global power relations in question. It puts the focus on the privileged and extraordinary life and reinscribes the distant Other, in this case in Africa, as one who is primitive and without agency. This sets the stage for us to believe that any help, any investment, any charity at all is better than none and that if it weren't for the white savior there would be no hope. Thus Africa can remain in our minds an object for our noblesse oblige, as well as a source for raw materials and cheap labor.

This is not an argument against the infusion of ways of knowing that are not built upon the idealized notion of the rational as distinct from the emotional or affective. It is to suggest that the affective power of celebrities is not the stuff of everyday life. Celebrities cannot simply sub in for the eyewitness perspective. They are powerful brands that operate as thought leaders and there is always an element of commodification that attends their doings. Journalism's use of them as recontextualized sources does not for the most part treat this power as something that must be questioned and examined with a critical (not necessarily cynical) eye to the ways in which they are speaking for Others.

Notes

1. "Anderson Cooper 360," Cable News Network. Cooper interviewed Barr and Nugent on January 5, 2011 and Rivers, among other comedians, on January 4, 2011.
2. One of the most cited arguments is Herman and Chomsky, *Manufacturing Consent* (1988).
3. For an analysis of racial representation using the concept of bifurcation, see Joseph, *Transcending Blackness* (2012).
4. In a frequently cited live interview in 2005, Cooper challenged Senator Mary Landrieu of Louisiana on her stock answer praising the government helping Katrina victims; he repeatedly asked her about the dead bodies in the streets and the homeless people without food and water.
5. For example, Frankenberg (1993), Haraway (1988), Rowe (2000).

Further Reading

Celebrity has become a key focal point of scholarship in media and cultural studies. A number of edited volumes provide a good overview of the issues of representation, commodification and globalization discussed in this chapter. The *Celebrity Culture Reader* (London: Taylor & Francis, 2006), edited by P. David Marshall, includes a selection of excerpts of foundational writings on celebrity and its historical contexts. It looks at the phenomenon from a variety of perspectives, including its public sphere implications, fandom, and celebrity as industry. A collection by Liza Tsaliki, Christos A. Frangonikolopoulos, and Asteris Huliaris, *Transnational Celebrity Activism in Global Politics: Changing the World?* (Chicago: University of Chicago Press, 2011) explores the issues of celebrity intervention in global politics and the use of celebrity diplomacy in conflict zones, among other important subject areas. *Commodity Activism: Cultural Resistance in Neoliberal Times* (New York: NYU Press, 2012), a book edited by Roopali Mukherjee and Sarah Banet-Weiser, analyzes the commodification of activism in general, including the commoditized relationship between celebrity and citizenship. The book examines the relationship between branding and activism, the implications for social movements and politics, and the racial implications of commodity activism.

References

Avlon, J. 2011. "A 21st-Century Statesman." *Newsweek*, February 21: 16–23.

Baym, G. 2005. "The Daily Show: Discursive Integration and the Reinvention of Political Journalism." *Political Communication* 22(3): 259–76.

Benjamin, W. 2006. *Walter Benjamin: Selected Writings. Vol. 4, 1938–1940.* Cambridge, MA: Belknap Press.

Braudy, L. 1986. *The Frenzy of Renown: Fame and its History.* New York: Oxford University Press.

Burton, A. M. 1994. *Burdens of History: British Feminists, Indian Women, and Imperial Culture, 1865–1915.* Chapel Hill: University of North Carolina Press.

Cho, A. 2009. "Madonna and Malawi." *American Morning, Cable News Network*, http://www.firstpost.com/topic/person/alina-cho-madonna-and -malawi-video-LqTxMtpiQMs-33474-4.html.

Chouliaraki, L. and Fairclough, N. 1999. *Discourse in Late Modernity: Rethinking Critical Discourse Analysis.* Edinburgh: Edinburgh University Press.

Compton, J. R. 2004. *The Integrated News Spectacle: A Political Economy of Cultural Performance, Media, and Culture.* New York: Peter Lang.

Cooper, A. 2006. "Angelina Jolie: Her Mission and Motherhood." *Anderson Cooper 360*, Cable News Network, http://transcripts.cnn.com /TRANSCRIPTS/0606/20/acd.01.html.

Corner, J. and Pels, D. 2003. "Introduction: The Re-styling of Politics." In J. Corner and D. Pels, eds., *Media and the Restyling of Politics: Consumerism, Celebrity and Cynicism.* London: Sage, 1–18.

Daston, L. 1992. "Objectivity and the Escape from Perspective." *Social Studies of Science* 22(4): 597–618.

Delli Carpini, M. X. and Williams, B. A. 2001. "Let us Infotain You: Politics in the New Media Environment." In W. L. Bennett and R. M. Entman, eds., *Mediated Politics: Communication in the Future of Democracy.* Cambridge: Cambridge University Press, 160–81.

Diehl, J. 2010. "PostPartisan – George Clooney yells 'fire!' about Sudan." *Washington Post*, http://voices.washingtonpost.com/postpartisan/2010/10/george _clooney_yells_fire.html.

Dionne, E. J. 1996. *They Only Look Dead: Why Progressives Will Dominate the Next Political Era.* New York: Simon & Schuster.

Dyer, R. 1986. *Heavenly Bodies: Film Stars and Society.* New York: St. Martin's Press.

Frankenberg, R. 1993. *White Women, Race Matters: The Social Construction of Whiteness.* Minneapolis: University of Minnesota Press.

Fraser, N. 1992. "Rethinking the Public Sphere: A Contribution to the Critique of Actually Existing Democracy." In C. J. Calhoun, ed., *Habermas and the Public Sphere.* Cambridge, MA: MIT Press, 109–42.

Furner, M. O. 1975. *Advocacy & Objectivity: A Crisis in the Professionalization of American Social Science, 1865–1905*. Lexington: University Press of Kentucky.

Gans, H. J. 1979. *Deciding What's News: A Study of CBS Evening News, NBC Nightly News, Newsweek, and Time*. New York: Pantheon Books.

Gitlin, T. 1980. *The Whole World is Watching: Mass Media in the Making and Unmaking of the New Left*. Berkeley, CA: University of California Press.

Grigoriadis, V. 2011. "Our Lady of Malawi." *New York*, May 1. http://nymag.com/news/features/madonna-malawi-2011-5/.

Hall, S. 1997. *Representation: Cultural Representations and Signifying Practices*. London: Sage.

Hallin, D. C. 1986. *The "Uncensored War": The Media and Vietnam*. New York: Oxford University Press.

Haraway, D. 1988. "Situated Knowledges: The Science Question in Feminism and the Privilege of Partial Perspective." *Feminist Studies* 14 (3): 575–99.

Heller, Z. 2011. "The Accidental Activist." *New York Times Style Magazine*, March 25, 83–7.

Herman, E. S. and Chomsky, N. 1988. *Manufacturing Consent: The Political Economy of The Mass Media*. New York: Pantheon Books.

Hollar, J. 2007. "Bono, I Presume? Covering Africa Through Celebrities." Fairness & Accuracy in Reporting, May/June, http://www.fair.org/index.php?page=3119.

Holson, L. M. 2010. "Charity Fixer to the Stars." *New York Times*, December 5, http://www.nytimes.com/2010/12/05/fashion/05TREVORNEILSON.html?pagewanted=all.

Hume, M. 2005. "Africa: A Stage for Political Poseurs." *Spiked*, June 10, http://www.spiked-online.com/index.php?/site/article/329/.

Joseph, R. 2012. *Transcending Blackness: From the New Millennium Mulatta to the Exceptional Multiracial*. Durham, NC: Duke University Press.

Lippmann, W. 1965. *Public Opinion*. New York: Free Press.

Lury, C. 2004. *Brands: The Logos of the Global Economy*. London: Routledge.

Marshall, P. D. 1997. *Celebrity and Power: Fame in Contemporary Culture*. Minneapolis: University of Minnesota Press.

McGirt, E. 2011. "Can Matt Damon Bring Clean Water to Africa?" *Fast Company.com*, http://www.fastcompany.com/magazine/157/can-this-man-save-this-girl.

Michaels, S. 2010. "Bono Could Have Been Prime Minister, Says Tony Blair." *Guardian*, September 3, http://www.guardian.co.uk/music/2010/sep/03/bono-prime-minister-tony-blair.

Mindich, D. T. Z. 1998. *Just The Facts: How "Objectivity" Came To Define American Journalism*. New York: New York University Press.

Mindich, D. T. Z. 2005. "The Rise of Journalism's Scientific Mindset, 1832–1866." In S. R. Knowlton and K. L. Freeman, eds., *Fair and Balanced: A History of Journalistic Objectivity*. Northport, AL: Vision Press.

Mirando, J. A. 2001. 'Embracing Objectivity Early On: Journalism Textbooks of the 1800s. *Journal of Mass Media Ethics* 16(1): 23–32.

Nagel, T. 1986. *The View From Nowhere*. New York: Oxford University Press.

O'Neill, B. 2006. "Brad, Angelina and the Rise of 'Celebrity Colonialism'," *Spiked*, May 30, http://www.spiked-online.com/index.php?/site/article/327/.

Peterson, L. 2009. "White (Wo) Man's Burden: Madonna, Malawi, and Celebrity Activism." *Jezebel*, http://jezebel.com/5391099/white-womans-burden-madonna-malawi--celebrity-activism.

Richey, L. A. and Ponte, S. 2011. *Brand Aid: Shopping Well to Save the World*. Minneapolis: University of Minnesota Press.

Ross, D. 1991. *The Origins of American Social Science, Ideas in Context*. Cambridge: Cambridge University Press.

Rothschild, N. 2010. "Live Aid 25 Years On – Time to Change the Record." *Spiked*, July 13, http://www.spiked-online.com/index.php/site/article/9197/.

Rowe, A. M. C. 2000. "Locating Feminism's Subject: The Paradox of White Femininity and the Struggle to Forge Feminist Alliances." *Communication Theory: A Journal of The International Communication Association* 10 (1): 64–80.

Said, E. W. [1978] 2003. *Orientalism*. London: Penguin.

Schiller, D. 1981. *Objectivity and the News: The Public and the Rise of Commercial Journalism*. Philadelphia: University of Pennsylvania Press.

Schudson, M. 1978. *Discovering the News: A Social History of American Newspapers*. New York: Basic Books.

Smith, M. C. 1994. *Social Science in the Crucible: The American Debate Over Objectivity and Purpose, 1918–1941*. Durham, NC: Duke University Press.

Street, J. 2006. "The Celebrity Politician: Political Style and Popular Culture." In P. D. Marshall, ed., *The Celebrity Culture Reader*. New York: Routledge, 359–70.

Tuchman, G. 1972. "Objectivity as Strategic Ritual: An Examination of Newsmen's Notions of Objectivity." *American Journal of Sociology* 77 (4): 660–79.

Turner, G. 2004. *Understanding Celebrity*. London: Sage.

Turner, S. P. 2003. *Liberal Democracy 3.0: Civil Society in an Age of Experts*. London: Sage.

Tyrangiel, J. 2002. "Music: Bono." *Time*, March 2, 62–8.

USA Today. 2006. "CNN Gets High Ratings for Jolie Interview." July 3, http://www.usatoday.com/life/television/news/2006-06-27-jolie-interview_x.htm.

Ward, S. J. A. 2004. *The Invention of Journalism Ethics: The Path to Objectivity and Beyond*. Montreal: McGill-Queen's University Press.

Warner, M. 2002. *Publics and Counterpublics*. New York: Zone Books.

12

Global Media Ethics, Justice, and Indian Journalism

Shakuntala Rao

Globalization defines our era. It is what happens when the movement of people, goods, or ideas among countries and regions accelerates. In recent years, globalization has come into focus, generating considerable interest and controversy in the social sciences, humanities, and policy circles and among the informed public at large. Throughout most of history, the vectors that organized and gave meaning to human lives and human imaginations were structured primarily by local geography and topology, local kinship and social organization, local worldviews and religions. Today the world is another place. While human lives continue to be lived in local realities, these realities are increasingly being challenged by and integrated into larger global networks of relationships. Media is at the heart of such changes. The multidirectional flow of media and cultural goods is creating new forms of convergence and identities. These forms are often received either with exhilaration or panic (Mattelart 2002). Yet no one can disregard the fact that there is an acceleration of media convergence exemplified by various intersections among media technologies, industries, content, and audiences.

If we are to consider justice, and the institutions of justice to be key institutions which "hold democracy together," an analysis of media globalization must include understanding the connections between journalism ethics, democracy, and justice (Muhlmann 2010: 222). While journalism is not necessary to democracy, where there is democracy, journalism can provide different services to bring about a just society. Those functions, Schudson (2006: 12) writes, could provide initiatives of justice, public interest, and accountability by "informing the public, investigation, analysis, social empathy, public forum, and mobilization." Journalism thus provides spaces of public reasoning.

This chapter will focus on Amartya Sen's (2009) philosophy of justice as articulated in his book, *The Idea of Justice*, in which Sen locates justice and injustice in the context of Hindu beliefs and Indian history. While Sen

Global Media Ethics: Problems and Perspectives, First Edition. Edited by Stephen J. A. Ward.
© 2013 Blackwell Publishing Ltd. Published 2013 by Blackwell Publishing Ltd.

is well recognized, in and outside of India, as a public intellectual (having won the Nobel Prize for Economics in 1998), I limit my discussion to this book, where Sen gives us a blueprint of a workable philosophy of justice. In my thinking through issues of ethics, justice, and injustice, I focus on Sen's analysis and expansion of two concepts from early Indian jurisprudence: *niti* (strict organizational and behavioral rules of justice) and *nyaya* (the larger picture of how such rules affect ordinary lives). Sen accounts for the role of media in the process of enacting *nyaya*. Media enables the public to hear diverse sections of the society, allows for reasoned deliberations, and communicates injustices. If indeed *nyaya* is integral to the democratic process, as Sen asserts, and if media and journalism can contribute much to the discursive construction of justice, this chapter addresses the following questions: What is the relevance of *nyaya* as articulated by Sen to journalism ethics and practices in the newly globalized and liberalized media in India? What is the relevance of *nyaya* in developing a workable philosophy of ethics for global journalism?

Sen's Interpretative Use of *Nyaya*

"Justice" writes Sen (2009: 19) "is ultimately connected with the way people's lives go, and not merely with the nature of institutions surrounding them." Sen argues that justice is relative to a situation and that instead of searching for "ideal justice" (2009: 20), a society should strive to identify, ameliorate, and eliminate structural, but redressable injustices, such as subjugation of women, poverty, and malnutrition. Sen takes issue with his predecessors, such as John Rawls, who emphasize the *niti*-oriented political philosophy. While Sen writes that his own approach can be understood as not a radical foundational departure from Rawls's own program, Sen draws on the Sanskrit literature and treatises by outlining the distinction between *niti* and *nyaya*; both of these terms can be translated as justice, but *niti* refers to correct procedures, formal rules, and institutions; *nyaya* entails a broader, more inclusive focus on the world that emerges from the institutions we create, and is central to creating a sustainable and just society. The recognition, Sen observes, is that the realization of justice in the sense of *nyaya* is "not just a matter of judging institutions and rules, but of judging the societies themselves" (2009: 20). Arguing for a "realization-focused perspective on justice," Sen wants a global citizenry to be not merely about trying to achieve, or dreaming about achieving, some perfectly just society or social arrangements, but "about preventing manifestly severe injustices or *anyaya*" (2009: 21). He writes:

> When people across the world agitate to get more global justice…they are not clamoring for some kind of "minimal humanitarianism." Nor are they agitating for a "perfectly just" world society, but for the elimination of some outrageously unjust arrangements. (Sen 2009: 26)

In agreeing with Rawls that "Democracy is an exercise in public reason" (Sen 2009: 323) and not just about elections and balloting, Sen writes:

> The crucial role of public reasoning in the practice of democracy makes the entire subject of democracy closely relate to justice . . . if the demands of justice can be assessed only with the help of public reasoning, and if public reasoning is constitutively related to the idea of democracy, then there is an intimate connection between justice and democracy, with shared discursive features. (Sen 2009: 326)

Here Sen critiques *niti*-oriented political philosophy which understands democracy in narrow organizational terms, focusing primarily on the procedures of balloting and elections. "The effectiveness of ballot," writes Sen, "depends crucially on what goes along with balloting, such as free speech, access to information, and freedom of dissent" (2009: 341). In formulating his close connection between *nyaya*, reasoned deliberation, and democracy, Sen critiques the claim that democracy, like reason, is a quintessentially European or Western idea. Sen gives the example of Emperor Ashoka, from third-century BCE India, who had attempted to codify rules for public discussion by organizing meetings of Buddhist scholars. Similarly, by giving examples from *Akbarnama*, the recorded words of Mughal emperor Akbar from the fifteenth century, Sen recounts that the path of reason or the rule of intellect was, for Akbar, the basis of good and just behavior as well as of an acceptable framework of legal duties and entitlements.

The history of *nyaya* philosophy has provided the concept of reasoned deliberation in India. Pāṇini, the great Sanskrit grammarian, thought that the term *nyaya* came from the root *ni* and has the same meaning as *gam* which means "to go" (Saha 1987: 107). Hence *nyaya* in the local sense of the word can be the same as *nigaman*, or the conclusion of a syllogism. In Sanskrit different terms have been used to express the science of conclusions and logic: *Hetu castra*, or the science of causes; *Avviksiki*, or the science of inquiry; *Pramana castra*, or the science of correct knowledge; and *Vadartha*, or the science of discussion.

Nyaya philosophy originated in the times of *Vedas* (ancient scriptures of Hinduism) and evolved in the disputations and debates among scholars trying to ascertain the meanings of the Vedic texts. Such studies resulted in the writing of *nyaya sutras* (books), written to discuss the conditions of valid thought and the means of acquiring true knowledge or *buddhi*. The nyaya philosophical tradition in India, in its four thousand years of history, comprised various thinkers and texts such as *Nyaya sutras* of Guatama, *Bhasya* of Vatsyayana, *Nyaya Vartika* of Uddyotakara, and *Tarkasam-graha* of Annambhatta. Many of these *nyaya* texts, as in other schools of Indian philosophies, were *atman* (soul)-centered. "Nyaya philosophy is *atman*-centric," writes Chatterjee (1950: 188), "Everything originates from the *atman* and is dissolved in it. It is the center of interest, the central

principle of metaphysics, psychology, ethics, aesthetics, and religion."
While the liberation of *atman* from pain and pleasure is the ultimate goal
for *nyayayikas* (*nyaya* philosophers), the question, posed by Guatama, in
the beginning of *Nyaya Sutra* was, "What is the nature of knowledge?"
(Saha 1987: 9). *Nyaya* philosophy, its logical and dialectical technicalities,
breaks away from the existence of the ideal in Indian thought by showing
that the external world does not exist independent of thought but that the
world is intelligible; our reason could reach its reality and could know
its true nature. The process of *nyaya*, for *nyayayikas*, was a multilayered
path that began with *Anubhava* or presentation of facts through *Smirti*
or memory. There existed a distinction between *Prama* (valid knowledge)
and *Aprama* (invalid knowledge); the recognition of *Yathartha* (truth)
or *Ayathartha* (falsehood) in speech; reaching *Buddhi* was a process of
samcaya (doubt), *Viparyyaya* (error), and *Tarka* (hypothetical argument),
along with *Pratyaksa* (perception), *Anumana* (inference), *Upamana* (comparison), and *Sabda* (testimony). These levels and practices in speech and
thinking gave a clear path to reasoned knowledge (D'Almeida 1973).

Sen takes *nyaya* philosophy away from its focus on *atman* and supreme
happiness into the realms of the ethical-societal and of justice but his
interpretative and pragmatic use of *nyaya* as a path of reasoned deliberation closely resembles its historical formulations by Gautama and
Vatsyayana. While making outstanding points of philosophical thought,
especially against the more dogmatic and instrumental views of society in
various traditions of Indian philosophy, *nyayayikas* have been critiqued
for not reaching the most important and essential characteristic of human
knowledge, namely its transcendence. Because the material and objective
world is known through reason, critics argue, *nyayayikas* seem to treat
knowledge as they would treat many physical phenomena. "Knowledge
reveals for us the facts of the objective world and this is experienced by
us," writes Chatterjee,

> But that the objective world generates knowledge can hardly be demonstrated
> by mere experience. Knowledge is not like any other phenomena for it stands
> above them and interprets or illumines them all. (Chatterjee 1950: 55)

Sen, in the line of other great *nyayayikas*, argues against trying to find
an ideal justice, and instead emphasizes a more tempered *nyaya* position,
recognizing and considering comparative and feasible alternatives, and
choosing among them. Sen gives us a deceptively simple example of a
pragmatic interpretation of *nyaya* when he writes:

> If we are trying to choose between a Picasso and a Dali, it is of no help
> to invoke a diagnosis that the ideal picture in the world is the Mona Lisa.
> That may be interesting to hear, but it is neither here nor there in the choice
> between Dali and Picasso. Indeed, it is not at all necessary to talk about
> what may be the greatest or most perfect picture in the world, to choose

between two alternatives that we are facing. Nor is it sufficient, or indeed of any particular help, to know that the Mona Lisa is the most perfect picture in the world when the choice is actually between Dali and Picasso. (Sen 2009: 122)

For Sen, as for other *nyayayikas*, reflective and objective cognition (*Anu-vyavasaya*) brings the self (*Manas*) in direct contact with the knowledge of the object and leads to knowledge, justice, and ethics. The comparative analysis of Picasso and Dali provokes a choice between two alternatives rather than invoking the presence of Mona Lisa as the ideal. The public reasoning and practice of *nyaya* envisions a just society, but not in its transcendental manifestations, nor in its search for *atman*-centered happiness.

Nyaya and *Anyaya* in Indian Journalism Practices

It is in the context of reasoned deliberation, and its significance for achieving *nyaya*, that Sen locates the importance of an "unrestrained and healthy media" (2009: 254). The absence of free media, writes Sen, and the suppression of people's ability to communicate with each other, have the effect of directly reducing the quality of human life even if an authoritarian state happens to be rich in terms of gross national product. Without media's ability to disseminate information, it would be difficult to engage in any form of public reasoning and deliberation and to achieve *nyaya*. A free and unrestrained media can directly contribute to free speech, allows for dissemination of knowledge and critical scrutiny, and provides a protective function in giving voice to the neglected and disadvantaged. If democracy is a history of people's participation in public reasoning, it is in a well-functioning media that one finds the most important space of public reasoning. Rejecting the idea of "discussionless justice" (2009: 255), Sen asserts that it is a free, energetic, and efficient media in which one can facilitate the needed discursive process about democracy. "Media is important," writes Sen, "not only for democracy but for the pursuit of justice in general" (2009: 254).

Indian journalism practices and media environment have been radically transformed in the last two decades of dramatic economic globalization and privatization. While, immediately after independence, Indian journalists and publishers hoped and endeavored to fulfill the Gandhian vision of a free and independent press, the postcolonial Indian government was not as eager as these journalists to establish a free press (Ravindranath 2005). Journalists battled, unsuccessfully, to add a "free press clause to Article 19(1) (a) of the constitution," which gave the republic freedom of speech and expression but no guarantee of a free press (Natarajan 2000: 87). When the Prime Minister, Indira Gandhi, declared emergency rule in 1975 her government began to strictly censor all political news, and arrested and jailed more than 300 journalists. Since the end of the emergency in 1977, print news media in India have functioned relatively free from government intervention and there have been no attempts to "muzzle the press or expression of dissent" (Sonwalkar 2002: 825).

Television news, however, had remained under state control. Until recently Doordarshan, the state-operated television system, and the only one allowed to broadcast, started its modest operations on September 15, 1959. For 12 years, when the rest of the world's television media gained momentum in terms of quality content and freedom, India had a one-hour twice-a-week experimental service in Delhi until the second television center began in Mumbai in 1972 (Bhatt 1996). Without any competition, Doordarshan's news programming remained dull and uncontroversial, as the government approved and censored it; the news covered few stories about justice issues, and did not interest viewers. It was only with the deregulation, privatization, and commercialization of the broadcast industry in the 1990s that television news became an important source of information. In the past decade, commercial television has established itself as the vanguard in news-making though it has also been accused of "copying US-style sensational journalism" with an entertainment-oriented news agenda (Thussu 1999: 129). There are now more than 300 cable news channels, broadcasting in 16 different languages, catering to vast audiences in the subcontinent and among South Asian diasporas. Having depended solely on Doordarshan to provide news, viewers have access not only to the major international cable television news stations such as CNNI, BBC World, MSNBC, Bloomberg, and Headline News, but also a plethora of Indian news channels such as STAR News, Zee News, NDTV 24 × 7, and India TV.

The Use (and Abuse) of Hidden Cameras

The new broadcast journalism in India has heavily invested itself in questions of democracy, democratic institutions, and justice. Broadcast journalism, in the age of privatization, liberalization, and globalization, has begun to address questions of social justice and political accountability. The rise in the use of hidden cameras in Indian journalism is one such example. Journalism practices have been transformed with the phenomenal rise of hidden cameras in the past decade. Indian news channels have aggressively used hidden cameras to gather news, calling resulting news-stories "sting operations." The television media has used hidden camera revelations to expose violations of trust and abuses of power, and to debate the morality of the activity captured in such stories and, thus, to further the practice of *nyaya* and democracy.

Tehelka.com (an online magazine) started the trend in 2001, airing video footage that revealed professional cricketers fixing matches and taking bribes. In another hidden-camera story, *Tehelka* sent two journalists, who posed as agents from a fictitious arms company called "West End," and tried hawking a nonexistent product – hand-held thermal cameras – to politicians and bureaucrats. The journalists proffered bribes and prostitutes to push the deal through, captured all transactions on a spycam, and exhibited the footage at a press conference. In both of these news stories, hidden cameras revealed an abuse of power and forced influential men and women to surrender their power and reputations. Democracy is well served by such stories, if it is indeed true that, as Sen contends, democracy succeeds not only by striving to have the most perfect institutional structure (*niti*), but also by integrating our behavior patterns and the direct contribution of press freedom into the quality of our lives (*nyaya*). In such a context, the use of hidden cameras for watching, and freely and energetically criticizing, immoral behavior, makes justice possible and helps strengthen the functioning of democracy.

One recent example of a hidden camera story concerned Nithyananda Swami, a self-styled guru or holy man whose devotees included politicians and movie stars. Founder of the Life Bliss spiritual movement, Nithyananda headed Dhyanapeetam, a group of Ashrams in Bangalore and in other Indian cities. News channels received a hidden camera video of Nithyananda having sex with two women, one of whom was an actress. The footage was first broadcast on Sun TV, a Tamil-language network based in Chennai; several news channels broadcast parts of the video. NDTV 24 × 7, a Delhi-based English and Hindi news network, ran a lengthy story entitled, "God men, good men, and bad men." Prior to his arrest, Zee News, another Delhi-based Hindi news network, ran a story titled "Tainted Swami tracked down." In this news story, the visuals show Nithyananda walking out into a hotel lobby followed by 20 to 30 journalists and videographers. Nithyananda appears on camera to say, "I will go into the vow of silence from now on to heal all the people and I don't wish harm to anybody... I feel only peace." The reporter continues:

> He might preach silence to the media but he will have to have a reply ready when he appears before a court in Bangalore... In a youtube video [Swami] has admitted that the bedroom scenes with the Tamil actress were experiments... Vow of silence or not, the Swami has a lot of explaining to do.

Media coverage focused on the injustice of his violation of trust; *nyaya* was well served when he was exposed and arrested.

Another such "sting operation," the spycam video footage of Narayan Dutt Tiwari, an 83-year old veteran politician, and the governor of the southern Indian state of Andhra Pradesh, showed that hidden-camera coverage could expose a person's abuse of power, and support the justice of removing such people from power. The video, first broadcast on a local news channel, Amoda Broadcasting Network (ABN), was later broadcast on news channels around the country. In the video, Tiwari is seen with three young women performing various sex acts. The faces of the women were blurred and the broadcast had no audio. Despite first denying the authenticity of the video, Tiwari resigned two weeks later. In a Zee News story titled, *"Tiwari ka antim sanskar"* (Tiwari's end), the reporter pointedly discussed the details of Tiwari's abuse of power. She says:

> [The governor] was 83, and the women ranged between the age group of 17 and 25. It is reported that usually those girls were brought from different parts of the country to be employed in Raj Bhavan [the governor's mansion] giving them tax-payers' money to provide a variety of sexual comforts. Radhika, a woman, has admitted that that she sent the young women on Tiwari's request. In return, she claimed, the governor failed to keep his word to provide her a mining license in Andhra Pradesh.

The television news channels covered Tiwari's public denial and, subsequently, covered his resignation. Zee News ran a special, "End to a Distinguished Career: The Life of N.D. Tiwari" and Star News broadcast a more provocatively titled special, "The Old Man and Sleaze: The N.D. Tiwari Scandal."

In a special story titled, *"Tasveer ka toofan"* (Photographs create storm) Zee News covered women's group protests in Hyderabad, the capital city of Andhra Pradesh. Visuals showed protestors standing in front of the Governor's office, shouting slogans, and holding up placards reading, "Tiwari must resign." The voiceover of the reporter said, "These voices are speaking out... [the Tiwari] video is creating controversy in Hyderabad and women's organizations are protesting." Zee News then interviewed a local women's rights activist, identified as Sandhya, who said:

> These women [in the video] it is shameful for them as to what has happened... the women would be willing to come out in public if there is an inquiry but only under police protection.

Protests by women's groups and reporters against Tiwari's denial both stoked and reflected ordinary people's sense of outrage and injustice, and Tiwari's resignation seemed justified given he had abused the trust and power they had afforded him.

Nyaya is served in the coverage of Tiwari and Nityananda's cases where the behavior of each, their abuse of power, is harshly criticized by a free and energetic media. If the hidden camera in India has become the "weapon of the weak," media practices in these two cases reflect its ability to bring about social and political justice (Rao 2008: 194). It is in media that justice should manifestly and undoubtedly be seen to be done for there is a "clear connection between the objectivity of a judgment and its ability to withstand public scrutiny" (Sen 2009: 394).

While Indian media has easily located injustices in corruption cases, it sometimes disagrees on criteria for judging hidden-camera stories and, thus, to fully contextualize *anyaya*. In the case of the death of Srinivas Ramachandra Siras, a professor in the Modern Language Department at Aligarh Muslim University (AMU) in Aligarh, a city in Northern India, it was unclear as to who was the victim of injustice: the professor who had been unfairly fired and had died under mysterious circumstances, or a university which had employed a man engaged in immoral activities. Unlike in Tiwari's and Nithyananda's cases, reporters and producers determined the moral criteria of establishing the victim and perpetrators of injustice, which affected the ways in which the story was told. Professor Siras had been suspended by the university administration after they had been provided a videotape in which Siras was seen having sex with another man. The professor accused two independent video journalists, Adil Murtaza and Shiraz, of surreptitiously entering his apartment and taping the sex act. None of the news channels broadcast any part of the tape. Siras was found dead in his university apartment weeks after he had been suspended from his job. Police reports first claimed that he had committed suicide, but later suggested that his death had been a case of homicide. While NDTV 24 × 7, in a report titled, "Fired for being gay?" suggested that unfair targeting of gays by the university and the media's "sting operation" had victimized Siras, Zee News suggested that the professor had been justifiably fired for "molesting men in his university-provided apartment," and that the men were victims. While the NDTV 24 × 7 report described the sex as "consensual sex," Zee News reported that it was "molestation."

Coverage of Siras's death suggests that *anyaya* remains ill-defined in the Indian media; a widely accepted cultural taboo against homosexuality affected media assessments of Siras's firing and death. This case highlights the often invoked "cultural values" which explain and even justify the deficiencies of public reasoning about minority rights. The media's obligation to give voice to the minorities, even sexual minorities whom the public despises and fears, suggests that a free media must challenge widely held cultural notions, such as that homosexuality is an immoral act, and open up a discussion of human rights. According to Sen (2009: 254), a free press has and must fulfill a "perfect obligation" not only to report about oppression and marginalization of minorities, but also to prevent ways in which oppression takes place. In depicting competing claims of freedom, between those who assert majority cultural rights over those who seek individual minority rights, media can succeed in advocating public reason and *nyaya* only when journalists recognize inclusiveness as part of democracy and as a common principle.

Uneven Injustices: Coverage of Crime

While the highly censored Doordarshan news had rarely covered any types of crime, and seldom focused on injustice of any sort, liberalization and privatization of television news has resulted in 24-hour, seven-day–a-week continuous news, and has created a cycle of uninterrupted reporting about violent crimes such as rape, molestation, murder, assault, incest, and child abuse, but less coverage of poor victims and the victims' families than coverage of wealthy victims.

The first high-profile murder case widely covered in the postliberalized Indian media was the 1999 murder of a fashion model, Jessica Lall, by Manu Sharma, the son of a wealthy politician, where journalists discovered that the police and judiciary had committed systemic injustices. Another high-profile murder, that of Aarushi Talwar, the 14-year-old daughter of a successful dentist couple, occurred in 2008, and like the Lall murder case, garnered much and continuous coverage from television news over several years. On the morning of May 16, 2008, Talwar was found dead with her throat slit in her parents' home at Jalvayu Vihar in Noida, Uttar Pradesh, an affluent neighborhood on the outskirts of Delhi. Suspicion immediately fell on the family's live-in manservant, Hemraj, who was found missing from the home. But, two days later, the police found the dead body of the missing man on the terrace of Talwar's residence. After a disorganized and drawn-out investigation, the police arrested Rajesh Talwar, the father of the deceased girl, and charged him with having committed the double murder. Rajesh Talwar, however, was released two months later because the police had failed to produce any credible evidence against him. The coverage of the Aarushi Talwar murder case focused on the police's failure to collect evidence, tampering with and losing physical evidence, and failing to follow viable leads. The Central Bureau of Investigation (CBI) took over the investigation in June 2008 in an attempt to solve the case. In December 2010, two years after the murders, CBI closed their investigation without any new findings.

On the day of the release of the CBI report, all the news channels broadcast interviews with Aarushi's parents, who spoke fluently in English and Hindi. Zee News ran a story titled "Rajesh Talwar: Justice has been denied to my daughter"; Star News ran a poll for its audiences and asked them to text the answer to the question, "Has there been justice for Aarushi Talwar?"; Star News ran a story titled, "Aarushi's Family and Friends Want Justice"; NDTV 24 × 7 interviewed a well-known Indian film star, Rani Mukherjee, who said on camera she was "praying for justice for Aarushi." Journalists interviewed Rajesh and Nupur Talwar, often in their spacious and markedly wealthy surroundings, such as in their living room and front lawn. Several journalists used the word *anyaya* (injustice) in their report. One reporter said, on camera, after covering the press conference conducted by the Talwar family,

> This is a story about injustice. It is also a story [that] speaks to every family's heart. Parents want to know about the relationship between a child and parents. Children are interested to see what was happening to their peers.

In the newly commercialized news media, it is not unusual to find stories about injustices against children. Some recent examples include NDTV 24 × 7 footage of a nine-year-old drug addict found beaten after having been tied to a tree; the report mentions that the mother of the child had asked for intervention from local goons after she had unsuccessfully tried to wean the child off drugs. Zee News did interviews with six-year-old Shah Rukh, who had been abandoned by his father on a train because he was suffering from a chronic disease. In one case, a 10-year-old girl who had been raped and stabbed was found in the lower middle-class neighborhood in Delhi. The father, who, unlike the educated Talwar family, spoke only in a rural dialect of Hindi, was interviewed briefly by Zee News and Star News. Television news channels frequently run stories of purposely blinded children turned into beggars, street children run over by cars, and children trafficked from Nepal.

While such television news coverage of crimes against children show the reporters', producers', and audience's continuing interest in and concern about *anayaya*, no one case received the kind of continuous and extensive coverage that the Aarushi Talwar case did. The class status of the victim or, if known, the victim's family, seems to have made a difference in the amount of coverage any case received. The intensity of the focus on injustice was mitigated by the social class of the victims. Any case, such as the Aarushi Talwar case, in which the victim was wealthy, received far more coverage than similar crimes in which the victim was poor. Crimes against poor children were widely reported as a systemic failure of the government, police, and judiciary to check abuses, but none received continuous or in-depth coverage. The media coverage of crimes against lower-class children showed neither commitment to nor consciousness of class equality, nor substantive analysis of the complicated issue of child labor in India. Such coverage, that treats violence against children as an individual psychopathy of abusers, supports Sen's (1999: 69) contention that "the battle against class divisions has substantially weakened in India." New coverage suggests that class stratification gets intensified in discourses of injustices. If news discourses can play a critically important role in facilitating public reasoning, and if Sen's idea that justice ought to be theorized through our experience of injustice is right, media narratives about violent crime need to be contextualized and substantively analyzed in terms of class, gender, and sexual inequalities which underlie both crime and television news coverage of it. Further, in a country like India where caste continues to pervade every aspect of social life, the media's inability to fully cover caste-based crimes keep such experiences marginalized.

Nyaya in Global Media Ethics

Journalism practices in India show us a complicated scenario in advocating *nyaya* and in addressing *anyaya*. For instance, in some cases hidden cameras have been successfully used to uncover the abuse of power by the powerful and to strengthen democratic institutions; other uses of hidden cameras seem to highlight the biases which underlie cultural experience. Cultural values, in certain instances, overshadow advocacy of public reasoning and minority rights. Similarly, the coverage of crime, which is omnipresent in India's commercialized news media, shows a troubling amount of coverage on injustices against the rich and powerful while ignoring injustices against the poor and weak. While the practice of *nyaya* in media coverage of crime and hidden camera stories in India remains uneven, I see the relevance of *nyaya* to discussions of global media ethics.

Grappling with changes in technology, globalization, and ethical theory during the past decade, journalism and media professionals have made various efforts to develop a philosophically rigorous and epistemologically sound ethics for the global media (Christians and Traber 1997, Couldry 2006, Silverstone 2007, Ward 2010). In one attempt to formulate global media ethics, the *Journal of Mass Media Ethics* published a special issue titled "Search for a Global Media Ethics" (2003). In this issue, Callahan writes that the profession's global scope and transnational media provokes the question of whether there can be "universal ethical standards for journalism to meet the challenges of globalization" (Callahan 2003: 3). Similarly, Ward (2005: 4) states that a global media ethics would imply that responsibility "would be owed to an audience scattered across the world," given the increasingly global reach of media corporations facilitated through new technologies. Christians and Nordenstreng (2004) have proposed a theoretical formulation which re-examines the search for global media ethics, and proposes the social responsibility theory as a possibility for the press to adopt internationally. They offer the possibility of establishing several universal principles which they ground in "a morality rooted in animate nature" (2004: 20). Stating that "global social responsibility needs an ethical basis commensurate in scope, that is, universal ethical principles rather than the parochial moral guidelines represented by codes," Christians and Nordenstreng list respect for human dignity based on sacredness of human life, truth, and nonviolence as three universal principles (p. 20). Ethicists, journalists, and scholars alike agree that any invention, evolution, or construction of global media and journalism ethics should be highly nuanced both in its epistemological approaches and in practical applications.

Christians et al. (2008), in their article on global media ethics, propose a cross-disciplinary theoretical perspective. The article does not presume to provide conclusive answers to theoretical questions about the relationship between the self and the other, the local and the global, or the universal and the particular, but puts forward an argument about ways in which current disagreements about the nature, possibility, and desirability of a global media ethics could be addressed. "Progress in developing a global media ethics is stymied by a number of wide-spread beliefs and presumptions," write Christians et al. The authors contend that "One issue is whether there *are* universal values in media ethics." Their answer is a qualified "yes"; they write:

> It appears there are universals. Even a cursory survey of many codes of journalism ethics would find agreement, at least on a denotative level, on such values as reporting the truth, freedom, and independence, minimizing harm, and accountability. Yet, a survey would also find differences. Some media cultures emphasize more strongly than other such values as the promotion of social solidarity, not offending religious beliefs and not weakening public support for the military. Even where media systems agree on a value, such as "freedom of press" or "social responsibility," they may interpret and apply such principles in different ways. (Christians et al. 2008: 138)

In opening up these tensions, the authors describe several theoretical positions which might coalesce to form our current understanding of global media ethics. In their attempts to avoid errors of the past, Christians et al. propose an outline of a theory of ethics consisting of levels, "the levels of presuppositions, principles, and precepts" (p. 140), that interact dynamically in experience. Rooted in a holistic conception of theory in which basic values and ideas emerge from a "common humanness in concrete contexts," Christians et al. see such values as "context-influenced articulations of deep aspects of being human" (p. 139). The most deeply embedded disagreements between factions (antifoundationalist, poststructuralist, accounts of pluralism and multiculturalism), the authors argue, should not necessarily detract from the fact that they also come together at notable junctures and that most theories of ethics usually subscribe to a modicum of universalization and to some universal extension of nonviolence and sacredness of human life. Within such a conversation, Sen's interpretative use of *nyaya* can be most effectively used in global media ethics in two spheres: one, to seek relevance for global perspectives of justice and two, to centralize poverty (and the question of class) as a deprivation of justice.

"The world beyond a country's borders must come into the assessment of justice in a country for two distinct reasons," writes Sen, "First, what happens in a country, and how its institutions operate, cannot but have effects, sometimes huge consequences, on the rest of the world" (2009: 347). He writes that each country's or society's parochial belief might call for global examination and scrutiny; the world can establish common principles and question presumptions that lie behind particular ethical judgments. Sen's concept of *nyaya* makes justice not only a national process, but also an international and global one. As applied to journalists, Sen's emphasis is on transnational considerations of justice, that media ethics can establish common principles of nonviolence and the sacredness of human life, and apply such principles to free media and its coverage of justice/injustice issues, such as crime and corruption. The media's focus must remain, according to Sen's *nyaya* principle, on injustice. He writes of the importance of actual behavior (*inter alia* combining the operation of the principles of justice with the actual behavior of people) and grounding the assessment of injustice by combining social behavior with social institutions. "What really happens to people," writes Sen, "cannot but be a central concern of a theory of justice" (2009: 200). Only then *nyaya* will have applicability in guiding the choice of institutions in actual societies. For reasoned deliberations to take place in the media about *nyaya*, both vested personal interests and local parochialism must be questioned.

Nyaya, for Sen, is ultimately a focus on human lives (which is different from ancient Indian philosophical traditions of *nyaya* overly focused on the *atman*) and a person's actual ability to do different things. One of the central issues of Sen's philosophy of *nyaya* is its connection to poverty. In rejecting previous claims of poverty as merely income-based, Sen accounts for a poverty in "capability deprivation" which he recognizes as much more intense than what we can deduce from income data. Moving away from income-based approaches to poverty, Sen gives an example – that even in high income families, girls or women can be deprived of resource allocations (as seen in many parts of Africa and Asia). Thus women in these families suffer from greater mortality, morbidity, undernourishment, and medical neglect than can be found simply on the basis of comparing incomes of different families. Understanding the nature and source of deprivation and inequity is central to the removing of *anyaya*. If one identifies reducing the deprivation of resources or poverty as a principle in global media ethics and juxtaposes it with nonviolence and sacredness of human lives, reasoned deliberation in the media would require a concerted effort to be cognizant of providing a space for discussions of not only class inequity, based on low income, but also the deprivation of capability to live a flourishing life.

In this chapter, I have limited my discussions to Sen's formulation of a theory of *nyaya*, its use in journalism practices in the newly globalized, commercialized, and liberalized media in India, and to its possible theoretical relevance in developing a workable framework for global media ethics. As media worlds get increasingly rearranged, globalized, and interconnected, discussions of justice and injustice become imminent. Sen's analysis and use of *nyaya* can illuminate our understanding of justice in profound ways and can be a hugely constructive part in developing a theory of justice. Nyaya, however, cannot become an intellectual "standstill"; media scholars and journalists are obligated to achieve *nyaya*, and redress *anyaya*, in practice as much as in theory, but with continuous critical scrutiny.

Further Reading

Amartya Sen's work in economic theory is well known in and outside of India. Most recently, Sen has emerged as more of a philosopher-economist, advocating the "capabilities approach," which points toward a nuanced understanding of how best to tackle deprivation. In this view, raising incomes is of secondary importance; what really matters is increasing the "capability" people have to achieve their goals in life. A person's "capability" may be impaired not only by poverty but also by disability, discrimination, or illiteracy, for example. Sen situates himself in a tradition of thinkers who have pressed for radical change in philosophies of justice: Mary Wollstonecraft, Karl Marx, John Stuart Mill. It is only in the past few years that Professor Sen's work on justice and *nyaya* has been used by media scholars. Sen himself has written about ethics in the Indian media in a lengthy editorial in the newspaper, *The Hindu*, in January 2012 titled, "The Glory and the Blemishes of the Indian News Media" (http://www.thehindu.com/opinion/op-ed /article2781128.ece). Beyond Sen, many authors are now addressing the intersections between justice and media ethics in Indian journalism. These include Nirja Jayal's book *Democracy in India* (New York: Oxford University Press, 2001), Robin Jeffrey's book *India's Newspaper Revolution: Capitalism, Politics and the Indian Language Press* (New York: St. Martin's Press, 2000), and Nalin Mehta's *India on Television: How Satellite News Channels Have Changed the Way We Think and Act* (New Delhi: HarperCollins, 2008).

Further readings in this area include the following: C. Bertrand, *Media Ethics and Accountability Systems* (New Brunswick, NJ: Transaction Publishers, 2000); W. Crawley and D. Page, *Satellites Over South Asia: Broadcasting Culture and Public Interest* (Delhi: Sage, 2001); M. Firoz, *Television in India: Values and Concerns* (Delhi: Saad Publications, 2005); D. V. R. Murthy, *Development Journalism, What Next? An Agenda for the Press* (Delhi: Kanishka Publishers, 2006); N. Sevanti, *Headlines from the Heartland: Reinventing the Hindi Public Sphere* (Delhi: Sage, 2007); R. Oza, *The Making of Neoliberal India: Nationalism, Gender, and the Paradoxes of Globalization* (New York: Routledge, 2006); S. Poolani, *Rape of News? The Ethics (or the Lack of it) of Selling Editorial Space* (Mumbai: Frog Books, 2004); S. Rao and N. Johal, "Ethics and News-Making in the Changing Indian Mediascape," *Journal of Mass Media Ethics* 21 (2006): 286–303; K. M. Shrivastava, *Media Ethics: From Vedas to Gandhi and Beyond* (Delhi: I&B Ministry Publications, 2005); B. Zelizer, *Taking Journalism Seriously* (London: Sage, 2004).

References

Bhatt, S. C. 1996. *Satellite Invasion of India*. Delhi: Gyan Publishing House.

Callahan, S. 2003. "New Challenges of Globalization for Journalism." *Journal of Mass Media Ethics* 18: 3–15.

Chatterjee, S. 1950. *The Nyaya Theory of Knowledge*. Calcutta: Das Gupta.

Christians, C. and Nordenstreng, K. 2004. "Social Responsibility Worldwide." *Journal of Mass Media Ethics* 19: 3–28.

Christians, C. , Rao, S. , Ward, S. J. A, and Wasserman, H. 2008. "Toward a Global Media Ethics: Theoretical Perspectives." *Ecquid Novi: African Journalism Studies* 29: 135–72.

Christians, C. and Traber, M. Eds. 1997. *Communication Ethics and Universal Values*. Thousand Oaks, CA: Sage.

Couldry, N. 2006. *Listening Beyond the Echoes: Media, Ethics and Agency in an Uncertain World*. New York: Paradigm.

D'Almeida, A. 1973. *Nyaya Philosophy: Nature and the Validity of Knowledge*. Chennai, India: Pontifical Institute of Theology and Philosophy.

Mattelart, A. 2002. "An Archeology of the Global Era: Constructing a Belief." *Media, Culture and Society* 24: 591–612.

Muhlmann, G. 2010. *Journalism for Democracy*. New York: Polity.

Natarajan, J. 2000. *History of India's Journalism*. Delhi: Sage.

Rao, S. 2008. "Accountability, Democracy and Globalization: A Study of Broadcast Journalism in India." *Asian Journal of Communication* 18: 193–206.

Ravindranath, P. K. 2005. *Regional Journalism in India*. Delhi: Authors Press.

Saha, S. 1987. *Perspectives on Nyaya Logic and Epistemology*. Calcutta: K. P. Bagchi.

Schudson, M. 2006. *Why Democracies Need an Unlovable Press*. New York: Polity.

Sen, A. 1999. *Development as Freedom*. New York: Random House.

Sen, A. 2009. *The Idea of Justice*. Cambridge, MA: Harvard University Press.

Silverstone, R. 2007. *Media and Morality: On the Rise of the Mediapolis*. New York: Polity.

Sonwalkar, P. 2002. "Murdochization of the Indian Press: From By-line to Bottom-line." *Media, Culture & Society* 24: 821–34.

Thussu, D. K. 1999. "Privatizing the Airwaves: The Impact of Globalization on Broadcasting in India." *Media, Culture & Society* 21: 121–31.

Ward, S. J. A. 2005. "Philosophical Foundations for Global Journalism Ethics." *Journal of Mass Media Ethics* 20: 3–21.

Ward, S. J. A. 2010. *Global Journalism Ethics*. Montreal: McGill-Queen's University Press.

Part IV

Theoretical Foundations

13

Global Media Ethics?
Issues, Requirements, Challenges, Resolutions

Charles M. Ess

What were once the concerns and province of a few specialists in computer science and philosophy have increasingly become the ethical challenges and issues faced by billions of people around the globe. As is obvious, computational devices in particular and digital devices more generally are increasingly commonplace appliances in the developed countries, where they serve primarily *communicative* rather than computational goals. Accordingly, computer ethics has morphed into a much broader digital media and information ethics. These ethics attend to digital media *per se*, whether within the compass of computer-mediated communication (e.g., the Internet and the World Wide Web) and/or our use of digital devices such as cameras and cell phones.

Along the way, digital media ethics includes profound transformations, for example, in journalism ethics. As but one instance: smartphones allow their owners to serve as "citizen journalists" whose eye-witness recordings, for example of police violence, once uploaded to the Web, thereby radically change earlier forms of news gathering and reporting. These and related developments (e.g., blogging) are quickly changing journalism ethics. Once a professional ethics for a relative few, journalism ethics is increasingly hybridizing to incorporate an ethics "for the rest of us," one that addresses both amateur and professional responsibilities and rights (Ward 2011, Ess forthcoming).

These developments highlight a first challenge for a global media ethics. Because these devices and their affiliated ethical challenges confront every person who takes them up, such an ethics must serve as an applied ethics "for the rest of us." Candidates for a global media ethics must be accessible and useful for the vast majority of those who use these devices, not just philosophical ethicists. A second immediate challenge is one of the defining themes of this volume: Such an ethics must be *global*.

Global Media Ethics: Problems and Perspectives, First Edition. Edited by Stephen J. A. Ward.
© 2013 Blackwell Publishing Ltd. Published 2013 by Blackwell Publishing Ltd.

It must present a palette of ethical norms, decision-making frameworks, and examples that conjoin globally shared values and principles with the norms and practices reflecting the distinctive identities and traditions of a given cultural group.

Happily, much recent work suggests that these daunting challenges can be met, at least partially. Philosophers and their collaborators are finding ways of presenting diverse ethical issues evoked by digital media in ways that are accessible and useful to those outside professional philosophy (e.g., Ess 2009, Heider and Massanari forthcoming). In addition, on both theoretical and practical/applied levels, an ethical *pluralism* has emerged in important domains of digital media ethics, beginning with online privacy. This pluralism, I have argued, helps meet the requirement of a global information ethics that must hold together both shared norms and local applications of those norms that thereby preserve diverse cultural identities (Ess 2007).

Nonetheless, enormously complex ethical issues remain that do not appear to be easily resolvable. Still more fundamentally, our engagements with new digital media appear to bring in their wake important transformations in our sense of self and identity. Most briefly: The foundational conception of the autonomous self in the modern "West" – one that legitimated both Western conceptions of privacy as well as modern liberal-democratic states – appears to be shifting toward a conception of self more characteristic of (among others) "Eastern" traditions, meaning a *relational* self. Simultaneously, however, we find in "Eastern" countries (specifically China, Japan, and Thailand) an increasing shift *away* from such traditional relational selves and toward more "Western"-like individual selves.

To begin to address these issues and challenges, I first offer a "primer" in common ethical frameworks – namely, utilitarianism, deontology, and feminist and virtue ethics. In the following section I show how these frameworks apply to issues of privacy and then pornography. Along the way, and then brought to the foreground in the final section, I illustrate how our changing responses to these sorts of issues correlates with a changing sense of selfhood and identity, followed by considerations of what these changes imply for a future global media ethics – and politics.

Digital Media Ethics: A Primer

Initial definition and questions

Digital media ethics intersects both applied ethics generally and information and computing ethics specifically (see Floridi 2010: ix). Digital media – with increasing rapidity and diversity – evoke a wide range of ethical issues suited to analysis (and, occasionally, resolution) within these ethical domains insofar as digital media (1) generate data, for example, as text, as recording sounds and/or pictures, as GPS-determined locations, and/or (2) transmit digital data, most usually by way of the Internet, the Web, and wireless and telephone networks.

Many of the ethical challenges here are (painfully) familiar. The focus here is on privacy and pornography: These are but prominent tips of a growing iceberg of ethical concerns. This list would further include matters of identity theft and cyberbullying, along with increasing surveillance (Fuchs et al. 2011). It further seems inevitable, for example, that contemporary work in robot ethics and the ethics of biometric devices and security will increasingly concern "the rest of us" as these devices become increasingly ubiquitous in our lives (Wallach and Allen 2010, Turkle 2011). There is also the question of what happens to our notions of ethical responsibility – notions that, during Western modernity, were increasingly attached to an autonomous, *individual* (and primarily *rational*) human being – as our networked lives increasingly distribute the ethical responsibility for any given act across a complex range of networks, for example as increasingly controlled by artificial agents (Taddeo 2011) and defined by the design decisions of specific programmers and technologists (Grodzinsky, Miller, and Wolf 2008).

Moreover, as the Internet and the Web continue to weave more and more people and cultures together around the globe, the range of *ethical frameworks* that come into play likewise expands and grows. What is most obvious – often in painful, if not bloody ways – are the contrasts between these frameworks. While applied ethics coupled with an ethical pluralism might help resolve some of these conflicts (Ess 2007), some of these conflicts seem intractable. Consider a well-known example. When the Danish newspaper *Jyllands-Posten* published the now (in)famous Muhammed cartoons in 2005 and early 2006, it did so in the name of high Western ideals of freedom of speech and expression. But for millions of devout Muslims worldwide, the cartoons represented a direct assault on deeply held beliefs concerning the sanctity of the Prophet Muhammed and Islamic prohibitions against the depiction of human beings (Ess 2009: 105f.). This conflict thus took place at the fault line between premodern religious worldviews and regimes, on the one hand, and modern Western democracies as secular institutions which subordinate religious belief (as private) to primary civil rights, including rights to privacy and freedom of expression. As the continuing fallout of the cartoons suggest, such foundational differences may be intractable.

Ethical decision-making frameworks

Nonetheless, one or more basic ethical frameworks enable us to analyze, and in many cases resolve, a significant portion of our ethical challenges.

Up until the middle of the twentieth century, much of modern Western ethics was divided between two distinct ethical frameworks – *utilitarianism* (as a form of consequentialism) and *deontology*.

Utilitarianism emerges within the Anglo-American tradition and specifically the work of Jeremy Bentham (1748–1832) and John Stuart Mill (1806–73). Utilitarianism aims to secure the greatest good for the greatest number by way of an ethical cost–benefit analysis of our possible choices (Sinnott-Armstrong 2011). As a simple example: A friend invites you to a party for a new group of students in her area of studies. Under ordinary circumstances you would agree to go. You certainly like your friend and her parties, but the following day you have a major presentation in one of your classes. You quickly do some ethical accounting: What are the possible *positive* and *negative* consequences of attending the party, and thereby, of being less than 100 percent prepared for the presentation the following day? And how do these compare with the possible positive and negative consequences of not attending the party, but thereby being as fully prepared as possible for the presentation? In classical utilitarianism, you would assign each set of outcomes a quantitative measure – either positive *utils* (for pleasures) or negative ones (for pain). Perhaps attending the party will result in +20 utils, countered by some unhappiness for yourself and your cohorts as you do less than splendidly the next day, say 10 utils. By contrast, missing the party may be significantly painful, say 10 utils. But doing well on the presentation will make you, your cohorts, your professor, and your class very happy indeed, worth say +60 utils. Hence, attending the party would result in a net of +10 utils; focusing on the presentation should net +50 utils. And so, from a classic utilitarian approach, you go on developing your presentation (however grudgingly).

The simplicity of this example should not mislead. Utilitarian calculations have become central in the modern West, especially regarding choices in social policy and war. Consider, for example, the horrific costs and tremendous benefits (at least to Allied soldiers and their commanders) of using atomic bombs on Hiroshima and Nagasaki versus the horrific costs to the Japanese civilians and the (more uncertain) benefits of attempting to close the war in the Pacific with conventional forces. Presuming that a conventional invasion of Japan would have cost the lives of about 500,000 Allied soldiers, while the atomic bombings would cost "only" 200,000 Japanese lives – it is perfectly sensible from a utilitarian perspective that the bombings were chosen as bringing about a greater good than failing to use them.

At the same time, however, these examples also highlight important limitations of utilitarianism. First, everything depends on our ability to accurately predict the morally relevant consequences. In many cases, this may be straightforward, but human affairs can also be notoriously unpredictable. Perhaps if you had attended the party, you might have had either a much better time or a much worse time than you anticipated. Indeed, what if the guests turned out to include someone especially interesting and attractive, perhaps so much so as to lead to marriage, children, and life happy ever after? But having made your first calculations without predicting this important set of (presumptively) positive utils, now you will never know. Alternatively, you might have conscientiously prepared for class but your cohorts decided to play instead, resulting in a in-class disaster. Analogously, one of the unforeseen costs of the atomic bombings of Nagasaki and Hiroshima was a Cold War that extended over generations, a Cold War which at times brought the world to the brink of nuclear holocaust. If the latter had taken place, would those left in a postholocaust world consider these cost still outweighed by the benefits of the Allies winning the Pacific war more quickly? Again, we are simply not always capable of predicting important and relevant consequences. Yet this is what utilitarianism requires.

Certainly, every moral framework enjoys both its strengths and limitations, so none of these objections should be considered as fatal. Rather, they help us get an initial sense of when utilitarianism might be appropriate, and when it should be complemented with or set aside in favor of other ethical frameworks.

Deontology. A further difficulty with utilitarian considerations is that they may justify what seem to be violations of basic ethical values. The greatest good for the greatest number can be bought, in the worst case, at the cost of tremendous suffering, even death, of the few. Again, this is a calculation we may be willing to make and find justified in the case of warfare. Soldiers are by definition those who are willing to pay the final cost of their lives for the greater good of the greatest number. The rest of us, more or less willingly, accept their sacrifice as it leads (ideally) to greater security, comfort, and so forth.

But are there any rights, duties, or values that we may think or feel to be somehow absolute – that is, these cannot be overridden, no matter the consequences? For example, most of us in the modern world seem to think or feel that slavery is no longer a justified practice. But a utilitarian can straightforwardly argue, analogously with the example of the soldier, that the sacrifices of a relatively small number of persons (insofar as slaves were ever regarded as such), as they lead to greater pleasure for the greater number (as compared to not having slaves), are thereby justified.

We may, however, think there's something wrong with slavery, despite its benefits to the majority. Deontologists provide some of the most important accounts of just what that wrong is. Most centrally, modern deontology – initially in the ethics of Immanuel Kant – begins with the conception of the human being as a *person*, understood specifically as an agent who has moral freedom or rational *autonomy*. This autonomy means more precisely our *free* capacity to give ourselves our own rule or law. At the same time, this means that we must recognize that the Other is a free human being, capable of determining his or her own goals or ends, and thereby of choosing the *means* to achieve those ends. We are then required to respect others as persons, as "ends-in-themselves," never as a means (only) to our own ends. If one of us, however, should use the

Other as only a means to ends or goals that we have chosen for ourselves, then we fundamentally deny the capacity of the Other as essentially the freedom to choose his or her own goals or ends (see Ess 2009: 176–80).

Such a deontological analysis helpfully undergirds our intuitions of what's wrong with treating others as "objects," as just things, whether we are thinking of slaves, or, to anticipate the discussion of pornography, of women and children as sexual objects. More strongly, deontology supports the claims in modern political theory that human beings, *qua* citizens, enjoy a set of basic human *rights* that are to be defended and fostered by the state. These rights cannot (ideally) be compromised, even for the sake of significant benefits for the majority. From the time of John Locke (1632–1704) and Thomas Jefferson, this view that human beings are endowed with certain "inherent and unalienable rights" (Jefferson [1776] 1984: 19) has grown alongside the expansion of democratic societies, initially in the West. By the end of the twentieth century, most countries in Europe recognized a series of *positive* (or entitlement) rights, such as equal access to public transportation, education, unemployment benefits, and healthcare. There has also been much important debate as to how far these conceptions of rights, especially as they turn on distinctively modern Western conceptions of the (rational, autonomous) *individual*, may be claimed to be universal. Nonetheless, the United Nations' *Universal Declaration of Human Rights* (1948) makes just such a claim. And, as we will see below, it is precisely in the non-Western states that *individual* privacy rights are gaining increasing recognition and protection.

Feminist ethics and virtue ethics. The rise of both feminist and virtue ethics in the latter half of the twentieth century highlighted a primary difficulty with various forms of modern deontologies. Broadly, numerous feminists criticized the deontological conception of the individual *qua* rational. Specifically, Carol Gilligan (1982) documented the ways in which, when confronted with difficult ethical choices – including considerations of abortion – women as a group would characteristically consider how their choices would affect not simply themselves as individuals, but rather an often extensive and complex "web of relationships." Moreover, these decisions were shaded by the *affective* dimensions of the relationships involved, not simply rational calculations of utilitarian outcomes and/or deontological principles of respect and autonomy.

Gilligan's work, soon followed by other important contributions such as Nel Noddings's "ethic of care" (1984), highlighted one of the main limitations of Kantian deontology: Rationality, while important, is only part of how we both know the world and make our ethical judgments therein. A more complete account must acknowledge the affective dimensions of our knowledge and ethical decision making – first of all so as to recognize the legitimacy of the knowledge and choices made by women, children, and "others" outside the comparatively narrow and privileged sphere of male rationality. Beyond their service in environmental ethics (i.e., where the rights of nonsentient beings and eco-systems are claimed and defended), these critiques have been dramatically reinforced especially over the past two decades in phenomenology and neuroscience (Wilson and Foglia 2011).

Moreover, the emergence of feminist ethics and attention to the emotive dimensions of ethical decision making was further reinforced and broadened by the parallel (re)emergence of *virtue ethics*. In some ways, virtue ethics is among the oldest of ethical traditions, and also the most globally shared. This may be in part because virtue ethics starts – and seeks to end with – the very sensible question: What must I do? This includes: What must I *become* – that is, what habits and facilities must I acquire through practice – in order to be happy or content?

This question is not as self-interested as it may first appear to be: When it was initially raised – in ancient Greece as well as in ancient China, India, and in many indigenous traditions – the question arose for people who, in contrast with Western moderns of the Cartesian or Hobbesian conception, were fully aware of themselves as both *individuals* (i.e., persons possessed of a singular and unique identity, one distinct in defining ways from the identities of those around them) and as *relational* beings. As relational beings, our sense of identity and personhood is defined by the various relationships that mark out our origins and (current) place(s) within a given community and society. If one of these relationships changes dramatically – when our parents die, for example – then the defining relationships are removed, and thereby, our very identity and sense of self is (dramatically) changed (Ames and Rosemont 1998: 20–35). For such a self to ask the question "What must I do – and *become* – to be content" immediately involves these relationships. Hence the question is always also a question of "what must I do – and *become* – to ensure community harmony," that is, a community sense of well-being, not simply my own.

The virtue ethics focus on contentment or happiness thereby restores the emotive dimensions of ethical decision making. Ethics is not simply a matter of determining on purely rational grounds what is right (deontology) or what will benefit the many (utilitarianism); *in addition* (note, not *instead of*), ethics is about a sense of contentment and harmony that is as much felt as it is rationally considered. Moreover, in part because of its sources in teachers such as Socrates, Confucius, and Jesus – teachers who only spoke, but did not write – virtue ethics emphasizes the development of one's own *judgment* in ethical decision making. That is, in contrast with modern utilitarianism and deontology – highly rationalized systems of principles and rules that lend themselves to a kind of deductive approach to ethics – virtue ethics traditions are rooted in writings that collect for us many sayings and particular examples, but not much in the way of general rules and principles. The result is a somewhat impressionistic picture of how these ethical masters thought, *felt*, and judged in specific contexts. But this picture must then be applied by us through a complex process of interpretation and application to the issues we ourselves confront. For example, what does it *mean* when Socrates tells Crito, in effect, that it is better to die at the hands of unjust men rather than to break the law to save oneself (Plato 1926)? Is this simply a *particular* argument intended for Crito, who is otherwise eager to save his teacher Socrates by bribing the guards and helping him escape Athens? Can we somehow apply this particular example to one or more of our contemporary concerns, as many have done in the West in the subsequent millennia, including, for example, Martin Luther King, Jr. (1964)? The pursuit of virtue ethics thus always forces us to ask such questions, as suggested, for example, by the once popular phrase among US Christians, WWJD ("What would Jesus do?"). That is, given what these written sources tell us of the character and actions of these teachers, not simply their principles, what *judgments* can we draw regarding how we ourselves should behave in the face of current challenges?

A singular advantage of virtue ethics is its global and historical scope. That is, we find extensive developments of virtue ethics in the major philosophical and ethical traditions of the world, both ancient and contemporary. Moreover, these traditions are characterized by a *pluralism* that builds on recognizing the central role of judgment. That is, we acknowledge that there may be more than one legitimate judgment in the face of a given ethical quandary: A plurality of legitimate "judgment calls" can be made. But at the same time, not just any response will do (thereby opening the door to whim, arbitrary power, and ethical relativism). Moreover, the global diffusion of these traditions makes them strong candidates precisely for a shared, global, but still pluralistic ethics in a global information ethics (Ess 2007).

Cases and Issues in Contemporary Digital Media Ethics

We now turn to two specific cases, privacy and pornography, to illustrate both contemporary issues in digital media ethics and how to apply the ethical frameworks introduced above.

Privacy and data privacy protection

Contemporary Westerners tend to take the notion of individual privacy as a positive good that is ethically and politically absolute. Indeed, privacy is included in the UN *Declaration of Universal Human Rights* (1948) as a basic human right. In historical and cultural terms, however, this understanding has made only a very recent and, it may be, a relatively brief appearance.

Certainly, the Western conception of the individual, as the foundation of contemporary notions of individual privacy (and, correlatively property) rights, has deep roots. Foucault, for example, marks its beginning with the emergence of writing as a "technology of the self," first expressed in the

Socratic dictum to care for the self. This dictum evolves through the Stoics and first-century Roman elite to bloom dramatically in the Protestant Reformation and the diffusion of literacy and print to the majority of populations in the modern West by some time in the nineteenth century (Foucault 1988). But individual privacy was not defended as a legal right until 1890, in a landmark paper by Samuel Warren and Louis Brandeis (Tavani 2007: 130). Such individual privacy is justified in Western contexts on a variety of grounds. First of all, such privacy is seen as carving out a personal space in which the self may express and develop itself precisely as an individual (DeCew 1986). More broadly, such privacy thereby fosters the sorts of autonomous (and primarily rational) individuals who are taken to both justify and require the modern liberal state. The modern liberal state is a state in which individuals determine for themselves what it means to live "the good life." That is, what the good life means for individuals is *not* determined by the community, religious authorities, traditions, or even the state itself (Johnson 2001: ch. 3).

By contrast, those societies and cultures characterized by more *relational* selves have uniformly regarded individual privacy as something strongly negative. Individual privacy is desirable only for protecting what must be evil or seditious thoughts and activities on the part of those who thus "have something to hide." For example, in Thailand, as a strongly Buddhist society, the traditional conception of privacy as a positive good has been that of *collective* privacy – the privacy of the family vis-à-vis the larger community (Kitiyadisai 2005). Otherwise, until recently at least, individual privacy has been regarded in North Asian countries as something shameful (Lü 2005) or something to be purged – along with the (from a Buddhist perspective) illusory self that it protects (Nakada and Tamura 2005).

At the same time, individual privacy rights have increasingly come under attack in the contemporary West. To begin with, insofar as our personal information is digitized, it is more or less effortlessly copied and instantaneously transmitted across globally extended networks. Moreover, the dilution or outright suspension of individual privacy rights are consistently justified by state interests – whether in the name of fighting crime (hence police surveillance, wiretaps, physical searches, etc.) or of fighting terrorism. Especially after the 9/11 attacks in 2001, numerous plans for state collection and surveillance of personal data have been developed, all justified in the name of state security (and, to be fair, thereby at least some measure of individual security). In the same direction, the rise of social networking sites especially is affiliated with what Anders Albrechtslund has characterized as "voluntary surveillance" and "participatory surveillance" (2008). That is, such sites work by making available in at least a semipublic forum all sorts of information about the individual that, in the pre-Internet era, would have been considered personal and thus private. Simultaneously, while most users appear not to notice or to care, the terms of service for such sites generally make the data freely uploaded by users the property of the site's owners. This data is, of course, valuable first of all as information for which advertisers pay good money; otherwise these sites would not exist or remain in business. In these ways, individual privacy rights appear to be eroding in the face of increasing intrusion and control over personal data by both states and corporations.

Certainly, a utilitarian calculation of "the greatest good for the greatest number" can justify individual privacy and, correlatively, property rights, insofar as such privacy can be shown to lead to both individual and collective happiness. Presuming that individuals *enjoy* privacy and the activities that it affords them, then privacy contributes to the happiness of the individual. And insofar as the activities protected by individual privacy thereby either contribute to the happiness of the many (by producing pleasure or positive utils) and/or do not detract from it (through activities that result in pain or negative utils), then the resulting calculation is easy: Privacy contributes to both individual and collective pleasure or happiness, and so is justified.

But as the examples of warfare foreshadow – utilitarians (more precisely, *act* utilitarians who apply utilitarian calculations to each specific act, in contrast with *rule* utilitarians who attempt to develop more general rules) can also justify sacrificing the interests and pleasures of a few if such a sacrifice would lead to greater good. Hence utilitarians can justify the sacrifice of a relatively small number of soldiers, especially if the soldiers themselves consent to these sacrifices, for the sake of the greater happiness of a nation whose security is thereby (ostensibly) defended (i.e., a greater happiness results than would follow upon a military defeat of the nation-state). Similarly, act utilitarians can justify sacrificing the privacy rights of a few (or perhaps even many), if such a sacrifice, however painful, nonetheless leads to a greater net happiness (again, beginning in the form of a secure nation-state).

By contrast, deontologists provide a more straightforward defense of privacy rights, insofar as these can be shown to be necessary to our basic existence and practices as ethical autonomies. Again, such rights are not to be sacrificed by the state in the name of the greater good. So we find rights to privacy – including data privacy protection – spelled out in much greater detail, for example, in the Constitution (*Grundgesetz*) of the German Federal Republic. Privacy rights are seen to protect a range of *individual* rights, including private autonomy (*Privatautonomie*), freedom of expression (*Meinungäußerungsfreiheit*), a right to (develop) personality (*Persönlichkeitsrecht*), and the freedom to express one's will (*Willenserklärungsfreiheit*; see Bizer 2003). The pressures of terrorism have certainly issued in efforts to reduce the very strong privacy protections established in Germany and in the EU more broadly. So far, at least, these pressures appear to be resisted more successfully in the United States, whose ethics and legal practices are more firmly grounded in the Anglo-American traditions of utilitarianism (Burk 2007: 97f.).

Finally, at least Western feminists and virtue ethicists would generally insist on strong (but perhaps not absolute) individual privacy protections because such privacy serves to protect individual expression and development (e.g., Virginia Woolf's *A Room of One's Own*, 1929). Moreover, individual privacy establishes a space in which the individual is free to develop, without fear of critique or suppression by others, virtues that are central to both individual contentment and community well-being, including our capacities to initiate and sustain intimate relationships, reflective judgment, critical thinking, and so forth. Hence individual privacy rights will hold a very high place in the virtue ethicist's scale (Ess 2010: 112f.).

As we will see in the final section, this picture of privacy quickly becomes more complicated, and in surprising ways, as we return to Eastern conceptions and practices.

Pornography and virtual child pornography

Concerns over online pornography have accompanied the rise of the Internet and the World Wide Web fueled first of all by the perception that pornography "drives" much of the traffic online. As Susanna Paasonen points out, however, both because of the intensely secretive nature of the pornography business, and because it largely remains a topic that few academics are willing to research, we have no reliable data to support such perceptions (2011: 424). Moreover, the most recent "EU Kids Online" study documents that for children and teens in the EU, exposure to pornography is lower than would be expected in light of "media hype." Indeed, young people are more concerned with potential harm from, for example, cyberbullying, than from unwanted exposure to sexually explicit materials (Livingstone et al. 2011: 42).

That said, there is a long tradition of feminist critiques of pornographic materials – first of all, as they reinforce patriarchal stereotypes of women as primarily sexual objects. These critiques, however, are countered by the "antiantiporn feminists" who argue that pornography may open up new spaces for the exploration of historically marginalized and repressed forms of sexuality, beginning with women's sexuality *per se*, and extending through gay, lesbian, bisexual, transgendered, and queer sexualities (Ess 2009: 145–9, Bromseth and Sundén 2011). Moreover, as we should expect of anything affiliated with gender and gender roles, both definitions of and responses to "pornography" vary widely from culture to culture (Ess 2009: 147f.).

So what might our *ethical* responses be to the easy production and availability of "pornography" online? Litska Strikwerda (2011) develops a striking exploration of some of the issues at work here in her analysis of virtual child pornography. To begin with, in contrast with other forms of pornography, child pornography represents an ethical "bright-line rule": We (more or less) agree universally that this is an intolerable wrong. Hence, child pornography is universally criminalized, whatever cultural and ethical variations we might find regarding pornography more broadly. By contrast, *virtual* child pornography, that is, materials that are produced digitally without harming flesh-and-blood children, thereby calls into question the fundamental justifications for criminalizing child pornography. We hence must both re-examine those justifications and determine whether or not new ethical arguments might come into play that would help us resolve these challenges.

As Strickwerda points out, liberal societies, that is, those devoted to maximizing individual freedom and self-development, have pursued two primary routes to justify criminalization of specific activities, materials, and so forth. The first is the basic principle from utilitarianism: The greatest good for the greatest number implies preventing harm (as generating pain or, worst-case, loss of life). On this view, however, "victimless crimes" such as prostitution, as not leading to at least direct harm, should not be criminalized. By the same token, the production of virtual child pornography does not involve direct harm to real children: hence on this approach, we have no justification for criminalizing its production (Strickwerda 2011: 144f.).

But what about materials that *lead* to harm? In particular: What if we could demonstrate that the distribution and consumption of virtual child pornography are causally linked to direct harms to children, as such distribution and consumption ostensibly assures pedophiles of the normalcy of such acts? In this case, *paternalism* – the role of the liberal state to prevent such harms – would justify criminalizing such materials. But there is, as yet, insufficient evidence to prove a direct link between the consumption of such materials and direct harm to children (Strikwerda 2011: 144).

So far, then, Strikwerda finds neither strong utilitarian nor deontological grounds for criminalizing virtual child pornography. From a utilitarian standpoint, if no harm can be demonstrated, then no negative utils can be counted against the larger sum of presumptively positive utils generated from pedophiles' enjoyment of such materials. Certainly, deontologists would insist that the rights of children to be treated and respected as persons should be paramount, and certainly override any utilitarian considerations of maximizing pleasure. But again, if no direct harms in the form of violation of such rights can be demonstrated, the deontologist can offer no objection.

Strikwerda then turns to virtue ethics. She argues that we should pursue those attitudes toward and practices of sexuality that reinforce our care for the Other as an equal person (a deontological respect conjoined with an ethics of care) – what she characterizes as a "sexual mentality based on equality" (2011: 158). Both the production and consumption of virtual child pornography clearly seem to work against such virtuous practices: Hence a virtue ethicist will condemn both. Moreover, Strikwerda notes that even in liberal societies, moralism justifies criminalizing the *representations* of immoral acts if they generate a level of offense that itself (closely) amounts to harm. She draws here on the work of Hugo Bedeau, who argues that such representations may be criminalized if they

> can cause offense to persons … by virtue of flouting deeply held convictions, and that in being offensive these activities are harmful or something sufficiently akin to harmfulness as to be virtually indistinguishable from it. (Bedau 1974: 97, in Strikwerda 2011: 158)

Strikwerda thus demonstrates a unique strength of virtue ethics vis-à-vis an ethical issue (virtual child pornography) that occupies an otherwise very gray zone in the moralities of utilitarianism and deontology. That is, in light of the current lack of convincing evidence that such materials cause direct harm, neither utilitarianism nor deontology seem able to justify prohibiting materials that most of us would condemn as unethical. By contrast, virtue ethics is able to argue an ethical approach that succeeds where deontology and utilitarianism appear to stall – thereby helping to clarify the limits of utilitarianism and deontology. At the same time, Strikwerda's virtue ethics analysis, as bolstered by a specific form of moralism, further articulates and supports widely shared moral intuitions regarding such materials as "somehow" wrong.

Changing Media, Changing Selves – Changing Politics?

We have begun to see that our ethical decision making turns not simply on the ethical frameworks that we rely on (perhaps as fostered in our native cultures and traditions). Even more fundamentally, much of our ethics turns on our conception of the self – beginning with whether we emphasize a more individualistic or more relational sense of self. At the same time, our root conceptions of selfhood and identity further drive our sensibilities and preferences as to what sorts of social and political structures we require or tolerate.

As the discussion of privacy helps make clear, the modern Western sense of self as an autonomous individual not only undergirds strong notions of individual privacy (and property) rights as positive goods; it also requires and justifies modern democracies and conceptions of the liberal state. By contrast, relational selves – whether in indigenous traditions, those of the premodern West, or those of Asian societies up through the twentieth century – are affiliated with hierarchical and nondemocratic societies. While there is nothing intrinsic to the relational conception of the self that would prevent it from exercising autonomous self-rule, such self-rule has emerged only in the modern West, and that in affiliation with the communication modalities of literacy and print (Ess 2010, Taylor 1989). Again, as we have seen, Eastern societies have historically held a clearly *negative* conception of and attitudes toward individual privacy. Only after a very long period of interaction with Western societies and, specifically, trade agreements with EU countries that, following the provisions of the EU Data Privacy Protections, require similar levels of privacy rights and protections of Eastern trading partners, do we see the emergence of a positive conception of individual privacy, if not its protection in law.

But interestingly enough, the situation on both "sides" of what was once a clear line is now changing rapidly. On the one hand, as we have already noted above, Western ideas of individual privacy as a near absolute value and basic right are rapidly shifting toward what one researcher describes as "the privately public" and the "publicly private" (Lange 2007).These terms refer to how once individually private sorts of information are now voluntarily shared in the quasi-public spaces of social networking sites such as Facebook. These shifts, moreover, cohere with shifts away from individual to increasingly relational emphases in selfhood (Gergen 2011). Historical correlations then suggest that more relational selves will further express greater comfort with more hierarchical and nondemocratic regimes. Certainly, there have been, for example, some notable protests against, say, Facebook's now familiar habit of violating users' senses of privacy (Opsahl 2010). On the other hand, there appears to be ever-greater comfort in the West with both state intrusions into privacy (in the name of fighting terrorism) and with voluntary submission of private information in the name of social networking and consumer convenience (Baym 2011: 399f.). And contra optimistic claims that the enhanced interactivity of "Web 2.0" applications would lead to greater citizen engagement – a claim most dramatically realized recently in the so-called "Arab Springs" (Howard et al. 2011) – in the West the results so far are decidedly mixed. For example, Shannon Vallor (2010) shows how the affordances of contemporary communication media, including social networking sites, work *against* our acquiring some of the virtues basic to deep friendship and long-term commitments, such as patience, perseverance, and empathy. Similarly, Sherry Turkle (2011) argues that we are increasingly inclined to engage more with such technologies and less with one another, precisely in the name of convenience, but we thereby undermine the human fabric essential to democratic governance. Perhaps most troubling, significant recent neurological evidence shows that our increasing engagements with new media, whatever other benefits we may point to, weakens our capacities for inductive analysis, critical thinking, imagination, and deep reflection (Carr 2010).

Alongside these developments and in the face of evidence accumulated over the past 15 years or so, a number of scholars and researchers are increasingly pessimistic with regard to how far the democratization potentials of the Internet and the Web are generally realized (e.g., Thorseth 2011). And within the domain of religious uses of new media, the most recent research shows that those religious denominations and traditions most adept at exploiting the advantages of new media, including those clustered under Web 2.0, are characterized by emphases on emotion over reason, and hierarchy, including patriarchy, over more egalitarian and democratic values and processes. By contrast, those traditions and denominations characterized by more egalitarian norms and democratic processes and rooted in primarily rational conceptions of the individual remain more at home in the media technologies of literacy, print, and the less interactive forms of the Internet and the Web (Cheong and Ess 2012).

Surprisingly, however, Eastern societies show opposite patterns. As we have seen, there is an observable increase in the demand for individual privacy rights. This is apparent, for example, in the development of positive conceptions of individual privacy in the Chinese law dictionary (Lü 2005), as well as in increasing legal recognition of individual privacy rights, especially in North Asia (Greenleaf 2012). Most significantly, there is now discussion of introducing due process rights in the People's Republic of China (Sui 2011), rights dramatically weakened in the USA and the EU in recent years. These transformations appear to correlate with increasing democratization in these societies more broadly if slowly (Lü, personal correspondence, 2011).

These developments suggest an emerging convergence between what was once West and East, specifically in terms of a hybrid self that conjoins both emotive and rational, both individual and relational, emphases. This convergence, in particular, may be facilitated specifically by cell phones – now available to about four billion people. These devices are the most individual of our communication technologies, and we use them to reinforce our close-tie relationships even more strongly than our weak-tie relationships (Ling 2008). Simultaneously, Web 2.0 media appear to favor the emotive over the rational. A key question is how far the hybrid selves fostered by new media will cultivate the *rational* autonomy historically correlated with democratic regimes – and how far these selves will rather pursue the more *emotive* and relational. As we have seen, feminist shifts toward more balanced conceptions of the self and moral reasoning – that is, as engaging both reason and emotion – are crucial developments. At the same time, however, overly emotive selves move easily from the wisdom of the crowd to the madness of the mob, whether as racist lynch mobs or the party faithful carried away by the skillful manipulations of propaganda and mass rallies designed precisely to fuel emotive enthusiasms for the Great Leader and the Fatherland. Somewhat more gently, overly emotive selves may find it difficult to break into individual ethical autonomy and political maturity if doing so will hurt or offend the Others caught up in one's web of relationships (see Gilligan 1982).

To be sure, there are grounds for at least modest hopes that some version of democratic processes will remain possible in "the West," especially in reaction against a growing awareness of how much of our online lives literally belong to the corporations who use our data – indeed, our very identities – for the sake of their profit (e.g., Bechmann and Lomborg forthcoming). In a media landscape of powerful multinational corporations and nation-states less inspired to and/or capable of protecting the individual rights requisite for democratic processes, it may well be that the best we can hope for are civic engagements of the sort that Maria Bakardjieva (2009) has helpfully identified as "subactivism." While not fulfilling online the more grandiose ideals, for example of (Habermasian) deliberative democracy, subactivism nonetheless identifies important new forms of "making sense of public issues and getting involved in civic activities that evolve at the level of everyday life" (2009: 91).

All of this suggests that we are in a unique place of choice: We can still *choose* carefully what sorts of selves we seek to cultivate, in part by way of our media usages. Presuming we want to sustain liberal democracies and their norms of equality, including gender equality; and insofar as literacy and print have served as the premier "technologies of the self" – of the cultivation of especially the rational autonomy undergirding modern liberal states and these core values – it would seem imperative to continue to pursue these sorts of literacies and cultivations. This is most especially true if, as some evidence suggests, at least unwitting uses of new media work to privilege the emotional and relational rather than the rational and the individual.

Further Reading

While somewhat dated in the face of rapid technological and cultural developments, my *Digital Media Ethics* (2009) still serves as a useful first introduction to global media ethics. A second, extensively updated, edition of the volume is scheduled to appear in 2013.

Global media ethics draws from a wide range of disciplines and fields, beginning with information and computing ethics. Luciano Floridi is among the most significant philosophers in this area, and his *Information: A Very Short Introduction* (Oxford: Oxford University Press, 2010) provides a comprehensive but quite accessible overview of the field.

In the domain of Internet studies, the Introduction and section overviews in *The Handbook of Internet Studies*, edited by Mia Consalvo and Charles Ess (Oxford: Wiley-Blackwell, 2011) provide readers with an extensive map and first orientation to this young but rapidly growing field. An important extension and update of these domains will appear soon in the forthcoming *Oxford Handbook of Internet Studies* edited by William Dutton.

Readers wanting to know more about changing Buddhist conceptions of selfhood in the age of digital media and their ethical implications will be well served by several of Soraj Hongladarom's recent articles, including his "Pervasive Computing, Privacy and Distribution of the Self." *Information* 2(2): 360–71 (2011).

Readers interested in current explorations of Confucian thought vis-à-vis digital media will find the work of Pak Wong especially helpful, including his "Dao, Harmony and Personhood: Towards a Confucian Ethics of Technology." *Philosophy and Technology* 25(1): 67–86 (2012).

References

Albrechstlund, A. 2008. "Online Social Networking as Participatory Surveillance". *First Monday* 13(3). http://www.uic.edu/htbin/cgiwrap/bin/ojs/index.php/fm/article/view/2142/1949.

Ames, R. and Rosemont, H. 1998. *The Analects of Confucius: A Philosophical Translation*. New York: Ballantine Books.

Bakardjieva, M. 2009. Subactivism: Lifeworld and Politics in the Age of the Internet. *The Information Society* 25: 91–104.

Baym, N. 2011. "Social Networks 2.0." In M. Consalvo and C. Ess, eds., *The Handbook of Internet Studies*. Oxford: Wiley-Blackwell, 384–405.

Bechmann, A. and Lomborg, S. Forthcoming. "Mapping Actor Roles in Social Media: Different Perspectives on Value Creation in Theories of User Participation." New Media and Society. Special issue on "Internet Studies."

Bedau, H. A. 1974. Are There Really "Crimes without Victims"? In E. M. Schur and H. A. Bedau, eds., *Victimless Crimes / Two Sides of a Controversy*. Englewood Cliffs, NJ: Prentice-Hall, 55–105.

Bizer, J. 2003. Grundrechte im Netz: Von der freien Meinungsäußerung bis zum Recht auf Eigentum. In C. Schulzki-Haddouti, ed., *Buĕrgerrechte im Netz*. Bonn: Bundeszentrale fuĕr politische Bildung, 21–9.

Bromseth, J. and Sundén, J. 2011. "Queering Internet Studies: Intersections of Gender and Sexuality." In M. Consalvo and C. Ess, eds., *The Handbook of Internet Studies*. Oxford: Wiley-Blackwell, 270–99.

Burk, D. 2007. "Privacy and Property in the Global Datasphere." In S. Hongladarom and C. Ess, eds., *Information Technology Ethics: Cultural Perspectives*. Hershey, PA: IGI Global, 94–107.

Carr, N. 2010. "The Web Shatters Focus, Rewires Brains." *Wired Magazine*, May 24. http://www.wired.com/magazine/2010/05/ff_nicholas_carr/all/1.

Cheong, P. and Ess, C. 2012. "Introduction: Religion 2.0? Relational and Hybridizing Pathways in Religion, Social Media, and Culture." In P. Cheong, P. Fischer-Nielsen, S. Gelfgren, and C. Ess, eds., *Digital Religion, Social Media and Culture: Perspectives, Practices, Futures*. Oxford: Peter Lang, 1–21.

DeCew, J. 1986. "The Scope of Privacy in Law and Ethics." *Law and Philosophy* 5: 145–73.

Ess, C. 2007. "Cybernetic Pluralism in an Emerging Global Information and Computing Ethics." *International Review of Information Ethics* 7: 91–119. http://www.i-r-i-e.net/inhalt/007/11-ess.pdf.

Ess, C. 2009. *Digital Media Ethics*. Cambridge: Polity Press.

Ess, C. 2010. "The Embodied Self in a Digital Age: Possibilities, Risks, and Prospects for a Pluralistic (Democratic/Liberal) Future?" *Nordicom Information 32*(2): 105–18.

Ess, C. Forthcoming. "Digital Ethics Past, Present, Futures." *Foreword to Don Heider and Adrienne L. Massanari, eds., Digital Ethics*. New York: Peter Lang.

Floridi, L. Ed. 2010. *The Cambridge Handbook of Information and Computer Ethics*. Cambridge: Cambridge University Press.

Foucault, M. 1988. "Technologies of the Self." In L. H. Martin, H. Gutman, and P. Hutton, eds., *Technologies of the Self: A Seminar with Michel Foucault*. Amherst, MA: University of Massachusetts Press, 16–49.

Fuchs, C., Boersma, K., Albrechslund, A., and Sandoval, M. Eds. 2011. *Internet and Surveillance: The Challenges of Web 2.0 and Social Media*. London: Routledge.

Gergen, K. 2011. *Relational Being: Beyond Self and Community*. Oxford: Oxford University Press.

Gilligan, C. 1982. *In a Different Voice: Psychological Theory and Women's Development*. Cambridge, MA: Harvard University Press.

Greenleaf, G. 2012. "Major Changes in Asia Pacific Data Privacy Laws: 2011 Survey" University of New South Wales Faculty of Law Research Series 2012, Working Paper 3. http://law.bepress.com/unswwps/flrps12/art3.

Grodzinsky, F. S., Miller, K. W., and Wolf, M. J. 2008. "The Ethics of Designing Artificial Agents." *Ethics and Information Technology*10(2–3): 115–21.

Heider, D. and Massanari, A. L. Eds. Forthcoming. *Digital Ethics*. New York: Peter Lang.

Howard, P. N., Duffy, A., Freelon, D., Hussain, M., Mari, W., and Mazaid, M. 2011. "Opening Closed Regimes: What Was the Role of Social Media During the Arab Spring?" Project on Information Technology and Political Islam, http://dl.dropbox.com/u/12947477/publications/2011_Howard-Duffy -Freelon-Hussain-Mari-Mazaid_pITPI.pdf.

Jefferson, T. [1776] 1984. "A Declaration by the Representatives of the United States of America, in General Congress Assembled." In M. D. Peterson, ed., *Thomas Jefferson: Writings*. New York: Library of America, 19–24.

Johnson, D. 2001. *Computer Ethics*, 3rd edn. Upper Saddle River, NJ: Prentice-Hall.

King, M. L., Jr. 1964. "Letter from the Birmingham Jail." In Martin Luther King, Jr., ed., *Why We Can't Wait*. New York: Mentor, 77–100.

Kitiyadisai, K. 2005. "Privacy Rights and Protection: Foreign Values in Modern Thai Context." *Ethics and Information Technology* 7(1): 17–26.

Lange, P. 2007. "Publicly Private and Privately Public: Social Networking on YouTube." *Journal of Computer-Mediated Communication* 13(1), article 18. http://jcmc.indiana.edu/vol13/issue1/lange.html.

Ling, R. 2008. *New Tech, New Ties: How Mobile Communication is Reshaping Social Cohesion*. Cambridge, MA: MIT Press.

Livingstone, S., Haddon, L., Görzig, A., and Ólafsson, K. 2011. "EU Kids Online Final Report." www.eukidsonline.net.

Lü, Y. H. 2005. "Privacy and Data Privacy Issues in Contemporary China." *Ethics and Information Technology* 7(1): 7–15.

Nakada, M. and Tamura, T. 2005. "Japanese Conceptions of Privacy: An Intercultural Perspective." *Ethics and Information Technology* 7(1): 27–36.

Noddings, N. 1984. *Caring: A Feminine Approach to Ethics and Moral Education*. Berkeley, CA: University of California Press.

Opsahl, K. 2010. "Facebook's Eroding Privacy Policy: A Timeline." Electronic Freedom Foundation, https://www.eff.org/deeplinks/2010/04/facebook -timeline.

Paasonen, S. 2011. "Online Pornography: Ubiquitous and Effaced." In M. Consalvo and C. Ess, eds., *The Handbook of Internet Studies*. Oxford: Wiley-Blackwell, 424–39.

Plato. 2002. "Crito." In *Five Dialogues*, 2nd edn., trans. G. M. A. Grube. Indianapolis, IN: Hackett, 45–57.

Sinnott-Armstrong, W. 2011. "Consequentialism." In E. N. Zalta, ed., *The Stanford Encyclopedia of Philosophy*. http://plato.stanford.edu/archives/win2011/entries/consequentialism/.

Strikwerda, L. 2011. "Virtual Child Pornography: Why Images Do Harm from a Moral Perspective." In C. Ess and M. Thorseth, eds., *Trust and Virtual Worlds: Contemporary Perspectives*. Oxford: Peter Lang, 139–61.

Sui, S. 2011. "The Law and Regulation on Privacy in China." Rising Pan European and International Awareness of Biometrics and Security Ethics (RISE) conference. Beijing, October 20–21.

Taddeo, M. 2011. "The Role of e-Trust in Distributed Artificial Systems." In C. Ess and M. Thorseth, eds., *Trust and Virtual Worlds: Contemporary Perspectives*. Oxford: Peter Lang, 75–88.

Tavani, H. 2007. *Ethics and Technology: Ethical Issues in an Age of Information and Communication Technology*, 2nd edn. Hoboken, NJ: Wiley and Sons.

Taylor, C. 1989. *Sources of the Self: The Making of the Modern Identity*. Cambridge, MA: Harvard University Press.

Thorseth, M. 2011. "Virtuality and Trust in Broadened Thinking Online." In C. Ess and M. Thorseth, eds., *Trust and Virtual Worlds: Contemporary Perspectives*. Oxford: Peter Lang, 162–77.

Turkle, S. 2011. *Alone Together: Why We Expect More from Technology and Less from Each Other*. Boston: Basic Books.

United Nations. 1948. *Universal Declaration of Human Rights*. www.un.org/en/documents/udhr/.

Vallor, S. 2010. "Social Networking Technology and the Virtues." *Ethics and Information Technology* 12(2): 157–70.

Wallach, W. and Allen, C. 2010. *Moral Machines: Teaching Robots Right from Wrong*. Oxford: Oxford University Press.

Ward, S. 2011. *Ethics and the Media: An Introduction*. Cambridge: Cambridge University Press.

Wilson, R. A. and Foglia, L. 2011. "Embodied Cognition." In E. N. Zalta, ed., *The Stanford Encyclopedia of Philosophy*. http://plato.stanford.edu/archives/fall2011/entries/embodied-cognition/.

Woolf, V. (1929) 1989. *A Room of One's Own*. New York: Mariner Books.

14

Global Ethics and the Problem of Relativism

Clifford G. Christians

The complicated cases and issues in media ethics are increasingly international in scope. Important news events are routinely transnational conflicts at their core, and cannot be domesticated without distorting them. The diaspora, common now around the world, means that communities attached to local news live and work elsewhere. Global digital technologies make national boundaries irrelevant for news events, and the media institutions that produce news are themselves typically multinational. Their global reach tends to frame news in international terms. The bulk of our work in media ethics has been predigital and tidily national. Today's electronic globalism requires a repositioning of media ethics from print-and-broadcast domestic to cyber-international.

Rupert Murdoch's News Corporation with 64,000 employees is designed organizationally to meet today's world challenges. But the phone-hacking scandal in Britain discredited it as immoral to its structural core. Closing its London tabloid, *The News of the World*, was not a British event but an act of desperation to save the Murdoch empire worldwide.

A 21-year-old Iranian student, called the Comodohacker in the news media, recently cracked 300,000 Gmail accounts in his home country. He claims to have the algorithms to break the encryption of Google and Yahoo, putting the world's financial system in a panic.

Anders Behring Breivik terrorized Norway, murdering seven with a car bomb in Oslo and shooting 86 at a youth camp on Utoya Island. With alleged links to the far-right English Defence League and opposing his country's immigration policy, Breivik was not Norwegian news only. It reverberated across the United States with its parallels to Timothy McVeigh's bombing in Oklahoma City as political protest. And the three-day massacre in Mumbai, by Pakistani members of Lashkar-e-Taiba, spoke to the world about terrorist assaults on the financial centers of democratic governments everywhere.

Global Media Ethics: Problems and Perspectives, First Edition. Edited by Stephen J. A. Ward.
© 2013 Blackwell Publishing Ltd. Published 2013 by Blackwell Publishing Ltd.

Australian Julian Assange launched the website WikiLeaks.org in 2006, aiming to uproot investigative reporting from its home in city and nation. In releasing nearly two million leaks on every topic imaginable – from classified government material to financial records of banks and businesses – it transforms raw documents from their natural habitat to a global data bank. The international scope of WikiLeaks material (from 100 countries) provides a central repository of documents of international interest to compensate for the lack of on-the-ground reporters overseas.

As we rework media ethics so it is strong enough to take international issues seriously, moral absolutism stands in the way. We need an international ethics to match global technologies and news events, but moral relativism is our most serious impediment to achieving it. Martin Luther King declared in March 1965 that "the moral arc of the universe is long but it bends toward justice." Only a macro theory can tell us whether the "bend toward justice" is true of the global media universe. If our thinking is encumbered by ethical relativism, no such macro theory is sustainable. In this electronic era of relentless change and confusion, a premier issue is relativism. Unless we can resolve it intellectually, the future of global media ethics is limited.

This chapter confronts ethical relativism directly, positioning it against moral relativism. It then demonstrates that moral universals can be nonabsolutist, by grounding them in human existence rather than in metaphysics, divine commands, or natural law.

Philosophical Relativism

In philosophical relativism, moral principles are presumed to have no objective application independent of the societies in which they are constituted. To get our thinking straight on it for global media ethics, we need to work out of its intellectual history. David Hume in the eighteenth century and Friedrich Nietzsche in the nineteenth century established the conceptual categories that continue to dominate our thinking.[1]

The Enlightenment idea of a common morality known to all rational beings had its detractors. David Hume, for example, took seriously the multiplying discoveries of other cultures as sea exploration discovered the planet. He recognized that these diverse conceptions of the good might turn out to have nothing in common.

Hume, as a British empiricist, insisted that humans know only what they experience directly. In opposition to rationalism, he argued that desire rather than cognition governed human behavior, and morality is therefore based on emotion rather than abstract principles. Moral rules are rooted in feelings of approval and disapproval. Such sentiments as praise and blame are motivating, but cold abstractions are not (Hume [1751] 1975). From his ethical writings in Book 3 of his *Treatise of Human Nature* ("Of Morals") (1739) and Book 2 ("Of the Passions") of his *Enquiry*

Concerning the Principles of Morals (1748), this typical quotation shows how Hume limits the role of reason in morality: "Morals excite passions and produce or prevent actions. Reason itself is utterly impotent to this particular. The rules of morality, therefore, are not conclusions of our reason" ([1739] 2000: 3.1.1.6).

Hume limited reason's territory. Facts are needed in concrete situations and the social impact of our behavior needs to be calculated, but reason cannot judge whether something is virtuous or malevolent. Good and evil are not causally connected nor are they related as abstractions. Reason judges quantity and number; it calculates resemblance and difference. But virtue is not a product of reason and vice irrational. Hume's *Enquiry Concerning Human Understanding* (1751) condemns speculative metaphysics that goes beyond the bounds of experience and abets superstition and religious doctrine. The influence of Hume's philosophical naturalism on Adam Smith, Jeremy Bentham, and Charles Darwin is well known, and he is still widely cited in the West today.

While Hume initiated in modern terms the long-standing philosophical struggle over ethical relativism, Friedrich Nietzsche (1844–1900) made it inescapable.[2] Nietzsche developed a totalizing assault on moral values. Since there is no transcendent answer to the "why" of human existence, we face the demise of moral interpretation altogether. In his first book, *The Birth of Tragedy*, Nietzsche insisted that "only as aesthetic phenomena are life and the world justified" ([1872] 1967a: 5, 24). He announced a philosophy beyond good and evil that places morality not only "in the world of appearances but even among deceptions, as semblance, delusion, error, interpretation" ([1872] 1967a: 22–3; see also Nietzsche [1887] 1967b, [1886] 1966). In a world where God has died and everything lacks meaning, morality is appearance, even a fool's paradise.

In contrast to the traditional belief that ethics was essential for social order, Nietzsche argued that moral values had become useless. His *Will to Power* presented a nihilism that means "the end of the moral interpretation of the world" ([1880] 1967c: 1–2). Nietzsche put ethics permanently on the defensive. Because he was questioning God's existence, and with it the validity of moral commands, Nietzsche turned to aesthetic values that need no supernatural sanction. "One can speak of beauty without implying that anything ought to be beautiful or that anybody ought to create the beautiful" (Nietzsche [1883–5] 1968: 130).

One hundred years later, in summarizing the postmodern argument against ethics, Zygmunt Bauman uses Nietzsche's perspective directly: Ethics in postmodern times has been replaced by aesthetics (1993: 178–9). In more general terms, today's understanding of ethical relativism lives in the Nietzschean tradition. The right and valid are only known in local space and in native languages. Judgments of right and wrong are defined by the internal criteria of their adherents. Moral propositions are considered to have no validity outside their indigenous home. Defending an abstract good is no longer considered beneficent, but seen as imperialism over the moral judgments of diverse communities. The concept of norms itself has eroded. The Enlightenment's metaphysical certitude has been replaced by philosophical relativism.

In this second decade of the twenty-first century, a number of sociological factors have combined to give this tradition of relativism an urgency and comprehensiveness that threatens conceptual progress in media ethics.

Social constructionism dominates the social sciences and is one factor (Miner 2004). A constructionist methodology abets relativism by its operating presumption that knowledge and reality are constituted by contingent variables rather than a phenomenon's inherent quality. Bertrand Russell's epistemology, Nelson Goodman's world-making, Foucault's narrative, and Emile Durkheim's functionalism are explicit models of pervasive constructionism. In social scientific approaches to communication, the notion of humans as cultural constructors is ubiquitous.

Another factor is cultural anthropology. For over a century, it has been axiomatic to accept all of the world's cultures in their own terms. As a given of scientific research, honoring cultural diversity enriches human life and promotes tolerance. But, as George Marcus and Michael Fisher (1999) argue, after World War II, cultural relativism was popularized to mean moral relativism. Reflecting Hume and Nietzsche, since cultures are equal in principle, value systems are equally valued no matter how different they are. What is considered good is approved by the majority in a given culture. Cultural and moral relativism are distinct categories, and it is a logical fallacy to conflate them. Intracultural and intercultural diversity in institutions such as monogamy does not in itself prove that gender relations have no transnational moral dimensions. Plato's allegory of the cave in his *Republic* teaches us not to confuse the fire with the sun. Regardless, cultural relativity now typically means moral relativism.

As another factor, the profusion of media worldwide has typically allowed cultural relativity to slide into philosophical relativism. The media's penchant for daily affairs tends to follow this conflation and exacerbate the problem of relativism rather than resolve it. In the news we emphasize specifics. The media's preoccupation with visual narrative usually leaves cultural relativism unattended. Moral commitments are embedded in the practices of particular social groups, and they are communicated through a community's stories. The media as a cultural phenomenon and social institution prize diversity. But in doing so, their programming typically intermixes cultural and moral relativism, rendering cross-cultural and transnational principles incoherent for their audience.

As we work on ethical principles for the global media, believing them to be more crucial than ever, ethical relativism is deep, wide, and largely unattended. Cultural relativism as epistemology is indispensable for curbing ethnocentrism. It enables us to see other cultures as only different, not inferior. It is critical to social scientific research. However, in the moral domain it is both misused and erroneous.

Moral Absolutism

Philosophical relativism – in the ruminations of Hume, totalized by Nietzsche, and ubiquitous today – is pitched against moral absolutism. Ethical relativism is an argument against absolutes. It objects to universal truths that are typically used to control or convert dissenters. Absolutes are said to threaten diversity, whereas relativism liberates us to reject all oppressive claims to truth. Ward (2010) puts the fundamental question in these terms: "Is ethics relative or absolute?" He argues correctly that our work on ethical judgments must "adequately address the debate between relativism and absolutism. This debate introduces additional, higher-order questions about the status of the conceptual schemes themselves" (2010: 93).[3]

Moral absolutism is a normative ethical theory that certain actions are absolutely right or wrong, regardless of the context or consequences or intentions behind them. There are principles that ought never to be violated. Lying is immoral, for instance, even if its purpose is a social good:

> Absolutism in ethics seeks a set of ethical criteria that are objective in an absolute manner. The set is known to be true or reasonable per se. It is not relative to a particular conceptual scheme, among many potentially rival schemes. There is only one conceptual scheme, and it absolutely grounds our judgments of right or wrong. (Ward 2010: 95)

One source of or justification for an absolutist ethics is the demands of reason. The deontological rationalism of Immanuel Kant is a notable form of such absolutism. Kant argued that all cognition entailed time and space, and categorical imperatives were true across history, therefore absolute, and true for all rational beings everywhere. In 1755, Kant's first major book, *Universal Natural History and Theory of the Heavens* explained the structure of the universe exclusively in terms of Newtonian science. What is called the Kant–Laplace theory of the origin of the universe is based on it. Newton's cosmology meant that absolutes were unquestioned.

In the *Critique of Practical Reason* (1788) and *Groundwork of the Metaphysic of Morals* (1785), Kant assimilated ethics to logic. He demanded that moral laws be universally applicable and free from inner contradiction. Society was presumed to have a fundamental moral structure embedded in human nature as basic as atoms in physics, with the moral law the analog of the unchanging laws of gravity. In a context-free rationality, moral principles are derived from the essential structure of a disembodied reason. For ethical rationalists, the truth of all legitimate claims about moral obligation can only be settled by formally examining their logical structure. Nietzsche opposed moral absolutism of this secular kind, based as it is on the rationality inherent in human beings and on the structure of the universe itself.

Many religions have morally absolutist positions, rooting their system of morality in divine commands. Both Hume and Nietzsche's relativism opposed religious moral systems considered to be absolute, without contradiction, perfect and unchangeable.

Hume's opposition to divine command theories is elaborate and influential. His philosophy as a whole seeks to unmask the dogmas of religious belief and he critiques the metaphysics of seventeenth- and eighteenth-century theology. His skepticism and naturalism appear throughout his work and culminate in his books devoted entirely to philosophical issues in religion: *Natural History of Religion* (1757) and *Dialogues Concerning Natural Religion* (1779).

The heart of Nietzsche's objection to religious mandates is his famous quotations on the death of God, by which he means the Christian God is no longer a credible source of absolute morality. In *Thus Spoke Zarathustra* (1883–5), for those who have given up their belief in God, Christian morality is no longer self-evident. And for societies, how can a system of values be retained in the absence of a divine order?

Richard Rorty understands the significant stakes here, defining truth not as "a mirror of nature" and "privileged contact with reality" (1979: 10), but as "what comes to be believed" in everyday happenstance (1979: 61). He scourges foundationalist views of truth as "the quest for certainty over the quest for wisdom.... Science, rather than living, became philosophy's subject, and epistemology its center" (1979: 365, 394). Rorty abandons those moral problems that appeal for their salience to an abstract order beyond time and change. In his *Contingency, Irony, and Solidarity* (1989) he situates moral theory within language. For making life worth living, he looks for those values that emerge when we clear the deck of normative ethics, Enlightenment epistemology, theology, and metaphysics. Rorty seeks those autonomous conditions within which we contribute our own vocabulary to the ongoing human experiment. In language, we rehearse our common doubts, affirm our mutual contingencies, and push away every kind of fundamentalism that purports to be the final answer. Literature rather than philosophy awakens us to the cruelty of particular social practices and to human solidarity. "Since there is nothing beyond vocabularies which serves as a criterion of choice between them," our doubts about ourselves or our culture "can be resolved or assuaged only by enlarging our acquaintance" (1979: 80). In pleading for morality as contingent rather than epistemically certain, Rorty does a wholesale housecleaning of an ethics of absolutism (cf. Rorty 1998, 1999).

Universalist Theory

Moral absolutism and moral universalism are not identical. Peter Singer's *One World: The Ethics of Globalization* (2004) is a utilitarian universalism without being absolutist. A defensible universalism holds that what is justified or blameworthy is independent of custom or opinion, as opposed to relativism. But that assertion does not mean that whatever is morally permissible or impermissible is independent of context, as in absolutism.[4] Since Nietzsche, ethical relativism has been arguing against absolutes, that is, against ethical objectivism.

For global media ethics to be possible and meaningful over the long term, moral universals must be dislodged from rationalistic absolutes. With the concept unencumbered, the primary issue is identifying a different kind of universal, one that honors the vast diversity of human life and in so doing undermines the argument for philosophical relativism. The challenge is a normative model of universalism that keeps ethics close to people's everyday experience, so that variety in cultures is recognized rather than buried under an abstract metaphysics.

Instead of working with the intellectual framework established in the Global North by Hume and Nietzsche, a universal paradigm needs to be constructed on totally different grounds. Therefore, the retheorizing of theory must be done without presuming rationalist foundations, without the luxury of a noncontingent morality from which to begin. Transformational work on universals understands norms to be historically embedded rather than formalistic and abstract. As such they belong to a different category, philosophically speaking, than that of objectivist absolutes.

The centerpiece of a twenty-first-century theory of global media ethics is presuppositional in character. Rationalist ethics is a single-strand theory presuming the noncontingency of starting points.[5] Absolutist models rest on foundational a prioris, generating theorems considered true without exception. However, instead of rule-ordered prescriptions, worldviews ought to be interwoven into theory making. With presuppositions – values, as they are commonly called – considered sine qua non, a new generation of global media ethics is possible that is multicultural and transnational. No theories are neutral, even though scientific theories since the Enlightenment pretend to be (Christians et al. 2009). Theories are a problem of axiology rather than epistemology. Theories reflect core beliefs about human existence. In Levinas's terms, ethics is not a vassal of philosophical speculation, but is rooted in human existence. We seize our moral obligation and existential condition simultaneously (Levinas 1985).

Making beliefs transparent establishes dialogue among competing worldviews rather than empowering the knowledge of empires. It opens a dialectic between the transnational and the local, between sameness and difference. As Stephen Ward puts it:

> One of the negative consequences of extreme relativism is to discourage cross-cultural dialogue . . . The social danger of extreme relativism is passivism and an inability or reluctance to judge. If no cultural or ethical traditions are better than any other, then why not passively acquiesce to whatever tradition one was born into? Why bother to reform? On what basis can I judge another view or practice to be incorrect? (Ward 2010: 98–9)

Nonabsolutist universals can be verified through hermeneutics.[6] Hans-Georg Gadamer, for example, replaces the foundationalist conception of knowledge with the idea of understanding that is neither dogmatic or relativistic. For Gadamer, language originates in and with humans, so that the human species' existence is primordially linguistic (1989: 443). As the one species constituted by language, humans can embed universals and diversity in each other. They know themselves through their symbolic expressions, in the process generating patterns of value along the boundaries between norms and actual behavior, the conscience and socially constructed principles (Wuthnow 1987). Transcendental criteria are thus shifted from a metaphysical, vertical plane to the horizon of community, world, and being.

In Thomas Nagel's *View From Nowhere* (1989), while humans have the unique ability to view the world in a detached way, the subjective is always with us and cannot be rationalized away. We can step back from our *persona* and place ourselves, along with our subjective points of view, in a broader conception of the world. The attempt to understand everything as objective, and construe the subjective as mere appearance, is manifest in overreaching forms of scientism and metaphysical absolutism. Symbols enable us to reside simultaneously in the internal and external (Ricoeur 1974).

In Susanne Langer's (1957) striking book, *Philosophy in a New Key*, symbolization is used to understand the human mind. Symbolic thought sets up a new theory of the arts and gives coherence to our piecemeal struggles with issues of life and consciousness. Symbolic action, this distinctive feature of the human species, comes into its own in ethics in our theory making. Theories are symbolic constructs. The human world is made accessible, nurtured, and integrated into social units through symbol, myth, and metaphor. The meaning of theoretical statements derives from an interpretive, historical context that humans themselves supply. Symbols open up the human spirit where our worldviews are inscribed. They permit us to express levels of reality that otherwise remain hidden. In symbolic theory, concepts are not isolated from their representations. The social and individual dimensions of language are a unified whole.

In symbolic terms, theories are not authoritative canons of self-evident truth, but catalysts for critical thinking. They enable moral agency. Theories are meaningful portraits of reality and not statistically precise formulations derived from artificially fixed conditions. Theorizing in these terms is not an examination of external events, but the power of the imagination to give us an inside perspective on reality.

Herbert Blumer (1954) usefully distinguishes definitive and sensitized concepts. Absolutist theories generate definitive concepts, that is, law-like abstractions from artificially fixed conditions isolated from people's experience and language. In theories that represent the idea of understanding in hermeneutics, sensitized concepts generate an insightful picture that capture the original meaning and explicate it to maximum impact. Sensitized concepts display an integrating scheme from within the data themselves. Examples well known in the literature are Ellul's "efficiency," Gramsci's "hegemony," Baudrillard's "simulacra," and Innis's "monopoly of knowledge." Theories of moral universals represent this alternative view of human knowing. Such moral universals enable researchers to handle cultural complexity with *savoir-faire* and competence.[7]

Theories of Global Media Ethics

Several initiatives are under way to establish a global media ethics without being trapped in philosophical relativism. They follow a trilevel theory of universals rather than the foundationalism of absolutist ethics. Below are illustrations of a Gadamer-style pathway between objectivist dogmatism and subjectivist relativism.

Philosophical anthropology

Christians (2010) proposes the sacredness of life as a universal theory not subject to relativism. This theoretical model does not obstruct cultures and inhibit their development. It represents a shift from an absolutist ethics of reason to an ethics of being. The paradigm's credibility is rooted in philosophical anthropology which gives priority to the necessary and sufficient conditions of being a member of the human species.

The sacredness-of-life model emerged from a study of ethical principles in 13 countries with six languages from Latin America to Africa, to Islamic and Judeo-Christian ethics, to Hinduism and Native American mythology (Christians and Traber 1997). The search was for a first starting point in ethics regardless of national identity, religions, and cultures. Philosophers, theologians, and social theorists were asked the questions: "What is the basic principle that is nonnegotiable among your people, in your culture, in your moral theory? What is the bedrock value for you, the presupposition from which you begin?" This research on four continents is a limited sample, and ideally the question about basic presuppositions should be asked of all 6,500 living languages in the world and all 20,000 people groups. But this study is explicitly international and cross-cultural, and points us in the right direction.

Aristotle taught us that there must be an unmoved mover. There cannot be infinite regression or knowledge is indeterminate. One cannot act or think without taking something as given. All knowledge begins with presuppositions because it must start somewhere, not because such presuppositions have been demonstrated to be unequivocally true. They represent the researcher's beliefs about what's best for the world.

The basic commitment in all the groups that were studied is the sacredness of life. The sacredness of life is a pretheoretical given that makes the moral order possible. Living nature reproduces itself in terms of its very character. Therefore, within the natural order is a moral claim on us for its own sake and in its own right. As Hans Jonas concludes, "Nature evinces at least one determinate goal, life itself.... With the gaining of this premise, the decisive battle for ethical theory has already been won" (1984: 78). It is a universal principle that contradicts moral relativism.

The veneration of life is a protonorm. *Proto* here means "beneath." A protonorm in ethics is similar in kind to the proto-Indo-European language, a lingual predecessor underlying the Indo-European languages as we know them in history. Reverence for life on earth establishes a level playing field for cross-collaboration on the ethical foundations of a responsible press. It represents a universalism from the ground up. Various societies articulate this protonorm in different terms and illustrate it locally, but every culture can bring to the table this fundamental norm for ordering political relationships and such social institutions as the news media. In this sense, universal solidarity is the basic principle of ethics and the normative core of all human communication.

Human responsibility regarding natural existence contributes the possibility of intrinsic imperatives to moral philosophy. This is a protonorm that precedes its elaboration into ethical principles. And its universal scope enables us to avoid the divisiveness of individual interests, cultural practices, and national prerogatives. The primal sacredness of life is a protonorm that binds humans into a common oneness. Out of this primordial generality basic principles emerge for media ethics such as truth, human dignity, and nonviolence.

Rather than rational abstractions, this is an ethics of being in which the organic realism has a taken-for-granted character. Ontological ethics of this sort makes no appeal to essentialist human nature or to universal reason, that is, to the primary assumptions of an absolutist ethics. In Helmut Peukert's terms, given the oneness of the human species, our minimum goal must be:

> a world in which human beings find ways of living together which enable every individual to work out a lifestyle based on recognition and respect of others, and to do so ultimately in a universal perspective not confined to small groups or nations. Universal solidarity is thus the basic principle of ethics and the normative core of all human communication. (Peukert 1981: 10)

Moral psychology
Patrick Plaisance is developing an international media ethics based on recent advances in moral psychology and virtue theory. Moral and cognitive psychology are challenging the mainstream view of moral agency by identifying the multiple factors involved in approaching and resolving ethical dilemmas (Plaisance 2011: 107). Its inductive methodology and cultural orientation represent another alternative to the abstract, deductive framework of absolutist ethics. It seeks to demonstrate that empirical research is crucial for normative theory in media ethics of the future.[8]

Moral and cognitive psychology are included broadly, and virtue science and neuroethics are referenced, but the centerpiece of Plaisance's project is the work of psychologist Donelson R. Forsyth (1980, 1981). Professor in the Jepson School of Leadership Studies at the University of Richmond, Forsyth is a social and personality psychologist who studies ethical thought and moral judgment. Ethical ideology is an important domain of journalism culture, and Forsyth organizes ethical ideologies along the dimensions of relativism and idealism (Plaisance et al. 2012: 643–6).

The relativism category assesses "the extent to which journalists base their personal moral philosophies on universal ethical rules" (Hanitzsch et al. 2010: 276). Probing the question of relativism enables comparative research on the extent to which journalists depend on the situation or on universal principles in their ethical decision making. The idealism category

> refers to the importance of consequences in journalists' reasoning about ethical dilemmas. Highly idealistic journalists... believe that desirable consequences should always be obtained with the "right" action. Less idealistic journalists... admit that harm will sometimes be necessary to produce a greater public good. (Hanitzsch et al. 2010: 276)

The Forsyth Ethics Position Questionnaire (FEPQ) measures degrees of relativism and idealism by assessing responses to a series of 20 statements.[9]

Plaisance, with colleagues Elizabeth Skewes and Joanna Larez, is using moral psychology measures to study the ethical commitment and virtuous behavior of professional exemplars in journalism. The participation of Plaisance and Skewes in the World of Journalism project – headed by Germany's Thomas Hanitzsch – demonstrates how cognitive moral development and moral ideological orientations work internationally (Hanitzsch et al. 2010). The culture of 1,800 journalists and media organizations in 18 countries is being studied to understand multidimensional influences on news production and to identify distinct journalism cultures around the world (Hanitzsch et al. 2010: 5). By examining the moral connections and disparities among journalists across the globe, the study contributes to the question of moral universals without being caught in philosophical relativism.[10]

On the epistemological level, the World of Journalism research project indicates that impartiality, and the reliability and factualness of information, are valued worldwide. By including the Forsyth index of relativism and idealism, the project makes morality a crucial dimension of journalism culture. There is wide cross-cultural agreement that questionable methods of reporting ought to be avoided, even if it means not getting the story (Hanitzsch 2010: 284). Most journalists in the countries surveyed tend to obey universal principles regardless of situation and context, though there is approval of less universal and more scattered principles that allow for flexibility and personal latitude in solving dilemmas.

Sonia Livingstone rightly accuses journalism and media studies of "methodological nationalism" instead of mapping transnational flows.

> The field of media and communication – its phenomena, questions, and concerns – is focused on clearly demarcated, tradition-bound, institutionally integrated countries widely recognized and referred to by their self-identified publics, media and culture. (Livingstone 2012: 416)

Cross-national research should be critiqued for "inadvertently privileging the dominant norm over the norms of 'others'" (p. 422). Nation-by-nation studies tend to idealize the degree to which states are politically and culturally homogeneous. Risto Kunelius (2009) puts the issue in different terms: "Economic and political developments have begun to reposition the nation as the basic ingredient of international politics," and the news media facing transnational conflicts and communities in diaspora are reorienting themselves "in relation to the state and national identity" (2009: 139). The World of Journalism project, while explicitly nation-state in its structure, seeks to avoid these issues by not using professional Western values as the yardstick by which to measure success or failure. Its psychosocial framework is geared toward diversity in the global arena of journalism, and claims to present only a rough picture of a level playing field – Europe, North American, and non-Western democracies, and countries North and South (Hanitzsch 2010: 274).[11]

This World of Journalism research faces the long-standing is–ought dilemma. What is described cannot be considered normative without committing the naturalistic fallacy. Plaisance writes eloquently about this problem of inductive research, recognizing the complicated issues in the relationship between data-gathering and normative theorizing. He insists correctly that philosophical theory and social science research cannot be a zero-sum game (2011: 96–101, 108–10).

Christian Smith's *What Is a Person?* (2011) is helpful here. Smith argues that the nature of persons is the fundamental question of philosophy and ought also to be the social scientist's starting point. To interpret and explain social life scientifically requires a social theory that does justice to the humanistic vision of people and society. The World of Journalism research has a reasonably sophisticated concept of persons. By the study of culture, moral judgment, ideals, and values are included; moral agency is correctly seen as multidimensional. Hanitzsch (2007) has integrated roles, epistemologies, and ethical ideologies to get beyond functions and behavior in isolation. To the extent personhood is made ontologically explicit and social-psychological measures are refined further to reflect holistic humans, an intellectual pathway is opened from descriptive to normative ethics.

Contractualism

Stephen J. A. Ward proposes a contractualist view of ethics. In his summary, "Ethical principles are humanly constructed restraints on social behavior" (2005: 6). Ethics is a never-ending project of "inventing, apply-ing, and critiquing the basic principles that guide human interaction, define social roles, and justify institutional structures" (2005: 7, cf. 2010: 13, 22). In opposition to absolutism, Ward bases ethical principles on "intersubjective agreement obtained from rational, public deliberation, in light of common purposes, values, and facts" (2005: 7). As with John Dewey's (1927) experimentalism, concepts and principles are shaped and tested as "tools of inquiry" and policies "treated as working hypotheses" (1927: 202–3; see Ward 2005: 18). For contractualism, absolutist ratio-nalism is wrong in its claim "that all ethical differences can be shown to be variations on major common principles. Substantial and non-reducible differences exist in ethics" (Ward 2010: 97).

Based on the philosophical foundation of contractualism, Ward adopts naturalism as his meta-ethical theory. Ethics, he says,

> is a natural activity of humans, explained and justified by natural concepts, phenomena, and causes...A natural theory of ethics does not appeal to supernatural authority, transcendent absolutes, or the intuition of non-natural, moral properties. Naturalized ethics is ethics within the limits of human experience. (Ward 2010: 27)

Ethics is a rational construction that changes over time, "not a discovery of absolute principles" (2010: 52).

Instead of rejecting journalism's historic core – objectivity, for example – Ward reconstructs it in naturalistic terms. He recognizes that "traditional news objectivity is, by all accounts, a spent ethical force, doubted by journalists and academe" (2004: 261). Rather than abandon-ing the concept, he redefines it as pragmatic objectivity. He recognizes the central roles of values and presuppositions in human knowing and does not insist on detachment. Ward's naturalism calls for the best available "scientific knowledge of human interaction with media technologies, and the best available knowledge of the economics and sociology of human communication" (2010: 167). Pragmatic objectivity keeps "truth as a goal of inquiry and redefines truth in a modest, realist manner. The search for truth does not require the presumption of an absolute view of truth or reality." Instead of one-track neutral reporting of facts, multidimensional pragmatic objectivity understands truth "as the slow process of coming to know more and more things about our empirical world and to grasp them in a more accurate and comprehensive manner" (Ward 2004: 271).

In the same spirit, contractualism transforms professional journalism standards into a new global ethics for journalists as world citizens. The main principle is the flourishing of humanity at large, with cosmopoli-tanism its central doctrine. Ward describes cosmopolitanism as an ancient ethical theory affirming the equal value and dignity of all people, but he rejects the idle claim that the moral community is borderless. He demon-strates that cosmopolitan's central axis is respect for humanity's moral capacity, however manifested (2010: 154–67, 2011a: ch. 7). Cosmopolitanism reinterprets the media's aims and principles for the global age as promoting a transnational human good. The cosmopolitan journalist has a "multisociety contract" to reject extreme patriotism and advance what Ward calls both rational and reasonable goals: those that promote the creativity, freedom, and fulfillment humans share as a species (2010: 165, 168–71). In this sense, ethical flourishing

> gives priority to the right in the sense that the pursuit of our goods occurs within the bounds of justice. Ethical flourishing is a composite good where the good and the right are as congruent as possible. (Ward 2011b: 739)

As today's media landscape is being realigned again – this time around mixed media platforms that include citizen journalism sites, interactive chat, and professional news – Ward's contractualism calls for an ecumenical approach to ethics (2011a: 216–17). "Ecumenical ethics should articulate a number of principles that integrated newsrooms embrace"; this is an open ethics "that seeks ever new ways to enhance participation, discussion, questioning, and interaction between the group and those outside the group" (2011a: 218, 225).

In sum, Ward does not respond to objectivist absolutism with the extreme relativism of Nietzsche. His naturalism instead leads to what he calls "moderate relativism." Not all moral schemes are equal:

> In ethics, it is not "anything goes." Some schemes are better than others . . . Not all values are to be doubted; not all values are to be accepted. One works critically from within the best tradition available and remains open to other traditions. (2010: 97, 100)

Ward's formal label for this moderate paradigm is "contractual universals," where "fair and rational deliberation shows (or could show)" that such principles as ethical flourishing "should be recognized and honored by all parties" (2010: 175). His *Global Journalism Ethics* does not merely correct the weaknesses of traditional journalism ethics but develops a new foundation and structure for it in universalist terms. His contractualism enables an authentic global perspective to emerge, "not a colonial or national perspective disguised as a global philosophy" (2010: 183).

Neuroscience

Lee Wilkins (2010, 2011) is developing a nonabsolutist theory of universals for media ethics based on neuroscience. For Wilkins, a crucial question for twenty-first-century ethics is this:

> Does the human being through evolution and genetics, have a species specific and hence universal, hard-wired capacity to consider right and wrong in a way different from animals, including the higher apes and intelligent species such as dolphins? (2010: 26)

Wilkins finds among neuropsychologists an affirmative answer to this question. Neuroscientific research documents that, through evolutionary naturalism, the human species has developed a sense of right and wrong. Harvard's Marc Hauser contends that a moral instinct has evolved in humans, "a capacity that naturally grows with each child, designed to generate rapid judgment about what is morally right or wrong based on an unconscious grammar" (Hauser 2006: xvii). Hauser's experiments with both children and adults in various cultures suggest a moral capacity "that enables each individual to unconsciously and automatically evaluate a limitless variety of actions in terms of principles that dictate what is permissible, obligatory, or forbidden" (2006: 16). As Wilkins elaborates:

> This does not mean that human beings don't make ethical mistakes, just as human beings make grammatical or word usage errors or misunderstand some statements entirely; nor does Hauser's concept of "a moral faculty" mean that there is one right answer. Hauser concludes that human beings are hard-wired for "fair" in much the way that John Rawls (1971) described justice as fairness. (2010: 26)

Hauser exemplifies what neuroscience is clarifying for us – the linkages between the organic brain and the moral mind (Gazzaniga 2005). Philosopher Patricia Churchland (2011) argues that moral values are based in the caring for offspring that is true of all mammals. The processes and chemistry of the brain as it has developed in humans moves them beyond self-preservation to social ties with other humans. Morality is not an abstract system, but neurobiological in origin. Wilkins considers this biological inheritance, identified in the theory and research of neuroscience, the ground for universalizing moral development and an ethics of care throughout the species. Actual, lived relationships rather than intellectual and theoretical constructs are the origin of philosophical feminist ethics, with neuroscience verifying why relationships should have the supremacy.

Wilkins's theoretical work on universals in media ethics seeks to account for both neuroscience and philosophy. But, in order to make that integration possible, she contradicts the tradition of ethical rationalism. From Descartes through Kant to much of the contemporary era, she observes, "rationality was both necessary and sufficient for ethical action... This reliance on rationality worked in tandem with a principle-based and top-down approach to ethical thinking"; in this ethical paradigm, "logic and rationality were intended to supersede the emotions, which were viewed as an impediment to rational thinking and subsequently to appropriate moral behavior" (Wilkins 2011: 805).

Contrary to philosophy's formal models of ethical rationality, Wilkins adopts a counter-Enlightenment tradition: from Hume's sympathy and Adam Smith's moral sentiments, to Darwin's "moral organ" and biology's genetic basis for virtue, to psychology today that has documented "how emotions influence, sometimes profoundly, human decision-making"

(2011: 806–7). Now in the twenty-first century, interdisciplinary research has converged around the core understanding that emotions bound and sustain human rationality, that the human organism and the environment are mutually interactive on multiple levels, and that the moral sense is primordial to the mind-enhanced brain (Wilkins, 2011: 807). Wilkins finds Gilligan's feminist philosophy of care and empathy,[12] and the communitarian philosophy of protonorms, the best way to defend and elaborate on these core understandings (2011: 809–11). Wilkins's theory is human-centric and therefore dynamic, rather than presuming the static and formal abstractions of natural science.

What neuroscientists understand about human morality – extended into non-Enlightenment epistemology and ontology – is a universal approach for Wilkins that links the literature of moral development and feminist ethical theory.

> If there is a bedrock of instinctive moral understanding, . . . then studying moral development and its influence on it can help articulate the complexity of moral thinking and growth throughout the human lifetime. (Wilkins 2010: 28)

The goal of her theoretical work is "to delineate one fruitful path by which a universal (or at least international) understanding of media ethics could be first articulated and then investigated both philosophically and empirically" (2010: 24). If human beings have a capacity for moral thinking similar to the biological capacity for language, "then some understandings of ethics can be universalized through the species" (Wilkins 2010: 28), in the same way that all humans learn languages of equal phonemic complexity at a similar age. But, in contrast to the essentialist rationalism of the absolutist paradigm,

> we should look not for a universal ethics comprising hard-and-fast truths, but for the universal ethics that arises from being human, which is clearly contextual, emotion-influenced, and designed to increase our survival. (Gazzaniga 2005: 177)

Conclusion

One could argue that philosophical relativism ultimately founders on Mannheim's paradox, summarized this way: Relativists claim that truth is situation-bound, but they cannot proclaim relativism without rising above it, and they cannot rise above it without giving it up (Geertz 1973: ch. 8, cf. Mannheim 1936: pt. II). As with the classical "liar's paradox," relativism contradicts itself in asserting itself. For relativism there must be at least one nonrelative truth, that of relativism. Furthermore, to advocate relativism in its traditional terms is stultifying. If moral action is thought to depend on a society's norms, then the norms of society must be obeyed; to diverge from them is to act immorally. The distributive fallacy is inescapable:

Without moral norms of universal scope, one ideological bloc presumes to speak for the whole.

The illogic of relativism ought itself to be convincing. But rather than debate the tradition of Hume and Nietzsche in the epistemological terms set by philosophical relativism, the revolutionary idea is to start over intellectually with theories not trapped in metaphysical abstractions across time, but which do take seriously universals across space. Instead of concluding that no moral universals are possible, scholars today doing credible work on global media ethics understand norms to be historically embedded rather than grounded in metaphysics, divine commands, or natural law. The primary issue is identifying a different kind of universal, one that honors cultural diversity while articulating cross-cultural norms. In fact, protonorms, journalism cultures, cosmopolitanism, and neuroscience seek universal frameworks in exactly these terms. They step outside professional media ethics to develop normative models rooted in philosophical reflection (Euben 1984).

These theories are multileveled reflections of core beliefs about human existence. As Guba and Lincoln argue, the issues in theory and research ultimately must be engaged at the worldview level:

> Questions of method are secondary to questions of paradigm, which we define as the basic belief system or worldview that guides the investigation, not only in choices of method but in ontologically and epistemologically fundamental ways. (Guba and Lincoln 1994: 105)

The conventional view of theory as extrinsic is a truncated and unsophisticated paradigm. The theories of global media ethics represented here stake their legitimacy on their parsimony and coherence, but find their ultimate defense in their commitments to universal human solidarity, idealism, ethical flourishing, and life-in-relation.

The four theories of global media ethics presented above open a pathway out of relativity that is intellectually credible. They represent a different model of moral universals, constructed from the ground up and not imperialistic in character. They have met the challenge for media ethics in a global age – whether cultural diversity can be honored while moral relativism is rejected at the same time.

Notes

1. Ward (2011a: 29–33) reviews the intellectual history of philosophical relativism since the Greek sophists, elaborating the concept in terms of his own work on journalism objectivity (2004) and connecting it theoretically to Audi (2007) and Wong (2006). My historical review of the one-many problem situates this version of philosophical relativism in the Hindu Vedas (eighth century BCE) and the Greek Presocratics (sixth century BCE) (Christians 2008).

2. Relativism is given a different orientation in Christians (2009) and (2011).

3. Ward examines the philosophical issues in the debate over absolutes and relativism in his *Global Journalism Ethics* (2010: 93–102).

4. As Jürgen Habermas (1990, cf. 1993) understands so clearly, external appeals rooted in universal pragmatics are necessary cross-culturally. Competing normative claims can only be adjudicated in the public sphere under ideal speech conditions such as reciprocity and openness.

5. For a trilevel theory of moral universals that overcomes the weaknesses of mainstream single-strand decontextual theories, see Christians et al. (2008).

6. For an elaboration of the role of hermeneutics in communication generally, see Grossberg and Christians (1981); for a review of hermeneutics applied to theory, see Christians (2007).

7. There are notable searches for universals in philosophical ethics that do not promote transcendental metaphysical abstractions, but recognize diversity in culture by keeping ethics rooted in everyday experience. The feminist ethics of Seyla Benhabib (1992, 2002) has shown that the ethics of relation is particular and universal at the same time. She calls it interactive universalism. As we ground ethics in everyday human experience, we are speaking about our common humanity. Dialogic relations are rational and principled, so the values we identify in everyday life we generalize as true about ethical interactions throughout the human race.

   Martha Nussbaum (1999, 2000) uses extensive research into the daily lives of women to argue for overlapping capabilities that are true of humans universally as they work out their existence in the real world. The common values that emerge from people's daily struggles are bodily health, bodily integrity, normal life span, affiliations of dignity and compassion, recreation, political participation, rights to goods and employment. Human beings are the type of creatures who are fully capable of all these functions and they provide a basic minimum for constitutional principles that should be respected by all governments.

   Kwasi Wiredu (1996) writes out of an African philosophical perspective. The human species lives by language. All languages are similar in their phonemic complexity and all languages serve not merely functional roles but cultural formation. Through language we arbitrate our values and establish our differences and similarities. Through the commonness we share as lingual beings, we can believe that there are universals at the same time as we live in our particular communities.

8. For a review of the literature on contemporary moral psychology and the universal moral sense, see Young and Saxe (2011).

9. Relativism and idealism (being idealistic about consequence) are categories for moral psychology that do not engage directly the relativism versus absolutism issue in philosophy. Relativism in the FEPQ is defined in terms of universal rules and as such resembles philosophical relativism, but moral absolutism and concern for good and bad consequences are distinct domains.

10. This conclusion is correct as long as the findings continue to show no substantial moral agreement across cultures in journalism values.

11. The relationship between social-scientific comparative studies and philosophical universals is contentious and unresolved. Nikolaev (2011) develops

the debate in terms of social science's internationalism and philosophy's universalism.

12. In giving primacy to the relation-in-between, rather than to individual actors, feminist ethics has moved the concept of caring to the center as the most powerful way to describe our duty to one another. For journalism, it mandates other-regarding care for the audience and readers. The public is considered active and responsible. Citizens themselves arrive at their own solutions to public problems, and an ethics of care is especially concerned how well that process functions. Journalists need to care about how democracy is working. Carol Gilligan, for example, has been researching the role that patriarchy plays in government and social institutions. With patriarchy as deep a contradiction to democratic life as slavery, overcoming patriarchy so democracy can be realized more fully will be one of history's most important events of the twenty-first century (Gilligan and Richards 2009).

Further Reading

Several theoretical works on global ethics respond to the challenge of relativism by developing approaches to universalism that are credible philosophically. Seyla Benhabib's *Situating the Self* (1992) is one example. She has developed the principle of interactive universalism, that answers Lyotard's claim that master narratives are no longer possible. Martha Nussbaum's *Women and Human Development* (2000) uses extensive research into the daily lives of women in India to argue for overlapping capabilities that are true of humans universally as they work out their existence in the everyday world. Kwasi Wiredu, while chair of the philosophy department at the University of Legon in Ghana, wrote from an African philosophical perspective in his *Cultural Universals and Particulars* (1996). The human species lives by language, and through our common lingual character, it is possible to defend the idea of universals at the same time that we live in our particular communities.

In global media ethics, Stephen J. A. Ward's *Global Journalism Ethics* (2010) is theoretically informed and develops a cosmopolitan perspective while dealing with the philosophical issues that a global perspective raises. Christians, Rao, Ward, and Wasserman work through the intellectual challenges in developing theories of universals in their 2008 essay in *Ecquid Novi*, "Toward a Global Media Ethics: Theoretical Perspectives."

Alexander Nikolaev proposes a comparative strategy for theorizing in international terms. His *Ethical Issues in International Communication Ethics* (New York: Palgrave Macmillan, 2011) argues that comparative studies are the best alternative in a relativistic age. This edited volume illustrates the kind of research and scholarship necessary for effectively comparing the communication systems that exist today in different parts of the world.

References

Audi, R. 2007. *Moral Value and Human Diversity*. New York: Oxford University Press.

Bauman, Z. 1993. *Postmodern Ethics*. Oxford: Blackwell.

Benhabib, S. 1992. *Situating the Self: Gender, Community, and Postmodernism in Contemporary Ethics*. New York: Routledge.

Benhabib, S. 2002. *The Claims of Culture: Equality and Diversity in the Global Era*. Princeton, NJ: Princeton University Press.

Blumer, H. 1954. "What Is Wrong with Social Theory?" *American Sociological Review* 19 (February): 3–10.

Christians, C. 2007. "Hermeneutics and Philosophical Reflection." In D. W. Hatley and P. F. Furr, eds., *Freedom Fighter: A Festschrift Honoring John C. Merrill*. Natchitoches, LA: Northwestern State University Press, 149–68.

Christians, C. 2008. "The One-and-the-Many Problem in Communication Ethics." In P. Lee, ed., *Communicating Peace: Entertaining Angels Unawares*. Penang, Malaysia: Southbound Press, 45–62.

Christians, C. 2009. "Theoretical Frontiers in International Media Ethics." *Australian Journalism Review* 31(2): 5–17.

Christians, C. 2010. "The Ethics of Universal Being." In S. J. A. Ward and H. Wasserman, eds., *Media Ethics Beyond Borders: A Global Perspective*. New York: Routledge, 6–23.

Christians, C. 2011. "Cultural Diversity and Moral Relativism." In A. G. Nikolaev, ed., *Ethical Issues in International Communication*. New York: Palgrave Macmillan, 22–34.

Christians, C., Glasser, T. L., McQuail, D., Nordenstreng, K., and White, R. A. 2009. *Normative Theories of the Media: Journalism in Democratic Societies*. Urbana: University of Illinois Press.

Christians, C., Rao, S., Ward, S. J. A., and Wasserman, H. 2008. "Toward a Global Media Ethics: Theoretical Perspectives." *Ecquid Novi: African Journalism Studies* 29(2): 135–72.

Christians, C. and Traber, M. Eds. 1997. *Communication Ethics and Universal Values*. Thousand Oaks, CA: Sage.

Churchland, P. S. 2011. *Braintrust: What Neuroscience Tells Us About Morality*. Princeton, NJ: Princeton University Press.

Dewey, J. 1927. *The Public and its Problems*. New York: Holt.

Euben, P. J. 1984. "Philosophy and the Professions." *Democracy* 1: 112–27.

Forsyth, D. R. 1980. "A Taxonomy of Ethical Ideologies." *Journal of Personality and Social Psychology* 39(1): 175–84.

Forsyth, D. R. 1981. "Moral Judgment: The Influence of Ethical Ideology." *Personality and Social Psychology Bulletin* 7(2): 218–23.

Gadamer, H. G. 1989. *Truth and Method*, 2nd edn., trans. J. Weinsheimer and D. G. Marshall. New York: Seabury Press.

Gazzaniga, M. S. 2005. *The Ethical Brain: The Science of Our Moral Dilemmas*. New York: HarperCollins.

Geertz, C. 1973. *The Interpretation of Cultures*. New York: Basic Books.

Gilligan, C. and Richards, D. A. J. 2009. *The Deepening Darkness: Patriarchy, Resistance, and Democracy's Future*. Cambridge: Cambridge University Press.

Grossberg, L. and Christians, C. 1981. "Hermeneutics and the Study of Communication." In J. Soloski, ed., *Foundations for Communication Studies*. Iowa City: University of Iowa Monograph Series, 57–81.

Guba, E. G. and Lincoln, Y. S. 1994. "Competing Paradigms in Qualitative Research." In N. K. Denzin and Y. S. Lincoln, eds., *Handbook of Qualitative Research*. Thousand Oaks, CA: Sage, 95–117.

Habermas, J. 1990. *Moral Consciousness and Communicative Action*, trans. C. Lenhardt and S. W. Nicholson. Cambridge, MA: MIT Press.

Habermas, J. 1993. *Justification and Application: Remarks on Discourse Ethics*, trans. C. Cronin. Cambridge, MA: MIT Press.

Hanitzsch, T. 2007. "Deconstructing Journalism Culture: Towards a Universal Theory." *Communication Theory* 17(4): 367–85.

Hanitzsch, T., Folker, H., Mellado, C., Anikina, M., Berganza, R., et al. 2010. "Mapping Journalism Cultures Across Nations." *Journalism Studies* 12(3): 273–93.

Hauser, M. D. 2006. *Moral Minds: How Nature Designed Our Universal Sense of Right and Wrong*. New York: HarperCollins.

Hume, D. [1751] 1975. *Enquiry Concerning Human Understanding*. Oxford: Clarendon.

Hume, D. [1779] 1990. *Dialogues Concerning Natural Religion*. New York: Penguin. Original

Hume, D. [1757] 1992. *The Natural History of Religion*. New York: Macmillan.

Hume, D. [1748] 1998. *An Enquiry Concerning the Principles of Morals*. Oxford: Clarendon.

Hume, D. [1739] 2000. *Treatise of Human Nature*, ed. D. F. Norton and M. J. Norton. Oxford: Clarendon.

Jonas, H. 1984. *The Imperative of Responsibility : In Search of an Ethics for the Technological Age*. Chicago: University of Chicago Press.

Kant, I. [1788] 1997. *Critique of Practical Reason*, ed. M. Gregor. Cambridge: Cambridge University Press.

Kant, I. [1785] 1998. *Groundwork of the Metaphysic of Morals*, ed. M. Gregor. Cambridge: Cambridge University Press.

Kant, I. [1755] 2000. *Universal Natural History and Theory of Heaven*, trans. I. Johnston. Arlington, VA: Richer Resources Publications.

Kunelius, R. 2009. "Lessons of Being Drawn In: On Global Free Speech, Communication Theory and the Mohammed Cartoons." In A. Kierulf and H. Rønning, eds., *Freedom of Speech Abridged? Cultural, Legal and Philosophical Challenges*. Göteborg, Sweden: Nordicom, 139–51.

Langer, S. K. 1957. *Philosophy in a New Key: A Study of the Symbolism of Reason, Rite, and Art*, 3rd edn. Cambridge, MA: Harvard University Press.

Levinas, E. 1985. *Ethics and Infinity*, trans. R. A. Cohen. Pittsburgh, PA: Duquesne University Press.

Livingstone, S. 2012. "Challenges to Comparative Research in a Globalizing Media Landscape." In F. Esser and T. Hanitzsch, eds., *Handbook of Comparative Communication Research*. New York: Routledge, 415–30.

Mannheim, K. 1936. *Ideology and Utopia*. New York: Routledge.

Marcus, G. and Fisher, M. 1999. *Anthropology as Cultural Critique: An Experimental Moment in the Human Sciences*, 2nd edn. Chicago: University of Chicago Press.

Miner, R. 2004. *Truth in the Making: Creative Knowledge in Theology and Philosophy*. New York: Routledge.

Nagel, T. 1989. *View From Nowhere*. New York: Oxford University Press.

Nietzsche, F. [1886] 1966. *Beyond Good and Evil*, trans. W. Kaufmann. New York: Random House.

Nietzsche, F. [1872] 1967a. *The Birth of Tragedy*, trans. W. Kaufmann. New York: Random House.

Nietzsche, F. [1887] 1967b. *On the Genealogy of Morals*, trans. W. Kaufmann and R. J. Hollingdale. New York: Random House.

Nietzsche, F. [1880] 1967c. *Will to Power: Attempt at a Revaluation of All Values*, trans. W. Kaufmann. New York: Random House.

Nietzsche, F. [1883–5] 1968. *Thus Spoke Zarathustra: A Book for All and None*, trans. W. Kaufmann. New York: Viking Press.

Nikolaev, A. G. 2011. "The Essence of the Debate." In A. G. Nikolaev, ed., *Ethical Issues in International Communication*. New York: Palgrave Macmillan, 1–19.

Nussbaum, M. 1999. *Sex and Social Justice*. New York: Oxford University Press.

Nussbaum, M. 2000. *Women and Human Development: The Capabilities Approach*. New York: Cambridge University Press.

Peukert, H. 1981. "Universal Solidarity as the Goal of Communication." *Media Development* 28(4): 10–12.

Plaisance, P. 2011. "Moral Agency in Media: Toward a Model to Explore Key Components Of Ethical Practice." *Journal of Mass Media Ethics* 26: 96–113.

Plaisance, P., Skewes, E. A., and Hanitzsch, T. 2012. "Ethical Orientations of Journalists Around the Globe: Implications from a Cross-National Survey." *Communication Research* 39: 641–61.

Rawls, J. 1971. *A Theory of Justice*. Cambridge, MA: Harvard University Press.

Ricoeur, P. 1974. *The Conflict of Interpretations: Essays in Hermeneutics*, ed. D. Ihde. Evanston, IL: Northwestern University Press.

Rorty, R. 1979. *Philosophy and the Mirror of Nature*. Princeton, NJ: Princeton University Press.

Rorty, R. 1989. *Contingency, Irony, and Solidarity*. New York: Cambridge University Press.

Rorty, R. 1998. *Truth and Progress: Philosophical Papers*, vol. 3. New York: Cambridge University Press.

Rorty, R. 1999. *Philosophy and Social Hope*. New York: Penguin.

Singer, P. 2004. *One World: The Ethics of Globalization*. New Haven, CT: Yale University Press.

Smith, C. 2011. *What Is a Person? Rethinking Humanity, Social Life, and the Moral Good from the Person Up*. Chicago: University of Chicago Press.

Ward, S. J. A. 2004. *The Invention of Journalism Ethics: The Path to Objectivity and Beyond*. Montreal: McGill-Queen's University Press.

Ward, S. J. A. 2005. "Philosophical Foundations for Global Journalism Ethics." *Journal of Mass Media Ethics* 20(1): 3–21.

Ward, S. J. A. 2010. *Global Journalism Ethics*. Montreal: McGill-Queen's University Press.

Ward, S. J. A. 2011a. *Ethics and the Media: An Introduction*. New York: Cambridge University Press.

Ward, S. J. A. 2011b. "Ethical Flourishing as Aim of Global Media Ethics." *Journalism Studies* 12(4): 738–46.

Wilkins, L. 2010. "Connecting Care and Duty: How Neuroscience and Feminist Ethics Can Contribute to Understanding Professional Moral Development."

In S. J. A. Ward and H. Wasserman, eds., *Media Ethics Beyond Borders: A Global Perspective*. New York: Routledge, 24–41.

Wilkins, L. 2011. "Journalism's Sentiments: Negotiating Between Freedom and Responsibility." *Journalism Studies* 12(6): 804–15.

Wiredu, K. 1996. *Cultural Universals and Particulars: An African Perspective*. Bloomington: Indiana University Press.

Wong, D. 2006. *Natural Moralities*. New York: Oxford University Press.

Wuthnow, R. 1987. *Meaning and Moral Order: Explorations in Cultural Analysis*. Berkeley: University of California Press.

Young, L. and Saxe, R. 2011. "Moral Universals and Individual Differences." *Emotion Review* 3(3): 323–4.

15

Global Media Ethics
Utopian or Realistic?

Stephen J. A. Ward

The chapters of this book have explored specific problems for the construction of global media ethics, from differences among media cultures
to parochial coverage of global issues. In this concluding chapter, I step
back and ask a larger question: Is the creation of global media ethics as a
whole a realistic and desirable goal?

We noted in the Introduction that globalists who promote the project
hold at least two beliefs in common: (1) media ethics must "go global";
(2) news media should adopt a global attitude toward themselves and their
practices. Global media ethicists believe the project is desirable, necessary,
and realizable. However, there are skeptics who regard the project as
utopian and undesirable. This skepticism goes to the heart of the matter. If
the project is undesirable or unrealizable, why are books on global media
ethics published? Why do smart people spend their time discussing global
media ethics?

I will proceed by exploring, and responding to, several criticisms of the
project and the idea of a universal media ethics. I then present a realistic
conception of what can be achieved in global media ethics. My aim is not
to prove that the project is possible and realizable, since no such proof
is possible for future-orientated projects. The world is too uncertain a
place to guarantee our wishes. However, I attempt to clear a path for
future work by setting aside some familiar objections. I contend that the
objections are not persuasive and do not show that a universal media
ethics is impossible or undesirable. Hence it is rational and practically
worthwhile to support the project of global media ethics.

Skeptical Objections: Utopianism

The objections to be considered complain that the project is conceptually
incorrect and practically utopian. In addition, the project, even if it were

Global Media Ethics: Problems and Perspectives, First Edition. Edited by Stephen J. A. Ward.
© 2013 Blackwell Publishing Ltd. Published 2013 by Blackwell Publishing Ltd.

realizable, is an undesirable approach to ethics. If these complaints were valid, it would undermine the project.

What is the charge of utopianism? It is the realist's charge that a project (or theory) seeks to bring about a state of the world which is so perfect or far from reality that the project is practically impossible to realize. The word "utopia" comes from the Greek meaning, literally, "no place" although it came to mean a perfect place in terms of its political, social, and moral aspects. For the critic of global media ethics, "utopia" and "utopian" have a negative meaning. It means working toward an ideal state of the world that can never be. Therefore, it is idle (if not harmful or counterproductive) to engage in such speculation about the future. Better to work on what has a chance of becoming a reality, given the nature of the world and human society.[1]

From a realist perspective, utopian thinking about global media ethics can make one or more of three mistakes. (1) The project may set the wrong goals for action. For example, global media ethics may assert that its goal is that all journalists rigidly adhere to one code of ethics; and critics may question that goal. (2) The project may be too hazy and speculative to be of much use in guiding conduct and theorizing. For example, global media ethics may be explained in ways that make it sound like nothing more than a dreamy spirituality about the "brotherhood of mankind," with no concrete details on how it would make a difference in theory or practice. (3) The project cannot be realized to any significant degree. For example, perhaps a global media ethics can only prompt conversations about media ethics across the borders of a few countries.

With respect to (1), it is not apparent that global media ethics proposes wildly inappropriate goals. A survey of recent writings would show that the goals being proposed, from Christians's principles of respect for life and nonviolence (Chapter 14 in this book) to Ward's (2010) four levels of human flourishing, do not appear to fall into the category of obviously inappropriate aims for global ethics. As for (2), it is implausible to claim that all or most work on global media ethics fails to say anything important about practice. The chapters in this book refute that contention. Mistake (3) however is more difficult to assess. It may be that global media ethics offers reasonable goals with practical implications but the project will never reach these goals due to the nature of today's media, the world it inhabits, and the forces that determine news media. The objections considered below fall under mistake (3).

Objection #1: The project is practically utopian

This objection articulates a common belief about news media: Many news organizations are profit-driven businesses where ethics is not primary. Therefore, ambitious ethical projects on a global scale will receive a lukewarm response. I call this belief the "principle of the supremacy of nonethical factors" in media production. The principle is strong. In journalism, for example, the principle asserts that nonethical factors, such as economic and organizational structures, determine what journalism is done and how it is done. Nonethical factors cause unethical conduct or give ethical considerations a low priority.[2] It is not difficult to imagine how these factors might undermine the project of global media ethics. Stories that adhere to global norms may be costly to produce, or editors may be nationalists who reject cosmopolitan attitudes, or even-handed global reports on a war or a global issue may be deemed unpatriotic and likely to offend audiences.

Objection #2: The project is normatively utopian

Objection #1 argues that there are overwhelming economic and organizational forces against the project. Objection #2 argues that there are overwhelming normative and cultural factors that block the project. This is what I call the "principle of unbridgeable normative differences." The principle states that the norms of media practitioners and media cultures across the world are so different that it is unrealistic to think that they will ever agree on a common global ethics. Also, the differences are irreducible. The differences are substantial and cannot be bridged by general principles that all cultures share.

Objection #3: Universalism is undesirable in a global world

Objection #3 contends that, even if global media ethics is not utopian, it should not be developed. This is because universalism is conceptually incorrect and it promotes an undesirable approach to ethics.

Conceptually, universalism – the belief in universal moral principles – is incorrect because (1) there are no universal principles in ethics, or at least not in media ethics. And/or (2) we cannot agree on what those principles are. This objection often relies on an implicit or explicit cultural relativism, which we will discuss below. Combined with the principle of normative differences, this criticism is a formidable objection to universalism.

Universalism is undesirable because it consists of abstract principles, is rigid about rules, is insensitive to social differences and contexts, and is, too often, a tool of imperialism.

Let's spell out these complaints about abstract universalism a bit further. It is claimed that, in media ethics, ideals such as an aggressive free press and news objectivity are imposed insensitively on media practices in different countries. Imposing universal principles leads to a questionable "top-down" or "deductive" approach to media ethics. For example, Fair's chapter 8 in this book indicates one way these values are imposed – media development agencies may impose Western ideas of a free and democratic press on African countries like Liberia. Wasserman's chapter 7 shows that it is too often assumed that the Western notion of serving democracy is universal and can be easily imposed on media in transitional democracies.

Top-down, abstract universalism does not fit well with a global, plural world. It fails to encourage a cross-cultural conversation where the values of all participants are given due consideration. Further, universalism is sometimes charged with being a rigid deontological approach that insists on following rules and carrying out duties without sufficient consideration of social context and consequence.

These three types of objection appear to show that the project of global media ethics is utopian and undesirable.

Responses

These objections question the value of working on global media ethics, theoretically or practically. I defend the project by noting some reasons for questioning the objections.

Principle of supremacy questioned

Objection #1 states that the project is practically utopian, given the supremacy of nonethical factors. The principle rightly notes the influence of economic and other factors in media production. But it goes too far. If accepted it would invalidate all of media ethics, not just global media ethics.

To begin with, the principle of supremacy says nothing new about ethics and media. We are all aware that the influence of ethics in news media is diminished by unethical forces, from biased journalists to "get-the-story-at-any-cost" news organizations. The tension between ethical and nonethical imperatives defines media ethics. Media ethics is concerned with the ethical use of the power of media (Ward 2011). However, the supremacy principle does more than note the tension. It contends that nonethical forces always (or almost always?) are the primary determinants of what content gets produced and how it gets produced. Ethical projects are unrealistic if they aim at wide-ranging reforms. They are naïve if they believe that ethics will become a dominant influence on newsrooms and other centers of media production.

The supremacy principle may seem obvious, a matter of common knowledge. The unethical practices and scandals of news media have been well documented over many years. This common knowledge, however, ignores counterevidence. For instance, it ignores the moral impulses at work among journalists worldwide. In recent years, hundreds of journalists have been killed or imprisoned for revealing official wrongdoing; others have led democratic movements against tyrants. The principle ignores the fact that many journalists struggle every day to do the right thing, even if the public image of the journalist is that of an unethical professional. The supremacy principle does not mention that, in the United States and Canada alone, dozens of major news organizations – from the *New York Times* and *NPR* to the *Toronto Star* and the Canadian Broadcasting Corporation – follow extensive ethical guidelines. Ombudsmen and public editors monitor how well these newsrooms follow their guidelines. The principle also ignores a crucial cultural factor: Many newsrooms, such as the newsrooms of public broadcasters, make ethics a significant factor because of the importance of maintaining public trust in their reports.

The history of news media provides additional counterevidence. For example, in the early 1900s, as the mass commercial press arose in the United States and Canada, journalists organized themselves into professional associations and wrote the first codes of journalism ethics (Ward 2005). This exercise was motivated by a concern that nonethical forces were leading to biased and unethical journalism. This professional movement led to the entrenchment in newsrooms of such ethical principles as objectivity, truth telling, and editorial independence. The ethical project of creating a professional, objective journalism had a major impact on practice. The supremacy principle lacks the conceptual resources to adequately explain the success of this earlier ethical project – the project of professional journalism ethics. The principle fails to acknowledge that social and cultural forces such as professionalism and public expectations (and criticism) can be significant countervailing forces against unethical pressures.

In summary, the supremacy principle is too strong and too simplistic to provide a persuasive refutation of the project of global media ethics. The supremacy principle places too much emphasis on one or two factors in media work, while underestimating the power of countervailing forces, such as reform movements made possible by the agency of individuals, civic groups, professionals, and concerned citizens.

We should not allow this piece of common knowledge to be raised to the status of an unquestioned generalization, a generalization that dismisses (or discourages) ethical work in media. The supremacy principle is a counsel of despair. It says: Good people should not waste their time on ethics and new ethical projects. But what is the alternative? To acquiesce in the status quo? The existence of unethical factors requires us to do the opposite. We should find ways to make ethics more influential in media practice. Given the necessity for a global media ethics, described in the Introduction, we have an ethical obligation *not* to accept the supremacy principle. We should not dismiss global media ethics as impossible until we have at least made an effort to bring it into existence.

But what about objections #2 and #3, that the project is conceptually incorrect and culturally undesirable because it is a suspect form of universalism? I want to defend the idea of universalism as a general approach to ethics. It is, I argue, a more attractive understanding of ethics than cultural relativism. Then I will respond to criticisms of universalism as abstract, rigid, and culturally insensitive.

Universalism and cultural relativism

Ethical universalism maintains that there are some moral values that are valid for all members of a group or for all humans (Caney 2005: 26). One way to state this fact is to say that universal principles may be of restricted scope or of unrestricted scope. Principles of restricted scope apply to all persons of a particular group or profession but not necessarily to people outside the groups. Consider the principle, "thou shalt not commit adultery." It does not apply to all humans. It applies to people who are married. Take another example: Journalists should not compromise their editorial independence by accepting substantial gifts and other benefits from the source or subject of a report. This principle is of restricted scope. The principle is not meant to apply to all human beings, although the principle of editorial independence may apply to media professions outside of journalism.

Principles of unrestricted scope are principles of "the common morality" (Gert 2004) – a morality that applies to all people. The applicability of unrestricted principles is not restricted by culture, class, profession, or context. Candidates for unrestricted principles include injunctions to avoid harm, for example, prohibitions against murder, rape, torture, and abhorrent cruelty. Other candidate principles are positive injunctions to do good in various ways, such as the principles of kindness and charity. Unrestricted universalism can be found in theories of human rights, religious appeals to universal commandments, and humanistic philosophies which hold that all humans are owed dignity, rights, and opportunities.

A global media ethics has an interest in both restricted and unrestricted forms of universalism. It will seek principles that apply to all media practitioners, whether it is the principle of truth telling, editorial independence and transparency, or serving democracy. These restricted universals may be justified, ultimately, by the unrestricted principles of a global ethics. For example, the restricted universal principle that journalists should act as watchdog on the human rights practices of countries may be grounded in the unrestricted cosmopolitan principle that all humans everywhere deserve respect and dignified treatment by their governments. A global media ethics weaves together restricted and unrestricted universal principles.

The idea that restricted media principles are based on unrestricted principles should not strike one as curious. In ethics, specific principles are often justified by more general principles. We should expect this type of justification of media values because the principles of journalism and other media practices are not epistemologically self-sufficient (Ward 2010). Journalism ethics often appeals to principles of common morality, including broad social and political values. For example, the value of media truth telling or media promise keeping may be justified by unrestricted principles which hold that all humans should tell the truth and keep promises. The belief that informing the public is a primary ethical role for journalism is based, ultimately, on the belief that the public needs accurate and insightful information to be self-governing in a democracy. Belief in the unrestricted political value of democracy supports the restricted journalistic belief in the value of informing a public.

Ethical universalism is opposed to cultural relativism. The latter asserts that there are no universal ethical principles. That is, there are no principles (and no one set of principles) that can be shown to apply to all people around the world. Principles and norms are valid *within* cultures but not beyond them. There are other forms of relativism, such as subjective (or individual) relativism which holds that the justification of ethical beliefs is relative to individuals. As the saying goes, we all (each person) have our own ethics. Global media ethics is more interested in cultural relativism than subjective relativism because differences among cultures are frequently cited as the main obstacle to universal ethics.

Many forms of relativism take as their starting point the *fact* of ethical variation and change (Christians and Ward forthcoming). Relativists are impressed by differences in ethical beliefs around the world. They note that some cultures stress individualism, others stress social solidarity and fitting into social schemes; some cultures stress the impartial duties of justice, while other cultures make primary our partial attachments and duties to parents, family, and friends (Wong 2006). Relativists also note how ethical beliefs change. Slavery was once widely accepted; now it isn't.

Cultural relativism may contain an empirical and/or an epistemic claim. The empirical claim argues that universalism is wrong because, as a matter of fact, we do not discover common ethical values among cultures of the world. At the very least, there are more differences than commonalities. To modify our earlier saying: Cultures have their own ethics. Relativism in a plural world seems obvious. Since each culture has its own values, and cultures differ in values, it is unlikely that different cultures will agree on a common ethics in general or a common ethics for specific activities such as journalism.

Cultural relativism usually includes, implicitly or explicitly, an epistemic claim about how we justify ethical values. And this relativistic view of justification puts serious limits on how far one's principles apply to other cultures. For cultural relativism, we are inculcated into a system of values by our culture. Values have force and meaning because they derive from the communal life of a culture. Hence, the justification for values is local – the values are valid because they belong to and are supported by the culture in question. The justification for an ethical belief is relative to a specific culture. An ethical belief is valid if it conforms to the values and practices of a culture.

A local (cultural) theory of justification in ethics leads to a radically nonhierarchical view of the worth and validity of ethical beliefs in different cultures. If ethical beliefs are valid for the culture in which they are held,

302 Stephen J. A. Ward

then it seems to follow that every culture's ethical system is as valid as every other culture's ethical system. No ethical system of one culture is better or worse than the ethical system of any other culture. No set of principles in one culture is superior to a set of principles in any other culture.

Now, if all systems are relatively true or valid, cross-culture comparison and critique is not possible. The basis of such a comparison is either universal principles or the presumably superior principles of another culture. But cultural relativism denies the existence of universal values, and it denies that the principles in one culture may be better than the principles in another culture. Therefore, the values of one culture do not extend (and should not be extended) beyond that culture. Assume that one culture prizes the communal values of solidarity and conforming to authority, while another culture prizes individual freedoms and the right to criticize authority. According to cultural relativism, neither of those cultures has a right to critique the other because there is no basis for saying that one set of principles is better than another. Where values differ among cultures, there is no higher culture or higher set of principles to adjudicate the dispute. All criteria of evaluation are culture-bound. And, if there is no higher ground, then any attempt to identify universal principles is a faulty approach to ethics. Therefore, all forms of cross-cultural evaluation of values are questionable. In many cases, they incorrectly impose values on other cultures. "Imposing" here includes a wide range of activities, from intellectually criticizing the values of another culture to trying to stop certain practices deemed unethical. Every attempt to extend my principles to other cultures is an invalid imposition of my beliefs on others.

If cultural relativism is correct, then we should eschew any attempt to build a cross-cultural ethics based on universal, culture-transcending principles. The best (or only?) approach to ethics is tolerance and respect for the values of other cultures. Ethics is not universal. It is parochial. It is culture-bound. The justification for and critique of ethical principles is limited to what can be justified from within specific cultures. The project of global media ethics is incorrect because it violates the limits of ethics as established by cultural relativism.

These are the obstacles that cultural relativism throws across the path of global media ethics. If valid, these objections would invalidate global media ethics. But cultural relativism has serious internal problems, and therefore its arguments are not persuasive.

Problems of cultural relativism

Critics have argued that relativism is conceptually inconsistent. When relativists attempt to formulate their thesis, they contradict themselves (Todorov 1993: 389). Thomas Nagel in *The Last Word* (1997) claims that relativism is self-defeating. Nagel says the relativist can claim that relativism – the claim that all beliefs are relative to culture – is universally true. However, if this is so, relativism is self-defeating. There exists at least one universal principle, the principle of relativism. To avoid this problem, the relativist can say that the thesis of relativism is relatively true. However, if this is so, then those who are not persuaded by relativism have no reason to embrace it. They may legitimately stick with their own beliefs, which are also relatively true (Nagel 1997: 15).[3] Other critics note that cultural relativism often assumes the validity of some universal principles, such as the principle that all cultures should be tolerated and/or respected. Tolerance becomes a significant restraining principle. For example, Rawls argues against cosmopolitan theories of liberalism by claiming that liberal societies should not seek to impose their political values on other "decent" (but not liberal) peoples because this would violate the principle of tolerance (1999: 59–60, 67–80, 82–4).

Beyond these conceptual questions about relativism, there are questions about its empirical and epistemic claims. Empirically, there are studies (Christian and Traber 1997, Hanitzsch, Plaisance, and Skewes in chapter 2 of this book) which indicate that a significant number of common values exist across cultures and media cultures. In addition, cultural relativists may assume that variation and change among ethical values refute universalism. This is false. Universalists *agree* that there is variation, but they also contend that universal values exist. Furthermore, the universalist may argue that the differences are exaggerated and that many of the differences are not ultimate or unbridgeable. Many apparent differences may be "reducible" to universal values. In such a case, differing beliefs are different interpretations or expressions of a common principle. For example, all cultures believe in the value of education for their youth but how cultures go about educating youth varies. So the cultural relativist has to do more than point out the fact that differences exist.

Cultural relativism's notion of ethical justification – its ethical epistemology – is questionable. One problem is that it is often difficult to clearly identify a culture, let alone identify *the* ethics of that culture. Cultures are amorphous entities, straddling borders and containing conflicting ethical traditions and views. Another problem is that the cultural relativist fails to distinguish between consent and rational justification. Why should the fact that a belief or practice conforms to the current value system of a culture justify that belief or practice? Is it not the case that cultures can contain immoral practices, such as violating human rights? And what does consent consist in? Would a majority vote decide what is ethical for a culture? But can't majorities act unethically towards minorities?

Why is acceptance or conformity the criterion of ethical validity? When we discuss universals, we do not presume that they are valid simply because all (or most) people in a culture accept them, or that the universals conform nicely to the value systems of every culture. Beitz, for example, argues that to claim that human rights are universal is not to claim that they are accepted necessarily by everyone (2001: 274). Ethical validity must go beyond consent or conformity to notions of informed and well-reasoned consent. Scanlon (1998) argues that correct moral principles are those that reasonable people could not reject. The idea of "reasonable people" is a normative notion, going beyond the fact of acceptance. I have argued (Ward 2010) that the ground of universal principles is whether they can be proposed as a reasonable and effective conceptual framework for our ethical beliefs and practices. Universal principles are those principles that we think *should* be adopted as our basic principles. We propose universals to others, with good reasons. We don't demand social conformity.

Cultural relativism portrays itself as a tolerant form of ethics, respectful of ethical variety and change. Yet a closer look shows that, as an approach to ethics, it struggles to deal with ethical variety and change – the features that are supposed to make cultural relativism obvious.

A central fact of ethics is that, over time, the ethics of people change. Confronted with new situations and problems, people invent new norms and principles. But the idea of ethical validity as conformity to a culture's values doesn't seem to leave room for invention and reform. Conformity means conforming with what exists, the status quo. This problem within cultural relativism becomes clear when we deal with tensions between subcultures and traditions within a culture, or where there is a movement to challenge existing values, such as a movement toward greater equality for women. If conformity is the basis for ethical validity, then all such attempts at reform are invalid since they are nonconforming.

Finally, the cultural relativist's appeal to tolerance and respect is dubious. The first problem is that, as the previous paragraph suggests, to insist on conformity to one set of values within a culture can also be a form of imposition. The general principles of tolerance and respect seem to preclude criticism of specific cultural values and practices. The second problem is that the idea of tolerance and respect of other cultures is, as it stands, too general. When questions arise, we cannot fall back on a general demand for tolerance and respect for all cultures. Instead, we need to ask, in each case, *who* is demanding respect from other cultures. Are they tyrants and undemocratic leaders seeking to stay in power? Also, we need to ask *what* beliefs or practices are demanding respect? To decide whether a practice deserves respect requires us to evaluate the practice in detail. In addition, I would argue that any evaluation of practices across borders will, consciously or unconsciously, use universal ethical principles of human rights (and other universals). Therefore, cultural relativism provides an inadequate basis from which to question existing norms and practices in our own culture and in other cultures.

In summary, universalists have good reasons to doubt cultural relativism as a meta-ethical perspective. Cultural relativism does not provide persuasive arguments against universalism and, by implication, against global ethics. This is not to say that cultural relativism could not be reformulated to avoid my responses. However, as we have seen, some of the most popular and potent arguments currently leveled against universalism fail to persuade.[4]

Abstract universalism

Even if cultural relativism is rejected, there remain other objections against universalism. We have noted these objections. Critics, many of whom are not cultural relativists, have contended that universalism can become top-down and abstract, ignoring context and preferring a rigid deontology of rules. It seems we need to look for a different form of universalism, for example, a bottom-up, nonabstract universalism. I agree that we need to develop a universalism that avoids the faults of top-down, abstract universalism. Yet we need to do so carefully. We need to note the limitations of some of the objections against abstract universalism, and we need to explain how some of the objections, as stated, can be misleading.

Consider the complaint that ethical universalism is abstract. Ethical universalism *is* abstract. It consists of principles of great generality. The principles abstract from the details of specific situations and the identities of moral agents. For example, the universal principle against murder abstracts from the many types of people who may murder and the many ways of committing murder. This abstraction is welcome in ethics (cf. Ward 2011). Given the large number of situations and contending rules in ethics, we rightly seek guidance from general principles.

Abstract principles are an essential part of ethics. An ethics is a complex scheme which ranges from specific beliefs, for example, intuitions that action A is wrong in situation S, to general principles, for example, the principle of utility. When we reason ethically, any or all levels of that scheme may come into play. The idea that we can dispense with abstract principles is incorrect. They will play a role in our reasoning, for example as unconscious assumptions, even if we are skeptical of abstract principles.

So when is abstraction used incorrectly? Abstraction has a negative influence on ethical thinking if the thinker believes that abstract principles are sufficient for deciding what action is best. Two mistakes are common: We believe that abstract principles are clear and can be applied without interpreting their meaning for certain situations; or we believe that in applying abstract principles, we do not need to take into account the facts of the case. For example, we might be absolutists and believe that the application of general principles is the same always and everywhere, and does not require careful consideration of the situation's context or consequences. This faith in abstraction is misplaced because many cases are so complex that the abstract principle must be interpreted as to its meaning in this situation. Also, abstract principles often come into conflict in a situation and one has to look to interpretations, context, and consequence to weigh the principles. Therefore, no reasonable universalist holds that citing abstract principles is sufficient for ethics. No reasonable universalist believes that we do not have to consider context or consequences. To admit the relevancy of context is not to embrace a form of relativism or "situation ethics." It is to embrace the reasonable view that, to apply general principles, "apply" means bringing together the principles at issue and the facts of the case. The same process happens in applying legal principles. Therefore, the objection against abstract universalism is misleading if it is interpreted as an objection against abstraction per se. Instead, it is a warning about exaggerating the power and sufficiency of abstract principles. It is better to accept the need for abstract principles and to be aware of their limitations than to complain about their abstractness.

What about the objection that abstract universalism imposes principles on other cultures? A true universalism rejects any use of ethical principles as tools of ideology and imperialism. Universalism should seek an inclusive conversation across cultures about what universals are most important and how they may be instantiated in different cultures. The fact that some people or countries have claimed their values to be universal so as to support their imperial actions does not show that all forms of universalism are guilty of unethical, hegemonic intentions. However, the abuse of universal ethics reminds us to examine claims of universality critically.

Then there is the view that universalism cannot take cultural variation into account. This view is questioned by recent theorizing. For example, in Christians et al. (2008), the authors agree that, historically, alleged universal principles have been imposed on other cultures in an insensitive manner. However, the authors explain how it is possible to conceive of universals as inclusive of cultural differences. Universal principles such as respect for life and a commitment to nonviolence can be expressed in many ways by different cultures. This approach rejects the idea of universals as transcendent of human experience and culture. Instead, it thinks of universals as incorporating (and being consistent with) the local and the particular. Universalism restricts the number or variety of ethical values in a culture. Principles can be instantiated in many ways and, in any case, universal principles are a relatively small subset of the values and rules expressed by a culture. A universalism of principle leaves plenty of room for variety among the values, norms, and practices in cultures and among cultures.

Finally, it is a mistake to portray universalism as a rigid deontology of rules that pays insufficient attention to context or consequence. Many forms of universalism are consequentialist (or nondeontologist), such as utilitarianism. Some forms of consequentialism, for example Mill's utilitarianism, regard a deontological sense of duty as an important part of ethics. Reasonable forms of deontological ethics do not hold that we should follow rules blindly, without looking to context or consequence. It is a mistake to think the defining feature of deontology is a rigid love of rules and duties. Instead, the defining feature of deontology is its attempt to restrain consequential thinking, not dismiss it. Deontology insists on the importance of rights and duties to prevent the maximization of good consequences from violating individual rights.

Consequential reasoning, especially a focus on the common good, may lead us to ignore our duties to others, whether they are individuals or minorities. Deontologists want the consequentialist pursuit of the good (however it is defined) to be restrained by rights and duties. Therefore, it is misleading to portray universalism's ethical options as a choice between a pure consequentialism and a pure deontology. A third option is possible: a mix of consequentialism and deontology. The choice becomes this: Which form of thinking – promoting the good or promoting what we owe to others – should receive the most emphasis in ethics? Consequentialism is not necessarily antiduty or antirights. But it will construe talk of duty and talk of rights as means to good consequences. Deontologists, in contrast, will make duties and rights primary, and will use duties and rights to restrain consequential reasoning. In Ward (2010) I argued that the best approach to universal ethics is a system that makes primary a deontological concern with justice. Yet the approach also has a consequential emphasis on promoting the human good, defined as human flourishing. The goal is to pursue the human good within the bounds of justice. Therefore, we must be cautious about characterizing universalism (negatively) as "deontological" or "rigidly deontological" as if these terms were synonymous. There are forms of universalism that are not deontological, and universalism can be deontological in emphasis without being rigid.

I have presented these responses to show that familiar objections are not persuasive and so it is rational to believe in the project of global media ethics. There are forms of universalism that are conceptually coherent, not utopian in a negative sense, and avoid the faults of a rigid abstract universalism.

Realistic Expectations

So far I have been arguing from a defensive position. I have tried to show how certain objections do not vitiate the idea of global media ethics. I conclude this chapter by examining, briefly, how we might actually go about developing the project. I will talk about the ideal fulfillment of the project, and then contrast it with what we can realistically expect.

Ideally, we can state the goal of the project as the simultaneous promotion of two related ideals – an ideal having to do with ethical content and an ideal having to do with the endorsement and application of the ethical content. Under the ideal of content, the goal is the articulation and defense of a set of universal principles (plus more specific norms and standards) for responsible global media. This ethical content is meant to be a new addition to media ethics. The content will extend, reformulate, or replace the ethical content of nation-bound media ethics, as found, for example, in the editorial guidelines of news organizations. A global media ethics should help media practitioners determine their duties to global audiences and how to improve the public's understanding of global issues. A global media ethics should promote human rights and global justice, and avoid excessive patriotism, nationalism, and xenophobia.

Under the ideal of endorsement, the goal is an ever-increasing endorsement of global media ethics by professional and citizen journalists, plus news organizations and journalism associations. The endorsement should come from practitioners who work in all forms of media, online or offline, traditional or "new media." The endorsement must lead to the application of principles to everyday practice. The level of endorsement and application should be sufficiently widespread so that the ideas come to have substantial, positive influence on global media and its coverage of global issues.

This is the ideal of global media ethics. How much of this ideal might be realized? What parts of global media ethics might be developed first? It is crucial that we have realistic expectations for the project and how it might unfold.

What would be some realistic expectations? Let's start by saying what would be unrealistic. First, it would be unrealistic to confidently assert that global media ethics will develop inevitably because we have a global media and it needs an ethics. There is no necessary link between having a global media and having a global ethics. It may be that a nonglobal ethics will continue to dominate the field. Globalists need to acknowledge the possibility that the project may fail. The ideas discussed in this book may fade away, for whatever reasons. It also would be unrealistic for globalists to believe that the project will be realized in full, at least in the foreseeable future. The validity of the project is not dependent on the belief that the ideal will be fully achieved. After all, it *is* an ideal.

So what is realistic? Globalists may realistically expect over the long-term that global media ethics will be realized in terms of content and endorsement to a significant extent.

The project of global media ethics may evolve as follows:

Stage 1: Injecting ideas into public discourse

Stage 1 – the stage we currently occupy – is an initial stage where the project needs to introduce global ideas and attitudes to public discourse about media, while showing the inadequacies of nonglobal ethics for today's media. The goal is a gradual widening of the ethical attitudes of increasing numbers of journalists and people who write about (and teach) news media. To achieve this evolution in attitudes, globalists, media ethics institutes, and educators need to put the topic of global ethics on the agenda of conferences. Global media ethics needs to be discussed on television and radio programs. It needs to be the subject of a growing number of articles and books. Global media ethics needs to have a place in the curriculum of communication and journalism schools. Meanwhile, journalism organizations, media ethicists, human rights workers, and others should continue to hold media practices up to global standards. Coalitions of journalists and citizens can work together to maintain constant pressure on media organizations to view their work from a global perspective. In this manner, we will be sowing the seeds of a global ethics attitude. This is the first practical step in making the project a significant part of media culture and media ethics.

As for endorsement during this period, the most important endorsements would be from global news organizations such as CNN, newspapers with an international focus, Al Jazeera, worldwide public broadcasters such as the BBC, the major international wires services, and major global websites and bloggers. Initially, local, regional, and even national news media will be less interested in global media ethics than will global organizations. Global news organizations need to lead the way.

Stage 2: Codifying the principles

Stage 1 is a stage of discussion, debate, and experimentation with the many approaches to global media ethics. Stage 1 should lead to stage 2 where there emerges an increasing "overlapping consensus" (Rawls [1972] 1992) on the content of a global media ethics. It is plausible (and realistic) to expect that intense discussions on what global ethics means will converge on a significant set of common ideals, aims, and principles. We see the same convergence of content happening in the other important areas of contemporary media ethics, for example, the development of norms of practice for mixed media (Ward 2011) online and offline.

This convergence will result in widely discussed editorial guidelines for global media ethics, perhaps first formulated by international news organizations and media associations. Hopefully, these guidelines and codes will become templates for other guidelines and codes. At some point, the guidelines may be consolidated into a smaller number of widely accepted codes of global media ethics. The guidelines and codes would receive elaboration and critique from ethicists, scholars, and researchers. At this stage, nonglobal and global media ethics will coexist in an uneasy tension. Global media will be a new and ascendant ethical approach.

It is unrealistic to expect that all media practitioners, all journalists, and all news organizations in the world will adopt *one* code of global ethics. It may be that media practitioners will accept the need for global ethics and hold a core of principles in common. However, they also may differ on some principles and on how those principles are interpreted and applied. For example, journalists in the West and East may hold different conceptions of what is meant by a socially responsible media. These variations in realizing global ethics would not invalidate the project. The variations would be in line with the notion of universals expressing themselves differently across cultures.

Stage 3: Completion of the ethics revolution

In the long run, we can speculate about a third stage where global media ethics becomes the dominant approach to media ethics. Ethical content will be clearly formulated and receive substantial endorsement. At this stage, the current ethical revolution will be over and a new (global) media ethics will hold the field.

Convergence of theory and practice

The dual nature of the ideal of global media ethics – content and endorsement – entails that the project must be a combination of the theoretical and the practical. To be successful, the project should not ignore one or the other. A global media ethics will not emerge from theory alone, even if the theory is a brilliant philosophical work. Any proposed theory will have to be seen as useful and important by working media practitioners. Nor will global media ethics emerge solely from emergent problems of practice encountered by journalists, for example, problems in covering global issues. A rigorous global media ethics will not emerge from workshops and conference discussions among working journalists only. Discussions among practitioners about global norms need to be stimulated by, and grounded in, the best available theories of global media ethics. Without the support of theory, well-meant declarations of global principles by practitioners will be inadequately grounded in philosophy and ethical theory.

My view is that, in developing ethical content theoretically, globalists should work in this manner: First, we develop a philosophical framework that specifies the global social and political values that media should promote. For guidance, we can look back to previous attempts to formulate international media guidelines, such as the effort in the 1970s and 1980 to state the principles of a new world information and communication order.[5] The ultimate principles of a philosophical framework will not be journalistic principles, such as reporting the truth. They will be unrestricted universal principles drawn from ethics per se, especially cosmopolitan ethics.

Second, once we have these global concepts, we should reformulate media norms and practices to give them a new global meaning. This is the approach I used in Ward (2010) for journalism ethics. I proposed that the ultimate aims of global journalism were best described by a consequentialist theory of human flourishing across borders, plus deontological ideas of human rights and global social justice. Then I gave global interpretations to existing journalistic principles such as objectivity and serving a democracy. Journalistic objectivity became a global impartiality that resists the undue influence of nationalism and patriotism. Serving a democracy was translated into promoting global democratic institutions and communities.

Third, with global values and reinterpreted media norms at hand, the project of global media ethics must show how an endorsement of such values would change practice, through case studies and other means. For instance, in Ward (2010), I showed how the adoption of my global ideas implied significant changes to how journalists regard patriotism and how they cover war. In this way we create the conceptual superstructure of global media ethics.

As I have warned throughout this chapter, the long-term success of forward-looking ethical labors cannot be predicted with any certainty. Only time will tell if these (or other) ideas are useful for designing a global media ethics. In the end, my approach may be shown to be a false step forward. However, even a failure or a partial success may be of help to a community of scholars and practitioners who care about responsible global media.

For those who remain skeptical about the prospects for global media ethics, I ask them to remember the power of new ideas and of pioneering movements over the course of history. As philosophers, we plant ideas like seeds in the hope of germination in the future.

Notes

1. This negative view ignores the real-world impact of utopian literature in the West at least since Thomas More first used "utopia" as the title of a book in 1516, and created a literary genre. Since More's *Utopia*, over 3,000 works of utopian literature have been published, although examples of the genre go as far back as Homer's *Odyssey* where some of the dead enjoy a wonderful life in the Elysian Fields. Some of this literature has had a positive impact, inspiring social reform and encouraging criticism of corrupt government. More's Utopia described a world in which there is religious tolerance, support for the aged, and state ownership of land. It has since been interpreted as a Catholic work of literature or an argument for communism.
2. Nonethical factors such as competition, attracting advertising, capturing a sufficiently large audience, and increasing profits can lead to unethical conduct such as inaccuracy, sensationalism, fabrication of sources, unfair representation of social groups, and so on.
3. I will not, in the space of this chapter, attempt to adjudicate the complex arguments about the conceptual coherence of relativism. I am content, for my purposes here, to note that these arguments against relativism should be taken seriously, and the arguments help to weaken our belief in relativism as clear and obvious.
4. Christians and Ward note that Wong (2006) and others have recently attempted to develop a nuanced form of ethical relativism based on presumptions that ethical systems, in varying ways, serve the same social and human needs across cultures. See Christians and Ward (forthcoming) for criticisms of this form of relativism.
5. This international project, sponsored by UNESCO, to create media principles for the world information system foundered on politics, power, and political

ideology. The McBride Commission, which led the project, produced a valuable document in 1980, *Many Voices, One World*. The publication contains ideas that could stimulate renewed efforts to create a global media ethics.

Further Reading

Several books provide accessible entry points for individuals who wish to know more about the project of global media ethics, including some works of my own. Richard Shapcott provides a useful and reliable overview of global ethics in *International Ethics: A Critical Introduction* (Cambridge: Polity Press, 2010). Shapcott provides a clear analysis of the main contending views such as cosmopolitanism and anticosmopolitanism.

Simon Caney offers a robust defense of global ethics and cosmopolitanism in political philosophy against realism and other sources of skepticism in *Justice Beyond Borders* (2005). For a criticism of Caney's perspective and a defense of national responsibilities, read David Miller's *National Responsibility and Global Justice* (Oxford: Oxford University Press, 2007). For individuals interested in specific concepts used in these debates, they could begin by reading Michael Rosen's recent analysis of the notion of concept of dignity in *Dignity: Its Meaning and History* (Cambridge, MA: Harvard University Press, 2012).

If one's main interest is global media ethics, I provide a framework for thinking about this topic in *Global Journalism Ethics* (Ward 2010). For a collection of writings on the various issues of global media ethics, I would suggest *Media Ethics Beyond Borders: A Global Perspective* (New York: Routledge, 2010) by myself and Herman Wasserman.

This chapter critiqued the mainstream forms of cultural relativism. Sociologist Steven Lukes provides a clear, general introduction to moral relativism in his *Moral Relativism* (New York: Picador, 2008). For a nuanced explication and defense of ethical relativism, the reader can do no better than to read David Wong's *Natural Moralities* (2006).

Much has been written on the idea of moral universals and culture. A good place to start is Kwasi Wiredu's *Cultural Universals and Particulars: An African Perspective* (Bloomington: Indiana University Press, 1996). In *Frontiers of Justice* (Cambridge, MA: Belknap Press, 2006), Martha Nussbaum outlines a cosmopolitan approach to global justice amid cultural differences by developing the "capability" approach to defining quality of life.

References

Beitz, C. 2001. "Human Rights as a Common Concern." *American Political Science Review* 95(2): 269–82.

Caney, S. 2005. *Justice Beyond Borders: A Global Political Theory*. Oxford: Oxford University Press.

Christians, C. G., Rao, S., Wasserman, H., and Ward, S. J. A. 2008. "Toward a Global Media Ethics: Theoretical Approaches," *Ecquid Novi: African Journalism Studies* 29(2): 135–72.

Christians, C. G. and Traber, M. 1997. *Communication Ethics and Universal Values*. Thousand Oaks, CA: Sage.

Christians, C. G. and Ward, S. J. A. Forthcoming. "Anthropological Realism for Global Media Ethics." In N. Couldry, M. Madianou, and A. Pinchevski, eds., *Ethics of Media*. Basingstoke: Palgrave Macmillan.

Gert, B. 2004. *Common Morality*. Oxford: Oxford University Press.

McBride Commission. 1980. *One World, Many Voices*. Paris: UNESCO.

Nagel, T. 1997. *The Last Word*. Oxford: Oxford University Press.

Rawls, J. [1972] 1992. *A Theory of Justice*. Oxford: Oxford University Press.

Rawls, J. 1999. *The Law of Peoples with "The Idea of Public Reason Revisited."* Cambridge, MA: Harvard University Press.

Scanlon, T. M. 1998. *What We Owe to Each Other* Cambridge, MA: Harvard University Press.

Todorov, T. 1993. *On Human Diversity: Nationalism, Racism, and Exoticism in French Thought*. Cambridge, MA: Harvard University Press.

Ward, S. J. A. 2005. *The Invention of Journalism Ethics: The Path to Objectivity and Beyond*. Montreal: McGill-Queen's University Press.

Ward, S. J. A. 2010. *Global Journalism Ethics*. Montreal: McGill-Queen's University Press.

Ward, S. J. A. 2011. *Ethics and the Media: An Introduction*. Cambridge: Cambridge University Press.

Wong, D. B. 2006. *Natural Moralities: A Defence of Pluralistic Relativism*. Oxford: Oxford University Press.

Index

Page numbers in italics refer to figures; page numbers followed by n refer to chapter notes.

Global Media Ethics: Problems and Perspectives, First Edition. Edited by Stephen J. A. Ward.
© 2013 Blackwell Publishing Ltd. Published 2013 by Blackwell Publishing Ltd.